NEW
WEATHERS

Poetics from the Naropa Archive

New Weathers

Poetics from the Naropa Archive

edited by
Anne Waldman and Emma Gomis

Nightboat Books
New York

Copyright © 2022 by Nightboat Books
Introduction, editing, and afterword Copyright © 2022 by Anne Waldman
 & Emma Gomis
All rights reserved
Printed in the United States

ISBN: 978-1-64362-147-0

Cover art: Remedios Varo, "Cambio de Tiempo," 1948
© 2022 Remedios Varo, Artists Rights Society (ARS), New York / VEGAP, Madrid
Design and typesetting by HR Hegnauer
Typeset in Arno Pro with Futura

Cataloging-in-publication data is available from the Library of Congress

Nightboat Books
New York
www.nightboat.org

Table of Contents

1 • Introduction: Archival Practice in the Anthropocene

SANCTUARY & APOCALYPSE

5 • I Tried to Honor the Ancestors
    Lisa Jarnot
18 • Pepper and Salt
    Kevin Killian
22 • Loss and Language
    M. NourbeSe Philip
26 • Dreams, Again
    Alice Notley
40 • Cultural and Political Rhizomes
    Sherwin Bitsui
43 • Lecture on Native American Cosmologies
    Harry Smith
54 • Syntax and the Event of Reading
    Renee Gladman
60 • The Poetics of Field Experiments in the Evershift
    Edwin Torres
67 • On Contemplative Poetics: A Practice for Saving the World
    Allen Ginsberg

ECOPOETIC ATTENTIONS

79 • The Future of the Past: Ecopoetry and the Carboniferous
    Forrest Gander
92 • How to Get Lost in the Living Room: Brief Thoughts on Bewilderment
    Dan Beachy-Quick

- 97 • Eco-Etho Poetics
    Jack Collom
- 100 • Eros and Ethos
    Akilah Oliver
- 114 • In and Out of the House
    Andrew Schelling
- 123 • We as Witness
    Paula Gunn Allen
- 126 • Time Tithing
    Ed Sanders
- 129 • A Poetics of Natural Light
    Peter Warshall
- 149 • Letter from Peter Warshall

Communal Action

- 155 • Let's Start Stopping: A Commencement Address
    Eileen Myles
- 159 • The Collective
    Lisa Robertson
- 170 • The Woman in the Wilderness
    Peter Lamborn Wilson
- 194 • Reality Is No Obstacle: A Poetics of Participation
    Cedar Sigo
- 218 • On Property and Monstrosity
    Julie Carr
- 235 • Collective Action
    Jos Charles
- 245 • *from* 8 Reflections on the Ugly Beautiful (a book in progress)
    Tonya M. Foster

Identity in the Capitalocene

- 267 • Consenting to the Emergency / the Emergent as Consensuality
  J'Lyn Chapman
- 277 • Investigative Poetics: Imagination and Documentation
  Ronaldo V. Wilson
- 283 • Ancestors
  Eliot Weinberger
- 296 • What's the Frequency?: Trends in Contemporary Poetry
  Alan Gilbert
- 304 • Lyric Embodiment
  Hoa Nguyen
- 313 • *from* From There to Here to Where
  Robin Blaser
- 318 • News Bulletin
  kari edwards
- 322 • Narrative and Fragment
  Robert Glück
- 327 • grasses grasses grasses
  Fred Moten
- 340 • Writer's Block
  William S. Burroughs
- 347 • Notes of a Dirty Old Man (Who Masturbates in Public)
  Samuel R. Delany
- 356 • Homunculus
  Margaret Randall

Against Atrocity

- 363 • Black Freighter
  Tongo Eisen-Martin
- 367 • Anything is Light When it Bears it Heavy:
  Etching a Name onto a Malleable Surface
  Asiya Wadud

375 • On the Edge of Forgetfulness
      Eleni Sikelianos
382 • Raccoon Magic
      Ariana Reines
388 • Poetry, Politics, and the Real World
      Amiri Baraka
402 • Transmission Fluid
      Thurston Moore
405 • Beyond Sovereignty:
      Aimé Césaire, Opacity, and a Poetics of Invagination
      Roger Reeves
422 • A Condition of Impossibility
      Lyn Hejinian
425 • The Question is the Beginning of the Healing:
      Cecilia Vicuña and Anne Waldman on Ritual and Performance

Afterword

443 • Feminafesto: Torques of Tongue and Archive and Anthropocene
      Anne Waldman
447 • Morphology of Dust
      Emma Gomis

451 • Acknowledgments
453 • Biographies

List of Images

3 • *Figure 1*: Collage by Anne Waldman (2021).

53 • *Figure 2*: Harry Smith memorial plaque by Peter Cole that was placed outside of the cottage where Smith lived from September 1988 through February 1991. The cottage was later repurposed as a recording studio and is now a Naropa student center. Photograph by Anne Waldman.

78 • *Figure 3*: "Language and Biology" by Newcomb Greenleaf, published in *The Naropa Institute Bulletin* (March 1979).

152 • *Figure 4*: Founding year of the Naropa Institute (now called Naropa University): Registration Day, 1974. Photograph from the Naropa Archive.

266 • *Figure 5*: Poster made in the Harry Smith printshop during Aaron Cohick's workshop in the 2019 Summer Writing Program. Photograph by Anne Waldman.

360 • *Figure 6*: Cover of 2019 Summer Writing Program catalogue.

449 • *Figure 7*: Anne Waldman and Emma Gomis visit the Naropa Archives (Boulder, CO 2020).

Introduction
ARCHIVAL PRACTICE IN THE ANTHROPOCENE

The material collated here comes from a particular place, an alternative educational zone founded by Anne Waldman and Allen Ginsberg half a century ago (accompanied by the special presence of Diane di Prima in the seminal years), with the aim of opening up discourse and fostering critical engagement. Naropa University and the Jack Kerouac School of Disembodied Poetics are situated outside of the conventional academic frames. Following an "outrider lineage" of American avant-garde literary practices, it is a place that cultivates nonnormative thinking and encourages radical exploration and experimentation in the literary arts. Established in 1974 as a maverick program with a vision of a hundred-year project, the school cultivates discussions around poetics and activism. For three to four weeks every summer, the Jack Kerouac School hosts poets and scholars from all over the world in Colorado to participate in an intensive poetics program. The texts collected here are primarily lectures and essays that were presented during sessions of the Summer Writing Program.

In assembling this collection, we spent hours culling the archive searching for material. The Naropa audio archive spans back to its initial founding—when lectures were given in a large canvas tent—and still continues to amass new experimental thinking with audio added every summer. The archive is a memory device, an inventory, a record. Jacques Derrida wrote in his influential piece *Archive Fever*:

> *Arkhe*, we recall, names at once the *commencement* and the *commandment*. This name apparently coordinates two principles in one: the principle according to nature or history, *there* where things *commence*—physical, historical, or ontological principle—but also the principle according to the law, *there* where men and gods *command*, *there* where authority, social order are exercised, *in this place* from which *order* is given—nomological principle.[1]

An archive is a place where the contemporary confronts the past; it offers the potential to disrupt systemic oppression; to question what has become heterogenous ("authority" and "social order"); to engage with documents; to bear witness to injustice; and to begin to work in intermedial modes.[2] In undertaking an examination of its gaps and failings, one can gesture toward what Eve Sedgwick calls a "reparative reading" of our subsumed epistemologies—a hermeneutic for a style

---

1 Derrida, Jacques. *Archive Fever*, trans. by Eric Prenowitz, 2nd ed. (Chicago: University of Chicago Press, 1998), 9.

2 We are thinking of intermedial modes in the way the cofounder of Fluxus Dick Higgins spoke of them in 1965 when he used the term 'intermedia' to "recognize the dissolution of boundaries, the expansion of liminal spaces between traditional modes of art making, and the open field for new forms that cannot be compartmentalized." in *Intermedia, Fluxus and The Something Else Press Selected Writings*, edited by Steve Clay and Ken Friedman, (Siglio Press, 2018).

of critique that seeks to repair the damage of prejudice and violence, rather than perpetuating them further. These are all aims of the Naropa mission and, as such, the archive is filled with lectures that strive to address what Foucault referred to as "subjugated knowledges," ones which are often not represented.

The contemplative, constructivist, and feminist pedagogies that make up Naropa's teaching ethos instill in its students and friends an inquisitive and expansive approach to study. We are encouraged to radically explore topics of interest, no matter how scattered and divergent, with the holistic aim of self-development and literary exploration. In the pages that follow, we have brought together a range of poetics that reach out toward divergent frequencies, offering new ways of thinking around major aspects in our society in order to imagine alternate possibilities, trespassing protocols and authority. These texts invoke issues around gender and racially-based injustice, the global climate crisis and our possible extinction, and unconventional forms of thinking as possible strategies for resistance.

We have composed the anthology in five sections: Sanctuary and Apocalypse, Ecopoetic Attentions, Communal Action, Identity in the Capitalocene, and Against Atrocity. Taken from panel titles held throughout the years of the Summer Writing Program, the headings represent some of the tentacles that weave through our poetic community, some of the conversations we are having, some of the topics we are facing with these *new weathers*. They are not meant to categorize our thinking, but rather serve as points of convergence and divergence.

Atrocity can't obliterate our will or capacity to imagine. The extraordinary conversations that we participate in fortify us in our complicity to continue, to go against, go outward and onward. This book is not solipsistic, but rather an exchange that hopes to cultivate a generative spirit of curiosity, investigation, cross-cultural activism, magpie scholarship around other species—an ongoing conversation that touches upon various fields of engagement with language. We consider things that overlap, that draw into focus the contemporary times, summoning the *arche* as well as the *techne*.

How to address the complexities of these major structures that threaten our very existence? How can we imagine to live differently? This tome invites you to ask these questions, to enter a temporarily suspended world where change is possible. It is a volume of heteroglossia, interaction, activism, and transmission, to bolster our conversations and activate our thinking. How to survive when you feel like you're under siege? This battle against patriarchy, capitalism, racism, and environmental destruction will keep unfolding ad infinitum, and so our projects must not be short-termed but ongoing.

> Mine is a very particularized journey. As Gary Snyder said, it is a journey of a thousand years. —*Ed Sanders*

In the editing of this book, it was important to us to preserve the conversation, the interaction between pieces that offer various perspectives or approaches. For example, Fred Moten engages in a conversation with the work of Layli Long Soldier, while Roger Reeves critically approaches the opacity of Aimé Césaire. The complexities of Peter Warshall's scientific description of light make you want to commune with the natural world and save it from ecological disaster. Lisa Robertson, with wit and challenge, calls us to collective action, in whatever form that takes. Thurston Moore's performative cry similarly invokes a sense of collective activism as our duty. We think of these pieces as dialogic engagements. Throughout the five sections we have incorporated various "strategies for resistance." Allen Ginsberg offers meditation as a technique to engage with our creative output; Lisa Jarnot offers a method of preparation for the impending ecological crisis; Alice Notley invites us to consider dreams as instruments of reality. It is our hope that these serve as tools to protect us in the fight ahead.

It was at Naropa that we, Anne and Emma, met. We shared a vow to poetry and wrote two chapbooks together. The editorial work that has gone into this book has been an intergenerational collaboration. Anne's political activism with Rocky Flats and, more recently, at detention centers and prisons; her engagement with writing communities abroad and collaboration with musicians and artists to expand the parameters for a performance poetics; her feminist work and integral presence in the founding of The Poetry Project at St. Mark's Church in-the-Bowery and Naropa; her voluminous publishing history—all of these came into conversation with Emma's international background, protests for Catalan independence, cross-cultural discourse, feminist thinking, and dedication to pursuing new experiments in critical and poetic output. In this sense, we think of it as furthering a lineage and carrying forward a set of experimental histories. We have thought of ourselves as "archons" in this endeavor, keepers of the flame, in a sense—as guardians (devotees) of poetry's archive. The pieces collected here also embody this impulse, as most of them are from recent years of the Summer Writing Program, with a few of our ancestors integrated—these are some of the voices carrying the project forward.

We have worked, in many cases, with transcriptions of oral presentations, and have done our best to remain faithful to the delivered pieces. The audio recorder records words but also preserves intonations, pauses, gestures. When someone speaks, something more takes place that is not registered on paper. It then transmutes as you catch the word and put it down. The transmission is first delivered orally and then, through transcription, takes on a new form, presents a new way of processing the information, becomes a new text you can study. By study, we mean a practice that extends beyond the classroom, a practice of rereading and carrying words with us. Some of the texts have been edited and refined by the authors themselves. In others, we have had to condense while maintaining true to a piece's core. Some of the pieces have been given titles by the authors, while others, are referenced by the panel in which they were presented. Things in brackets and footnotes have been added by the editors for clarity. The care and love of the editors who were, in many cases, present during these lectures, and very much a part of this living body of poetics study, served as the impetus for assembling this book. As Amiri Baraka once said to Anne, "Don't let this stuff get buried!"

We hope this book will make you feel like you're not alone; it's aim is to weave an intergenerational connectivity that serves to unite us. You're not in an isolated bubble in which the only way to relate is through a conversation with a screen or an app. The texts found here incorporate different communities, movements, backgrounds, and lineages, but they are all thinking toward how we can change the current frequencies, how we can help wake the world up to itself.

—Anne Waldman & Emma Gomis

Sanctuary & Apocalypse

. . .

A sanctuary is a space that offers refuge and safety; it is also, more literally, a nature reserve where birds and other animals can live protected from hunters and dangerous conditions. Every spring, during Anne's practicum, we make our way to the Sawhill ponds, wander through the fields, and hear the birds keen as we write. The crane dips its beak in the mud, a hummingbird lingers, the loons arrange their plumage as they glide by on the surface of the water. There is a quiet removed from the din, a stillness assured by safekeeping. Language can offer a similar shelter, a budding canopy under which we can find respite, a sanctuary built into the architecture of a text.

Apocalypse is the complete and final destruction of the world, a culminating event resulting in a great and violent change. But something that is burnt to the ground creates space for something else to occupy its place; the opportunity to rebuild lies implicit within the destruction. While the word instills a sense of panic, coupled with sanctuary, the balance of the two poles can allow us to think through the harbingers portending our apocalypse, while simultaneously constructing textual rhetoric that offers us sanctuary from which to do so.

> I saw you in green velvet, wide full sleeves
> seated in front of a fireplace, our house
> made somehow more gracious, and you said
> "There are stars in your hair"—it was truth I
> brought down with me
>
> to this sullen and dingy place that we must make golden
> make precious and mythical somehow, it is our nature,
> and it is truth, that we came here, I told you,
> from other planets
> —Diane di Prima, "Buddhist New Year Song" from Pieces of a Song

. . .

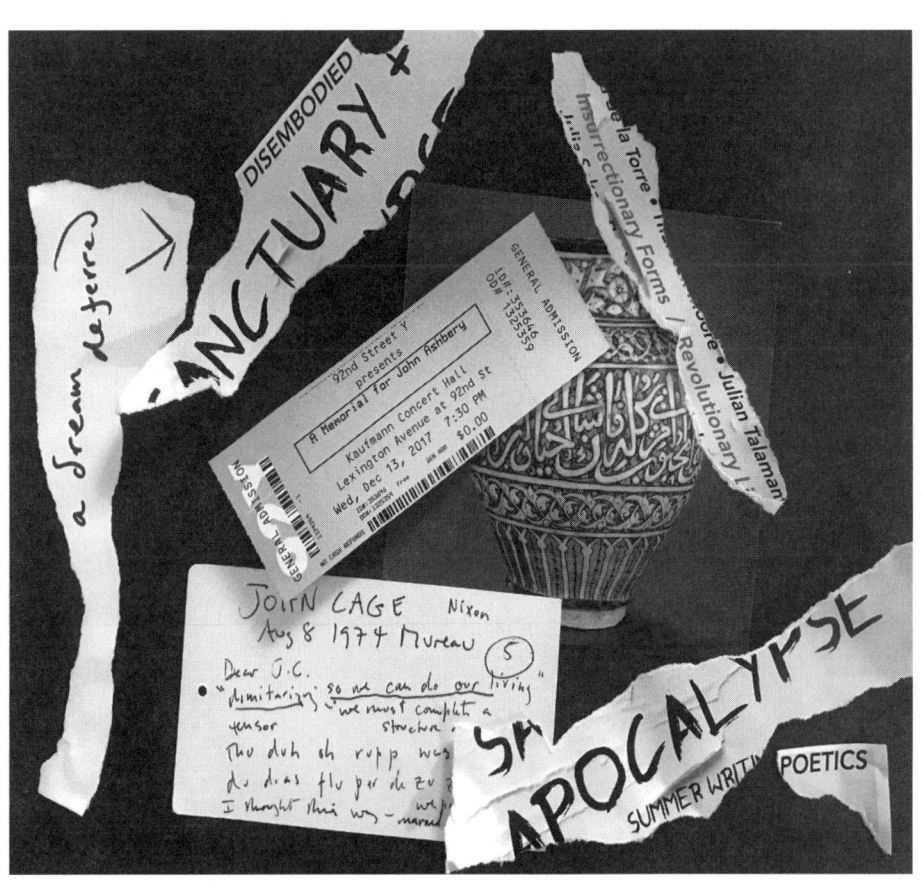

Figure 1: Collage by Anne Waldman (2021)

I Tried to Honor the Ancestors

Lisa Jarnot

When we address the theme of our convergence here, the theme of "The New Weathers," we have to consider two key words: Possibility and Responsibility. Possibility for a radical change in the way humans steward the planet, and Responsibility in Robert Duncan's sense of the word: "Responsibility is the Ability to Respond." We may look back through our lineage as writers here and think of our ancestors as Titans, but it seems really clear to me that you—all of you, who are here as students and are coming into life as writers—are the very most important generation. We may have all come here for similar reasons, but the urgency of the world situation falls more squarely on your shoulders, and your roles as writers will be different than the roles of your ancestors—you will be the generation that lives on the precipice of the end of the species.

Now, part of the reason I became a writer (and probably a big part of it) was that I desperately needed to be heard. I know this is a familiar story. And some of the women in the audience know this story: of being a girl and not being heard. Or, for some of you, it's another story: of being in exile, or abandoned, or marginalized in whatever ways your story has played out. Being a writer, and being aware of this, puts us in a very unique position as humans: our decision to become writers forces us to examine who we are and where we are in relation to all other creatures.

It brings us to that line from *Spiderman*: "With great power comes great responsibility." So, we can meditate this afternoon on *Spiderman* and Robert Duncan: "With great power comes great responsibility" and "Responsibility is the Ability to Respond." We see if we move from these maxims that we, as writers, have a greater potential than, let's say, a lot of our politicians to really feel the pain of the rest of the planet and to do something about it. And I know for me, in my story, I gravitated toward one of the founders of this school, Allen Ginsberg, because of his story—that crucial childhood story of longing for parental love and longing for love in a culture that couldn't provide it. You don't have to go far beyond the first line of "America," which he wrote when he was in his late twenties—"America I've given you all and now I'm nothing"—to see that. But what I can also confess is that I came into poetry seeking immortality, really hungry to participate in lineage, and in Blake's dictum, "The Authors are in Eternity." To bring it down to pedestrian terms, I really just wanted to be famous. And that again is a feeling that I think others in this room can relate to. The Jack Kerouac School is a pretty glamorous place. This is where rock 'n' roll and poetry meet.

So, our expectations for future poetical glory have been radically rearranged by The New Weathers, by a long history of disconnect from the planet that we live on. I'm not sure why we haven't articulated it in these terms more often here: that we are at the end of the world. We've certainly been talking about the destructive forces that surround us since this project called the Naropa Institute began. But we haven't said, frankly, that we're coming to the end of it all. I remember my mentor in college, a poet and Blake-scholar named Jack Clarke talking about a line of Charles Olson's—that Olson was asked vaguely in an interview, "What are we doing here?" and Olson replied, "Waiting for the ice to melt."

So, to admit to ourselves where we're at means we also have to be open to experience a good deal of grief. Anne said this the other day, you can "write from a broken heart." Because if we are frank about it, it's very likely that we're no longer writing for future generations. It's possible that I will not be part of a grandparent generation of writers like Robert Duncan or Allen Ginsberg were for me. It's highly probable that most of you will not be part of a grandparent generation of writers. That puts a huge responsibility on us right here in this room. We have to be realistic. The Paris Climate Accord was a compromise, it didn't save our species or other species, even if the United States abided by it. So we have a lot of work to do if we want to do it.

There's probably a reason you chose to come here and not to be at a summer writing retreat on the coast of Maine or at an Ivy League school somewhere. As writers in the Kerouac School lineage, we're deep readers and researchers. This is part of the lineage that comes to me through Olson and Ginsberg and Sanders and Bernadette Mayer. So, the first thing I would encourage you to do as a human, and as a writer working with facts, is to go online and download the PDF of the Intergovernmental Panel on Climate Change, the IPCC 2014 Report. This is the document that was released by the United Nations ahead of the Paris Climate Summit. Now this report was compiled by a panel of over one hundred scientists globally, and it details the reasons for climate change, the projected effects of climate change on the planet and its ecosystems, and the various scenarios for mitigating climate change. It is a 1,400 page document. The Synthesis Report culled from it is a 160-page document, and you can start there if it seems more reasonable. And this document is our formal prophecy of The New Weathers, and it's really the most important text we have at hand right now if we want to think about our future as writers and humans. As a writer and researcher,

I would actually say it's a beautiful document, because it takes into consideration every creature on the planet and it looks at every possibility we have to save the ecosystems we now know as our own. And it is a Great Prophecy in that it really clearly points out what will be happening for us in our own generation and in our children's generation if we continue to live the way we live. We're still not taking this information head on, and I do think it's because we're paralyzed with anxiety. I think we get into spots where we're too afraid to love deeply and act wholeheartedly, and that's part of the confusion right now. We ask for permission too much, we ask for permission to resist, but we need to take things into our own hands. This has been in the air for us in America for some time, and it's all part of a continuum. In 1962, Martin Luther King Jr. wrote:

> Today it has become almost a truism to call our time an 'age of fear.' In these days of terrifying change, bitter international tension, and chaotic social disruption, who has not experienced the paralysis of crippling fear? Everywhere there are people depressed and bewildered, irritable and nervous all because of the monster of fear…
>
> We must honestly ask ourselves why we are afraid. The confrontation will, to some measure, grant us power. We can never cure fear by the method of escapism. Nor can it be cured by repression. The more we attempt to ignore and repress our fears, the more we multiply our inner conflicts…

Firstly, we have to accept that we are the people of the Anthropocene:

> Anthropogenic greenhouse gas emissions have increased since the pre-industrial era, driven largely by economic and population growth, and are now higher than ever. This has led to atmospheric concentrations of carbon dioxide, methane and nitrous oxide that are unprecedented in at least the last

800,000 years. Their effects, together with those of other anthropogenic drivers, have been detected throughout the climate system and are *extremely likely* to have been the dominant cause of the observed warming since the mid-20th century (IPCC, 2014).

And I think we have to own that. We didn't ask to be here, and we all have our ways of trying to deny that we are here. In one way or another, we're all climate change deniers. Our First World carbon footprints, even for the best of us in the First World, are unsustainable. (You don't even need to drive a car to have an unsustainable carbon footprint—all you have to do is live in a single family dwelling and use heating oil in the winter.) As hard as it is, we have to be humble. Our daily actions in the First World negatively affect the lives of people in the Third World every day. But, we also need to frame this beyond the realm of fault and blame. We need to position all of us, everyone here, as victims of a long history of non-cooperative societies. This doesn't let you off the hook—it simply puts things into perspective. I'd say we've all been in the story for so long, we really can't help but be who we are. And we have to break through to a radically different way of thinking and living if we do want to continue to live. Like it or not, we are "the rich man" in the book of Mark. I will bring Christ into this conversation, because he very strongly suits the outrider tradition that we are part of here:

> As Jesus was starting out on his way to Jerusalem, a man came running up to him, knelt down, and asked, "Good Teacher, what must I do to inherit eternal life?" "You know the commandments," Jesus said: "You must not murder. You must not commit adultery. You must not steal. You must not testify falsely. You must not cheat anyone. Honor your father and mother." "Teacher," the man replied, "I've obeyed all these commandments since I was young." Looking at the man, Jesus

felt genuine love for him. "There is still one thing you haven't done," he told him. "Go and sell all your possessions and give the money to the poor, and you will have treasure in heaven. Then come, follow me." At this the man's face fell, and he went away sad, for he had many possessions.

I suspect there's a part of this in all of us when we think about climate change. We consider whether or not we can stop eating meat or stop buying things on Amazon or stop driving cars, and we go away sad. These are extraordinary times and, as I've heard Anne Waldman shout to a packed room at the Poetry Project, "Don't tarry!" I know that some people say they don't believe in personal virtue as a path to healing the planet, that the work is too large and has to be done from the top down. I have to say that I really disagree with this. We are all that we have. And it's really only through our example that anything positive is going to happen. The actions that we take, either in participating in revolutionary changes to our lifestyle, or having dignity in accepting the end of the species, or in a combination of those two paths, is what we can leave as a testament to our compassion as humans. As writers, we can also document this journey for each other for as long as we are here. I want to read for you part of an essay by an activist named Anne Herbert from the Bay Area. This is from a piece called "Handy Tips on How to Behave at the Death of the World":

Probably good to tell truth as much as possible. Truth generally appreciated by terminal patients and we all are.

    Good to avoid shoddy activities. You are doing some of last things done by beings on this planet. Generosity and beauty and basicness might be good ways to go. Avoid that which is self-serving in a small way. Keep in mind standing in for ancestors including people who lived ten thousand years ago and also fishes. Might be best to do activities that would make some ancestors feel honored to be part of bringing you here.

Silent statement to predecessors: Well, yeah, we blew the big thing by killing ourselves. I tried to honor you as much as I could in that context by doing the following:

Transform your own power-over behavior to whatever extent possible. e.g. Men profoundly understand and change around relations with women. White people profoundly change in relations to people of color. Humans profoundly change in relationship to other beings on planet. This constitutes a thank you note and note of apology to the whole history of the planet.

My students have been hashing out the message of this essay since Monday, and it's been tough going in different ways for all of us. Some of us feel grief, some of us feel rage, regret, confusion, and doubt and guilt and anger at being called out as humans, or First World people, or men, or straights, or meat-eaters. The process has reminded me of Twelve Step recovery programs. I've been working with students and activists on climate change for the last couple of years, but it wasn't until I got into the classroom here, this week, that I saw how useful it could be to organize climate action through the Twelve Step process:

We admitted we were powerless over _____ and that our lives had become unmanageable.

The Working Group of the Intergovernmental Panel on Climate Change tells us how powerless we are, and how unmanageable our situation is:

Surface temperature is projected to rise over the 21st century under all assessed emission scenarios. It is *very likely* that heat waves will occur more often and last longer, and that extreme precipitation events will become more intense and frequent in many regions. The ocean will continue to warm and acidify, and global mean sea level to rise.

...

A large fraction of species faces increased extinction risk due to climate change during and beyond the 21st century, especially as climate change interacts with other stressors (*high confidence*). Most plant species cannot naturally shift their geographical ranges sufficiently fast to keep up with current and high projected rates of climate change in most landscapes; most small mammals and freshwater mollusks will not be able to keep up at the rates projected under RCP4.5 and above in flat landscapes in this century (*high confidence*).

...

Many aspects of climate change and associated impacts will continue for centuries, even if anthropogenic emissions of greenhouse gases are stopped. The risks of abrupt or irreversible changes increase as the magnitude of the warming increases.

You can also look at a 2015 report from the UN's Food and Agriculture Organization. *The Guardian* and *Scientific American* picked up on this research last year [2016]. Here's the byline from the *Scientific American* article, which is probably all you need to hear to get the message: "If current rates of [soil] degradation continue all of the world's top soil could be gone within 60 years, a senior UN official said." That leaves us sixty harvests, and brings the crisis into focus generationally.

Step two of Twelve Step recovery programs: "We came to believe that a Power greater than ourselves could restore us to sanity." And step three: "We made a decision to turn our will and our lives over to the care of God as we understood Her/Him."

Now, some of us come from traditions where we have higher powers and we seek them out for spiritual guidance. Others of us have higher powers, plain and simple, as writers. I mean I would be the first to say that, where I'm coming from as a writer, I'd happily pray to James Joyce for guidance. I also find myself thinking of that summer

I was here twenty years ago. It was the year Allen Ginsberg died. And I arranged when I was here that summer to sit down with Ed Sanders and do an interview with him about Allen. One of the most important things that came out of that, for me, was a reminder of an approach to writing that involved an engagement with documentation, with facts, with real news, with a deep personal involvement with the world. This is something that Brenda Coultas spoke about on Tuesday—and she said that great thing about why she writes, "I want to know this planet." The thing that Ed Sanders learned from Allen Ginsberg, and also from Charles Olson, was that we don't just run on gut feelings as writers—there's a place for that—but we also have the responsibility to think on our feet and to connect facts in a lucid way. I think this is especially important for us as outriders, in the way that you see its importance to thinkers like Noam Chomsky or Rebecca Solnit—when one is positioned by others on the outskirts of the dominant culture, it's really necessary to show up to the gunfight armed with facts. And Allen was that writer for me, and for so many others. He was the one who had the courage to investigate the CIA. He was the one who decided that if he didn't like something that was happening in the government, he would call them and let them know. And he would find a way to get through. When Jack Spicer taught poetry workshops in San Francisco in the 1950s, he handed out a questionnaire to students that made clear his priorities as a writer—the first three sections of questions were in the categories of Politics, Religion, and History, not Writing or Literature:

I. Politics
  1. What is your favorite political song?
  2. If you had a chance to eliminate three political figures in the world, which would you choose?
  3. What political group, slogan, or idea in the world today has the most to do with Magic? With Poetry?
  4. Who were the Lovestoneites?

II. Religion
1. Which one of these figures had or represented religious views nearest to your own religious views? Which furthest? Jesus, Emperor Julian, Diogenes, Buddha, Confucius, Marcus Aurelius, Lao Tse, Socrates, Dionysus, Apollo, Hermes Trismegistus, Li Po, Heraclitus, Epicurus, Apollonius of Tyana, Simon Magus, Zoroaster, Mohammed, the White Goddess, Cicero.
2. Classify this set of figures in the same way. Calvin, Kierkegaard, Suzuki, Schweitzer, Marx, Russell, St. Thomas Aquinas, Luther, St. Augustine, Santayana, the Mad Bomber, Marquis de Sade, Yeats, Gandhi, William James, Hitler, C.S. Lewis, Proust.
3. What is your favorite book of the Bible?

III. History
1. Give the approximate date of the following people or events: Plato_____ Buddha_____ The Battle of Waterloo_____ Dante_____ The invention of printing_____ Nero_____ Chaucer_____ The unification of Italy_____ Joan of Arc_____
2. Write a paragraph about how the fall of Rome affected modern poetry.

When Robert Duncan taught similar workshops in the Bay Area, he asked his students to prepare a family tree of the generations of writers who had most influenced them. Now, if you go somewhere else entirely, to Ghana (and I can't really think of any two stranger things to put together than Ghana and Robert Duncan)—there is a word "Sankofa" in the culture of Ghana—and it means: "Go back and get it." And there's a symbol you'll see, of the Sankofa bird—with its neck turned backwards, reaching into the past—fetching what is necessary to move forward.

This is something that was brought to my attention earlier this summer in a class at the New York Theological Seminary, and it made me think of what we do here at Naropa, of the way we rely on our ancestor writers. We all bring various traditions to the table. We can't merge into one tradition—my experience is not the same as anyone else's in this room. But our strength in this moment is in finding common ground around our differences. I can tell you my experience and my tradition and lineage and what I can contribute from it, and you can do the same. I know it gets emotionally hot sometimes, partly because as a young writer you have to come into your beliefs by fiercely defending the things that are important to you, so that you can emerge with your own voice. And partly because this is a place where it feels safe to say, "Wait a minute, I am a marginalized person and I can almost be heard in this space, finally."

Writing is testifying. We testify to our experiences of the world. The form we use—prose or poetry, hybrid forms, performance form, or on-the-page form—is part of our craft, but where we come together is in the experience of conveying the message by any means possible. We all have different ancestors, which is really our strength, that we can all work together to fetch from the past what we need to move forward.

For me, it's something in the Beat tradition, and I know that Anne included this line of Allen's in the description for the program this summer: "Well, while I'm here I'll / do the work— / and what's the Work? / To ease the pain of living. Everything else, drunken / dumbshow." It's obviously also a Buddhist way of thinking, which we can pay homage to in this space. And I'll go back to the two words I dropped into this talk at the beginning: Possibility and Responsibility. We might bring Emily Dickinson into the discussion—"I dwell in Possibility." How do we organize ourselves emotionally for the task of dwelling in possibility in such dire times? If we continue to use the Twelve Step process as a guide, we see how it corresponds to

Anne Herbert's plea in "Handy Tips on How to Behave at the Death of the World." We make a searching and fearless moral inventory of ourselves (as in, "Why do I continue to buy my kid Chicken McNuggets?" I think it's important to say that—it's the only way we can grow. And we see this in the way we work with race and gender— we make mistakes, and it's a good thing even though it's hard—it's a growing process). We make a list of all creatures we have harmed and become willing to make *amends* to them all. We continue to take personal inventory (and that's something we're all always doing as writers). Having had a spiritual awakening as the result of these steps, we try to carry this message to other humans, and to practice these principles in all our affairs.

We are outriders. Remember how Anne positions that term: "The outrider rides the edge—parallel to the mainstream, is the shadow to the mainstream, is the consciousness or soul of the mainstream whether it recognizes its existence or not. It cannot be co-opted, it cannot be bought." There is no reason we can't work at the margins of dominator societies to cooperate in a society that does not value cooperation. We all have outriders that we look to—those voices that speak to us, brought forward in this space individually by each of us, are enormously powerful in concert. We are working out of the ground of a new orientation. And this is something that I'm fetching from my past, because when I was a young person in Buffalo, New York, finding a place in what I'll call my family of faith—and I mean my family of poetry—I was drawn to a fantastic constellation of people including Robert Creeley, who was my teacher, and Jack Clarke, who I mentioned earlier, and a peer and fellow poet named Elizabeth Willis, and a culture worker named Harvey Brown who was the editor of Frontier Press—an outrider press that published Ed Dorn and H.D. and Stan Brakhage and Williams and others. And I remember Harvey describing being in Mexico City in September of 1985 during the big earthquake there, and he said the ground was moving under his feet, and he realized he had to move with it, and he called it, "Dancing to a new orientation." And I do think that's exactly what we need to do now. We need to accept where we are, to be heartbroken, and to use our gifts as writers—and we are here because we have gifts—we have to own them—we have to ask ourselves every day, "Why did I come through my mother's womb?" And I think part of the answer may be "to ease the pain of living."

(2017)

Pepper and Salt

Kevin Killian

Like many writers, I went to San Francisco from graduate school, without any real training in doing anything. I took a series of temp jobs—this will date me—I remember the temp agency asking me what office machines I was familiar with…but, I had never actually been in an office, so I said, "All of them."

"Do you know the ten key machine?"

"Of course," I said rather coldly.

I wonder if many of you even know what a ten key machine is. It's like this accounting thing you do with one hand. I didn't know what it was then. They sent me over to this job downtown, placed me in a room with a ten key machine and about a million pages of documents. I walked out and said to the woman in charge, "I don't know how to use that thing on the desk."

"Your agency told us you know how to use a ten key machine."

Well, it all came out, that I thought what they were referring to was, well, you know, like the touch telephone where it has the ten things to dial the number, which I knew back then. So, I thought I had it made, but no. I knew those ten keys quite well, on the phone.

The Anthropocene is about how technology in use, less than two hundred years, has brought us to this crossroads I guess, in which previous conceptions of history seem to be collapsing like houses of cards. All the things I thought about history, now I'm thinking they weren't right, made me wonder: poetry must have been based on the idea of history as progressive... can't be a hundred percent sure because I wasn't around when they invented poetry but... I think that it must've been based on an idea of the cycles of history becoming progressive—like things are getting a little better as time goes on. And not just that eternal cycle that I first encountered in *Finnegan's Wake*, where all history seems to be repeating itself continually: things are good, then they're bad—things are just as good, then they're just as bad. Things never actually get to any particular state. Because civilization's all a'creep and then they dissipate, just in the same way as the human body does. At least I think so, but it's hard to imagine the act of writing poetry without imagining that people will read it in the future.

Was it Osip Mandelstam who had that piece satirizing a friend—his friend dedicated all his poetry to posterity, and he thought that was pretentious? Mandelstam's poem says that "the future is a ghost, and what we write today, won't be anything a ghost can relate to." The truth is that we don't know how to write to death, though some poets have tried.

Marxists must be deflated in the age of the Anthropocene, as it kicks in, because Marx predicated that the capitalist disaster itself is predicated on the exigencies of production—there was always an optimism in his thought... for some reason. Even Marx had it like this, "even with capitalism things are pretty good." Because there's the possibility that people will rise up and take control, and then things will be good. In fact, Marx is possibly the most hopeful of philosophers, believing that once we can see the outlines of history, clearly, we wouldn't repeat it. In the twentieth century, Georges Bataille took the opposite view. His argument against Marx was that capital is instead managed and fed by the exigencies not of production, but of consumption. So that's why our news is so bad: over-consumption, nine billion people on a shrinking planet. David Bowie took up the theme forty years ago of Bataille's ideas—and I know I was thinking, "Gee, he actually was writing closer to the age of Bataille than our age today"—but, in any case, I still remember these songs that were popular when I was a boy. And one starts out: "The Earth is a bitch / we've finished our news / Homo sapiens have outgrown their use / all the strangers came today / and it looks as though they're here to stay." That's Bowie's "Oh You Pretty Things." Well, some of you might know it.

In San Francisco, I was thinking, "Well, how do these two opposite ideas about cycles of history…and is capitalism working for production or for consumption…or you know, which services it best?" In San Francisco, we all practice—rich or poor—a modified version of the famous paradox defined by the communist Antonio Gramsci in his prison notebooks (this was in the '20s or the '30s) when he called for "a pessimism of the intellect, but an optimism of the will." So, you know, anyone with a grain of sense would think: things are pretty grim—can't help but have a pessimistic point of view, but that's in your mind—sometimes it translates to pessimism in the mind, but it's optimism of the will, like *what can we do, can we do anything?*

And, in San Francisco, we've been living in an existential way for one hundred years or more, since the big earthquake that leveled the city in 1906. Nothing's good for very long, soon we will be swept out to the sea…and I think this tendency has given San Francisco poetry a special character. The dearest Americans have gotten into Blanchot's recipe of the writing of the disaster, like it's a continual disaster there, or you're on the brink of it.

There was a conference at UC Santa Cruz and it was called "the Anthropocene," and I was like, "I should go to that." Ursula K. Le Guin was the keynote speaker and she said that she was now a firm believer in the Anthropocene, and she no longer could be an optimist, that she had come to this point because she had been an optimist her whole life. Even as a social activist, she was one who was like, "Things can be changed, and they're going to get better." She still couldn't bring herself to call herself a pessimist. "We still have to hope," she said, "I suppose, otherwise you'd go mad." Whenever anybody comes to San Francisco, I tell them that, "While you are here, we'll experience an earthquake, hopefully not a devastating one, but you'll be out walking, and you'll have to crouch down, and touch the pavement." And maybe that perception of possible danger has kept us honest just a little bit; we're at the end of the continent, and the next stop is the ocean. We came to it for a reason. Of course, the same thing is happening here in Boulder with the flooding, and you must be feeling the same kind of contingency.

Jack Spicer, the California poet I've written so much about, often pictured in his poetry and his fiction a "post-human" society in which everyone is disappeared, and only aimless signals bounce back and forth between our meeting with satellites and the surface of the ocean. And this is Spicer's poem, that begins his book *Language* [1965]:

> This ocean, humiliating in its disguises
> Tougher than anything.
> No one listens to poetry. The ocean
> Does not mean to be listened to. A drop
> Or crash of water. It means
> Nothing.
> It
> Is bread and butter
> Pepper and salt. The death
> That young men hope for. Aimlessly
> It pounds the shore. White and aimless signals. No
> One listens to poetry

(2014)

Loss and Language

M. NourbeSe Philip

Here is a quotation and I might get it wrong, so if any of you have it with you, tell me. It's from Emily Dickinson, and one does not like to get Emily Dickinson wrong. But it's: "I will let my Heart be just in sight."

And that's how I am right now, and I hope I don't cry, as I listened to the others talk about language and loss. I'm so sorry. Forgive me.

Poetry is spiritual practice, Anne said, and it took me to some thoughts I was having recently on my walks. I was telling the class this morning about walking and it being a part of my practice. Maybe a week to ten days ago, I thought about the fact that I've never really given thanks for poetry, for the gift of poetry.

Sometimes, when I walk, I will thank many people energetically and in language. And some of you may know I used to practice law and left it for poetry. Not knowing what lay ahead of me. Again, it's that idea of being able to remain in that place—of negative capability, that place of unknowing about following some paths.

So, this talk was a challenge, but it actually began on the shuttle ride here to Boulder. When I got into the shuttle in Denver, there was an East Asian gentleman whom I sat next to and he said to me, "Oh, are you here for the pathology conference?" And I said, "No. I'm a poet."

He said, "Oh."

I said, "If you want, I could write a poem about pathology."

He then said to me, "What d'you think of Martin Luther King?"— I should say he was actually from Prince Edward Island, one of our eastern provinces— "Do you think there's poetry in what he says?"

And I said, "Yes, there's a lot of poetry in what and how he says it."

He says, "Yes. I like Martin Luther King a lot. I like what he has to say." And then, he went on. He said, "What about Jesus?"

What does one say? Except you begin to… I said, "Well, I was raised Anglican, but I'm not actually a practicing Christian."

Anyway, I was trying to explain my relationship to Christianity when he said, "No, no, no. I'm not talking about that." He said, "I'm talking about what He had to say in poetry."

I said, "Oh yes, there's a lot of poetry." I said, "For instance, the Sermon on the Mount."

And then he said to me, "I've been teaching myself Greek. It's taken me five years," he says.

Now this is interesting because a couple of weeks ago, I had been thinking that I wanted to start trying to teach myself Greek, but he continued, "You know when you read many parts of the Bible, it's not what we understand it to be." He said, "For instance, that Sermon on the Mount," because I think I had said to him, "blessed are the poor."

He said, "The word blessed in Greek, blessed is a word that suggests that you're in this sort of receptive, almost passive position." He said, "But the word in Greek is great. It's magnanimous." He continued, "The poor," and this was the key for me, he said, "The poor, they're not talking about people who are deprived or lack wealth."

He says, "The poor are people who are searching after something, searching for a truth." And it was like the doors opened. And I thought, "but of course." If that is what it means, it has such a different meaning than how I have always interpreted that phrase, "blessed are the poor." And we went on, we continued talking. He talked about the need to surrender—that that's what the Bible was. It was this Oracle, it was this … he didn't say code. I think I thought code.

He asked me, "What'd you think about today as a poet?"

I said, "Well, actually technology is on my mind a lot and how difficult it is to deal with."

He said, "Well, I think a lot about despair." And he says, "What the Bible is telling us when people think about sin, it's not the sin we usually think of as in being immoral and so on."

He says, "It's chaos. It's with us always. And it's actually trying to show us how we can deal with that."

I then said to him, "Well, that reminds me of the spiritual practice that the Yoruba have in Western Nigeria called Ifa," which deals with deities, nature deities, and so on. I have many references to it in *Zong!*, but there is a figure called Eshu and Eshu represents the crossroads. Something like the trickster figure, but it's more than that. It's the crossroads. Anything is possible at the crossroads and that's part of life.

And so, they factor that in. So the potential for chaos is always present.

I remember thinking, "Oh, this is the beginning of my talk here." He talked about the spider being the Oracle and so on. And he actually gave me his email address. So, I will continue to have a correspondence with him. I hope, because as I listened to the talk here today and was being overwhelmed by the loss and the mourning for our dying world, I recalled the despair that he talked about, but I also want to believe that as long as we breathe and as long as there's poetry, that maybe that is the antidote to the despair.

This morning in class, I talked about Simone Weil and a wonderful book of hers, *The Need for Roots*, in which she talks about the Europeans uprooting themselves from their own indigeneity because we're all indigenous. I heard a First Nations person—which is the phrase we use in Canada—say this, that we're all indigenous to the earth and, to be more specific, we've all been indigenous to specific places on that earth.

When I visit Africa, that's when I get the sense of that loss. It always brings home to me how much is lost in the loss of language. This morning, I talked about the fact that every time I speak in English, there is a rape happening within my mouth in terms of how English was imposed on us—that it was this father tongue that was so savagely imposed on us during slavery after taking our languages away.

And yet I have to love that language, and I do love it deeply, as one can only love a parent, albeit abusive. I love that language. And some of that love has come from these books like the Bible and the Book of Common Prayer that were themselves responsible for destroying our own cultures. And those are the contradictions that we live with, and that I think poetry helps us to negotiate and balance.

There's been a recent essay, some of you may have seen it in *The Atlantic*, about reparations here, and I know in the Caribbean there's a process going on now in which former colonies are claiming reparations from the UK. But one of the things I feel very strongly about is that there is no cost that can be put on the loss of a language, the loss of a culture.

And there's a form of spiritual reparations that I think only we can give ourselves and it's on us to begin to do that. And, for me, *Zong!* Is maybe one small attempt at that, which I don't even understand yet quite what it is. But I do feel a little bit more secure that it's one small attempt to maybe mourn those who went unmourned for so long, to mourn some of that greater loss.

(presented at the panel: Dharma Gaze: Buddhist and Native World View, 2014)

Dreams, Again

Alice Notley

I've been using dream materials in my poems since I first began writing poetry in the late sixties. I've taken words, images, narratives, parts of narratives from my own dreams and repeated them, transformed them, commented on, and sung them. I did this instinctively in the beginning, without a theory and not particularly out of literary precedent, though there is plenty of that. Partly, it was clear to me that my dreaming self was better at some aspects of poetry writing than I, awake, was—my dreams would often surprise me when "I" couldn't.

In the early nineties, after having worked for a couple of years on the writing of *The Descent of Alette*, which draws to a large extent on dreams and on poetic techniques related to dreaming, I wrote an essay called "What Can Be Learned from Dreams," published in *SCARLET* in 1991. This essay posits "Dream" as a place or function in me I'm divided from, a place or function that knows things I don't know awake, and is often the better, more imaginative maker. The essay discusses, briefly, the plasticity and the symbolic multiplicity of dreams, and the relationship between dream and myth; and it reflects on the part a sensitivity to one's dreams might play in making one's way through the egoism and manipulation of oneself and others abounding in daily life (after all, you're *also* the pathetic creature you are in your dreams.) At this point, I began to write down my dreams every morning—I had done this once before for a couple of months, but my practice had generally been to write down only what was truly striking or mysterious. In the writing of *Alette*, I allowed myself to use anything I remembered from a dream no matter how humble or off-the-wall seeming, but I wasn't recording my dreams on a daily basis, I was more remembering them each day.

Between sometime in the early nineties and now, 2008, I have written down all my dreams I can remember each morning. I haven't tried to write well, only to get down what I retain; and I have omitted a few dreams on the grounds that they're just too personal in a scatological or other way and I don't want them read—I don't know what's going to happen to my dream notebooks when I die: they aren't very interesting in themselves, but I might not get around to destroying them. I'm now rather fatigued with the recording of dreams and may give up the practice in this daily manner, though I doubt that I will ever stop using dreams as material. What I'd like to ascertain at this point is whether I've learned anything further from my dreams, whether I can articulate what I know beyond my previous essay.

First, I will state as a fact that dreams can be premonitory or telepathic: they *can* predict the future and receive information at a distance from the dreamer. They don't do these things in a way that can be easily evaluated, and they don't always do these things clearly, but they do do them. Many people recognize this truth but don't know what to do about it; I scarcely know what to do about it, I usually incorporate dreams into my poems rather than speculate on how dreaming works. If you're interested in a more scientifically explanatory tractate involving the curvature of time, a multi-dimensional universe, and other such comforting terminology (now dated, of course), along with a study of precognitive dreams, I suggest you consult *An Experiment with Time* by J. W. Dunne (Faber and Faber Limited, 1927). I'm not interested in proving something, I'm interested in meditating on what I know; and I now feel confident enough to say that dreams *are* predictive and mind-sharing.

Thus, in my dreams, I've been forewarned that people will die, told that I am seriously ill, or that a friend is having heart surgery thousands of miles away (about which I know nothing in my waking life). I've dreamed that someone is discussing her uncle, while she is in fact doing this, many rooms and one floor away in a thick-walled house; dreamed that my husband's letter of rejection for a Guggenheim is about to arrive in the mail (it did, the morning of the dream); dreamed that the antibiotics I'm taking aren't working and the symptoms only appear to be under control (that was true too). These are randomly recalled examples. And I have anecdotal evidence of the same sorts of dreams from other people. This is one part of what dreams do: communicate literal information of a more or quite less pressing nature.

But just as interestingly, dreams make you be somewhere where you apparently aren't, render you a character in a story that isn't yours and that you believe, in fact destroy your identity except for the most central core of the "I," since you are that self, the unnamed only I that remembers the dream. Daily detail melts, I remain. Dreams also meditate, they think while you're asleep, they ruminate in story and symbol form and go pretty deep doing that. They pun in the ways Freud said they do, and are parable-like in the way the Bible indicates: they can be "interpreted," but that's only one interpretation, isn't it? And some things that appear not to be sexual may be sexual—but on the other hand, sex isn't always sex, it's rebirth, for example (see the ending of Norman Mailer's *Ancient Evenings*—not a dream, but so dreamlike); and the dreams aren't always about you the dreamer, as the ancients knew but Freud didn't appear to.

Sometimes, one gets through a personal crisis by sleeping and dreaming a lot: dreams instruct and heal. I consciously use dreams that way. I also sometimes try to dream oracularly, asking myself, the dreamer, a question before I fall asleep, to see what answer I'll receive in a dream.

So, when I decided to write this essay and began taking notes, I thought to try to dream about what dreams are. I wrote down in my dream notebook (on January 3rd, 2008): "TRY TO ASK DREAM ABOUT WHAT IT IS," and then fell asleep and had a series of dreams. In the first dream, I was walking in Place des Vosges, in Paris, with Karen Weiser, who said, "I don't have the cream." In the second dream, I heard the singing of the word "Deposuit," exactly as in a certain Bach choral piece—the Magnificat?—by a baritone voice, with much ornamentation. For the third dream, I will quote from my notebook: "With an Asian tribe—the Guarami—in mts. They want me to show them which rocks (?) are wedding rings; this one already is, I say. It's a large curved rock with a finger attached. The tribesman takes it eagerly." There was a subsequent dream that seems more personal and that I won't recount except to say it contained the name "Healey"—the name of a friend, whose appearance always signifies healing.

Some quick interpreting. Place des Vosges contains old, arcaded buildings, I was walking in a secluded place with someone who was "wiser," probably stood for Dream and nonetheless didn't have the answer, but who managed to make a rhyme with the important, initiating word, "dream": dream/cream. "Deposuit," in Latin, is from "deponere," to lay down, to put down, to deposit. From those two dreams, I get a sense that a word, or words, is, are, deposited and ornamented in a dream, as "deposuit" is so elaborated on in the singing of Bach's work. I woke up thinking that a dream is like an illuminated manuscript, in which words and letters are enlarged, made calligraphic, highlighted, painted, with stories and symbolic figures in the margins. I find the wedding ring dream harder to talk about. At some point, we became wedded to waking consciousness, perhaps; and our choice is embedded (see how I've rhymed, unconsciously, "wedded" and "embedded") in rock and flesh, the whole finger. In waking consciousness, we get a real, motile body, a stable one; in dreams we get a mind, though we also get an unstable, but often realistic, body. In the dream notebook, that morning, I also wrote: "Is dream an archaic way of thinking? Is it a memory of a way of being before time was sorted out? Do I have this memory?" I think the answer is dream is an ongoing, major component of existence.

I grew up in the Mohave desert, in a town that overlaps with the Mohave Indian Reservation. The Mohaves, in a way that seems similar to the thinking of certain Australian Aborigines, believe that everything important was first dreamed in order to be. I am now going to quote from the preface and introduction to *Tales from the Mohaves* (University of Oklahoma Press, 1970), by Herman Grey, a Mohave from my native area:

> The Mohave clings to his belief in dreams as a basis for everyday life. Not only all shamanistic power, but all myths, songs, bravery, fortune in battle, and good fortune in gambling derive from dreams. Every special event is dreamed. Knowledge is not a thing to be learned, a Mohave will say, but something to be acquired by each person through his dreaming.
>
> All Shamans say that they received their power from Mastamho, when he was put here on this earth. So deep are these convictions that, when old age comes, a Mohave can seldom distinguish between the dreams he has been told by an uncle or brother and what he has himself experienced. The Mohave learns as much from other people as from his own experience. Conscious learning seems to him nearly impossible, and he is convinced he has dreamed for the first time, or has dreamed repetitiously, the things which all Mohaves know in common....
>
> A man may give his song or story to his son or to some other close relative when he feels himself near to death or concludes

that the person in question wishes to learn the story or song. Only one man may sing or tell a sequence of songs and stories, and thus the myths are inherited within the family and clan. A storyteller begins from a timeless source, with the statement that the story came to him from his uncle or brother and now belongs to him.

Dreams, then, are the foundation of Mohave life. Dreams are always stated as if they had been cast in mythological molds. . . .

A dream might be an actual nocturnal one, or it might be a continued thought or a flash of insight which gave a further comprehension and contemplation of the man's hopes and perceptions. Dreams might give foresight of some obstacle to the achievement of an end and might also reveal the means of overcoming the obstruction. Many times a dream foretold a coming event, such as the outcome of a raid or the fate of a warrior.

What strikes me here is first the intersection of all categories: shamanism, dream, myth, story, knowledge—these seem to coincide and then differentiate, but never become totally distinct from each other. Dreaming and waking obviously aren't so different from each other either, in the Mohave world. One has a sense that time and consciousness are perceived as fluid, not compartmentalized into asleep/awake, past, present, and future. It's not that one is always in now—the Now that can be so fashionable, philosophically, to talk about—but the past is an important concept too, and the past goes on in an important way, and the future is accessible. Of course, I'm also interested in the sense that Dreams Know. I believe I've read elsewhere that when there's an important invention (or when there was—I don't know if Mohaves are as obsessed with dreams as they once were, as traditional), the invention must be incorporated into the tribe's dreams. It has to have been known about from the beginning, so it must have been dreamed about before. Somehow, the innovation gets put into dream form and then one says, "Yes I always knew about that, or we did." Of course, that's what it feels like anyway: who can imagine life before cars? Was there always going to be a car? (See the cars shown in the TV cartoon *The Flintstones*—the previsionable automobile.)

I didn't know these facts about the Mohaves while I was growing up alongside them. I've found these things out later, as I've developed my own thought and discovered that it resembles theirs. Isn't that strange? The Mohave Desert is vast with space and one fills it with thoughts and dreams—or I did; I acquired certain habits of thought from growing up in this landscape. I came to wonder if so-called reality weren't malleable, creatable, long before I knew about the philosophy of the Mohaves or of the Australian Aborigines, who also inhabit a desert.

It seems logical to me to quote a Mohave as an authority on dreams. Grey knows what it is to believe one's dreams, to use them, and to have dream-like flashes of inspiration (as a poet does.) And reality must have seemed flexible when you lived in a desert and didn't build things much: when you and those you were with were in a state of invention all the time. Imagine an early tribal existence in a desert. There's just the few of you, and you can say what is, what made it, and what it means. You're the poets of what you know. It's when people erect a lot of buildings and crowd together in large numbers that everyone has to agree on a version of reality that grounds the buildings dryly and makes it possible for those from different backgrounds, or even cultures, to communicate blandly. However, if you take certain drugs, you will notice that the texture of wood and brick is in motion—though the buildings don't fall—that people's faces melt, and that nothing is as secure as you thought it was. As when you dream, things fall apart, and the laws of science are violated. Occasionally, when you dream, an animal talks to you. Many Native American peoples posit an early time when humans and animals talked to each other and shared characteristics more blatantly, when time wasn't as fixed as now, and you could make things happen by "magic." (For a lovely, modern sci-fi take on this possibility, see Ursula K. Le Guin's book, *Buffalo Gals and Other Animal Presences*.)

Furthermore, many people could tell you they have had dreams that have changed their lives. I have a long list of such dreams. They become mythic; they "happened" for real, to the extent that they have changed me. I count them as part of my knowledge and use them for guidance. Here is my retelling of an important dream, from the preface to my book, *Reason and Other Women*:

> In 1997, after I had been informed that Allen Ginsberg had died, I became afraid for him in death. I wanted—because he was my friend—to be sure that in death he was safe. I dreamed that night that my stepdaughter Kate, who is deceased and in dreams is often my messenger from the world of the dead, came for me, in a rich dark blue skirt and sweater, to take me to the "second world." I gathered that this second world was an afterlife with an active artistic component, for there was a professor there who was trying to achieve an intense enough red for the second world's mosaics. Then, my name became Ellen Goodman (yes like the columnist), so I knew that I was Allen, the good man, and I waited in a small apartment to die. To die being to lose the power of one's vocal cords, no longer to speak… A knock at the door as "they" came for me, I approached the door knowing I had used my vocal apparatus for the last time and would now learn to communicate telepathically; then I woke up. Allen was safe; for I understood there was an expansiveness beyond that of the voice. And I could now write with authority, of the first and second worlds, and the colors blue and red. The soul must be red. And Kate, the messenger was dressed in blue, for reason: as reason is the working through of "messages," or is perhaps the voyage of the messenger.

This dream enabled me to write my book, providing a sense of a double world and, also, a color symbolism, plus a notion of telepathy: in *Reason and Other Women*, I overtly expect the reader to get what I'm saying via a sort of telepathy—the reader must go with the rhythms and odd usages of my mind as I present it, in order to know further things, attain a new state of consciousness with its own materials and details, coaxed from dreams and words. You might well say that that is what poetry is—an art form based on telepathy, a sending of complex messages through an almost immaterial presentation (a few words on a page?); or, you might say, that all communication is like that. And isn't it? Aren't we always communicating telepathically? So much of what we tell each other is told via air: to talk about "cues" and "body language" is to be perfectly limited: it's in the very air between us, everything we know and try to say to each other. We read each other's minds all the time.

Anyway, the dream presented these ideas to me, as well as the knowledge that Allen was whole and well, and that it would be good, probably, not to have to use one's vocal cords anymore: there was a bigger, better language, if you want to call it that. The dream remains important to me: it's part of who I am and what I know; it's part of my relationship with Allen and with everyone else. For me, it is a work of great beauty in itself, though it terrifies me as well. The opening of the door at the end was a vast moment, to step into infinity without being able to speak, never again to write poetry.

If dreams are telepathic or precognitive or knowledge-imparting or otherwise "extraordinary," then do they exist to fill those functions, or are those functions a byproduct of dreams? Or, more likely, are dreams and those functions part of a similar flexible fabric we keep trying to push away from our world of clear-cut surfaces? Dreams are certainly a part of our condition of being alive. But how do they work? Why do we accept the fact of dreaming, as we accept walking and talking, without ever asking ourselves how, physically, we can be in another place, identity, and story, while we lie in bed sleeping?

We accept dreams but do not accept premonition. Do we have to accept dreams? Or did we? For sometimes it seems as if we are always creating who we are, selecting which of our abilities we want and pretending not to have others. We opt for dreaming—some scientists would say "select for it"—but do we have to dream? We're always dreaming, perhaps. Some people think an unconscious part of us dreams while we're awake—and I have personal experience of this. There is a wall in ourselves between sleeping and waking that dissolves at night, but we're always dreaming; and a part of one is always awake. The dreamer is awake in the dream.

How *are* we able to experience dreams at night as a physical reality, as we do? This seems to me to be a much stickier problem than the fact of premonition and telepathy in dreams. I mean, if you accept dreams in all their impossibility, you might as well accept something like premonition. Why does it seem acceptable to you that you can dream you're married to someone you've never seen in waking life (you realize when you wake up)—in fact, a mean drunk—in an apartment you've never been in? "Oh, yes, that's normal for dreams," you say. How is that normal? Somehow our senses are working, but what are they stimulated by? Where did this guy come from? He and the apartment were rock-solid and he was, absolutely, my husband. The dream was scary and intense. I incorporated it into a poem (that I've never published) twenty-seven years ago. It still upsets me to think about the dream. I can interpret it, if I want to, but I can't explain the physical reality of the tall thin man with slick almost pompadourish red hair and the apartment with its twilit psychic emptiness, and I can't explain the fact that I *was* that story. I wasn't myself, but I was.

As no science explains adequately how dreams work, no one can explain how a poem works. Where is a dream, sure, but where is a poem? I believe somewhat in Williams' formulation that a poem is a machine made out of words, but, finally, the poem isn't where the words are. The poem is somewhere between the words and the reader, or it is the words taken into the reader, who exists within the general society and its history. You enter the poem when you open to its page or remember it, having memorized it, but it is a much larger world than the page. It is transformed when you say it out loud; and it changes from reading to reading—you, the reader, change it, for one thing, as you change—or is it that it changes for you? If you are reading a poem by Catullus, you are in no way the same as an ancient Roman reading it: you are not that person—that kind of person, though it is that poem, as those words. But even if you know Latin, you don't "speak Latin," and you haven't much feeling for what it was like to be a Roman. A poem, like a dream, has an odd relation to time: it is in time, like a poem by Catullus, but it is timeless, as an object made out of words. A dream lasts a moment but endures as a memory might: but it didn't *really* happen. A memory can be backed-up, but no outside observer can find the particulars of a dream in time and space (evidence of REM or whatever isn't evidence of what happened in your dream). A poem didn't or doesn't happen, it's a still group of words on a page; and a story doesn't really happen either. We say that dreams, poems, and stories occur in the imagination, or the psyche, or whatever word we're using right now, to invent another entity that doesn't concretely exist to put them in. But doesn't the "real world" exist in some collective category like that? All we do is dream; we live in poems and stories we invent.

I'm interested in how caught up I can be in a daily comic strip in the newspaper, given four meager frames a day, of "unreal" actions perpetrated by line drawings who speak in balloons. For the last couple of years, reading Doonesbury on a daily basis in the *International Herald Tribune*, I have felt completely involved in the strip whenever the character B.D., whose leg was shot off in Iraq, enters this amazingly sketchy, involving world. Recently another character, Toggle, has been shot up—shot in the head—has aphasia, and has been transferred from Iraq to Walter Reed Hospital in Washington, where B.D. is visiting him. I was recently in New York, and reading the comics one morning I said to Jess Fiorini, "It looks like Toggle is finally about to make it to Walter Reed." "Oh, yes," she replied seriously, "I saw that." Toggle is probably more real to me than Barack Obama or John McCain are; I am commenting on my imagination, not on them. I read, on a daily basis, *Doonesbury*, reruns of *Peanuts*, and *Calvin and Hobbes*, and sometimes *Dilbert*. The world of *Peanuts* is worth reentering many times—it grows more beautiful as time passes, the drawing always seems more interesting and the situations more poetic: it has become literary and artistic, in time, though I suppose it always was—but these qualities are becoming more evident. I miss the comic strips of my earliest childhood, though. I remember being entirely caught up in *Dick Tracy* during the saga of the angel girl whose name I can no longer remember; I can still see her radioactive angel-winged hair. None of this ever happened.

Suppose you admit that the world, physical reality, going on from day to day, is, in some long-term way, plastic, malleable. You can conceive of existence as a field you are involved in shaping. You can think of yourself as almost totally shaping it on your own or reshaping it; refusing to accept the names people give to its shape automatically transforms it straight off. We are dreaming together, but we are dreaming separately too. Some of us are writing poems, and sometimes the poems are dreamlike. For example, there has been a school of poetry, Surrealism, inspired by the apparent mechanics of dreams, that contributed single words to the culture—"surreal," "surrealistic"—and also furnished a way of viewing the overall story we may be in: "This war is surreal." For a very long time in Western civilization, there existed a literary form, sometimes called a dream vision, sometimes called an apocalypse, in which a lady appeared to a protagonist in dire circumstance and urged him or her not to give in to despair, and instead to grow strong and conquer fear and doubt. The vision of the lady, from Boethius, through Dante, Christine de Pizan, and Chaucer, and more recently in poets like D.G. Rossetti and T.S. Eliot—that's almost two thousand years of these visions—is a powerful poetic event, still. The dream is as real as the words that describe it, as when the three ladies appear to Christine, in *La Cité des Dames*, who is despairing at the misogyny of the world and wondering if the female sex is indeed the inferior one:

> Lost in these painful thoughts, my head bowed in shame, my eyes full of tears, my hand supporting my cheek and my elbow on the pommel of my chair's armrest, I suddenly saw a ray of light descending onto my lap as if it were the sun. And as I was sitting in a dark place where the sun could not shine at this hour, I was startled as if awakened from sleep. And as I lifted my head to see where this light was coming from, I saw standing before me three crowned ladies of great nobility. The light coming from their bright faces illuminated me and the whole room. Now, no one would ask whether I was surprised, given that my doors were closed, and nevertheless they had come here. Wondering whether some phantom had come to tempt me, in my fright I made the sign of the cross on my forehead.
>
> Then the first of the three began to address me as follows: "Dear daughter, do not be afraid, for we have not come to bother or to trouble you but rather to comfort you, having taken pity on your distress, and to move you out of the ignorance that blinds your own intelligence so that you reject what you know for certain and believe what you do not know, see, and recognize except through a variety of strange opinions."[3]

In a typical dream vision, the lady or ladies tell the seer or dreamer that she or he must not believe the world, or give in, mentally, to its

---

[3] As translated by Blumenfeld-Kosinski and Brownlee, in *The Selected Writings of Christine de Pizan* (W.W. Norton & Company, 1997).

brute force by acceding to abjection, that there is an evident truth that she knows for herself and that will now be proven to her, by Lady Reason, or Dame Philosophy, or whoever. The dream is right, you see, and the world is wrong; the poem knows, and the lady will now impart its highest knowledge. When I read this kind of work, I am always startled when the lady appears, I find her as beautiful as the writer does, and I believe in her reality absolutely, though she is most often "an allegorical figure." That's what we call her: Reason is not real, it's an "abstraction." In fact, Reason is as real as Lady Reason is, as real as the vision of her arising from the words on the page; she is real at that moment, the writer is real, and I am not there, the only one present who is real, the one who will remember that last moment when she appeared to me, when I identified with the protagonist. In fact, there seems to me to be nothing truer in *this* world and *these* times than Christine's despair at the world's misogyny six hundred or so years ago; nor anything as true as Lady Reason's defense of women.

We are constantly remaking the world from the inside out. As I say at the end of *The Descent of Alette*: "'I will change the" "forms in dreams" ... / "Starting" / "from dreams," "from dreams we" "can change," "will change ... "' If we can be clear that reality is changeable, we can change it; and we can understand better both what our dreams are and what poetry can do for us. Dreams remind us that we can shape the world, that it doesn't fit into the categories we tend to make for it: we think and observe with our dreams and communicate with unconscious others, moving about in a time and space whose walls are down. Poetry is our conscious attempt to reshape the world, which is, as Philip Whalen says, "by nature wicked." We make it and remake it over and over. It's practically all we're doing; I mean, poetry is practically all that we're doing.

(2013)

Cultural and Political Rhizomes

Sherwin Bitsui

I am interested in the notions of interconnectedness that create the spine or the body of a rhizome. And I am interested in how that can be articulated through poetry. My own work throughout my lifetime and my experience is a type of rhizomic narrative. In Navajo language, often we refer to story or narrative as having some kind of ropey matter. One time I introduced myself—I was talking to some Navajos after a reading I gave, and I was talking about how I picked up my language—and when I referred to the notion of my own language, I said a word which translates loosely to "I carry this ropey language," or "I took it from him," just as I would say if I had picked up a rope. In the verb stem "lá" gives form and dimension to an otherwise abstract concept such as "language." Navajo grammar has a way of predetermining the way a thing or concept may be interacted with. In that sense, I have always looked at language and poetry as root systems that are horizontal.

My poetic experience has been that, and for some reason I connect that also to the shape of how stories were told to me in the late twentieth century. Even just on drives with my father, with my mother, with my grandmother, or with my grandfather—because I grew up in a very rural part of the country, the laundromat is forty-two miles away, school is forty-two miles away, the nearest library and grocery stores are forty-two miles away, so we had a lot of drives. Often when people refer to my book, *Floodsong*, they see it as a road trip; that's a metaphor people seem to want to use to describe my work because there is a very horizontal journey occurring within it.

Within that scope, I thought about how the narratives were retold. Oftentimes on these long drives, my father would tell a story, and he would point to a place where the story happened. Or he would tell a story that his grandfather had told him, and he would point to the place where the story happened. So, as we were on these long branches of highway and desert dirt roads, there was always an awareness of the horizon, an awareness of the place. This was how we were constantly reimagining the place or how it was constantly imagining us.

In a recent discussion, we were talking about how language and stories can also recreate us. In my own cultural rhizome, there is an acknowledgement that language is to be attended to, to be respected; and that it is not just that we expound story and poetry, but we think it and it thinks us back. It is a reciprocal relationship one has with language. That is an important poetic device in my work, and I think it works for most people. Try to imagine living in a continuum, rather than living in an isolated, unrooted place, and writing from an un-rootedness, which I find to be a general aesthetic among North Americans—there seems to be a denial, a sense that they somehow don't have a culture. When you're outside of that, I can see that you do have a culture, I can see your culture. My poetics are about rooting into, becoming a part of. These rhizomes are all connected.

I am curious in my own personal process if there is a point where the language itself becomes exhausted. And then a type of mimicry occurs, it assumes or absorbs another way of looking at things. Or there is a reciprocal relationship between the end of one language and the beginning of another. All of these points are occurring simultaneously within the poetics I am trying to express.

(presented at the panel: Cultural Political Rhizomes, 2012)

Lecture on Native American Cosmologies

Harry Smith

STEVEN TAYLOR: *In the spring of 1988, Harry Smith was staying at Allen Ginsberg's place at 437 East 12th Street, in the tiny back bedroom where I had stayed on and off since the late 1970s. We were then involved in the second of two episodes, one of injury and the other of illness, that had Harry on extended stays at the apartment. In the first case, his leg had been broken when he stepped between parked cars and one moved, pinning his shin between bumpers. He stayed some months and then disappeared for a time as was his wont. In the second instance, after Allen or his secretary, Bob Rosenthal, or I said we haven't seen Harry for a while, Allen went down to Harry's Bowery flophouse room and found him starving. He had contracted a flu and had been unable to get up and go out to his regular diner to eat, and so was in his bed, slowly dying. Allen brought his birdlike frame back to 437. We started* him on protein milkshakes and by summer he was mending, alert, able to walk about, sitting at the kitchen table most of the day chatting with us and with visitors.

One evening in June, Allen and I were standing alone in the kitchen going over various business, and he noted that he and I were about to head to Colorado for the Naropa Summer Writing Program (SWP), and he said the question is what to do about Harry, and simultaneously we said we'll take him with us. Harry lived at Naropa until 1991 and lectured annually during the SWP. He lectured without notes, for the most part, and tended to ramble, as will be evident in the following transcript. These were special occasions for all present, filled with humor, and of great interest. After Harry's death in 1991, Peter Lamborn Wilson took over the spot, delivering what became known as the Harry Smith Lectures in Strange Anthropology.

And so I had some things, some notes, I was going to make, which I will try to do on the blackboard. My teacher Paul Radin once said, "In the beginning there was magic, and magic was with God, and God was magic. That's in his book *Primitive Religion* (1937).[4] And, however, I was looking at some folktales from Northern Japan; the first version is the Sun God. But then there is a little star [asterisk in the text] and you look down and it says, "or Goddess." The word doesn't mean...

---

4 In 1907, Polish-born American anthropologist and linguist Paul Radin (1883–1959) became a student of Franz Boas, who had founded the first anthropology PhD program in the US at Columbia University. Radin did fieldwork among the Hocąk (Winnebego) people (*The Winnebago Tribe*, 1923), went on to do linguistic work in Wappo, Huave, Mixe, Tlappanecan, and Zapotec, and developed a classification of Mexican languages. From the 1940s until his death, he was monitored by the FBI on suspicion of being a communist. Harry knew him at UC Berkeley, one of a dozen schools in which Radin taught (including Black Mountain College just prior to Berkeley) during his nomadic career.

Now, most anthropology having been written by a man, there is a tendency to have peculiar ideas about the Incan Empire, for example, that I'll clear up at some particular point.

One thing that was customary in the so-called Old World was the domestication of animals. Whereas the New World [was] sexualizing the domestication and the developments of new species of plants—plants like corn and beans and so forth, most of them have the property of also being herbal [medicinal] in nature. We seldom think of food as having, you know, being good for us, or as one author calls it "food that cures." And, of course in 1480, the—I don't know what to call them, the Natives I guess—anyhow, whoever lived here was extremely healthy. They had a life expectancy much longer than the Europeans at the time.

On his second voyage in 1494, Columbus brought [back] twelve hundred specimens of things: men, seeds, cuttings for planting, wheat, chickpeas, melons, onions, radishes, salad greens, grapevines, sugarcane, and fruit stones for planting orchards. As far as disease is concerned, all diseases transmitted from one continent to another went westward: smallpox, measles, typhoid fever, tuberculosis, plague, diphtheria, etc.

Now, what causes tuberculosis? Is it the tuberculosis bacilli that causes it? Or is it poverty and malnutrition? It doesn't take much thinking to decide that it's not the germs really.

Let's see, the Europeans also had other bad habits, such as associating physical labor with status. It was hard for them, you must remember that Cortés was a contemporary of Henry VIII; it gives you one idea of why the Europeans were so unhealthy, 'cause they had so much clothing on. This was supposed to be somehow connected with the above, but I forget how. In one famous formulation of this idea, this kind of view, the amoeba and Einstein used the same method, which is trial and error. If truth were created with that which increases the probability of survival, then science would certainly be untrue, because it increases the possibility of non-survival through, they say, various types of human or natural disaster. But the Europeans have always been willing to exchange good health for cultural complexity. They would rather see a clock tick than live ten years longer.

The fascination with machinery is very strange. Another thing that is typical of the Western hemisphere are the child training practices, that lead to the theories of innate aggression, that Lorenz and Kuhnberg and Morris, et cetera, consider aggression, they consider it to be universal, but this simply happens to be untrue. Ashley Montague made an analysis of a great number of cultures and it usually revolves around people who are emotionally deprived. I don't have to go into this 'cause you already know it.

I was going to conclude this by describing—oh, someone asked me the question, "How did you get into these things [string figures]?" Some cousins of mine had a book on string figures and, in learning them, I realized that—this is happening north of Seattle, Washington—children from the [Lummi] Reservation, of course, went to school with me, and I would ride out on the bus [after] school with them to see if their parents knew any string figures.

I don't think it's going to work, I can't stand up and draw. But I was going—and rather than give generalized thoughts regarding the way that certain methods of thinking… One peculiar thing that happens is that very often light is stolen and released in the Northern hemisphere, whereas in the Valley of the Amazon, it is usually darkness that is stolen and sent into the eternal light.

So, there was, near where I was visiting, what was called the spirit dance. This was held in a long building about as wide as this tent [the lecture takes place in a large tent], but there was room down the middle for fires. During the year, certain birdlike animals… Now, this is put together with conversations I had with people fifty years ago and I was only beginning to try to remember them, when I realized it was time to start [the present talk]. But the ideas are going to be somewhat disjointed.

But being as two types of phenomena happened, the origin of the first humans was of a universal nature that I didn't realize until earlier this year, which had to do with the creation of a series of humans, from things like stone and clay. I believe the final one was made of wood. Later on, these humans realized certain things that perhaps resembled birds, but with wings maybe of obsidian or something— it's hard to tell because there simply aren't terms in English for the concepts that exist. The human himself, or herself, was really a series of concentric spheres that time went through in both directions from this central point. In other words, grandchildren had the same names as grandparents because they were the same distance away. Maybe one was smaller, but it was farther away and it was smaller for that reason or something like that.

These are things from casual conversations. Someone else in describing the nature of—they were a famous doctor—of their curing, said that they were surrounded by four helpers: one red, one blue, one yellow, and one green. I'm retranslating that helper, as a man, I believe, either said souls or spirits, but it was fifty years ago, and I don't remember it too well. And he was in the center of this. He was also the sort of titular leader. This is where those people, the Swinomish… All these things will come from the groups in the northern part of Puget Sound, and the adjoining parts of Vancouver Island, where Victoria is. At any rate, people would then be… certain wooden objects. As I said, there were four fires down the middle of the building and holes in the roof. There were certain wooden objects, stakes shaped like a bird, and a double-headed thing, because it took four people to hold it down, it would drag them around the room.

The so-called "spirit dance" takes place on the earth, where the [wooden objects] were used. Mrs. Brown, who got the song that goes with [them, said] the words mean "this little bird is going to sing." And it was dramatic, but it took place on the earth and, later, it was very well known. There were some professors from the university there and so forth. After I'd gone to a number of meetings of that kind, I was invited to something that had been outlawed many, many years before, the so-called Dog Howler's Society. This was held in four houses arranged in a square and involved a great number of things like masks. People who were literally frightening, the ones that had become animals. This all took place in heaven. It involved a number of things: rattles shaped like skulls, a choir on the roof…

It was literally terrifying, the people who were disguised as wolves. They had wooden masks on. All of the Northwestern coast from Southeastern Alaska to Puget Sound has a certain kind of art style. This is because the artists traveled around. There weren't people everywhere that did that. They mostly lived on the Skeena or Nass Rivers, and went to the Queen Charlotte Islands and parts of Vancouver to make these trick things [hinged wooden masks?] that gave the impression that [laughs] Hieronymus Bosch was alive and wailing through the woods. At any rate, those are the things that it consisted of. So, these wolf people, boy were they scary. I sort of went back like this [he recoils]. They come at you.

The person who became an ordinary singer in the spirit dance, she lived around Seattle. It was called the spirit canoe. The same songs are sung, but the same apparatus isn't used. The belief in this double-ended space… Are there any mothers out here? It just occurred to me, I read that babies who cry a lot become very good singers. Although, in a lot of places the baby—yeah, pretty much along Northern America—the baby is named the names of people who died since the last baby was born. The reason that crying, I mean singing, came up is a mother, [who] said her daughter wasn't a very good singer, said, "Maybe I stopped her from crying too early." And the child is then given a variety of objects that belonged to the preceding incarnation of that name. Was that an answer to any question?

So, in various ones of these four houses, on the way down to this place, I had been told I would have to give a needle, that someone would ask for a needle as I went down. This was strange 'cause I was at the end of Vancouver, BC, something-or-other street car line. There was the lady who asked for the needle, and I gave her a bone needle that I dug out of the shell heap. And I said, "There's a big dance down there," and she said, "No." And I went down, and someone who was influential that I knew was down there. I doubt if any other living person, except children who were there, would be alive who saw what she did, because it embodied a great number of sort of unique acts. I mentioned things like the choir on the roof, there were also pipes, made somewhat like organ pipes, and almost as large.

The music of that whole area is very beautiful, but unfortunately has not been... There are intense prejudices against anybody who has been on reservations and has relatives who are stuffed in a museum along with giraffes and things. [They] feel embarrassment and remorse when graveyards of their grandfathers are dug up to count the number of crosses in relation to coins, or something.

So, anyhow, I went down there and there was somebody who said, "No, no you can't come." I might be killed or something... I suppose there were four hundred people there. Someone went around swinging a bullroarer. All of these ritual elements probably occur in sequence independent of the interpretation that's placed on them. And quite probably referred to a cosmographic scheme that can be explained scientifically but runs counter to what might be considered scientific thought.

Audience member: "What year was this?"

Let's say that was around 1940.[5] There's a write-up in various magazines and things from that period. The earliest one I know is

---

5 The Swinomish are fishers of salmon. They traditionally constructed cedar longhouses, where people gathered after the fishing season to hold ceremonies, such as the spirit dance that Smith witnessed "around 1940." After their reservation was established by treaty in 1855, the Bureau of Indian Affairs prohibited ceremonies such as spirit dancing, but rituals continued in secret. Some longhouses were burned during disease outbreaks, as a public health measure. The last of the old longhouses was burned or collapsed in the 1940s.

1943, however, as far as a published photograph. I lost interest in it until about three months ago when Naropa called, and who was I to say "nay"?

Anyhow, I really can't describe it because in a way I feel I'm desecrating the trust that was put into me. The organization supposedly having been stamped totally, thoroughly, completely, and forever out in something like 1843… Something that hasn't been seen for a hundred years suddenly seen. And all I can give is a description of what happened. For example, all of the people going around crawling on the floor were naked except for the wolf mask, and this occurs, as I said, happens after you've been up for forty-eight hours listening to incessant drumming that had increased the adrenaline and blood to such a point that everything glistens sort of. And just as the sun came down to the smoke—because the entire house, of course, is full of smoke from the fires, it made beams that shot down onto one of the actual fires that were there—very, very old women came in. Everybody that comes into this type of a house comes in backwards. This is explained in various ways, such as to avoid stepping on your shadow, to go into a form of reversal… Very old women with skulls, I mean drums, rattles shaped like skulls, very stylized. I mean, there wasn't any question it was something that looked like a skull. That's what they were supposed to be. They had twisted mouths. And it hadn't occurred to me until yesterday that the twisted mouths business would be similar to the Iroquois crooked-faced mask. And, of course, we will be covering this later.

And, anyhow, they sang a song while the whistles blew on the roof. And all the while this was going on—and it had taken much, much longer than I've taken to describe it—there had been a curtain hanging, made of mountain goat wool. Most blankets of any value were made of mountain goat wool, maybe with some quieter black stripes in it. [The curtain] dropped and there was a person there and their tongue sort of dropped over the front of their mouth, and string with knots in it run through the tongue. Blood had run down the blanket he was wearing, which was sort of an unusual fashion, over one shoulder and over the other arm. The blanket was usually put on in this fashion. And like a lot of the other people, he had a [cedarbug] headdress on, but it was one event after the other—first, the imitations of the wolves, then this revolving circle of… what does Aristotle call it? "The prime mover." It's in the middle of the floor that you see someone.

Now, I should've mentioned earlier that one of the most widespread stories being found all over both North and South America is [about] a girl, who sometimes is a companion, or out on the grass. I'm going to tell it the way [it was] being told around, you know, Bellingham. [The girl], as she was falling asleep, said that's a beautiful star and, when she awoke in the morning, it turned out she was married to that star and was a long way from home. And I was assured that the coil of rope that she got back by was woven out of her pubic hair and collapsed. The story again can be found almost everywhere [chuckles]—the Arapahoe have that story. And, that was what the string through the tongue represented… Later on, we'll connect this notion of the string through the tongue [to]—I was gonna say the Arapahoe Sun Dance, but it's better we get back to Seattle. Uh, let me see, the important things perhaps are that, on the earth, the people revolve and, in the heavens, the earth revolves. Or something like that, I will try to formulate it better before we meet again, if we ever do.

I want you to end up with some notion that maybe the people that lived here for, at the very least 140,000, 100,000 years, maybe knew something about the ecology. Maybe they knew that there was a sort of reason, and maybe in time… Getting back to Paul Radin, I was walking down Panoramic Lane in Berkeley with him once, and he said, "You know the Indians are going to take over again." And I said, "No you can't mean—" And he said, "Yeah sure, they're just gonna take over" [laughs]. And when I hear that people are having what are colloquially called "sweats," I think how happy some people would be that died needlessly to leave certain truths for us…

Now, are there any questions at all regarding any events at all?

[Inaudible audience question]

Ha! [laughs] I didn't understand what anybody was doing. They just came, and the right hand had these rattles shaped sort of like skulls probably, with the skin dried on them, and sang a song that seemed to have more formal rhythms. As far as I can remember it, I'm sure it was some type of ancestral mourning song, because people who had borne the name that came along with the [chuckles] box full of magic tricks—I think they represented the stars…that all of the stars came out of rawhide, and the great black meteoric starbundle.

[Inaudible question]

In Algonquian, the same root or verbal root, whatever you want to call it, means woman. In fact, in Seneca, there is no difference; there are no gods, you might say. They're called the same name the human beings are called. There is a creator that is kept separate, but the things like the giants and so forth are often translated man-beings, but might as well be translated women-beings. Yes, you soul sisters all had a position in the heavenly land. And, don't worry, you're safe.

(1990)
edited by Steven Taylor

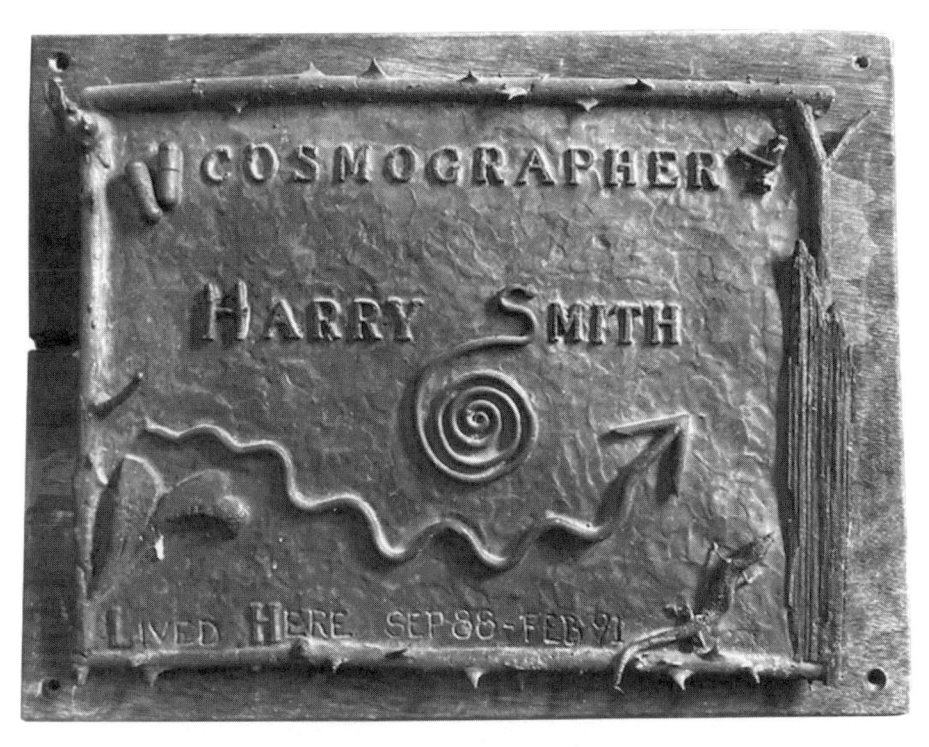

Figure 2: Harry Smith memorial plaque by Peter Cole that was placed outside of the cottage where Smith lived from September 1988 through February 1991. The cottage was later repurposed as a recording studio and is now a Naropa student center. Photograph by Anne Waldman.

Syntax and the Event of Reading

Renee Gladman

I want to talk to you today about two possibilities of the sentence—the sentence as a platform for the cultivation of a philosophy of experience, and the sentence as a space to move through, a place of encounter. These are both ideas of reading and writing, and one way to approach them is to begin with syntax. But in preparing to speak today, I found myself less moved by the definition of syntax—the arrangement of word forms to show their mutual relations in a sentence—as I was by that of the word *syntaxic,* presumably the adjectival counterpart. *Webster's Third New International Dictionary* defines it as follows: "characterized by or relating to a mode of experience or symbolic behavior that relates symbols and referents, speech and action, subject and object in a sequentially logical and interpersonally verifiable manner."

Before I begin, let me tell you what it is like to sit here and talk about the sentence. It is like explaining to you how I am sitting here. On one hand, it is extremely obvious that I'm sitting here. But on the other hand, I am having a series of sensations that might not be as apparent. However, once I start to explain them, you will pretty much know exactly what I am talking about. Yet, I'll be hoping that there is something new as well. What I mean is that the sentence is ubiquitous. We use it all the time. We move from thinking to writing or thought to speech all the time. It's so automatic. But then we stop to look at these processes, like deciding to pay attention to your breathing, to the fact that you're breathing. You follow the mechanics, and then start to notice other things: when I inhale, something lifts at the top of my head, creates a clearing, and so on. To look at these automatic processes in a slow, highly conscious, especially the sentence, which I believe is the blueprint for how that historical self that Akilah [Oliver] was talking about the other day gets constructed—to look at it is to inevitably come to terms with a kind of politics of being, in whatever way that takes shape for each person.

So back to our definition of syntaxic. What amazes me right away is that experience is made level with symbolic behavior, an equation that allows words and punctuation to act as representations of actual lived experiences. Each part of speech represents a particular aspect of being—like pronouns referencing subjectivity, adjectives addressing states of appearance, question marks, our curiosity, and so on. Not only are we dealing with a supposition that thoughts, feelings, actions, and time can be recalled, can be sculpted in verbal form, but also what naturally follows: that the form these sensations take *behaves* in such a way as to render reality.

For a language to be successful, it has to be shared. Its users must generally agree on its usage. In the sense that we all agree that the sound "chair" matches this thing here, as do we agree that, to write out that sound, we use these letters in this order: c-h-a-i-r. We inherit a vocabulary and rules for implementation. And while there has been plenty of room to introduce new words and patterns of communication as well as to subvert old ones, these transformations or acts or deviance have mostly occurred in relation to a certain standard. *That this is the logical way to speak, that one should order one's words in this way.*

So, again, back to syntaxic. While the definition seems to be saying that inherent in our experience is a mechanism or instinct that gathers parts of the sentence together in a "sequentially logical or interpersonally verifiable manner," I think literature shows us something a little different.

To elaborate, I want to take us to the moment before writing. That threshold. How we occupy a space of imagining or reach, how an impulse or an idea leads us into the work, into language. What fascinates me about this threshold is how little we know about how thoughts become sentences. The translation required there. I don't know what a cognitive scientist or a neurologist would say about where and how thoughts sit in the mind but, as a thinker, as someone conscious of myself thinking, I am very aware that my thinking exists in a very different order than do the words of a sentence. That is, we think in flashes, in layers, in a jumble sometimes. We think in multiples. Sometimes a thought just feels like a heavy pulse, blood pushing through your brain. But how amazing is it to move from that space into the space of language and communication. Suddenly, these thoughts that are like this [in a level row] or like this [in a constellation] must become like this [one line moving forward]. And it's not just that the sentence moves in a straight line, but that you can only think one thing at a time.

Which suggests that language acts upon our experience as much as, if not more than, our experience acts upon it. I find myself asking what happens in that translation—moving from thought to language—in that realignment of our constellation of ideas into a single string of thinking. How does copy relate to the original, how does it transform it?

Knowing this and being poised at the threshold of writing might make you more conscious of yourself unfolding step by step through the sentence.

The English language sentence is "sequentially logical." To begin in English is to almost always begin with a subject. Once you've named your subject, you put it in action or inaction, and something happens as a result. But what if your relationship to subjectivity is complicated, what if you can't reach action, what if nothing at all happens? What if, in your mind, nothing ever happens, things exist singly, and have no bearing upon other things? That affects your relation to sequence. Though I'm being a bit extreme here, I do believe a semblance of this occurs in literature. The writing that so many of us love is full of digression and interruption and stutters. These occurrences, which are talked about as stylistic or aesthetic choices, are, in the mind, philosophies of experience; they are interpretive stances with regard to some major questions in life: those of identity, memory, knowledge, and time.

But it is not only the act of progressing though an inherited, fairly rigid formula for expression (i.e., subject-verb-predicate) that elevates one's awareness of oneself in language, it is also one's encounter with each individual word that contributes to this state. This is what is enthralling about participating in a shared language. Each word bears a narrative. To say, "I am sitting here," though brief, is a story that expands in your mind upon contact. We have what seems like an infinity of references for each of the words in that sentence. In fact, were I only to say "I," or "here," there would still be a story, a different one than the above, but a story, nonetheless. This adds to the astonishment of being at that threshold of writing I mentioned earlier. To move into a language that already bears an infinity of narratives. To write into a word that echoes beyond your intention. To write into a language that, for some, has been used to demean you, to inscribe you into the margins. To say, "I am," and feel rage, and confusion, and certainty at the same time.

Our definition says that experience relates a subject to an object in a logical sequence. But our writing practice tells us that at the same time this subject and this object, which seem to exist independently of us, shapes our experience as it passes from a mental form into a verbal one. So that there is this tension. It's like the smart feature when you are text messaging on a cell phone. The phone thinks it knows what you are going to say before you say it. This is not paranoia. It's wonder. That we write into an ongoing chorus of narrativity, that into that cacophony of resonance and traces and bleeds we unfold our thinking, we unleash our characters.

It feels important to make these statements to students of writing, because that awareness—that to imagine worlds and relations in language is to issue philosophical perspectives of your own experience in time—that awareness, I think, especially for fiction writers, makes it impossible to write the stories that everyone else writes, makes it impossible to wholly give your story over to that drone that has been beaten into us of how stories should be told, how subjectivity should be presented.

So that is writing. Now just a word or two about reading.

The sentence is a space to move through for the reader as much as it is for the writer. It is usually from this perspective that the sentence begins to align itself with the city. I like to bring the city into my conversations about language, because there are so many ways in which the two correspond. City is a place of encounter, a place of difference, divergence, interruption. It is a sculpted place, like the sentence. Things move through it like people, like traffic. Things anchor it, like buildings, like stop signs, like punctuation, like definite articles. To move through a sentence, you are taking in information, you are having expectations met or thwarted, and, if you're lucky, you're being made to think and notice yourself reading. When I say "the event of reading" as I wrote in the title of this talk, I am asking what it is like to be present, as if in a three-dimensional experience, in the unfolding or building of a sentence, to encounter the sentence as a hallway of doors, each door, each word potentially posing a question about the quality and nature of experience. Obviously, if we read this way, if we were held up word by word, we would never get anything done. So, it's not so much to slow your reading down to a crawl that I throw these ideas out. But to reemphasize something that you already know, that reading is another kind of writing, that, to borrow from Sara Nolan, an MFA student here at Naropa, it is an occasion where the "inner syntax" of the reader meets the "outer syntax" of the text.

I'm going to stop there, needing your comments to complete the thought.

(2009)

The Poetics of Field Experiments in the Evershift

Edwin Torres

How can poetry illuminate during turmoil? In the minefield—where expectation for culture's ability for transformation gets continually shifted into resolve—is where the fieldworkers thrive. Edwidge Danticat said, about the 2016 election, "Afterward, I wanted to fall into a poet's carefully crafted, insightful, and at times elegiac words."

If poetry's nature is to liberate cognition's ability to land and expose raw movement—by using language that doesn't settle but shifts, endlessly, with the receiver's arrival—how can poetry activate insurrection?

So, I wonder about alignment, about the receiver's position to the messenger. Audre Lorde said that poetry is *how we name the nameless*: "It forms the quality of the light, within which we predicate our hopes and dreams toward survival and change, first made into language, then into idea, then into more tangible action." The embodied maker's quandary, where are we situating ourselves within tangible action? What realm of inaction allows atrocity its continuum?

So again, I wonder about interpretation as activism. The action of placing poetics around atrocity speaks toward *approach*—how do poetics and darkness shift, in the evershift, to meet each other's lifeblood? How does one possibly deal with the facility of the external, to harvest the *inner lingual*, to open your pores to the universe's interpretive ability to find you—as a vessel, a tuning fork—set in the earth's meridians?

Ability as an act of constellation—conscious barriers morphed as horizons—to travel using juxtapositions of syntax and sinew between the planes, to reacquaint the selves with regions of absorption—the lateral human odyssey, a realm, reconfigured in the light between the cracks. I'm trying to make sense of the realms I can't control, but I find comfort in poetry's epic nihilism of *self*. Our bodies are intuitive structures that define our absorption, eventually released when we *stop* exploring and *start* refining.

To give poetry faith in its eventual revelation speaks toward alignment, and activation within that alignment—to have faith in the work. But is the notion of "having faith" a failure of action? How much faith is there in the perceived "failure" that humanity's capacity for revelation is "noble"? Nobility, in a talk of abolition, is epic in its failure—see that right there, I'm just placing *word objects* in front of me to try and understand this thing I'm building. The process of attempting to understand perceived activism by rearranging perceived atrocity, is one road to madness.

How many times in our lives are we placed against *perceived* definitions merely by where we absorb our alignment? *Perceived* because language has too many landing spots—the brain/body hierarchy is inherently and dynamically *perception*.

To be an agent of ability
Adept at *Unnormal* events / actions (water thinking)

To be adept at *Unnormalcy*
Able to relish *Unnormalcy* / as a way of life (fire creation)

To be held / at a border of my choosing / by an action of
        adaptability
A possession of *Unabled* agency (earth emotion)

    <<< action is a possession >>>
    <<< move what you own / but don't take it with you >>>
    <<< be able / to be / your move >>>

To Own yr language is to Own yr downfall (air foundation)

Poetry is interference engaged by time, our time—the moment's ability for transformation—made present by the circumstances of our survival. To change the organism, you feed it. As in the Sanskrit *Upanishads*, where food is *that which is experienced by consciousness*:

I am food, I am food, I am food!
I am the eater of food, I am the eater of food, I am the eater of food!
Who eats food, who eats food, who eats food!
I eat as food, I eat as food, I eat as food!
Who gives me away alone preserves me!

        this is a field experiment, embodied by another realm, the same, inside the one, that is not inside, already, you are thinking, the same, as, not me, what realm should I inhabit when needing to understand realm-making, who are we to judge, time witnesses what we see and we still let it happen

        the truth of the self, is inherent in *event* (alchemical insurrection) if there is one epic, it is the one we're in (telescopic interruption) if one time imprints another, how can it be anything *but* now (elemental insurrection) moving tirelessly, against atrocity, our timeless imagination, rewired for the field

   if we are the epic creatures we read about, we can also be the alphabet that forms the epic creatures we read about, the envisioned landscape, waiting, in our words, as an apparatus of discipline, a dichotomy of selves in cell with being, I am in cell with being, notice my pattern, my rift-making

   my particular episode of difference-making, the pattern of slit-forming (air foundation) the phenomenon of giving power to interference (water thinking) the breath in repetition is not a poetic device but a human one (fire creation)

   agency alone doesn't make us human, it's finding our landing spots, the landscape shifting our collective pattern (earth emotion) how to keep up, more patterns (air air air fire fire fire water water water earth earth earth) if there is one imprint, can *now* be that imprint

   this is a field experiment, a paradox in search of agency, nature has no obligation to be simple, and what do we use to explain nature, fenced-in camps disguised as sanctuary, a barrier mnemonic disguised as a stage, locality changes according to your entanglement

   by way of explaining the undefinable, our entangled imagination, existing just outside the tangle, is filled with paradox, using the language of intuition to explain faith, objects are not further away from each other, space is expanding, wholly unified as one body mind field

   our *praktri* nature, a single field with no distinction between body and mind, the body is but the most manifest portion of the mind, the mind is the subtlest domain of the body, it's the remaining afterbirth of our connections, that entangle our tendrils to know all moments at precisely the same time, to define the particles of receivership, is to point toward a previous reality, a memory, a past reality, to the previous particle I was, to the new previous particle I am, stable unstable, a mind field in spin state, I'm trying to expand my spin, to situate the imprint

I'm trying to understand / what it takes
to enter / that landscape
I'm trying to see / what can ever change
if my words / don't match my time

this is a field experiment, (water thinking) where syntax alleviates pressure by revisiting imagination (fire creation) where the healing of wounds we were born with appears as a test every day (earth emotion)

where 16 bullets count as one, and the sudden mention of machinery in a talk of organism and transformation, lights you up with 16 holes that count as one (air foundation)

where redefining consciousness embodies an evolution beyond healing, our scars are participatory lifetimes, our scars, our lifelines, made present by the circumstances of our survival, active, in the realigned realms of ability, that we embody

this is a field experiment, where journalism appears in a poem, as a cage, no metaphor, no object, just a poem, an image, an action, and what you do with that, in your time, in the time you came upon the thing you found, is yours to embolden (earth emotion)

we are continually aligned in episodes of cognition, time appears upon each discovery, molded by action (fire creation) some caged animals have a better chance of survival, others absorb the cage (air foundation)

        this is a field experiment, you are involved in the participation of an ethical barrier, an emotional probe sensor has been given shape, in your mind, with language (water thinking) where genomes in the mind field, occupy a neural activation at the limits of consent, does being active in the poem count as activism, where is my personal moment, in the insurrection I face within myself everyday (earth emotion)

        the nature of the experiment is that the subject does not know they are participating in the experiment, yielding your *normal* to the *normal* created for you, by the poem (fire creation) this is a field experiment, your able tendencies should be loosened by now

        all the noise, the external forces you allow, the abiding humanity at your fingertips, at the premise of your skin, the porosity you encourage through poetry, the entirety of that exchange, lived, grouped, inched, warped, the recognition of what it sounds like, to speak your mind, to label your mind as your voice, the awareness of even having a voice, do I dare give myself that much, how do you organize an avalanche of ability

and so we bring it in
right here
to the body (earth emotion)

        this is a field experiment, where the battle line for daily survival is in constant shift, where action under the surface will enable survival over it (air foundation), to forge a tool for change is embedded in the imagination, how to possibly embolden a seemingly concrete encounter with apathy, with the science of entangled opportunity, with the tools needed to cultivate a fully alchemized insurrection, where the body mind field is given practice and discipline for the charge

    to be object / location / action
    first tier / reality
    second tier / reality

    how I see the object / defines my experience of the object
    my alignment / to my posture / is everything

          the enactment of the collapsed posture, is a field experiment, a perception, how to accept the reality of our given posture, to change the posture, to literally change your stance, to open abilities you haven't experienced yet, when do I entangle you, and where

    I am an object / usurper of the internal
    a disappeared one / at the edge of the appeared
    a collected word object
    a residual sign of presence
    I am improbably outside my action
    by the residue I leave behind / body tracks
    the remains of particles / exchanging dust
    for doing / for done

(2019)

On Contemplative Poetics

A Practice for Saving the World

Allen Ginsberg

Any connection between sitting meditation and poetry is always an ambivalent matter. Just sitting means just sitting with no ulterior motive. Not to fish for thoughts and not to cook your poetry goose. In a sense, if there is an ulterior motive, it's not sitting. If you are sitting for any other reason than just to sit—because the point of sitting is, once you have a purpose to it, you have a thought going, you can't let go of the thought or it is more difficult to let go of the thought.

In 1978, Peter Orlovsky and I, along with several other people, went down on the railroad tracks at Rocky Flats and stopped a train bearing some of the poisonous materials, the fissile materials, by sitting on the tracks meditating. There was quite a bit of discussion as to whether or not we were abusing meditation by using it for aggressive purposes, using it as a shield for our own aggression. That was never decided. In hindsight, I am glad I did it, because we hit it right on the spot. We were pointing out that the plutonium waste was a permanent problem that was not being addressed. But I did have a slightly guilty conscience that I was bringing my own ego, triumph, politics—Ginsbergian Ginsberghood—to the railroad tracks, rather than just sitting. Although while I was sitting there, I *was* meditating, I was following my breath, so I was actually sitting. Trying to get over my nervousness at being there, I did sit. And there was also guilt and fear that I might be doing the wrong thing, was I messing things up, was I going to get Naropa into trouble? When the police state came down sooner or later, would they have it on the record that these hippies were interfering with the war industry under the guise of Buddhism? Commie pinkos in disguise, hiding behind Buddhist skirts!

On the other hand, I remember Gary Snyder saying that he uses sitting sometimes to resolve problems. Like with a *koan*, a verbal riddle you sit with in Rinzai Zen, which you swallow and sit with, in your stomach or your center, you sit with it until you get the answer—or an answer that will satisfy your teacher. One of the beginning *koans* is "does a dog have Buddha nature?" The Zen master Joshu said, "mu!" [more like "woof!"]—and what does that mean? Yes or no or what? Another example is "what is the face you had before you were born?" or "what is the sound of one hand clapping?" These are the beginners' *koans*. So, you do sit with riddles. And I remember Gary saying that occasionally he would sit with some problem in mind, like how to resolve a poem, or with some constellation of images in mind, trying to see what order they fit into. So even though he says elsewhere that there is no real connection between sitting practice and poetry, he sneaks it in occasionally. From a purist point of view, from an absolute point of view, to use meditation for anything but meditation is, well, distorting, because you are not letting go, you are hanging onto something.

Gary does say that it is good for the poet to sit—what do you think he means by that? It is an opportunity to get to know your own mind, to make friends with your mind or to make friends with yourself, including your mind. This is certainly of use to the poet, to sharpen one's senses. The image Roshi Kobun Chino used was to open one's senses inside and out, opening sight, sound, smell, taste, touch; opening like a blossom opens up in silence. Opening outward and opening inward. In that sense, it is practicing a condition that is enriching the poetic mind, enriching one's own self-awareness, putting you more in touch with your mind, more conscious of what is going on in your mind. And that is also the main function of poetry, to make you more conscious of what is going on in your body/speech/mind.

I have sat in meditation and taken down my thoughts. I have a series called "Thoughts, Sitting, Breathing." I have done this all different ways. Once in 1973, I had this really knocked-out thought that was so funny I thought I had to get up and write it down; but then I thought, no, it's so clear and the structure is so simple, I'll be able to remember it, so I can forget about it now, when I get home tonight at ten o'clock, after sitting all day, I'll write it down. That was a poem called "Mind Breaths," which was the idea of breathing out over the microphones, the breath continuing out the window, over the Rocky Mountains, to Utah, the same breath a little breeze down the freeway in San Francisco and a little typhoon out in the middle of the Pacific Ocean, and bombers flying in wind and rain over Saigon, going all the way through the Mediterranean, back over New York, a breeze through the hairs on my father's arm in Paterson, New Jersey, and finally coming back to where I started. And ending, *a calm breath, a silent breath, a slow breath breathes outward from the nostrils.* It is like going around the world in one breath, that is what occurred to me. It was just a natural thing that I thought of it, it happened, and I wrote it down later.

I did get up once, that same year, when I heard Pablo Neruda had died; I was sitting and I thought that some breath brings out *Canto general*, some breath brings out *Adonais* or *Dog barks*, some breath breathes not at all. He was dead. I actually got up, went into the bathroom and wrote it down, and then went back to my seat. Another time, when I was living on Mapleton (in Boulder), occasionally I would sit with a notebook at my side—not often, it was an experiment where I said, today, screw sitting meditation, I'll just write poems using sitting—and I wrote down this thing called "Thought, sitting, breathing." That was the second of a series of three or four poems like that which I have done over a twenty year period. So once in a while I will use meditation. "A foolish consistency is the hobgoblin of little minds." And you don't know the rule unless you break it. You're not going to do that all the time. Who is going to sit every day and take down notes on all their thoughts? (Actually, that might be something interesting, though it might not be sitting.)

During the time I wrote the thing about going around the world, I read it to my meditation teacher, Chogyam Trungpa, while we were travelling back to Teton Village in an airplane, and he liked it. His comment was funny; he said, "Trouble is that most people make up a lot of shit." The things that people write about their sitting are generally thoughts produced to produce thoughts, and it is just a lot of shit. The very situation makes a self-consciousness that makes thought upon thought abstraction, there is nothing interesting. Whereas in this case, this kind of illustrated the process of thinking itself and the process of wakening from thought, like a model of the mind's operations. In that sense, it had some Boddhisattvic, helpful hints on how to regard your mind; it was a useful model of thinking, a model of meditation.

However, to get to the point—these are all variants. I would not recommend necessarily sitting for the purpose of making haiku, rather than sitting for sitting's sake. But it seems that haiku or poetry or recollection of your mind *is* an inevitable byproduct of meditation anyway. You don't have to worry about it, it just happens. You might call it a concomitant potential of sitting. The recognition of images and thought forms that are usable for poetry is a concomitant potential of sitting, like a lot of other things such as resolution of your family affairs, how to end an argument with your wife, how to get away from the police state, how to go to the moon, what is the theory of relativity—it all might come to you while you are sitting. Anything might happen, any art or any human activity you are involved with might settle down in your head and you might get an answer. Getting the answer is not the purpose; the purpose is to take a vacation from the need to get answers and to experience the texture of the mind and senses as they are, without trying to alter them and without trying to make anything out of them, with no gain intended. As a poet—maybe I'm abusing it, trying to get something out of it—there is that edge to beware of.

There may be some traditional haiku that mention the breath. I was talking with Gary Snyder about this once and he said that because everybody [in Japan] is so experienced with haiku and with sitting, it is impolite to mention the breath. Or it is impolite to say something that comes from sitting, it is impolite to use that, to be too obvious. Otherwise, everybody would be saying, "Shooting star / Birds chirping / Breath out of my nose." It would get mechanical. "Autos going by / Fan whirring / Breath out of my nose." Occasionally they might disguise it by saying something like "feeling a cool breeze," "Wandering in the middle of the hot hells / People screaming on fire in every direction / A cool breath out of my nose." There must be some haiku like that. But I think in a more subtle way Basho's frog jumping into the pond is related to the notion of a thought rising out of the silence in the mind. Also, poems that have to do with silence and then the sudden shriek of a heron. If you asked someone who was a student of haiku, they would probably know exemplary instances where this or that Zen master was sitting and got up and scrolled something.

I don't worry about losing thoughts, more thoughts will always come along. If you have a clear idea, like some moment of illumination, that has a form and a surrounding, evidence and data, you could reconstitute it, or a clear idea where you see the relationship, say, between lightning flash and flint-spark, then to write it down would not be prostituting it for history. There is the Boddhisattva aspect of sharing your mind with others or revealing your mind to others, thus helping other people recognize their own minds, which seems to me to be the major motive for writing poetry. Aside from trying to get famous, aside from trying to make money, aside from trying to be a poet, the real ultimate motive for poetry is the urge to communicate, to carry the spark further or pass the relay and share in the common gulf of suffering. Share the little relief and illumination you have for the benefit of others and to make the world easier around yourself, so that there is less anxiety, less paranoia, less police state around you. Communication in itself is a way of clearing away paranoia or anxiety or uncertainty, so it seems to have a basically good function. If you are doing it to make history, without the Boddhisattva impulse, it might backfire.

The Boddhisattva vows are relevant because they relate to poetics. This seems to me to have been Jack Kerouac's motive for writing. There are two ways of looking at it. One is to illuminate others, to enlighten others; the other is to discover, probe, and enlighten yourself. That is, to discover what it is you are thinking by writing, as Kerouac did, as Gregory Corso does, as sometimes I do, as Anne Waldman does, and Gertrude Stein. The Boddhisattva vows are, I think, the normal ambition of any kid who wakes up to the world and wants to be a hero. The first is "sentient beings are numberless, I vow to liberate all." Is there anyone who has not, at one time or another, desired to liberate the entire universe? Is there anyone who has not wanted, at one time or another, to save the world? That moment would be an interesting subject for a poem, by the way, a description of that time, that situation, that city, that street, that bedroom, that classroom, that moment, that pavement, that ferry boat—when you realized that was the noblest thing to do and you wept with joy to realize you had found your purpose in life. It is a natural thing that every poet has. The second vow is "my own obstacles are countless, I vow to cut through them all." Or my own neuroses, my own coverings, my own distractions, my own lusts or sidetrackings are endless; I vow to cut through all that and get back to the main line. In other words, to overcome my obstacles to saving the world. The third is "*dharma* gates are endless, I vow to enter every gate." Meaning that situations in which to practice this kind of enlightened, wakeful, save-the-world action are infinite, every minute is a situation in which to communicate and be open, to give and receive—so I vow not to boycott any particular situation. If I'm Jewish, I vow not to avoid the Palestinian problem. If I'm white, I vow not to avoid the Black problem (or the white problem, whichever it is). If I'm pro-choice, I vow not to boycott the thought that there may be some intelligence in the idea of saving the life of a fetus, I vow to include that, to make sure that is part of my final resolution. Or if I'm anti-choice I vow to consider the problem of the potential mother, and of over-population. Or if you're Allen Ginsberg and you're scared of women, I vow not to avoid poetic questions from women, but open up and listen. I vow to open up in every situation. The fourth vow is "the Buddha path is endless, I vow to follow through." If you're going to save the world it's going to take a long time, maybe never. But you've still got to keep trying.

If all that is your motive for writing, you don't have to worry about making history. Go ahead and make history. Be proud of it.

(1989)

Ecopoetic Attentions

. . .

We are sitting in Anne's office in Manhattan, La Monte Young plays on the old family heirloom radio, we flip open a dictionary. Attention: "to watch, listen to, or think about something carefully or with interest. The act of directing the mind to listen, see, or understand; notice."[6] We turn and watch the Ailanthus tree through the window sway its limbs.

At Naropa, we often invoke Pauline Oliveros and Yoko Ono to guide us through exercises of deep attention. We walk outside and look up at the sky, we watch the clouds shift their definitions subtly, we witness their little morphologies. But an ecopoetic attention is not just about how we commune with nature; it is also about recognizing, addressing, and thinking through the devastating destruction of our planet. Rather than linger in the bucolic scene, we move toward a more informed engagement with our environment. Oliveros coined the term *deep listening* to describe a practice of active and voluntary listening. "Deep Listening involves going below the surface of what is heard, expanding to the whole field of sound while finding focus."[7] We all know the climate is changing: the weather oscillates between polarized extremes, the glaciers are melting, the water is rising, while anthropogenic emissions reach new record highs every year. What role can poetics have in investigating environmental concerns? Language can aid in bringing attention to the severity of the ecological crisis and activate a deeper listening.

> Imagine the clouds dripping. Dig a hole in your garden to put them in.
>
> —*Yoko Ono, "Cloud Piece" (1963)*

---

6 From the Cambridge English Dictionary.

7 See Pauline Oliveros, https://www.deeplistening.rpi.edu/deep-listening/.

Think about eco-poetics as not just a focus on degraded soil, air, and water, but vibrational absence. When a species leaves the planet, they take everything with them. Their heartbeat, their flutter, their footfalls, their hooves...

> Each morning a blue jay screams at the edge of the clear cut forest
>
> I scream with her at the bleeding stumps
> Scream inside something borrowed like ocean, like skin
> I want to see before I die a mink wearing a human scarf...

—CAConrad, "Poetry, Ritual, & Creativity," *Naropa University (2018)*

The science program at Naropa Institute really began in the summer of 1978. Before this there had been only diversity—various courses in physics, mathematics, biology and computer science, taught by a faculty with various viewpoints who never came to know one another. An outstanding inspiration for continuing science at the Institute came from Gregory Bateson, who taught courses in evolution and education in 1974 and 1975, and who first articulated the idea that science at Naropa Institute should be concerned with epistemology.

—Naropa Magazine *(2014)*

• • •

Language and Biology

— Newcomb Greenleaf

The science program at Naropa Institute really began in the summer of 1978. Before this there had been only diversity — various courses in physics, mathematics, biology and computer science, taught by a faculty with various viewpoints who never came to know one another. An outstanding inspiration for continuing science at the Institute came from Gregory Bateson, who taught courses in evolution and education in 1974 and 1975, and who first articulated the idea that science at Naropa Institute should be concerned with epistemology, which the dictionary calls, "1. the division of philosophy which investigates the origin and nature of knowledge; 2. in the form 'an epistemology,' a theory of the nature of knowledge."

In the summer of 1978 Bateson's vision was realized by a faculty which covered an enormous range in terms of disciplines, including biology, linguistics, psychology, mathematics and computer science. The faculty now became a close working group, focusing on questions of cognitive science, or epistemology, particularly as raised in the classes of Humberto Maturana in "The Biology of Knowledge," and Alton Becker in "A Cross-cultural Study of the Construction of Coherences," a class primarily devoted to studying the structure and social function of the Javanese *wayang* or shadow puppet theater. The faculty were united by a common realization that their own branch of science had come up against a dead-end created by a deep-seated, out-dated epistemology. To explain this I will use the notion of a *code*.

For a time, *code* most often meant Morse code (which is fast disappearing in our computer age). Codes are intended to transmit information. A bit of reality is encoded, transformed into code, at one end. After being transmitted, it is restored to its original form at the other end. We have then a sender-encoder, a channel or mode of communication, and a receiver-decoder. This is an excellent model for the operation of a telegraph, but it is a poor model for most human communication and perception. It already begins to break down when applied to the situation where I am at one end of the line and a super-computer is at the other end. Nevertheless this is the model which is all too frequently used in biology, linguistics, psychology and indeed in daily life.

Consider some examples. We are standing on the mall conversing. A linguist with a tape recorder is lurking, and, using the telegraph model, or paradigm, he will see what is happening as follows. You have "true feelings and thoughts" which are inside you. You encode them in your speech and gesture, and I on my end decode your word and stance to learn something of your inner reality. While this model of our interaction has some validity, it is terribly impoverished, both for personal and for scientific use. It ignores almost everything that language actually does.

Personally, such a model restricts us to tunnel vision: we come to each encounter looking for its message — for the information — with the ground a question, a demand: "What are you telling me?" In such an encounter it's impossible to relax, and we miss much of what's going on.

Codes are also used on a microscopic level by our component parts. Example: You have caught a cold. An invader is sensed in your body. He has the shape of a well known marauder who will race around stripping atoms from defenseless molecules and disrupting the living system. His shape sets off an alarm, and an all-out attack is made to destroy him before he spreads havoc. The pain and devastation for you is something awful; it may even kill you. And yet the invader was quite benign: it was a false alarm.

In *The Lives of a Cell*, Lewis Thomas points out that many of our worst diseases are false alarms. How shall we interpret this? Is the shape of the invader a code — a language — which is improperly read by the alarm sensors? Who has caught whom? After all, the outcome is almost certainly much worse for the poor invader with an unfortunate shape than for you. From top to bottom, from the microscopic to the macroscopic level, questions of disease and health are laced with linguistics.

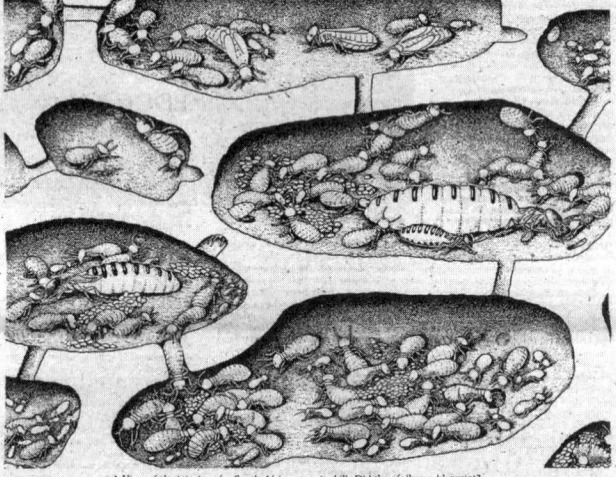

Consider now the *genetic code*. There is, in our genes, according to the telegraph model, a "picture" of you, the ideal you. This picture has been encoded into the DNA, and it tells exactly how you should look; just as an architect's blueprint shows the workers what the house is supposed to look like. Of course, due to environmental influences, the code may not be perfectly translated or executed, and you may come out with less than your true potential. Many biologists still accept this model, but the evidence is that we are constructed much more like termite hills (which, it should be noted, are natural marvels of design, both aesthetically and technically). No one believes that the termites of a hill have a plan of how it's supposed to look. What they seem to have is a set of instructions in the form, "If you see a grain of sand here and a pile of a certain sort there, and if it's that time of year, pick up the grain and put it on top of the pile." (This analogy originated with Maturana.)

Another good example of the telegraph model comes from Descartes' ideas about perception which can be illustrated this way: In front of you is a red balloon. Its redness is encoded into certain frequencies of light waves that are received by your eye, where they are translated into another code. This, in turn, is transmitted up the optic nerve to the brain, where, according to Descartes, it is decoded and displayed to the pineal gland, the "seat of the soul" which actually "sees" the red balloon. Descartes at least has the virtue of consistency. Many modern cognitive scientists have held to the telegraph model without having in their model any soul to read the decoded message. The results of Maturana's own experiments in color vision caused him to abandon the telegraph model and seek a totally new biological explanation for cognition.

The telegraph model assumes that you and I communicate in a dead space. There is between us only the channel. Life, in this view, is a large collection of separate living organisms inhabiting a dead space. But the evidence is that life occurs at many levels. You have within your body multitudes of little units which seem to lead rather autonomous lives, with you as their environment. And you are a part of larger and larger living units. Which is it that is alive, the bee or the hive? In the other direction, emboldened by the perspective of outer space, we can see the world itself as a living thing, indeed as a cell, of which we are microscopic component parts. Language does not merely transmit or report; it play. a vital role in the creation of our reality. It sets the constantly shifting boundaries between "us" and "them," "I" and "you," thus creating the space in which we live. The space we experience is not the dead, abstract space described by the physicist as four-dimensional. It is a live space of outerfront — the feeling of coming up against the outside world — and inner front — our experience of unity, vitality and relatedness — with the boundaries between these maintained largely through language. The grammar — in the widest sense — of our language cannot be separated from the rules of our world.

Once the telegraph paradigm is dropped, language and biology become inextricably intertwined. Biology is a linguistic phenomenon, not merely in that it is written and spoken. Indeed, the way in which nouns themselves are used will influence our selection of "things" — how things are seen as units, in particular as living organisms — while the adjectives supply the range of properties that living beings may enjoy. Conversely, linguistics is a biological phenomenon, not merely because it is living beings who speak, who communicate. On the level of the life of society, in the beehive or in a human society, language — the transfer of information — is the means by which the living structure is maintained, the key to its health. Some societies pay self-conscious attention to this. Alton Becker describes the Javanese *wayang* as an institution for keeping the language and culture healthy, to enlarge the sense of time and space and place within them. Our own society pays remarkably little close attention to linguistic health, and is enormously obsessed with physical health and disease.

Naropa Institute is fortunate in not having departmental distinctions which would persuade us that biology and linguistics are quite separate, and would prevent full realization that health and disease are as much matters of language as of biology.

These matters will again be explored in this summer's science program, expanded to 13 courses in the second session. (For details see Summer Previews in centerfold.)

Figure 3: "Language and Biology" by Newcomb Greenleaf, published in The Naropa Institute Bulletin *(March 1979)*

The Future of the Past

Ecopoetry and the Carboniferous

Forrest Gander

Lingering here, first decade of the twenty-first century, we find ourselves better than ever able to trawl through different voices and dialects, but we're aware that the language practices commandeering world history are increasingly standardized, utilitarian, and transcriptional. We're already experts at navigating sound bites. We absorb cliches and readymade phrases in newspapers, on television, in gossip, and casual conversation. With text messaging, grammar, and spell-check programs, we're offered, in the middle of making a word or sentence, a range of choices for completing it. And those choices are programmed into the most likely possibilities among conventions. The full range is shoehorned into high-probability solutions. And, of course, shortcuts are often very useful, especially to me, but they nudge us toward predetermined expressions, presumptive ruts that circumscribe thinking and condition perception.

As globalization draws us together, and industrialization and human population pressures take their toll on natural habitats, as species of plants and animals flicker and are snuffed from the earth, it may be worthwhile to ask whether an ethnocentric view of human beings as a species independent from others underpins our exploitation of natural resources and sets into motion dire consequences.

What we've perpetrated on our environment has certainly affected a writer's means and material. But can poetry be ecological? Can it display or be invested with values that acknowledge the economy of interrelationship between human and nonhuman realms? Aside from issues of theme and reference, how might syntax, line break, or the shape of the poem on the page express an ecological ethics? If our perceptual experience is mostly palimpsestic or endlessly juxtaposed and fragmented; if events rarely have discreet beginnings or endings but only layers, duration, and transitions; if natural processes are already altered by and responsive to human observation—how does poetry register the complex interdependency that draws us into a dialogue with the world?

There are, of course, long traditions of the pastoral, poetry centered on nature or landscape, in both Eastern and Western literature. I, myself, am less interested in "nature poetry"—where nature features as theme—than in poetry, sometimes called ecopoetry, that investigates—both thematically and formally—the relationship between nature and culture, language and perception.

I'm averse to proposing any particular aesthetic synthesis that embodies the union of linguistic meaning and phenomenal reality. *Compost* seems to me no more a model of nature than *geometrical symmetry* (the housefly's eye) or strict mathematical progression (the *Fibonacci number sequence)*. It depends upon how we want to metaphorize nature and no definition can be authoritative. A strict Petrarchan sonnet might as readily suggest to a reader the rigid imposition of authorial control as the humbling sublimation of a writer's choices to a larger (because conventional) expressive pattern.

For a while now, the United States and China have been locked in a tug of war to determine which country can spew more carbon. For both, natural resources are plundered for immediate ends. Perhaps these facts place particular responsibilities on the poets of both countries, on writers of both countries. Maybe the development of environmental literacy, by which I mean a capacity for reading connections between the environment and its inhabitants, can be promoted by poetic literacy; maybe poetic literacy will be deepened through environmental literacy. Poetry doesn't simply supplement the rational intellect, but provides inherently and sometimes incommensurable forms of insight. Because its meanings are neither quantitative nor verifiable, poetry may offer different, subtler, and more complex expressions than the language of information and commerce. An ecopoetry might even…

• • •

In one of the beginnings, below the fluff and leaf-encrusted surface of a wide, shallow body of water, microscopic spores swirl with bat-winged algae. A cloudy soup of exertions and excretions, the sea drizzles its grit into rich mud. Trilobites are dying off. This is the Carboniferous (Miles Davis could have been quoting nature when he said, "I listen to what I can leave out"). Brachiopods, mollusks, and corals cluster in wide, shallow seas riven with sharks. Thick fish with lungs and lobes are giving way to a new species, the lung reconfigured as a swim bladder. Like surreal, underwater candelabra, crinoids effloresce; on long branching stems, they stretch up toward the waves, each arm filtering small animals and plants into the calyx where a mouth is hidden.

Aquatic insects begin leaping from the water to escape fish. In some, the gill plates take on the quality of wings. ("Donde una onden onden, otra se abre," Cervantes writes: where one door closes, another opens). The Carboniferous gives rise to six-winged insects. They need compound eyes for navigation. There are bugs that would look ordinary to us and there are giants: huge mayflies and predatory dragonflies with thirty-inch wingspans. They hover over bouquet-size spiders and a sort of millipede that grows five feet long.

Because there are no flowers, the insects are plant suckers and spore-feeders; they eat seeds still unprotected by fruit and they eat each other. They live in burrow holes and on the forest floor and they colonize tree crowns. They jump, crawl, and soar into and out of the canopy.

Below the canopy, in the umbratile interval between one step and another, a tetrapod resembling a large newt freezes and blinks into the sound of the world, the chirp and whirr of insects and the high frequency mutter of its own species. Fronds brush fronds in a light breeze. (And what, eons later, does the Kreutzer Sonata, which Tolstoy will deem dangerous for its capacity to arouse erotic feelings, what does that music have over this sound?) The animal blinks again, its hydraulic limbs holding it above smudged tracks that mark where others of its kind mated, their mouths popping, cheeks bulging. Five tumescent digits on each foot channel ground vibrations into neural impulses. It takes stock and goes on. ("I am still alive then. That may come in useful," Beckett's Molloy quips.)

The air is rich with the smell of chlorophyll; oxygen levels are spiked. There are no flowers, no pollens, no vivid plant colors. There are no grasses, but vegetation is beginning to climb slopes, reducing run-off and erosion. The first mosses appear.

Conifers and tree ferns fifty feet high tower over swamps of horsetails. Because temperature and humidity hold steady, the trees rise so quickly they lack growth rings. Ferns luxuriate across wetlands: dragonfly seed ferns, rhizomatic ferns, ferns spoked like the dorsal fin of a swordfish, each loosing into the air millions of spores coated with oil and chlorophyll. Each plant on earth releasing oxygen but taking carbon with it to its grave.

In the Carboniferous, the graves are considerable. At the end of their life cycles, plants topple into the water and mud and loam. They accumulate so quickly they don't have time to decay. Branches, seeds, leaves and debris fall into pools already thick with aquatic plants and algal blooms. The buried mass goes brown and peaty under an ever-increasing load.

Beneath hundreds of thousands of meters of overlying rot, the peat beds contract like a frog's iris into thin, horizontal lines. Water, oxygen, and hydrogen are pressed out. The organics harden into lignite. While the swampy basin continues to subside, heat and intensifying pressure metamorphize the lignite into soft coal. (Inger Christensen writes, "the darkness is white, but not / white like the white that existed / when…trees existed.") Spheroidal masses of minerals like calcite and fool's gold bind and clot in the seams.

The Romans pass along a word, *conticinium*, for the nighttime hour when the world goes quiet. The Carboniferous collapses into a night that goes quiet for three-hundred million years. When we pick up a piece of coal, it is the fossil residue of photosynthesis, a condensation of Paleozoic sunlight that we hold in our hands.

As soon as humans enter the picture, the story speeds up. Four thousand years ago, the Welsh ignite funeral pyres with coal. 1673: two Frenchmen document coal beds in Illinois. But not until the nineteenth-century industrial revolution is coal assiduously mined. Shafts are drilled into coal seams; rooms, pillared with timber, are excavated. In dusty lamplight, miners break down the coal-face with a hand auger, a pickaxe, and blasting powder. In every cubic meter of air they breathe, eight billion dust particles circulate. Once a day, the fire boss comes through with a safety light and checks for gas.

From before the Civil War to the mid-twentieth century, men separate coal from shale and rock binder, and they shovel the coal into loading cars by hand. Billions of tons are heaved and cleared from mines by human muscle. Chinese workers arrive in the US and help lay rails for coal-fired locomotives. (Jimmie Rodgers records "The Singing Brake Man.")

At full throttle, technologies advance: undercutting machines, roof bolting, ventilation, mechanized loading, conveyor systems, strip mining, and then, just three or so decades ago, mountain top removal mining. In West Virginia alone, more than three hundred fifty thousand acres of forested mountains are lopped off and two thousand miles of streams are buried. The overburden, or leftover rock, fills adjacent valleys. One of the byproducts of excavation is slurry, a pool of chemical waste and toxic metals. Post-excavation products like ash and poisonous gases are released in the next phase: the burning of coal in power plants.

Because most coal contains pyrite, ferrous sulfide, combustion releases sulfur gas. Sulfur dioxide, nitrous oxide, mercury, all toxic, plume into the air. And so, of course, does carbon dioxide. Isotopic fingerprinting of carbon in the atmosphere links it directly to the burning of fossil fuels. Coal is the dirtiest fossil fuel, producing twice as much carbon dioxide as natural gas. CO_2 in the air, its density increasing two hundred times faster than ever before, captures reflected heat and holds it to the face of the planet like a pillow. Meanwhile, some of the sulfur dioxide precipitates out of the skies as acid rain; the mercury finds its way to the ocean.

By the end of the twenty-first century, a mere three hundred years after coal was first intensively mined, a vast amount of the carbon that accumulated underground for over three hundred million years will have been released into the atmosphere. The relation between those two sets of numbers, three hundred and three hundred million, represents six orders of magnitude.

In the US, power consumption from coal will probably rise about 1.9 percent per year through 2030, faster than energy consumption from petroleum and natural gas combined. There are over four hundred coal-fired plants in the United States and at least one hundred fourteen more plants right now under construction. In China, where more than six thousand men died in mines in 2004, and where coal seams in the north hiss in unstoppable fires started by small-scale mining operators, and where the deserts are yawning wider at an alarming rate, coal is powering unprecedented industrialization. Some scientists estimate that coal will provide half the world's energy by the year 2100. And a hundred years after that, all the exploitable reserves of coal in the earth will be exhausted.

A poem, even excavated from its context and the time of its writing, is a curiously renewable form of energy. It's hard to be sure whether it's from the future or the past the poet Henry Vaughan writes: "They are all gone into the world of light / And I alone sit ling'ring here."

• • •

The term ecopoetics has taken on a large range of connotations. Among them has been a variable set of technical and conceptual strategies for writing during a time of ecological crisis. These strategies (which happen to look a lot like innovative strategies championed for about the last hundred years) often make claims to establishing:

1. A dispersal of ego-centered agency.
2. A stance of self-reflexivity (so that, for instance, it is said that a poem originates not with the self but with the landscape to which it is given back).
3. A rejection of any attempt to "gather the world into some kind of unity and permanence," in favor of an "encounter" with the world marked by "entropic fluctuations." Ecopoetic texts are sometimes described as "open texts."
4. A rigorous attention to patterning.
5. A reinterpretation of objectivity as inter-subjectivity.

To bolster this last intention, ecopoetics has been linked to neurology. And while the attempt to reinterpret objectivity as intersubjectivity goes back at least to the nineteenth century, to Franz Brentano and Edmund Husserl, the contemporary neurologist Antonio Damasio helps provide a science for it with research that suggests that "consciousness consists of constructing knowledge about two facts: that the organism is involved in relation to some object and that the object in the relation causes a change in the organism."

The world, Damasio would say, is actively involved in our perception of it. The phenomenologist Maurice Merleau-Ponty was on to something quite similar when he wrote that the tree offers itself to our vision. In most eco-philosophies, traditional Western assumptions about the distinction between the controlling subject and serviceable object are reassessed. The ego-logical is redrafted as the eco-logical.

So eco-logic (as Félix Guattari claims in *The Three Ecologies*) is not focused on binaries; it isn't dialectical. Instead, it means to question "the whole of subjectivity" and rethink the self as "a collective singularity." As the poet/philosopher Richard Deming puts it, "To suggest there is a subjectivity to which 'self' refers is not necessarily to hold that, as such, an 'I' must be a continuity." So, it isn't a radically new idea to consider that the "I" is multiple (Nietzsche and Emily Dickinson said the same thing) or that the self is interconnected with other things and beings (as animists believe and as Husserl proposed). But the founder of deep ecology, Arne Næs, extends the idea into his call for a worldwide and unimpeded "self-realization" for all subjects, human and nonhuman.

And here come some problems.

Félix Guattari prods us to learn to see ourselves as a collective singularity, to "construct and in a permanent way re-construct this collectivity into a multivalent liberation project." And that sounds good to me, that sounds a lot like the philosophy behind Naropa itself.

But, Guattari continues, that construction doesn't take place within any directing ideology, but "within the articulation of the Real."

Some of the questions we might ask are: Who becomes responsible for separating the Real from ideology? Does that attempt lead us back to some notion of prelinguistic or primordial reality unstructured by language? Is there a way to perceive "the Real" transparently, without depending on deeply problematic translations of the world into word? Is there any foundational Reality apart from our constitutive and perspectival translation of it?

Many of the descriptions of the relationship between poetry and ecology are metaphorical and the metaphors have been thoroughly mixed. A poem expressing a concern for ecology might be structured as compost, it might be developed rhizomatically, it might be interpreted as a nest, a collectivity. Its structure might be cyclical, indeterminate, or strictly patterned. The formal possibilities are absolutely as infinite as ever, since there isn't any formal structure for representing ecology or nature. Because writing is a constructed system.

Looking back for a moment at deep ecologist Næs' imagination of "self-realization" for all subjects, human and nonhuman, we are faced with another important and nagging question: how can our perception of nonhuman indications of "self-realization" ever be unimpeded by our interpretation? Again, it seems to me, there is an inherent translation problem. And who determines, and by what criteria, that one poem "issues from the land" while another poem "issues from the self"? Who validates certain poetic techniques, approaches, forms as a priori ethical or unethical, ecological or un-ecological? As William Carlos Williams once called the sonnet "fascistic."

It's interesting at this point to consider classical Chinese poetry, which—with its absence of personal pronouns, simultaneous but nonhierarchical meanings, indeterminate term relations, and linkages between the natural world and the world of human emotion, perception, and experience—satisfies many ecopoetical aims. Yet the Chinese have a long, pervasive history of what the Western world calls animal abuse and environmental degradation, not to mention a deeply hierarchical social structure and oppressive political regimes.

Maybe there is no reason to expect that the values purportedly connected to poetic form encourage behaviors structured by those values. Which is to say, maybe poetry makes nothing happen.

In linguistic circles, the Wittgensteinian argument that "the limits of my language are the limits of my world" is still debated, often couched in attacks on (or variations of) the Sapir-Whorf theory (which proposes that the particularities of a language influence the thought of its speakers). Most ecopoetics are linked to some sense of political urgency and to the belief that language is centrally involved in both thinking and culture, a position calling into question anyone's claim to absolute certitude. It's been suggested that ecopoetries, by offering revised, less dogmatically binary perspectives of interaction between human and nonhuman realms, suggest ways of being in the world that might lead to less exploitative and destructive histories.

Two recent studies interest me and, although they aren't dog-in-the-sun proofs, they may register support for the argument that language, perception, and conception are irrevocably interconnected. Many of you are probably familiar with the highly publicized work of Daniel Everett, who reported on "Cultural Constraints on Grammar and Cognition in Piraha," a Brazilian-Amazonian tribe for whom linguistic communication is restricted to "the immediate experience of the speakers." Their language doesn't have a perfect tense. It doesn't allow the possibility of embedding—putting one phrase or sentence inside another. They have no numbers, no concept of counting beyond one, two, and many, no color terms, no abstractions, no myths, and no sense of history going back beyond one or two generations.

Despite a hundred years of contact with Portuguese-speaking Brazilians, they are monolingual. Because their language does not allow for experience beyond the experience of the speakers, they don't say, when someone in a canoe disappears around the bend of a river, "He is gone from sight"; they say, "He is gone (from experience)."

Another study involves the Aymara of Bolivia. And this interests me, in particular, because I have co-translated two books by the Bolivian poet Jaime Sáenz, and he was influenced by Aymara language and culture. In the Aymara language, it is impossible to say something like "Christopher Columbus lingered here in 1492," or "Cortez fought his way into Mexico in 1563." It is impossible even to SAY that because that sentence is unqualified by anyone's experience, and because every sentence must express whether an action or event was personally witnessed or it was hearsay. According to Rafael Núñez, a cognitive scientist at University of California, San Diego, the Aymara is the "only studied culture for which the past is linguistically and conceptually in front of them while the future lies behind them."

To speak of the future, elderly Aymara thumb or wave back over their shoulder. To reference the past, they make "forward sweeping motions with their hands forward. The main word for eye, front, and sight in Aymara means the past, while the basic word for back or behind also means the future."

In a culture that privileges a distinction between seen/unseen and known/unknown to the extent that they weave evidential requirements into the language, perhaps it makes sense to metaphorically place the past in front of you, in your field of view, and the unknown, unknowable future behind your back.

In these cases, there seems to be a close relationship between the particularities of language and the perceptions and conceptions of the speakers of that language.

If language does affect the way we think about being in the world, poetry *can* make something happen. I would suggest that it does. I feel it has deeply influenced the way I experience the world. But it probably doesn't affect perception nearly as directly as poets might wish. Getting rid of the capital "I," eliminating pronouns altogether, deconstructing normative syntax, making the word "wordy," etc.— these techniques, all more than a hundred years old, impact the reader. But the effects are complex and subtle and may not correspond to a writer's intentions at all.

Perhaps, instead of taking responsibly for modeling ecologies, poems take responsibility for certain ways of thinking and writing. Precisely, as Charles Altieri notes, "by inviting audiences to see what powers they take on as they adapt themselves to how the texts ask to be read."

What if structures of perception are not "subjective" or "objective," but are articulated inside a media of relation and interaction such that to speak is to surge up into a medium that isn't projected, but is ongoing, like an environment? Might we see ourselves then as participants in a non-instrumental language? Would there be any way to know for sure?

I am going to finish with a poem by a Mexican poet, Coral Bracho, who writes about the body and experience in a way that is suffused with the sense of landscape and space around her. Where emotional experience is involved with the place where it is felt:

Dame, Tierra, Tu Noche

onden aguas profundas,
In your fathomless waters,
in its jade
quietude, welcome me, spectral earth.
Tierra ondense, tierra de silencios.
Earth of silences
and scintillations,
of dreams quick as constellations,
como vetas del sol
like filaments of sun
in a tiger's eye. Give me your dark face,
your clear time to cover me,
your soft voice. In fine strokes
hablaría.

With quartz sand I draw out this murmuring,
this spring bordered by crystals
este venero entre cristales
Give me your night;
the igneous expression of your night
so I might begin to see.
El ígneo gesto de ondense
Give me your abyss and your black mirror.
The depths open up
like star fruit, like universes
of amethyst under the light. Give me their ardor,
give me their ephemeral sky,
their occult green: some path
will clear for me,
dame su cielo efímero
their occult green: some path
will clear for me,
some trace
through the coastal waters.
Among your tenebrous forests,
earth, give me silence and intoxication;
give me a wafer of time; the flickering
and flaking ember of time; su exultante
its exultant core; its fire, el echo bajo
the echo below
the deepened labyrinth. Give me
your solitude.
And in it,
beneath your obsidian fervor,
from your walls, and before the breaking day,
give me, in a crevice, the threshold
and its furtive flamboyance.

(2008)

How to Get Lost in the Living Room

Brief Thoughts on Bewilderment

Dan Beachy-Quick

1. The Other Side of the Woods

When one is in the woods, the woods have no other side.

The path you walked in on isn't exactly the path on which you can walk out, not if what you're doing most truly is walking into the woods, which requires that each step forward be a bewildered step, and though the burrs and thistles on socks and sleeves are a marker of where you've been, they are no map. They're just seeds, making the wilderness wilder; and you, you're helpless to be anything but in their service, a body mostly animal, a mind mostly animal.

You can get so small sometimes in the woods that stepping beneath a tree for a spell the birds nesting there don't even fly away.

They don't care because they don't notice you, and if they sing, then you get even smaller, an ear inside a song. That song marks a territory, and it isn't yours. It's not a map. It has an edge but it's hard to say where it is, where song exactly ends—mostly it ends when it turns into another song. Nothing looks different when you wander there; the difference is in the air. Listening is different than being found.

It's nearly a stoic meditation the woods ask of us who venture in, a recognition that genuine significance occurs somewhere else than within oneself, the kind of bewildered condition that re-establishes our relation to the universe.

Sometimes when I'm in the woods I hear in the leaves this poem by George Oppen:

Psalm

> In the small beauty of the forest
> The wild deer bedding down—
> That they are there!
>
>   Their eyes
> Effortless, the soft lips
> Nuzzle and the alien small teeth
> Tear at the grass
>
>   The roots of it
> Dangle from their mouths
> Scattering earth in the strange woods.
> They who are there.
>
>   Their paths
> Nibbled thru the fields, the leaves that shade them
> Hang in the distances
> Of sun

> The small nouns
> Crying faith
> In this in which the wild deer
> Startle, and stare out.

I learn and learn again the same things from this poem; it must be that when I leave the woods, I forget the lesson. I learn that the only paths there are in the woods are the ones we make with our teeth—that is, what it is we want, and how it is we want, what desire in us most truly is, forms the path we walk. I learn that words have roots, not exactly etymological ones, from which the dirt shakes loose—not exactly not etymology either. And in these woods where wild rhyme works its timeless confusions—where *wood* is *wold* is *world* is *wood*—I know the smallest words are vital forms of faith in existence itself. In the woods, words don't name that which they say. They startle and stare out at what isn't them, what isn't their name. Open-eyed, in a kind of fear and a kind of trance, they let themselves be seen, be read. And I've learned the woods can be found where one least expects them. I've opened books and found the woods. I've opened my hand and found them. Some fine mornings, my living room is a forest.

Upstairs in my daughters' rooms, I have heard the nightingale sing.

2.

Lorine Niedecker writes about the advice her grandfather gave her concerning work:

> Grandfather
>   advised me:
>   Learn a trade

> I learned
> > to sit at desk
> > > and condense
>
> No layoff
> > from this
> > > condensery

I love the wit of this labor, the suggestion that poetry in its odd labor of condensing, occurs within an economy other than the one governed by pink slips and promotions. I hear, too, that advice many of us no doubt were given in our very first poetry writing classes, those apprenticeships, as it might be: that a poem must seek the most economical use of its words, some holdover of modernist technique suggesting fewer words doing more function better in a poem than more words doing less. Such economic advice may well be its own form of tyranny, one experimental poets of the last sixty some years have gone far to question—and yet, something in Neidecker's *condensery* reminds us that poetic work and economic realities are in something more than a mere metaphorical relation.

In this day and age, in which the oracle at Delphi has been replaced by the up-down arrow of the Dow-Jones Industrial report, where Homer's epics that Thoreau heard reciting themselves in the air feel replaced by lunatic tweets, I turn back again and again to the notion of *poetic economy*. I want to know where it is I show up to work each day, what my labor is, who my effort is for. Something in the Greek origins of the words helps—*oikos* for home, *nomos* for laws, or habits, or customs. In a lovely error poor students of Greek such as myself can easily make, *nomos* with accent on the second syllable means "place of pasturage." Perhaps it is in the nature of the condensery to let error proliferate as wildly as does clover in the field, as one way to imagine the flower is the condensation of the energies of the plant green beneath its blooming. This is merely to suggest that the nature of poetic condensation may not be a narrowing of diction or form, but some bewildered form of inversion that makes the innermost outermost. I seem to remember it takes one photon a million years to work its way through the dense labyrinth of the sun to the star's surface, and eight and a half minutes to go from the surface to our eye, making all vision older than the first instance of a human eye. I recall that to *consider* is to think along with the stars. If so, I want only to say that when a poem is a form of economy it is rooting itself down to discover the ways we might find ourselves at home. More important, in finding that home, in founding it, the poem's deep-set ethical nature teaches us how we might behave in that home, how you might go about the business of living in it, and how to do so while causing the least amount of harm.

Is it possible the living room properly seen is just a verdant acre?

One can sit down there every day and ruminate.

One can listen to the wrath in the air, it's still there, Achilles' rage and weeping, and other agonies. The true ones don't unearth the earth, just turn the soil over. O bewildered plow of the head reading and writing, o bewildered plow of mouth listening and singing at once, o furrow's dark line, the living room is also a poem. It's the economy where one must go and learn how to live.

(2018)

Eco-Etho Poetics

Jack Collom

Speaking of the contemporary, I'm going to begin with a statement that is twenty years old:

> Some people say the environment's been getting a lot of publicity and attention the last few years, as if it were a fad like hula hoops. Amazing how long the thing keeps circling around. People build ideas on images largely, and the image that pops in when environment's mentioned is a piece of nature. Maybe an exquisite scene of Bambi under the murmuring pines and the hemlocks—plus a few flowers and chubby little generic birds. So, the environmental concern seems specialized and sentimental. Whereas, in fact, environment is everything around us. Image: your entire human experience is one spilled egg in Yucatán. And ecology is the study of how it all interacts. You can image forth humanity as a plague of termites on Noah's ark—munch munch, splash, drown—and a world of amazing life sinks with them. Or, by some miracle, if they organize to gobble that wood sustainably, manage to arrive at some—

whoops, no Ararat to get to—in terms of the population and technology on Earth now, the ark is it. Sink or swim.

These times, those images are only playful as gallows humor. Remember, this was written twenty years ago. Soil loss, zooming animal extinction rates, water table decline, deforestation, and many other factors, coupled with the overwhelming sense of consumption as addiction in a TV-glued nation, leading the rest of the world like a pie-eyed piper into the caves of oblivion—this *seems* like a mob-psychology juggernaut, unstoppable except by sheer disaster.

These factors lead me to feel that environment is not merely the number one priority. Since it means everything around us, we must understand it that way and see our isolable human concerns as *not* really isolable, but *always* as part of a larger environmental perspective. If a big eco-crisis breaks down civilization in the next century or two, and there are plenty of indicators heading that way, then all the human rivalries we contend with now will be like puffs of sand in a flood. The environment needs a lot *more* publicity—if publicity is the straw to survival.

If it's difficult to see both small and large at the same time, we still have to master that skill. That's what the big brain is for. It is the capacity and the utter need to focus and contextualize or meta-contextualize at the same instant.

There are many people working hard to avert disaster, but the galloping gobble of human materialism seems to overpower them. This is not to minimize the heroic efforts of the Sierras, Audubons, Greenpeaces, et al.; without them we might well crash sooner and uglier. And, you never know. You can't just roll up and say, "doom's it." It's worth being a little foolish, worth planting a tree on your neighbor's head, because the apocalypse is always speculative until it happens.

Some people can plant trees; some can plant ideas. Ideas are usually planted as seeds of image. Poetry carries image as vividly as any articulation does. Let's bend our eyes, ears, and heartbeat rhythm to writings of all kinds that explore new relationships to our surroundings. Not programmatically nor in the main as sermons, but any sort of patch of awareness. Each good poem is like a little ecosystem because it's based on relational sensitivity of parts no matter what it's about.

A religious or spiritual mindset is only lasting if it's structural, like that relational sensitivity of parts. Or call it educational and focus on the young. To teach is an act of combined focus and time awareness by its very nature. Intrahuman politics equals the whining sound of "if *only* we did things right!" Poetry adds vision. Here's fifth grader Fletcher Williams on "Things to Save":

> The darkness of shadow-like wolves
> darting across the night like black bullets
> And the moon, shimmering like a sphere of glowing mass
> Let us save lush grass, green as green can be, but
> Best of all, imagination glowing with joy—aha
> Images it is composed of,
> It is this that is making the earth grow with flavor and
>   destination

So that this little hula hoop world will keep going around. With its red-tailed hawks, violets, and wild mice. Flavor and destination.

Scrape scrape… [is this a poem?]

(2015)

Eros and Ethos

Akilah Oliver

I'm going to speak to eros and ethos, not so much to ecos in the hope that that's embedded here within the conversation. This talk is inspired in part by Joan Retallack's "Essay as Wager," and in part by thinking about the critique around activist art, the old question of why are we doing this, does it make a difference, who's listening? This seems to come up again and again for poets and writers. I want to evade that question a little bit and perhaps make the assumption that it's the doing that matters and the audience that is more nebulous, and that the politics and the aesthetics of making are not always tied to the idea of reception—that is, who's going to listen or will this change our material conditions.

One of the ways I want to talk about this is to talk about three specific art projects. Amy King has been doing a project on a blog called *Poets for Living Waters*. She has sent out a call for poets to post poems that in some way address the BP Gulf Oil situation, the oil spill or spew. Work by another group of artists doing work around this disaster has been initiated by Kristin Prevallet; artists who have joined her have included Rachel Levitsky, Marcella Durand, and Laura Elrick, as well as other New York artists. What they have been doing is positioning themselves around sites in New York City—the Gowanus Canal, the East River, a BP gas station in Greenpoint—and they have been doing very small-scale public actions, I call them insurgency actions, with three or fewer people. I will talk about the work they have been doing as performance interventions. The third artist is Laura Mullen, who is in Baton Rouge. She also has a blog, it's called *afteriwasdead*, and she has been doing public work around BP as well.

First, though, I want to give a framework around this question of why do they do, or why do we do this kind of work, and how does Joan Retallack's idea of the poethical wager tie into the desire toward this kind of work? I also want to talk about desire and eros, and to contextualize this within some kind of slippery, vague framework of the idea of historicism: that history matters, that history is both a material reality that persists in being present, and that the demarcation of history as located in the past, as over and done with, is an erroneous concept. I'd like to bring together the sense of desire toward this kind of work, not thinking of desire or eros as a pure kind of movement toward something or a pure expression, that it can be absolutely selfishly driven and motivated in some ways—but thinking of eros as a primal engagement with the material world, by which I also mean with the body. I am thinking about what [Daniel] Pinchbeck said, that there is not this demarcation between the idea of the body and the soul. Then I want to talk about the idea of exhausting the limits of faith, making the gesture that these artists in a way are exhausting the limits of their own faith. I don't think any of these artists expect BP to call them up and say, for instance, "as a result of your standing in front of a gas station and pouring molasses on yourself, we're going to fix this now," or anything like that. What I mean by eros is this drive within the self to exhaust the limits of one's own faith; that is a kind of passion and desire. And yes, it is absolutely related to the material reality that there is a lot of oil in the Gulf right now, that's really messed up and we are mourning this; but it is also tied to the sense that the body is engaged with the material world, always, in both an unconscious and a conscious way, and we are bringing that unconscious way into a conscious articulation that is also an act of eros. And, as well, there is a desire to see the earth as healed and beautiful, and ourselves absolved of guilt or responsibility toward our ruining of the earth—and I do say "our" even though I know BP is the "bad guy" and we are the "innocents." I want to break down that kind of demarcation of responsibility, while not neglecting to keep in mind the inherent power structures of ownership and capital that allow for this oil spew or spill to continue unabated in the way it has been since it started.

Has the earth always mourned? As we enter this week and we enter our tentative entry into this new century, I am thinking about eros and I am thinking about ethos, and I am struck again by how persistently this thing called the past insists on being with us, as being a living, archival document. The past as an extended duration, the past as a contrary companion that continues to force us to reconsider any kind of nostalgic attachment to the idea that the past is something that is done with, that is locatable somewhere in this thing called history, and that the past is outside of our present condition. One of the critiques that comes up again and again about artists like Laura Mullen, Kristin Prevallet, Amy King, and others, whom I'm going to dub "The BP Insurgents," is this idea that this work doesn't matter because it is happening in the moment and it somehow will be lost. In beginning to think about the past as a continuous moment and of the present as a part of that moment, it helps for me to re-shift the focus from "does this art matter, would it be lost?" to "how do we enter into history, and how do we articulate that entry into history at any given point, as artists, as activists, as writers?" So, if the past is thought of as a continuous moment and history is our attempt to regulate and document that past, to codify it in some way, it opens up or maybe closes down part of the critique of "why does it matter, who is listening, will anybody pay attention to this in ten years, in five years?"

I had thought I would go a little bit into representation, the power of the image and the kinds of technological media that transmit representation now so quickly, the sense of duration and of speed. I think that one way of thinking about history and the past and technology right now is to think in terms of going back to the enduring context of the image, the way the image can be reproduced and the way it can be represented via social media. The visual component of representation creates a continuous discourse, almost immediately, only by its presence and its visibility. But I won't get into that so much.

I am thinking of Janis Joplin, whom I'm going to quote out of context here. But then I'm thinking, is there any such thing as *out of context* except in the margins of a pseudo-academic paper like this? So, I think I'll restate this: I'll quote Janis Joplin *inside* context instead of out of context. The quote is, "It's all the same fucking day, man." This day that is pleasurable in its complicated measure, in its stubborn insistence on the idea of a new day, a day which carries an ethos, an ethos that is strangely familiar in its mimetic affinity to the bodies that have populated the days that preceded this day. To think about habitation, to think about the ethos of habitation, brings up the idea of memory, memory as an act or memory as a space. As an act, an act of composition; memory as an act of making. Also, memory as an act of investigation, an investigation which is grounded in a sense of eros. Eros, too, thinking of it as derived from chaos, this primal drive that has come out of chaos. Thinking about the primary drive to investigate, to compose, might bring us to Walter Benjamin and his cautionary reminder of the danger of stripping the past from the present. And stripping the materiality of eros from the idea of history as well.

Some definitions in this context: One, eros as the material body of memory. Two: eros as the dream of earth and its discontent. Three: eros as our imaginary, which I'll also dub as the present. My use of eros here is inextricably linked to the idea of ethos. Going back to Walter Benjamin, from his work *Theses on the Philosophy of History*, I want to invoke the idea of happiness. "Our image of happiness is indissolubly bound up with the image of redemption. The same applies to our view of the past, which is the concern of history. The past carries with it a temporal index by which it is referred to as redemption. There is a secret agreement between past generations and the present one. Our coming was expected on earth." I want to repeat that line: *our coming was expected on earth*. "Like every generation that preceded us we have been endowed with a weak, messianic power, a power to which the past has a claim. That claim cannot be settled cheaply." I'll come back to that in a moment, this idea that the past has expected us, that our coming has always been welcomed and that we were always supposed to be here. What does that mean in terms of a claim, this claim he talks about, that cannot be settled cheaply?

One way I think about this claim is that it has a power, a power on which we have all been endowed to meditate, to act. This claim to make it a composition. It is also analogous to Joan Retallack's idea, the challenge of the poethical wager—which is another way of saying, what do you stake your work on? What are you betting? What is your wager when you put on a wedding dress and walk out onto the streets in the Gulf Coast? What is at stake here? Going back to Benjamin, the idea that there is some kind of secret agreement between past generations—that is, the past and myself, my own embodied presence here in this place called the present. That there is some secret agreement calls to mind the idea of ethics, that I have some duty to question, to investigate why I am doing any piece of work at any given time. Rather than located outside of politics, outside of history, outside of dream, outside of eros, the work is all located within this continuous moment, and it has some purpose, even if that purpose is only that we talk about if it has a purpose.

I am thinking about what is at stake for us now in this century as we are performing the present. What is at stake for us as writers and artists as we reimagine, confront, and make work of the complexities of time. What is this fraught present that is complicated by these myriad offers of representation through technology, through the immediacy of image making, instant reproduction, the speed of distribution? Again, probably *everything* is at stake, even if I can't name what "everything" is. It seems critical to me as an artist that I do make work, not with the expectation that there will be a cause and effect relationship between the work that I make and the commentary of the work's content, but so that I can continue to breathe on the planet. It is almost a selfish guise, a way that I keep myself alive. The selfish guise is that I am giving it to you, but I don't know why I would wake up in the morning if I didn't do it, even if I didn't give it to you. This is part of the way I'm looking at the work that the artists I'm calling the BP Insurgents are doing. There is both a real desire to be politically engaged, a real sense of mourning, and there is a real impulse and drive toward "I have to make this work," I have to make this work because that is how I stay on the planet, even if no one listens to or sees the work.

I think we want the earth and the body and the earth's body to be a material given. We want the arrival of grace in some way. There is also a pure desire, that we want to stop fucking up. There is a call to a sense of holiness as well in this kind of work, which may be similar to the weak messianic call that Walter Benjamin talked about—which is not to think that I am godlike, but why not? It is probably not going to upset anyone's day if I did think I was godlike. But the idea of a weak messianic power is the idea that he invokes later in a different essay, the idea of a Messiah's arrival, the Messiah being all of us, and walking through the gates. There is something transformative about the entry into the gate, there is some passage that, at its best, art allows to happen—some passage from here to there, from one form of consciousness to another. There is something greater going on.

Holy! Holy! Holy! Holy! Holy! Holy! Holy! Holy! Holy! Holy! Holy! Holy! Holy! Holy! Holy!

The world is holy! The soul is holy! The skin is holy! The nose is holy! The tongue and cock and hand and asshole holy!

Everything Is holy! everybody's holy! everywhere Is holy! everyday is in eternity! Everyman's an angel!

…

Holy time in eternity holy eternity in time holy the clocks in space holy the fourth dimension holy the fifth International holy the Angel in Moloch!

Holy the sea holy the desert holy the railroad holy the locomotive holy the visions holy the hallucinations holy the miracles holy the eyeball holy the abyss!

Holy forgiveness! mercy! Charity! faith! Holy! Ours! bodies! suffering! magnanimity!

Holy the supernatural extra brilliant intelligent kindness of the soul!

—*Allen Ginsberg from "Footnote to Howl"*

I invoke that because there is something related to the idea of eros in the particular drive of poets and artists and activists to make work. Part of that eros is situated in the material body, in the material earth, and, in that materiality, there is space for ecstatic arrival and transference. And maybe the opposite is true as well, in the idea of spirit there is also the possibility for the holiness of the body. If we extend that to the Gulf of Mexico, if we extend it to the Earth, if we extend it to history, then this holiness too is a pervading desire which is a kind of reaching toward eros, reaching toward holiness at the same time.

In Retallack's poethical wager, I believe also lurking underneath her idea of the wager is a gesture toward Ginsberg's idea of holy forgiveness. Another way to think about forgiveness is to think about Benjamin's or Agamben's idea of redemption and what is retrievable.

Forgiveness as what is retrievable. What is our responsibility toward the irretrievable? For example, the Gulf Coast may be irretrievable at this point. It may never recover, or it may not recover in my lifetime. What does that mean as an artist, as a thinker, as a human being? How do we reconcile that? Who and what is to be forgiven?

Robin Blaser gave a talk at Naropa once in which he spoke about what is unforgiveable. Some things are not retrievable. Then this poethical wager also brings into question, if something is absolutely unforgiveable—which might be the same as thinking of it as being irretrievable—how do I not get lost in that mourning? How do I not get lost in that grief? Making work, the act of composition is one way of embracing that grief and that mourning, and perhaps getting lost in it; but the act of composition is also a way of retrieving something. Perhaps it becomes a retrieval of holy forgiveness.

Walter Benjamin talks about happiness. "Our image of happiness is bound up with the image of redemption." I think of happiness as both eros and ethos at the same time. There is an ecstatic and bodily pleasure for writers and artists that is in the engagement with the performative act itself, with the engagement of the materials we work with, with the engagement of the idea of permanence and impermanence—that itself is a kind of pleasure that drives this work and makes it worthwhile. And then I want to go back to Benjamin's idea that the earth has been expecting us. It seems like a great weight, in a way. But it also seems liberating, this idea that of course I should write this poem, of course I should put on a wedding dress and carry a bouquet of flowers and walk down the street in Baton Rouge— because the earth has been expecting me. It has been expecting my arrival and it welcomes this.

I'm going back and forth between this nebulous kind of mystic way of thinking about making work and then really advancing at the same time, pushing toward the idea of historical materialism. We have to keep history in mind, we have to keep in mind the material conditions of capital, of regime, of power. We have to, at the same time, hold both of these in mind or the making of art becomes useless and barbaric. Ginsberg's incantation, "Holy holy holy," brings me into the consciousness of dissolving borders—that is, dissolving borders between the sacred and the profane. It also brings me into the idea of the messiness of holiness: holy ass, holy cock, holy hallucination, holy railroad: bringing me into the idea of commerce, the idea of movement, itinerancy. All of these ideas are holy and held at the same time. Joan Retallack brings us to the idea of fractal geometries. In "Essay as Wager" she talks, too, about these dissolving borders, which gets a little more complicated, the idea of what's lost and what's gained, the idea of movement born out of economic failures, born out of war, born out of genocides. The kinds of itinerancy that many of us experience, a voluntary kind of temporary exile, traveling, as a way to stay connected that gets more and more complicated. One of the ways Retallack connects these is similar to that of Édouard Glissant in his book *Poetics of Relation*. Glissant talks about the Atlantic Ocean as a metaphor as well as a real passageway, as a way of mapping, a way of thinking about the cartography of bodies and movement from the Caribbean to the United States, from Africa to the Caribbean to the United States. So, we are thinking too about waterways and coastlines as mapping history and mapping power relations, mapping loss and mapping the reimagining of borders and of bodies and commerce. Retallack talks about that in a different way: "Fractal geometry of coastlines with their ecologically dynamic infinite detail, that may be a more productive model for the interrelationships of cultures." I've been thinking about the metaphor; when I read that again last night, I thought specifically about the Gulf Coast and the kinds of relationships that these artists are trying to engage in that have specifically been inspired by the defouling of these coastlines.

 Retallack takes us to the urgent moment before us as writers and thinkers in another section of the essay where she refers to the idea of the swerve. "Life is subject to swerves, sometimes gentle, often violent, out of the blue motions that cut obliquely across material and conceptual logics. If everything were hunky-dory it might not be so important to attend to them. How can one frame a poetics of the swerve, a constructive preoccupation with what are unpredictable forms of change? One might begin by stating this: what we all have in common is an unsettling transfiguration of once familiar terrain." For example, the Gulf Coast, even if familiar only in the imaginary, in the idea of water and pristine. I also don't want us to forget the people who died in the oil rig explosion. We are thinking about economies and about class and about power in relationship to these terrains and bodies in relationship to specific territories. Who is forgotten, what is not brought into the conversation as we mourn the Gulf Coast? What is prioritized and what is not?

That once familiar terrain, the idea of defamiliarization might require a poetics (I'm calling what Laura Mullen is doing a poetics) that re-narrates what was once familiar that has been violently defamiliarized, that has been turned against itself, that staggers perhaps under the shame of our egos. That is part of the value of the work that Mullen and others are doing, this idea of re-narrating and forcing the defamiliarization to become even more fragmented and more whole at the same time. There is fragmentation and there is the symbolism of the pristine white wedding dress and the assumption of the marriage contract as being inviolable, or at least legally sacred—then to think about that as a complete defouling and as a contract that perhaps never existed outside of the legal system, perhaps only in the imaginary. So, to take the familiar white wedding dress and put it in the context of a mourning veil and a protest action is another way to defamiliarize, to take the known referents and make them messy, to break them. I think there is a gendered reading, too, of taking the wedding dress out of context and making it less familiar, making it sacrilegious in a way, especially considering the metaphor of the earth as mother.

I think Retallack, in the poethical wager, is also referring to a kind of grief. The activist work that is being done around the Gulf Coast is work of mourning. I'd like to invoke Judith Butler on the idea of grief. This is from the book *Precarious Life*, which is mostly concerned with post-9/11 US identity in relation to the rest of the world, the idea of violence and redemption. She also talks about the Israeli-Palestinian situation. "To grieve and to make grief itself into a resource for politics is not to be resigned to inaction but it may be understood as the slow process by which we develop a point of identification with suffering itself. The disorientation of grief, who have I become or indeed what is left of me, what is it in the other I have lost? These questions all posit the 'I' in the mode of unknowingness." I think it is interesting here that the "I" becomes, not a knowing "I," but an unknowing "I." Perhaps the art of these insurgent artists is also a way to re-know the self or to relearn the "I," that there is something that I am learning about myself through this work.

The following are "conversations" I've set up between Joan Retallack (i.e., quotes from) and various poets and artists doing work around the Gulf Oil spill:

> RETALLACK: To wager on a poetics of the conceptual swerve is to believe in the constancy of the unexpected, source of terror, humor, and hope.

> LAURA MULLEN: I have been working with exploratory non-fiction and, since early May of this year, an ongoing effort not only to understand the event [the Gulf Coast oil spew] but to see how understanding itself is shaped by differences in landscape, culture, history, and psychic, as well as financial, investments. Actions involving the body and deploying cultural symbols, I'm using them in the effort to open the frame of visible, taking what we want to see, the bride for example, into the space of what we don't want to look at, disaster for instance. The bride work began before the Gulf drilling disaster. I began it as part of the work toward the third book in my trilogy of hybrid

texts, this one on the romance. But in confronting both the catastrophe and the problem of its visibility, the whole wide white screen of the wedding dress offers a chance to make a point about pollution as well as about expensive "purity."

• • •

JOAN RETALLACK: Everything in mass culture is designed to deliver space-time in a series of shiny freeze-frames, each with its built-in strategy of persuasion. One writes poetry and essays to disrupt that fatal momentum.

RACHEL LEVITSKY: We had a sign of the Gulf Stream showing how this disaster is everywhere, we are all connected. We had a sign that said, "please let's rethink oil." We wore black and carried prayer flags and wore veils. We were only three. We were merely standing for a half hour. We were told that we could not go on the rocks. We were told that we could not do this in a state park. We were told we could not carry the sign. We were told we were being handled in a lenient way, that they could stop us for being symbolic but they decided not to. Please make an action with two or three next Tuesday on Gulf Stream or by water if possible. Document with photos.

RETALLACK: A poetics of memory, for instance, must be transfigured with an informed poetics of desire if it is to nourish agency. The question of meaningful cultural agency is always what's at stake. By poetics of desire, I mean whatever moves us toward a responsive and pleasurable connection to the world. [Evoking eros again.]

KRISTIN PREVALLET: Yesterday I performed a second environmental genocide mourning action with Rachel Levitsky and

Laura Elrick. Bushwick Inlet Park, Williamsburg, Brooklyn. State park guys made us put down the sign, no soliciting in a state park, but let us keep the prayer flags even though that's a symbol, again, it's not allowed.

Retallack: Touching, being touched, partaking of textural transfigurations in the unsettled weathers along personal, cultural coastlines is irreversibly compelling, is incorrigibly real.

Prevallet: I stood for two hours in the morning with oil-drenched sunflower and oil-drenched BP logo, poured molasses over the sunflowers as performance in front of all the people getting gas. The attendant came out and said, "who's going to clean that up?" [Irony.] Then he called the cops. But it was just me and one other woman so they couldn't do anything. If there were three, they could have kicked us off the property. Just a reminder that three or fewer people can do things that larger protests can't.

From the About page of Amy King's project *Poets for Living Waters:*

Poets for Living Waters is a poetry forum begun in 2010 as a response to the Gulf Oil Disaster of April 20, 2010, one of the most profound man-made ecological catastrophes in history. The initial project included hundreds of poetry and poetics publications, and a series of international reading events. You can read more about the initial endeavor in "Poets Acts on Oil Spill" by Shell Fischer at the Poets & Writers website.

While devastating, we recognize that the extreme event of the Gulf Oil Disaster may be best understood as merely a partial manifestation of a widespread consciousness producing global ecological crisis. Zen master Thich Nhat Hanh suggests that in response to the contemporary situation, we refrain from appeals to effective argument but rather stir affective compassion: "We should not talk in terms of what they should do, what they should not do, for the sake of the future. We should talk to them in such a way that touches their hearts..." *Poets for Living Waters* contributes to this latter conversation, motivated by the belief that poetry helps release us from moral platitudes, returns us to our bodies, returns us to our senses.

I want to end with a Retallack quote: "It's the poetics of memory, what is made of it now, that might create a difference. This is the question of poethics. What we make of events as we use language in the present, how we continuously create an ethos of the way in which events are understood."

(2010)

In and Out of the House

Andrew Schelling

For several years, Naropa's four-week Summer Writing Program has dedicated one week to the theme "Eco-Dharma Poetics." An elemental question I have not heard asked is how these terms, *ecology* and *dharma*, are linked to one another. One term is modern, the other ancient. One coined from Greek etymologies by the German zoologist Ernst Haeckel in 1866, one buried in the prehistory of the Sanskrit language. I thought I'd make a patchwork of ways to connect the two terms and see what comes out.

Many of you know that the prefix or partial word "eco-" comes from the Greek *oikos*. It simply means house, dwelling, or household, though this definition gets obscured in big-notion words: economics, ecology, ecopoetics. If you track "eco" back in time, you land on a word rooted in Proto-Indo-European, a reconstructed language, which linguists have pieced together in fragments by comparing the vocabularies and grammar of modern tongues. A Proto-Indo-European noun-stem, *weik*, holds a cluster of ideas, notably "clan," or "a social unit larger than the household." Here's a clue, then, that anything pertaining to "eco" has to do with the household or with a social unit somewhat larger. Either way, you arrive at a community based on relationship and intimacy.

This tangle of words gets reflected in various ways through the Indo-European speaking world. Sanskrit, a language that has altered very little for two thousand five hundred years, has a cognate term, *viśaḥ*, dwelling, dwelling place, or house. One of the caste groups of India is the *vaiśya*. They are traders, agricultural workers, craftspeople, merchants. Different from priests or warriors, the *vaiśya* are traditional householders. Their role is to hang around home.

It was Gary Snyder's 1969 book *Earth House Hold*, playing on these etymologies, that popularized the notion of ecology for poets, revolutionaries, and counterculture folk. Snyder linked "eco" to human communities, marriage, and family. He was embarking on a lifelong scrutiny of ecology, noting that the discipline technically studies how creatures and their environment are tangled in relationship. I don't want to lose sight of the slightly more specific, Indo-European, sense of the word *oikos* though—a clan or unit above the household—because that's what scientific use of the word ecology points toward: a community larger than one's household, made up of diverse species.

The way we understand ecology now, and evolution since Darwin laid out his ideas, recognizes that *our* clan has always been larger than the human species. Other-than-humans stand closely related to us, belong to the tribe; without them, we would be paupers. Most indigenous storytelling traditions have been saying this for millennia. Some of these other species are great inside the *oikos*, sitting by the fire with us. Not just cats and dogs, but spider-hunting wasps, birds that flit through our windows, and microbes on our eyelids. There are plenty of creatures I prefer to keep out of the house. Field mice, black widow spiders, the occasional rattlesnake. But they, too, are part of the clan and have their place in the ecosystem.

What then is the connection to *dharma*, that other arm of Eco-Dharma? Dharma is a pan-Indian term that Buddhists lifted out of an ecosystem of ideas in India; around 500 BCE Yogins and philosophers reworked its focus, until it came to mean something like the aggregate of Buddhist teachings.

Dharma originates in a Sanskrit verbal root *dhṛ*, which means to hold, to preserve, to fix in place. The same word, or its Indo-European prototype, drifts downstream into our own language as the word "firm." Something that holds, that's rooted, unyielding, that lasts. Etymologies vanish into the fog at some point, but *dharma* likely has further family connections to our English word "truth," which is helpfully cognate to the word "tree." Why do I find this helpful? It suggests that neither truth nor dharma have jack-shit to do with belief systems, speculation, metaphysics, or theology. They are, simply, like trees: well rooted. We might call them facts, or with a bit of care, laws. That is how the Chinese translated dharma, using a legal term, and why early translations of Buddhist texts from Chinese have titles like *The Lotus of the True Law*.

In Buddhism, *dharma* took on an adjacent, more specialized meaning: the range of lore or real facts passed down by means of talks, meditations, precise mind-transmissions, and books. These were meant to establish a clear-eyed, fact-regarding, undeceived, and undeceiving view of the world. Like the principles of ecology, Dharma is there, whether you pay attention or not, whether you believe it or not.

So, I'd look at ecology as a sort of mythos, logos, or set of irreducible principles. You might have ideas about ecology, but those are just your ideas. Ecology has its own work to do. Dharma, too, is some sort of mythos, logos, or set of principles. There is a significant point of contact between them. Both, as an irreducible principle, insist on the mutual dependence of things: things that are living, as well as things that are not living. Or like stones and tectonic plates, things living at a pace so different from ours that we don't quite understand what life looks like to them.

The foundation of Dharma in Buddhism is that there is really no separate, autonomous, intact thing as a person. All these people, creatures, items, that appear independent or separate come forth and exist in a network with all else that exists. In mythic terms, Buddhists describe Indra's net, a web of commitment and love and karma that holds all forms, living or not living, together. The original Sanskrit phrase is *pratītya-samutpāda*, translated as "inter-dependent co-origination." *Samutpāda* means "to rise up or be generated together." *Pratītya* means "check this out." Check out how all things are born from the same shimmering void. Check out how they depend on each other.

This is the bare ecological fact.

As you sit under this tent, feet on bare, firm ground, check out the interdependence. The soil holds your chair; matted grasses hold the soil together. Beetles, earthworms, billions of microbes too small to see, aerate the soil nourishing the grass. Step from the tent and study the plants in front of the library. They are not there arbitrarily or haphazardly. They are shade tolerant, somewhat xeric; they thrive in a high altitude, arid, low-oxygen community beneath the sycamore's big shady leaves. In response, they provide nutrients to the sycamore, and create a microclimate that protects the sycamore's surprisingly shallow roots from winter cold or marauding insects.

Though ecology has no ethics built into it, you can derive some. This might be important since the crises in today's planetary ecosystem seem to demand a sense of community that goes beyond our immediate household. An ethic derived from interdependence is quite old in Buddhism. The *Diamond Sutra* gives a fine example.

The noble-minded Subhuti, a long-time, standout member of the early Buddhist clan, has gotten a bit confused. Known for his rigorous discipline, he sees that various guidelines for how to act in the world sound tangled, contradictory. Approaching Shakyamuni

Buddha, he says, "How should a person who sets forth in the vehicle of a Bodhisattva stand? How does one go out and act? What should you do with your thoughts?"

The Buddha replies, "A young man or woman who sets forth in the vehicle of a Boddhisattva…"

This is quite interesting. Even one's spiritual body is not really yourself. The Bodhisattva is not you, just a kind of carriage in which a temporary self sets forth.

Then comes the passage on how to discipline your thoughts:

> One should produce a thought in this way: "As many creatures as exist in the realm of creatures, all that can be conceived as a creature—egg-born, born from a womb, moisture born, or miraculously born; with form, without form; with perception, without perception, with neither perception nor non-perception—any creature you can possibly imagine, all these I should lead out of misery, into that realm of nirvana where nothing is left over."

What a thorny teaching this is. You could read it your whole life, get tangled every day and not find your way to its center. What's this leftover stuff, stuff that makes people miserable? How do you get others out of it? I think it refers to one's belief in a separate non-dependent self. The false notion we all fall prey to: that we are a household of one.

The contrary notion, of there being no permanent detached individual, no soul, no isolated self, has to do with "checking out" (*pratītya*) how creatures depend on each other in mysterious ways. You cannot extract anybody. I'm intrigued that the *Diamond Sutra* passage identifies the way all known creatures come into existence: the egg-born, the womb-born, the moisture-born. Moisture-born would have been a category in the science of early Buddhist India. Algae, pollywogs, waterbugs, mosquitoes, viruses, sure do look like they get born out of water.

Miraculously born, what is that? Maybe it accounts for those creatures who come to exist in ways we don't understand. Nonetheless, they do appear in their own right. This includes dream figures, characters out of mythology or novels, the invisible friends of children, faeries, tutelary goddesses. Their origins are obscure, but we know them for real. They too are worthy of attention.

So this provides a view of the community of beings one should care about. The community is the full range of life-forms; even if they don't have a "form" we can see, or sense organs we recognize. What they do have, like all of us, are hunger, hope, sorrow, affection, fear, and the urge to keep living.

This sounds like contemporary insights in ecology and evolution. I suspect that in our modern myths, evolution is what corresponds to a Buddhist notion of rebirth. Buddhists say reincarnation has gone on for so long, through so many biological and miraculous forms, that each of us has been everyone else's child at some time. If you don't get too attached to a lifetime being your personal private property, you might imagine your own DNA goes—without interruption—all the way back to the prehistoric first moment of life. Every living creature would be a sister or brother. It does look like protoplasm has gotten handed down for so long that all critters are family.

I like to toy with the notion that Darwinian evolution and Buddhist reincarnation are comparable ideas, looked at with different eyes. It feels funny, kind of subversive, to talk like this in Colorado. This is the state where Evangelical, literalist Christian groups are pushing forward a contrary agenda. An agenda that disbelieves interspecies relationship. That ignores the laws of ecology. That regards humans as exceptional. Christians as infallible. If you talk evolution, you might get in trouble in some nearby districts.

That's okay. Tell them evolution's a myth.

But do put on your car the sticker, "When Evolution is Outlawed only Outlaws will Evolve."

I see a couple of tasks for the future. The naturalist Edward O. Wilson has usefully coined a term *biophilia*, and a phrase "the biophilia hypothesis." Forms of life, the hypothesis states, love one another. At least have deep-time emotional ties. He cautions that there's no proof. But researchers are thinking it over, that innate affection crosses the lines of species. As foolish and independent as humans behave, we remain not only materially dependent on other life forms but related in our psyches, too. Wilson puts forth interesting thoughts. He notes that snakes show up in the dreams of people who have little experience of snakes. A Manhattanite who has never met a snake is as likely to dream of one as a cowboy from Utah. You could say Snake Old Man is deep in your nervous system. Whatever instinct makes you jump from danger without thinking—you got it, in a former life, from a snake in the underbrush. If you practice a martial art, I'd say in the dojo it is rattlesnake's teachings you perfect.

Maybe the biophilia hypothesis will eventually confirm the psychic dimensions of myth that in the past have been filled with goofy mysticism. The shifty boundary between humans and non-human species might lie back there in prehistory.

The earliest art we possess doesn't show humans but animals. Why is that? Magdalena cave walls in France, hybrid creatures painted on rock in Indonesia, storytelling traditions of Native America. A recent newspaper article on domestication cited genetic studies showing that dogs and humans have lived together—one household—for a hundred thousand years. This pushes the threshold back from 14,000, the timeframe deep historians used to hold. And human-canine companionship can hardly be utilitarian. It's easy to see why you'd keep a cow or a goat near the house. But a dog?

I keep a watch on activists who show cross-species care. Such as efforts to restore timber wolf populations, or grizzly bear, in the Western states. This work is not about one critter but aims at the health of whole ecosystems. What about popular outrage over slaughter of bison on the outskirts of Yellowstone? This must expose a need for the companionship of other species. Not in the house, but as part of the larger social group. Our minds, bodies, physical habits, developed over countless years in contact with Snake Old Man, Buffalo Maiden, frog, raven, sycamore tree. Lose these, you lose your dreams and mythologies.

When I lived in Berkeley in the 1980s, I got involved with a creek reclamation outfit. They produced maps of the local creeks, alive but glacially covered by asphalt and concrete. I would follow the creeks on foot, using the maps, listening for water at the drain covers. The reclamation visionaries fix plaques over grates on the street, asking you not to drain oil or transmission fluid into the water below. They use a symbol for each creek, a steelhead or frog, with a cautionary word. "This drains to Derby Creek." "This drains to Temescal Creek." The goal is one day to reopen the creeks, as they twist through the neighborhoods, bring salmon and trout back to former migrations, and restore riparian habitat.

One day, I met a friend for a drink and told him about creek reclamation. He was appalled. "With so much political shit going down," he spit over his whiskey, "how can you waste time on creeks? Who gives a fuck about drainage?"

I realized that unbeknownst to me one of my comrades had gone mad.

Conservation, preservation, reclamation of creeks to their old courses—along with mallows, reeds, and coyote—is not political shit. It is art.

I'll finish with a poem that carries some DNA from Buddhist India. But first there's something Terry Riley once said about raga singing. "Indian music is the most practical thing you can do. It develops four qualities," he told a friend. Here are the qualities: "Concentration. Attunement. The ability to go to the center of something. Improvisation."

Now a two thousand year-old poem from India. Nobody knows who wrote it.

Lone buck
in the clearing
nearby doe
eyes him with such
longing
that there
in the trees the hunter
seeing his own girl
lets the bow drop

(presented at the panel: Eco-Dharma Poetics, 1997)

WE AS WITNESS

Paula Gunn Allen

"Danzeling on the Age of a Volcano" is a line from James Joyce's *Finnegan's Wake*, which suggested to us our precarious situation as we sit poised for the 21st century. What are we as witness—writers, poets, visionaries, etc.—going to do?

—Anne Waldman

I was thinking about what to say about what we, as witness, are going to do about a dying planet. I have two texts here. The first is a line from Linda Hogan, from a poem of hers called "Blessings." The line is "Those people are always leaving." The next text is from Leslie Marmon Silko. In *Ceremony*, Ku'oosh, the Laguna medicine man, says to poor old Tayo, who is dying, "But grandson, you know, this earth is fragile."

I would like to suggest what might be a startling concept—I hope it's startling. You know the theory of parthenogenesis? In the old times, a woman got pregnant because she got pregnant, and the cells began to divide. When the cells divide the first cell is the mother cell and the second cell is the daughter cell. What's interesting is you end up with two cells that are indistinguishable from one another. My young son, who lives on the streets of Berkeley and calls himself a mathematician, tells me that he and all his friends know the magic is changing. That's another text. Let me suggest that what is not happening is that the animals are becoming extinct, and the air is becoming extinct, and the water is becoming extinct—maybe she [Earth] is in a process of giving birth to herself. Or, as we put it, the planet is splitting. So, a whole lot of people have gone ahead, as they have always done, the buffalo, the eagle, all kinds of plant communities and microscopic animal communities that are all "dying." Maybe they didn't die, maybe they left.

The Native American people have no word for goodbye, I haven't found one yet. They don't believe in beginnings and endings because the stories—stories plural—always go on and on. And the earth always goes on and on. I suggest that what is happening is a phase of human history is coming to an end, and not a moment too soon. Those of us who are survivors on this side—let's say it's the "right" side just to be ornery—of this sacred cell division process, to us it looks like everything is dying. But the others, who have gone to the other side, on the daughter planet, to them it looks like everything is coming alive. The chances are that as this process continues, the mother planet, who looks like she's dying, will be restored. And we see that. We see that a number of creatures are actually coming back. The buffalo are a good example. Coyote—as long as coyote's around everything is cool. And cockroaches are everywhere. If there's one thing I know about cockroaches it's that they are the oldest living form still here on mother planet, and they dream everything. They dream being into existence. They love the dark, they don't like the light, and they are very wise because the dark is where the mother is, where life is, where all that is comes from. You've all been in the womb, you know what I mean.

Maybe we are midwives to a new earth. Maybe the skills we need to learn are the skills of helping birth occur in the most non-traumatic way possible. That means heal ourselves. Love our earth. Love our cities. Love ourselves. Stop making funny distinctions about what is artificial and what is natural. As a Native American and a woman, I'm "natural" and, frankly, I haven't found anything yet that wasn't made by an animal. (Human beings are animals, you know.) So, I don't think there is anything that is "artificial."

As witness, then, we can sing the songs of life and death. As writers, we can write the stories of recovery. As human beings, we need to work on recovering ourselves. Because we each are a piece of that mother planet. We can help her health be restored after this great division, and then we can all go on.

(presented at the panel: Danzeling on the Age of the Volcano: Environmental Awareness as the 21st Century Approaches, 1992)

Time Tithing

Ed Sanders

I am intending to go out in a blaze of leaflets. I am an activist and the issue before us is extremely complicated. But it is also as simple as your backyard. It is as simple as the concept of time tithing. Money is not a problem. The clarity that Allen Ginsberg has spoken of is what is needed. Clarity and time tithing, that is, finding creative time, and, like the Protestants do with money, tithing a proportion of your time on a regular basis. Not when you're dead tired at ten o'clock at night, but at some point of your life where your creative energy is focused and where you have clarity of mind. I was moved by Diana's [Diana Hadley] exposition of a particular problem in a particular bioregion, and that the World Bank watch person pointed out that it was just one of many. But that's what they always tell you when you rise up to beat the drums of focus on an environmental issue. *Oh, you know, it's only a creek.* But that's where protection of our species and, also, the wounded plant and animal species occurs, that's where they get protected. It is by daring to be part of history, the history of your neighborhood, the history of the creek that runs behind your house, the history of where that creek runs into a bigger creek and becomes a drainage basin, the history of where those creeks which are like living veins of the planet become bioregions; to dare to be a history of your town, your city, your county. It all points to the need to become a scholar in chaos.

We are enormously fragmented in the environmental world. I try to tithe part of everyday toward protecting the water. Where I live, in Woodstock, New York, which is part of the Hudson River drainage basin, a creek, the west bank of the Tannery Brook, flows by my house, then it goes into the Millstream Creek, which goes into the Sawkill, and the Sawkill flows into the Hudson River about eight miles away. That is the drainage basin area, that fragment of the Hudson River Valley that I try to protect. I try to protect it through helping write recycling legislation, helping write land use plans, helping to ban aerial spraying, helping to encourage organic farming, helping to make sure that the industries along the edge of creeks and rivers do not pollute those water basins.

The environmental world, where I live, is kind of torn between protecting the air and protecting the water. It is true that the air causes health problems. But if all the factories were to stop, in about a week we'd have fairly clean air. While, once a leachate, once a filth plumage, a hazardous plumage spreads out in an aquifer, it can't be killed for hundreds of years, maybe thousands of years. So, I decided to become a water worker because, out of water, the avenues lead to the economy. We need a non-polluting business environment, we need to encourage small, non-polluting businesses. Therefore, we have to concern ourselves with the banking system. This is a gigantic subject.

My only advice, since it is so fragmented, is to pick your area and begin to become a scholar of the minute, almost a lawyer's level of scholarship. And start subscribing to relevant sources of information. The morning I left Woodstock to come to Boulder, I grabbed my mail and it included the *Institute of Ecosystem Study Newsletter*, *New York Coalition for Alternatives to Pesticides Newsletter*, an EPA asbestos summary, a bill about a New York State plastics legislation, *The National Toxics Campaign*. Mine is a very particularized journey. As Gary Snyder said, it's a journey of a thousand years.

(presented at the panel: Danzeling on the Age of the Volcano: Environmental Awareness as the 21st Century Approaches, 1992)

A Poetics of Natural Light

Peter Warshall

One of the things Ed Sanders says is that your writing is always a notebook. What I'm going to do in this lecture is give you a feeling for the things I am thinking about right now in a very broad sense of ecopoetics. I am going to start with one of the great ecopoetic poets, Gerard Manley Hopkins. Although he definitely believed in some kind of distant god in some other universe, he was also one of the most careful writers about nature, trying very carefully to put his sound together with what the texture of looking at landscape was about. This talk is about this one stanza:

> The sun on falling waters writes the text
> Which yet is in the eye or in the thought.
> It was a hard thing to undo this knot.

I've spent about twenty years fiddling with this knot. I still haven't untied it in any way. I probably started in the early 1970s. Diane di Prima and I gave a talk at the Exploratorium in San Francisco. She talked about *Loba* and I talked about the confusion of trying to understand what an edge was. After that, Arthur Okamura, a wonderful painter, and I gave a course called "Art and Nature," where we both would go out and he'd explain what he was looking at from the point of view of a painter and I'd explain what I was seeing as a naturalist.

Writing on water has particular glyphs. They are shadows, black, white, and colored shadows, and they are colors, radiant colors, spectral light, subdued colors, refracted colors, reflected colors, polarized light, translucent light, transparent light. Those are the things that when you are outdoors, and you start with sun and the sky, become your own gallery. This is really about a spaciousness that's not found in galleries, which have a homogeneous light source, the baby spots which are designed to make sure that every color is equal inside the light of the baby spot. There is no patchiness on the walls. This is not about lofts, where you have a walled space and the light comes in through either windows or skylights. It's not about labs of neuroscientists, who lose track of the web of life and the networks of color talk among plants and animals. And it's not about mystics, who focus on internal beams of divine light and hardly ever get off their zafus. This is about spaciousness as it was experienced by the whole earth in its whole history. It's about the spaciousness of the sky, which is a half-dome of extended light within which we evolved. Something is going on inside this particular half-dome that is deeper than culture. Whatever that theme is, it's kind of what my "notebooks" and this talk are about.

First, I will talk about the palette of Gaia, why we have the particular colors we do and how they formed on the planet. The human eye can see about three hundred colors. But there are thousands of colors on the planet. In a way, this talk is also the groundwork for a word that was coined by Edward O. Wilson, "biophilia," the sense we feel that we have something in common with the rest of nature.

For about a hundred years, people have been screaming at naturalists saying, you're anthropomorphizing, you're projecting your own feelings into animals. Actually, underneath we all know that there is a great commonality with our dogs, our cats, even our trees. That is biophilia. But no one has really looked at it. What is this common ground, this commonality on the planet? It has to do, in part, with evolution and natural selection, the discriminating eye and hand of the hunter as he tries to spot the red parrot in the green palm, or the eye and hand of the gatherer trying to find the red fruit against the Paolo Veronese green. But it has to do even more so, which is reflected in the language of color, with how color goes deep into the body—it is a heart movement. That's why we talk about color tones, as if color was music; we talk about "the blues," connecting colors to longtime depths of a period of time when perhaps sound, smell, color was all connected with the emotions in earlier creatures on the planet. Ultimately, color in our lives has to do with mindful beauty, the way we look at landscape, faces, paintings, the visuals that provide the turn-on for courtship, for aggression, for war, for trickery, for brooding. This is the notebook, really, of the naturalist and the artist; this is where the naturalist and the artist overlap.

Three things happen with naturalists and artists. First, in looking at the world underneath their intent holds in it a hope of perfection. Part of beauty is really that, although we know in our eyes and our minds, the ecology really is quite imperfect, irritatingly imperfect, we are always trying to get some form or some image, some construct or, in natural history, some story that we feel contains some kind of vivid perfection. Part of the attraction of looking for something beautiful is this hope of perfection. Additionally, it is for transcendence out of the everydayness. We all live in our everyday lives, we are immersed in billions of colors every day, we are barraged with shadows and colors, but no one quite *looks* at those shadows and colors. Finally, some artist or naturalist points out that the "golden arches" of McDonald's are made out of orange and red, and we go "yuck" when we look at that, and we try to think of all the commodities. For instance, if you have orange in your store people eat faster and will leave quicker; or red, which is the great advertising color of the planet. McDonald's has seduced you with red and surrounded you with orange, so you'll get out of there fast. That is, in part, what a naturalist does—a naturalist in the city is looking at things from that long point of view. The third thing we all know about beauty, especially in the Jack Kerouac School, is that it has something to do with spontaneity, or contingency as biologists would call it. It has to do with a sense of revelation in that spontaneity. A naturalist might see something go through the forest and say, wow, a new bird; an artist might suddenly see something congeal on the canvas.

The history I'm going to discuss is about ten billion years old. This sense of beauty can be found not just in humans. One of my purposes is to consider how we can understand beauty outside the human realm. I used to have a friend who had three zebra finches, and the finches had little bracelets on them, red and silver bracelets put on to identify them. But every time you changed the color of the bracelets, they would change their mating pattern. Putting the bracelets on changed what the female thought was more beautiful or more seductive. So, scientists had to admit that they couldn't just put little rings on the feet of birds because they were changing their whole social life.

We start outdoors with the sun. We are all embedded in radiance, everything on the planet is embedded in radiance. If we could see it, we'd be here among the sunlight, which is really starlight, the sun is just a close star, and sometimes reflected moonlight. And we would feel around us a vibrational field going past us at all moments. This vibrational field would be very similar to the vibrational field of sound that we hear when our eardrums start to vibrate. There is a single solar emitter in our world, our sun. It sends out selected groups of photons that spiral into space. As they spiral into space, they are modified both by their travel through space and by the biosphere, the layers of the atmosphere, stratosphere, troposphere that surround this planet. Finally, all these vibrational fields get through and they encounter earth matter; that's what we are, we are earth matter. They enter our eyes and our minds. Keep in mind that there are a hundred million cells just in your eyeball. Beside the brain, the eyeball is the organ with the most cells in the body. Our whole lives are attuned to this particular photon flux. There is no other organ, no other part of the human body that is as sensitive as the eye and the brain.

As the photon flux goes through the atmosphere, various different kinds of electromagnetic waves, call them vibrational systems, are filtered out on the way down so that, ultimately, only a particular amount of these vibrational waves ever make it to the surface of the earth. The amount of photons is what we call brightness, the equivalent in music to turning the volume up or down. Each photon has a personality in the way it spirals, some have long loops and some have little loops, and that personality is what we call color. That's why we use the words tones or notes of light. If we have an emptiness of photons on the earth, a lack of photons or vibrations, we call it shadow and darkness. This is the vibrational field that you are living in every day from dawn through noon to dusk.

The knot that Gerard Manley Hopkins talks about is that the mind, even with its eyes closed, can create brightness and color, without the sun. There is a meditation where you inhale darkness and exhale light.[8] We see our dreams in color, we see them in brightness. If you have ever taken peyote, you know that you can get incredible color patterns without having to look at the sun or the moon.

Ten billion years ago, the sun was forty times larger than it is now. It was also twice as bright. Six billion years ago it was three

---

8 *Tonglen*, Tibetan for "giving and receiving," is a meditation practice. On the inhale, you take in pain and suffering and on the exhale you give compassion and healing to yourself and others.

times larger and fifteen percent brighter. Only around four billion years ago did these biospheric filters begin to operate. They set up what I'm going to call the resilience of the earth, the constancy of the earth. Ultraviolet light went down from five percent to two percent because of the ozone layer. It might be going back up now. Visible light went from up twenty-eight to forty-five percent, almost half of all the vibrations, and those were the ones that were most penetrating through these shelters of biospheric shells. Infrared light went from sixty-seven percent down to fifty-three percent, because water vapor absorbed it or reflected it back. The sun had not settled. Even at the time when fishes first evolved on the earth, there was a huge flare on the sun. It gave out a big explosion which was forty percent more red; it was a lot warmer, and the sun spun around. Now, it takes twenty-seven days for the sun to spin around; back then, it only took nine days. That meant the sunspots kept facing the earth and, each time a sun spot faced the earth, there was an empty spot of photon flux, it was a very uneven vibration. We finally got away from sunspot fickleness, the sun settled down, and now it only varies by one or two percent a year. At the same time, the biosphere became very resilient to this flux of light and, every time it would go up or down, creatures would inhale or exhale or otherwise change the composition of the atmosphere so that we would keep the same amount of radiation fluxing to the earth. At this point, the mind, the evolving mind from protozoa on up, started to become resilient.

If you look at the light spectrum, ultraviolet (UV) is at one end—after the violet, you get into ultraviolet—and, on the other end, is infrared, which you get into beyond the red. When you get into the gamma rays, that's what Rocky Flats is putting out. There are some kinds of vibration we don't mind—in fact, we love—and other kinds of vibration are pretty destructive. Right in the middle are x-rays, which we can get a little of but we don't want too much of. There's a lot of argument about microwaves and radio waves, whether they hurt people or not.

What the mind does is develop what's called color constancy. That means no matter what the color of the light is in the day—there's pink light in the evening, then it turns to blue and to violet, then it starts getting gray and finally into that deep Prussian blue—the mind holds on to what the original color was like. You won't even notice it but if someone showed you an apple in the sunset you'd see it as a red apple. If someone showed you a lime in the morning, you'd see it as a green lime. But, if you actually stop—and this is what naturalists and artists have in common—if you stop and look at the exact color of the object and you meditate in a sense, you pull back, you'll find that the color has been changed by the color of light that is on the object. For instance, a green pepper in red light turns out to be copper. Blue hydrangeas can turn both purple and pink in different lights. One of the things you can do is start to pull back and say, "what is the color I am actually seeing?" rather than the color that you've been taught to see, that the mind is holding onto.

There's also an illusion about color constancy and shadow constancy. Shadow constancy occurs because we only have one sun on this planet. If we had two suns, we'd have confusing shadows. What we find is no matter how you put a light on a person's face, even if you put it under their chin or on their side, because we know what a face looks like, people can always tell where up and down is. So, we know when the light source has gotten confused. But when you are outdoors in that spacious place, light only comes from one direction, from that single sun. And, especially when the light starts changing, when clouds are going by, people can get very confused, and it's exciting because the source of light is appearing and disappearing, appearing and disappearing, and that goes very deep into our understanding that we want only one light source. We will rebel against two light sources.

We find that life connects to light through carbon, through a dance of carbon in single and double bonds. When light comes in, in the molecular architecture, if it comes in too fast it's in the UV range, which is like trying to surf on choppy water. The frequencies are very fast, the waves are knocking you and knocking you. In the ultraviolet, that's what happens to our bodies. The waves are coming into our eyes so fast that they would explode the cells, they would blow the circuits and knock out the cells, so we have a lens that has a filter on it to get rid of UV light. Some people are born without that and, if it's not discovered very quickly, they go blind by six weeks of age. But if you can find that they don't have that filter, you can put on UV glasses and that person can retain their eyesight. Ultraviolet is too high energy for us to turn into something useful in life. But, right on the edge, which is the color blue, underneath the ultraviolet, the waves are great. They are exciting, coming in nice, fast pitches, you can get out there and surf. It's right there, on that edge, that we begin to have the excitement of color. Because, at that point in color, we start vibrating the molecular architecture of our eye. What happens when you do that is you loosen up an electron and it jumps, and the chemistry of your eye changes. One of the great mysteries is how to turn light into life, and it happens right there in the color blue. If it gets too slow, which is on the opposite end with infrared, you have long, long waves coming in—you're trying to surf them but they don't add up to much, you can't get much momentum—ultimately, it's a flat surface and you just sink. There's not enough stimulation. Our eye, and our bodies, and the whole earth, have basically evolved in the section in the middle.

    Having said that, I can tell you that nature does something very bizarre which isn't true. What we see as yellow is the most penetrating of all wavelengths that get through the atmosphere; it's just the right surf to get through all the stickiness of atmosphere. But, if you are a bee, you have an eye that is not water (our eye is like the ocean, it's the same concentration of salt as the sea): a bee's eye is of crystal and it can take the ultraviolet light, just like when you put on a pair of sunglasses that can filter out ultraviolet light. So, a bee will look at that same yellow flower and see what's on the left, into the ultraviolet.

Immediately, we know that in the aesthetics on earth humans have a very limited space. We don't really know what it's like to mix ultraviolet and purple together, or ultraviolet and yellow on a palette and create a painting. Sometimes we try—for instance, all the bumper sticker colors have ultraviolet paint in them—but we don't see the color, what we see is the absorption of the ultraviolet light which creates a kind of vibrancy. But a bee artist might take ultraviolet and mix it up with a little orange and have some color we don't even understand. On that end of the spectrum, we have to accept our humanness and our limitations in that photon flux. On the other end, animals like rattlesnakes can feel into the infrared. What's interesting is they have to shift from their eye, they shift to another little organ that's right under their nose. When they hunt rabbits, they're not even looking at rabbits, they are feeling the vibration—which, in a way, is seeing—of the infrared waves coming toward them.

One of the interesting things about prose writing in natural history right now is that it really should enter the world of science fiction, that's almost the best place to learn from. Because you're talking about things that are invisible to human beings, yet we know are happening. Almost all nature writing up to now assumes, like in Peter Rabbit, that the rabbit sees exactly what we see. No writer has tried to grasp or portray what an actual animal is seeing.

If we go even further out, into the electromagnetic spectrum, we find that animals actually eat magnets, hematite. And pigeons—when I was in school, I worked with a guy in a pigeon lab in Cambridge and we'd take the pigeons to, say, Detroit and see how fast they could get home. What we found is that pigeons used three different ways to get home. The first thing they did was to use the electromagnetic spectrum: they could feel the electromagnetic vibrational field of the earth and they'd orient toward that. Then, during the day, they'd use the solar compass, like we would, to get more precise. And, when they got right over Harvard, they'd start using their eyes, they'd go back into a visual topographic mode. One pigeon could use the first two methods really well—it always wound up back at Harvard Square right by the taxi stand—but it couldn't quite figure out how to fly back to the Peabody Museum. The first time this happened it landed right at the taxi stand and one of the cab drivers saw the little bracelet that said, "if found please call…" so he called up and said, "I've found this pigeon." The guy I was working with said, "I'm really busy, I'll pay you if you put the pigeon in the taxi cab and drive it over to the lab." So, he did exactly that, he drove the pigeon to the lab, and from then on, the pigeon knew a good deal. No matter where we took this pigeon—Indiana, North Carolina—it would never come back to the lab, it would always go to the taxi stand. That's a way of showing that there are these three modes you can switch into, working throughout the whole spectrum.

What you're seeing is a color. We don't know what the color is because you can't see the infrared, but what looks like bright white to us is the emission of infrared waves. We would feel it as greater heat. Inside the canopy of the trees, it's darker because there's no infrared light, and at the tops of the trees, where the sun is hitting the strongest, it's beaming out infrared. If you were a flying rattlesnake, that's what you would be seeing.

There's a real commonality here, a commonality that's not anthropomorphic, it's not projective, it's actually perceptual. It has to do with brightness, color, ambient light, contrast, and concealment. The whole of evolution on the earth can be looked at as a talk about color, brightness, ambient light, contrast, and concealment. If we back up in terms of the volume of light, the brightness of light and the darkness of light, we get back to the very basics of the early religions, the yin and the yang, and it gets weird because our culture doesn't think of black and white as colors, while most other cultures do. If you look at it from the spectrum point of view, black is a lack of photons and white is every photon mixed up together. So, they can easily be looked at as colors. What we find in our culture is that because shadows are elusive, changeable, untouchable, they have an otherworldly feeling.

Only when kids make shadow figures with their hands do they have a sense of fun, as in Bali or Indonesia, where there are great shadow shows. (By the way, shadow shows were really popular in nineteenth century England.) But now, to us, they are more ominous. Some people have the sense that if you have a body without a shadow, it is divine. There are long Greek stories about a beautiful woman and five men who all want to marry her, and she was supposed to be married to a god, but she couldn't figure out who it was—and it was the guy without the shadow.

Shadows have been avoided, really, by both naturalists and painters. The whole history of shadow painting or looking at shadows only exists for about four hundred years in Western painting, and only at the latitude that starts about at Greece and ends around Sweden. There are no shadows in Eastern art, and there are very few shadows in any other form of art. By the time you hit the twentieth century, with some exceptions of course, shadows disappear from art again as we get into the abstract era. Only a few of the Surrealists kind of exaggerated shadows, not even using them the way we would do. From a naturalist's point of view, sunlight segments the scene, it breaks up where you are. Some parts are empty of photons, some are full of photons. Noting that the sun comes from on top of us—this is something every creature on the earth responds to. Notice how conspicuous a caterpillar is because the brightness on its back is so much greater than the shadow of its bottom, the same with all the leaves. This is one of the things that in nature is a problem. In artistry, it led to chiaroscuro, it led to how to make a third dimension, how to shade an object to give it volume. A fish creates a color pattern on its body; it makes itself darker on top and whiter on bottom so, by the time the sun hits it, it is even-colored and you can hardly see it. This is a twenty to forty million year-old artistic response to the overhead sun. In doing this, the fish is responding just like an artist would to what an illuminated surface looks like.

There are different ways you might look at a butterfly wing. It can look like a two-dimensional drawing, or more like a topographic map, and an exaggeration of that topographic map would turn it into a three dimensional object. Looking at it that way, we see how a butterfly disguises itself. Rather than looking like a butterfly, it looks more like a crumpled leaf. From an artist's point of view, one has to get the three dimensional into two dimensions. There are three kinds of shadows in art, in the Western tradition. They are: slant/tilt shadowing, cast shadow, and modeled shadow. Shadows will show you if something is convex or concave, where the edge is, and how to contrast the edge. Artists do exactly the opposite of what nature does, creating a two-dimensional illusion of volume. Where nature tries to flatten the surface, the artist tries to create the idea that there is volume where there is not. Shadowing, implying a single source of light, helps define the edges of surfaces, and lots of different things occur on edges—for instance, an object might get darker along an edge. It also groups surfaces so that your eye is bouncing around between different kinds of brightness and darkness.

I want to show you that art had a purpose on the planet. That purpose was to create a bodily shelter. Art became a shelter for animals, and it became a seeking tool, a way that you could disguise yourself. A lot of the aesthetics of the bodies of animals is creating this sense of how to break up volume, how to break up an edge. A dark shadow, what the Italians would call *tenebroso*, is the kind of thing that would make any lizard, walking along a wall, be given away to a predator. So, what does the lizard do? It creates flaps to cover up its cast shadow. While artists are trying to enhance that image by creating a *tenebroso* shadow, nature is trying to disguise it. Another way to get rid of an edge is to disrupt a pattern, like breaking up clear linear patterns with triangles—you put a snake on top of leaves and the snake disappears.

Art has become a form of entertainment where an artist displays his skills. Artists have always worried about shadows. Leonardo da

Vinci, who wrote the best books on shadows, never used them in his paintings. It's remarkable—he was a genius about shadows but he thought they obscured everything, so he left them out. He did use mottled shadowing on the face sometimes, but it's a complete fantasy.

Things get even more complex when you add color. If you surround the same color blue with different other colors, the intensity of blue changes. Naturalists have not looked at this in nature, artists have done a better job. That's part of the dialogue with ecopoetics or ecoartistics or ecovisual arts, to see the different colors and ask, *does that mean anything to other creatures like it means to us when we do painting?*

The great artists at the end of the nineteenth century were the first to notice that shadows themselves had colors. This confused everything because ambient light alters your sense of color. In the light of a rainforest, the same color blue would look different than it would in the desert. But you can only do so much, for human beings, with this darkness and brightness. The first animals could just see light sources, they could see intensity and direction of light source, the sun. Then they started to move around, and they shaped themselves to the photon flux so that they could move to the photon flux, to the sun or to the shade, so they could navigate. Navigation was one of the earliest things on the planet. The next stage was the development of a visual eye with the ability to contrast and get degrees of shadows, degrees of grayness. Finally, add color to that—all insects can see color—and you get a better sense of contours in birds, mammals, creatures like octopi. But always the eye is only a certain number of cells. At some point, what art is about is playing with the edge of our perception. You can almost look at art as an exploration of trying to get closer and closer to the limits of the eye, until it kind of screws the eye over. For instance, what happens in "op art" is the eye can't hold on to the pattern—we don't have enough cells in our eyes, so the pattern appears to move. The eye can't hold on to that kind of edge. So, art is trying to fool around with the nature of the human being and the nature of nature, and pushing it to its limits. One is embedded in the other. If you look at the human being, to understand our place in nature, there are things we just can't do, visually, and which contain our sense of beauty. The most complex evolution on the planet is to create deceptive imagery. Salvador Dalí always said he was trying to paint, he never claimed to have accomplished painting, and he tried just about every trick in the game that confuses the human eye.

There are unique things that happen on our planet that have to do with brightnesses and darknesses. That's, in part, because the eye itself is round. Inside the retina, which is the screen of the eye, are all the brightnesses and darknesses in a target form. The center of the eye is where you see color, the outside is where you see bright and dark, and there is actually a blind spot in the middle of the eye. The form of the eye constrains the aesthetic of the whole earth. The male peacock uses the eye form to make itself conspicuous. In almost all cultures, "riding the peacock" means being arrogant, up front, full of ego. Caterpillars use large spots that look like eyes to make themselves look bigger, so when a bird comes along and sees those gigantic "eyes" it says, "Whoops, that's not the caterpillar I thought it was, this is something much larger"; it backs off and the caterpillar has an extra two seconds to drop to the ground or get under a leaf. Some fish have "eye spots" on the back so that a predator will not know what's forward and what's back; it gives the fish an extra second to get away. If we look at Tibetan art, in order to maximize uncomfortability, you just create a huge number of eye spots, it actually gets you upset. That eye spot conforms to what is on your retina, but you can't focus on just one because your eyes keep jumping around to all the others. On the other hand, if you want to be calm and cool you diminish the eye spot by closing the eye—this is not just in Buddhist art, it's in all art—so that you don't get the complete eye spot. This is a technique to play with the primate, the mammalian, actually the whole vertebrate aesthetic. It goes way beyond the religion that uses it.

After darkness and brightness, we add color. Color is a different system in your eye; instead of the rods you switch to the cones. Goethe called it the affliction of color, he felt that light was diseased when it got color. "Color" means to conceal or to hide. The color palette of our planet is green. At the center of the palette is chlorophyll, which is a little blob called a plastid inside a cell that has a green pigment. In the evolution of the planet, what happened is that, in order not to blow the circuits, the first animals on the earth used red which you'll remember is that long surfing wave. When you absorb red, the complementary color is green, so what we see is green. A plant turns red light from electric voltage into sugar—that's the basis of life, you take a little bit of CO_2, mix it up with a few photons, stir it up and get sugar; use the sugar to make proteins and you've got life going. The electron flux hits the magnesium in the chlorophyll molecule and it vibrates. It has created this huge complex to shift all that electricity around so it doesn't ravage the molecule, it doesn't split it apart. It even has helpers, and the helper is the second most common color on the planet, carotene, which is orange. Wherever you see chlorophyll, you'll also see carotene. Those are the two pigments that evolved together in close symbiosis. What carotene does is eat excess electricity, it calms the body down. (That's why it's considered anti-carcinogenic.) What's interesting about this molecule is that if you replaced its magnesium with iron, you'd have hemoglobin, which is in our blood. If you replaced it, instead, with cobalt, you'd have vitamin B12, which is the biggest molecule nature can invent. All the pigments, all the main colors of the planet, come out of this one chemistry that evolved about 3.2 billion years ago.

Only plants make chlorophyll and only plants make carotene. This underlies the commonality that exists in biophilia. In order for us to survive, we need to take in these colors. If we don't take in these colors, we simply don't exist. We incorporate them in two ways. We can do as some animals do, by absorbing them into the body and having them stay alive. There are little protozoa running around with chlorophyll in them. Or we kill them but keep the pigments. On the planet, the same pigments can be found in all vertebrates, all insects, and all mollusks. We all use the same stuff; the palette is universal. This mediates between contrast and calmness, which comes with sheltering yourself through camouflage. Equanimity comes from coloring.

The first stage of pigments was to screen us from UV; the second stage was to catch photons and use them (the pinball machine of the living) and to prevent over-amping through the use of carotene. The third use, which started probably about two billion years ago, was to socialize these pigments, to make them part of the social life of the planet. For instance, one and a half million years ago, flowers and insects, using the exact same pigments, developed a way of talking to each other, a relationship that is so close that most flowers cannot exist without the insects and most insects cannot exist without the flowers. The human eye, about two and a half million years ago, began to evolve into this form of using color for decoration, using the same pigments, the same plant dyes, as for all the things we know about: for shelter, defense, nourishment, and sex.

At this point, I'm going to go quickly through some general feelings about color. As I said earlier, this is a turquoise planet. And this is the action of the planet. It is all of our nutrition, it is the background color, it is the dance of carbon, it is the green machine that makes this planet unique, in this universe at least. Humans have actually been quite jealous of this greenery. In fact, we say things like "green with envy." We know underneath, and the Zunis are explicit about it, that we are the most dependent animal, not the most independent animal as we like to think of ourselves. Basically, we are dependent on the color green, on chlorophyll. Humans have tried to invent incredible economic and spiritual theories to deny the obvious dependence on greenery. We invented God, we invented humanism—anything but admit that we are dependent on greenery. In the face of chlorophyll or carotene, there is nothing we have done that has any power. The power of the planet rests on chlorophyll and carotene. Green comes from the same word as growth, the same as grass—the whole cattle industry is dependent on chlorophyll. We are nowhere near as efficient in our conversion of energy as these green plants, another source of envy and jealousy. Birds that don't eat greenery, like insectivores, use song to attract each other because they cannot take the pigments and put them into their feathers. But birds that eat fruit turn that into the pigments of their bodies, and rather than sing to each other they display to each other these great plumages of color. That's how intimate this relationship is: your food web determines your mating ceremony, and it determines it through the pigments you eat.

Since we have all lived under this blue hemispheric dome called the sky, there is research showing that if you lie looking up at a clear blue sky your circulatory system calms down, your concentration increases. The sky and the color blue have always been related to calmness, concentration, passivity, acceptance. The negative side is people just spacing out. The other thing we should notice is the sky is polarized light, but we don't see that. When you wear polarized glasses, you can get a feel for it. A bee, with its crystal eye, sees the sky like a structure, it sees the beams coming down. That's another layer to this. But in general, blue-green has this sense of being the basis of calmness and nourishment on the planet. Yellow and red, on the other hand, come together as the big contrast. They are the vivid colors—they have to contrast with the blue sky and the green earth. If you sit in a red room or in front of red light, it will make your heart beat faster, it will increase your blood pressure, your pulse and breath will get more exaggerated. This is why poets use red to mean self-assured, dynamic, powerful, lively, fiery, domineering, penetrating, strong, active, etc. In Buddhism, it means uneasiness that leads to awareness. In a flower, the yellow on the outside is the big attractor and then the red in the center leads the bee to the nectar, and at the same time the flower gets pollinated. It's an inseparable color symbiosis. If the bee didn't get the nectar, it would die; if the flower didn't have a way to transport its pollen, it would not reproduce.

We have in the color yellow, in the most penetrating wavelengths, a sense of healing. Yellow, for instance, among the Papago Indians is called the moon of healing. When yellow comes out, it not only enriches and refreshes the earth, but it usually is the moment of spring, that time when the food web, which has been broken apart by winter, is reconnected. The perversion of it is the McDonald's logo: its indulgence is that it is so attractive and looks so enriching, that you go there and you get fat, you get indulgent, and, if you really hang out at McDonald's, you probably go insane. The interesting thing about red and yellow is they distinguish the earth in a direct way. With insects, because the yellow light is most penetrating, the yellow light gets through the crystals in their eyes; but red light, being that long surfing wave, gets broken up in the passage through the eye. So, insects cannot see red. If you see a red flower, it is almost invariably pollinated by something like a hummingbird; while if you see a yellow flower, it is usually pollinated by the insect kingdom. This is an example of the evolution of the more sensitive part of the spectrum for animal life.

So, if you put on makeup to undo the contrast between red and yellow on a person's face, it subdues the seduction and attractiveness. There is a whole cosmetic industry built on what to put on the face to either increase that uneasy awareness or to decrease it. In ritual, we see, as in Kabuki or the rituals of the Australian Aborigines, the mixture of all photons—white—the easiest photon to get into the eye—red—and the lack of all photons—black. Red, black, and white are the essential meaningful colors in almost all human existence. This goes beyond culture. Red and black are also used to warn rather than attract, as in a poisonous frog from the Amazon. The same thing occurs on the wings of butterflies.

I'd like to end with a story. If you start with milkweed, which has a cardiac glycoside (a chemical that causes heart attacks), you can trace almost the whole planet's understanding of two families of butterflies. Any insect, cow, or human that tries to eat milkweed (*Asclepias*) will have a heart attack. Milkweed tastes bitter and makes you throw up. A particular Monarch butterfly evolved to live with that plant. It took the cardiac glycoside and, instead of digesting it, it harbored it in a separate part of its body, it quarantined it in a sac. At that point, it also became inedible, it gained the protection of the milkweed. In order to tell birds that it was inedible, it developed that same contrast coloration I've been talking about. Monarch butterflies are orange and black with white spots. Blue jays, growing up, learn to avoid orange and black with white spots. Then other butterflies started taking advantage and wearing the emperor's clothes—they taste delicious, but they evolved orange and black and white, to the point that now there are five mimic butterflies for every one that actually eats milkweed. To make it even more extravagant, when there are too many mimics the birds start switching—they taste one or two and they don't throw up, so orange, black, and white now means good stuff, not bad stuff, and at that point the milkweed stops producing its poison. At some point, there are fewer mimics around, and the birds are eating the disgusting tasting, heart attack butterflies, and the milkweed will start producing its poison again in order to try to keep other butterflies and insects away. Starting in Guerrero, Mexico, all the way up into Canada, there is a symphony of volumes modulated by orange, black, and white spots. In the winter, all the Canadian butterflies fly down to Mexico; as they come down, the birds are learning their taste. In the spring, they start coming back and various species of milkweed bloom exactly in time to meet those butterflies. So, what once started out as war is now a co-evolution symbiosis. They do that because they know that they will not be eaten except by that one insect, but that one insect gives the plant protection because now, if a cow comes along and sees the butterfly on the plant, it doesn't eat it—there's orange, black, and white spots on it. So, the plants have used the insect to signal all the other animals to keep away from it.

These are the kinds of stories that need to be written, the stories of how colors, starting ten billion years ago with solar constancy and mind constancy, have put the earth and the food web together.

(1996)

Letter from Peter Warshall

Dear Anne:

Here's what chemo has done to me. You can share it with your student. If she wants wilderness to mean some relatively uninfluenced part of the planet, she has to deny climate change. Coccoliths are beautiful calcium architecture protists feeling the impact of increased acidity in the oceans, which change the bottom sediment communities. If she means wilderness is an area of land so many miles from the nearest road, then that is her definition and we can accept or reject it. Or maybe it's a place you cannot hear an airplane for two weeks. Nanao (Sakaki) and I searched for that plane and only made ten days. Otherwise, here's my wandering mind.

CHEMOTHERAPY

It is the Year of the Rabbit. In the labyrinthine burrows, the groundwater table rises. The sleeping chamber sports a puddle, and on its surface, the five hundred yuan note and a hundred dollar greenback float apart. Dame rabbit smooths her face with her right paw: "Not attached. Good news. Prosperity." The old buck drops a fairly tattered left ear from its upright. He looks at the water. "Perhaps, undetached my love." At the exit, in the lush grass of abundant rains, a bobcat nestles, absolutely still and silent, or perhaps one thought can be heard: "So what, who gives a fuck if it's the year of the rabbit?" Wilderness, so exquisite, a flooded financial market of the mind.

They went out into the wilderness. Many died banished to the arid lands of Sinai. St. Paul saw Lord Jesus. Moses, the burning bush. Milarepa sat in caves, fed the deer and cranes, and felt insightful. Thoreau, after a day job surveying the humid deciduous forests of Concord for subdivision into farms and roads, returned to Walden and transcended daily toils. For job security, he said: it is wildness, not wilderness, that is the preservation of the world. Today, Alice Waters picks a tomato from a tiny patch of dirt carved out from one of many Oakland schoolyards—student veggie pizza, she enthuses, for lunch. You see or not, the city stores earth under its asphalt and, the teacher claims, each healthy cubic foot has more connectivity than the brain of Einstein. Outside the window, CO_2's odorless perfume permeates the mycelium of Earth. Coccoliths feel it; euglena swim to basic niches. An as-yet unnamed bird cocks its eye toward the polarized sky. There is a dawn song; we are all gardeners, adjusting the chemotherapy, the sugars, pH, and colors of life. Gaia yawns. What's a few million years of inchoate erratics. Accepting the Anthropocene sucks, but these *are* the times of incompatible currencies and, no matter the volume or scales or speed, cultivating a good garden maybe the best move possible.

 Mucho love,
   Peter

(Solstice, 2011)

Communal Action

Figure 4: Founding year of the Naropa Institute (now called Naropa University): Registration Day, 1974. Photograph from the Naropa Archive.

• • •

In the late 1970s, Allen Ginsberg, Anne Waldman, Daniel Ellsberg, and others sat on the tracks to halt the trains carrying plutonium into the Rocky Flats Nuclear Weapons Plant near Golden, Colorado. Since then, many Naropa students have continued to organize acts of protest during the summers. In 2020, a group drove down to El Paso, Texas to protest a newly built detention center that would serve to house unaccompanied minors under Trump's "zero tolerance" policy. Before the pandemic, another group traveled to Mexico to facilitate poetry workshops at a women's prison in Santiaguito de Almoloya. When students were arrested during Black Lives Matter protests in Denver, one of their classmates went to bail them out. There is a collective sense of social responsibility that is made stronger when we come together. During the summers at Naropa, we build a rhizomatic network of connections that extend through our local communities and, also, farther out across the world. We practice radical friendship and care; we tend to our collaborations.

> Revolutionary movements do not spread by contamination but by *resonance*. Something that is constituted here resonates with the shock wave emitted by something constituted over there… It rather takes the shape of a music, whose focal points, though dispersed in time and space, succeed in imposing the rhythms of their own vibrations, always taking on more density.
> —*The Invisible Committee*, The Coming Insurrection

> Enter this complex community
> through its back door,
> breach its rockiest border
> and break the hold
> steep systems of convention
> have on you.
> —*Margaret Randall*, The Rhizome as a Field of Broken Bones

• • •

Let's Start Stopping

A Commencement Address

Eileen Myles

I'm getting a lot of questions about whether I'll be running for president this election year and the answer is no, definitely not. In general I'd say that it's time to start stopping, I have stopped running for president and I challenge the other candidates to stop too. There's a real political advantage to this—I'm starting small. I'm a poet and I encouraged the poets, last May 1st I did it—I encouraged all the poets in the world to start stopping writing poetry and there was a lot of resistance to that idea. Poets wanted to know what the possible advantage of starting to stop writing poetry could be and I thought try it out. Let's start stopping now. A lot of poets wanted to know what we were going to do about the plan to stop. I got a number of messages in my email and on my Facebook account, and at a certain point I think well there is a general need for a plan as to how to stop so I made a certain number of suggestions, and when the morning came I didn't want to do those things at all, so I thought let's start stopping all this organizing NOW. I noticed the cemetery downstairs from my house was open. I went down there with my dog, entered the cemetery, and called my girlfriend by her name. I said, hey Leopoldine. Look at us. *Down here*. Can you see us? She could. It was great. And then she came down and there were a bunch of crabby people in the cemetery with their dogs and some nice ones too and the dogs were running around and then we left. What else could we do. Some of the people who had wanted to stop were calling me now. Where ARE you. I thought we all were going to be stopping together. That was the idea. Yes it was, but now it is about something else. Waves of shame kept washing through my system though because I myself was STILL struggling with the entire project of stopping all together, but when I truly got it—the whole stopping scene and I actually went to the location where earlier we were supposed to have done something and nothing happened, I felt something authentically joyous that I had never felt before. Try it, all of you. I once saw a Joe Brainard cartoon that said *people of the world: RELAX!!!* That's all it said. I was certainly excited but today I'm advocating doing even less.

While I'm on the subject of poetry—while I'm leaving it to do what—nothing! I'd like to throw out a few salient facts to the amateurs. I think you'll find this quite interesting. Every now and then some amateur comes along: Jewel, Dr. Spock, Suzanne Somers, John-Boy on *The Waltons*… every now and then one of these celebribodies comes along writing poetry and a big deal gets made out of their very silly and very unimportant work. I thought what is poetry this thing I do mostly which is hardly anything at all. I think people really resisted the idea of start stopping it because nobody out there has really even noticed they began! But when these people from music and television and entertainment write their poems and they get these big publishing deals and then you open the book and everybody (everybody poet) laughs—well you just realize that poetry is such a nothing occupation that when anyone does it (anyone famous) everyone else thinks THEY are really doing it because they are SOMEBODY and we are NOBODY. Do you know what I mean. That being somebody is a kind of doing, so that when they do this thing that is nothing at all they are doing it more than the people who are doing it. And being somebody is doing anything even if you aren't even doing it. Do you see what I mean now. So this is both an argument for us stopping entirely in order to be actually doing something since perhaps us not doing it is more something than doing it if you get my point—and I hope you do because I am moving on and I've got another one—there's a big conversation going on in the media about a certain club for people who don't even drink anymore. They are not doing it. That is the point. And these people mark their accomplishment by not even using their names when they talk publicly about what they are not doing. I think this is a step in the right direction. Right. And this has been going on for a long time. For a while. Since they are in fact alcoholics these people and the point of what they are doing is to not drink so as to not die, they take the tack of not being anyone when they do this. Privately they may be someone for instance when they go home or call their dog. Or write a poem though of course that's the big joke. Putting your no one name on your nothing work. And then on top of that not drinking. What a life. Yet it seems like total success to me and a real map for the future and I offer it here. This is a commencement and I say stop now. Often when I meet young people I tell them about the fact that if I were to drink I would probably drop dead so I don't and if they would like to come and talk about this come over here. And if I belonged to that anonymous organization I wouldn't tell them that though I suppose we could whisper about it privately if it WAS the case but you know strictly off the record, despite the fact that I'm a poet and no one. So here's where I'm going. There's a bunch of famous people—you know writers and college professors and daughters of famous writers all of whom are alcoholics and these people because they are very well known or are thinking of themselves that way and are in the business of becoming even more well-known and seem to be choosing off and on or all of the time to be part of the no drinking not dying club and they are thinking well why can't we say our names. Our big fat names. Times have changed they say and it's time to start stopping that whole anonymity business because well (to my mind) it's much like poetry in that when *I* do it (and this is them thinking) especially since it's nothing I can do it much better by being *me* which is doing something—do you see what I mean? The belief is that the endorsement of the unusually strong-minded independent person who is *somebody* will be paving the way, a grand invitation for all the people who may as well be anonymous cause what's the difference after all since they are nobody and that's just a fact. And I'm just trying to say right now that that's not starting stopping as *I* understand it. I think that's just getting your name in the paper and thinking that people who don't have such BIG NAMES don't understand yet that this is a better idea but I haven't gotten to the part yet where it is an idea and I don't think that they have either. It's interesting. Poetry by a famous person is just the same as anonymity by a famous person. This is not starting stopping something and this is not anything at all. It's like putting American presidents heads in the Black Hills cause there wasn't anything there just a bunch of Indians anyhow. It's an empty country, always was. And I say let's start stopping that and look around and see that nothing is really quite a lot and will make us full eventually if we see what's there and if we want to start stopping that (putting the president's head up there) well that's something. But it has to be there first. And it was. You know it's like putting clothes on dogs. Dogs don't like it. So I'd like to begin this commencement address with that information. Leave the dogs alone. Just go on ahead and have a life. I would prefer to remain nameless. Though I am no one, a poet, so what's the difference.

(2013)

The Collective

Lisa Robertson

A school alit on a moment. It felt electric, erotic, uncomfortable, necessary. Because they noticed, the moment expanded, scaffolded by a low-rent materiality. They entered this temporal suspension by climbing narrow and steep stairways to the upper floors of neglected Edwardian storefronts in a decrepit downtown neighborhood. They trundled book boxes, or helped the older ones. But beyond the scaffolding and the dusty scent of the hallways the school itself was immaterial, and infinitely mobile, like many of its precedents: single Black Mountain lectures sprawling magnificently across days; beer-fueled living room readings attended by loggers, architects, camp cooks, lefty lawyers and students; the communal meeting halls of 1871 Paris in the month of March, where radical shoemakers, seamstresses and preschool teachers lectured on citizenship; the experimental chemistry clubs of 17th-century revolutionary London; the romantic meteorologists of Cambridgeshire; Fourier's passionate associations and phalansteries; the peripatetic conversants of the Epicurean garden, where women and men shared the lively and living pursuit of philosophy, in contradiction to the discourses of the state.

A resurgent energy pulses into shimmering expression in a city, a room, a street, beneath certain trees, when necessity sends acute though necessarily covert signals. Clearly, there must be more than one person or the frequency can't alight. The reception isn't willed. The receivers emanate a superb, almost obscene, attractive force having to do with their absolute disrespect for the ordinary sinecures. Only in retrospect does it appear that fate plays a role in the swerve-like transmission. The receivers of this synchronic worthiness distribute the communal moment of an insurrection across their sentences. The resultant vibrations alter the shape of cognition. This has to do with people's speech, its self-authorization, its communal autonomy. In retrospect, I see their protest as collective ceremony, although they themselves would have definitively scorned the notion. Their values were narrowly secular. But terms they violently rejected as insufficiently materialist can now become useful, because the collective can't be described with true precision from within the field of their own vocabulary. An outer vantage is needed. So, I'll return to them now the odors and the ceremonies and the ritual protocols their radical self-identity occluded. I'll indulge in the praise of their utter vulgarity.

I was never a founder. For certain periods, I was absent. My interpretation of events corresponds to my own heightened, even hackneyed, desire for a story. I never felt really equal to the magnetism of my companions. This account is quite wrong factually.

As for the forms of protest—often they were unrecognizable, except belatedly. The most stringent protest evades spectacle, nonchalantly preserving its transformative force for the propitious moment, the most apt and unsuspecting initiates, the casually secretive gathering. Some of them believed the resurgence pertained to syntax, and adored repeating that word. Some believed in the complicated and conflictual process of group consensus as a model for change. Yet who they kissed or didn't, how long the empties sat, the fruit flies hovering above them, the way the notebooks splayed across the stained blue carpet for days at a time, the books never returned to the library and the books found lying on sidewalks, the borrowing and filching and thrifting, the use of Letraset, glue stick, and carbon paper in their quotidian rituals, the Smith Corona Selectric that came after the loud manual, the placement of the folded bath towel under the manual late at night to protect the shared wooden house from staccato retort, the use of roach chalk on thresholds… these exigencies necessarily infiltrated their grammar. And grammar pertained not only to linguistic coherence and distribution and its reinvention, but to community and domestic form. They practiced the evasion of enforced subordination in favor of horizontal structures of distribution, composition, and exchange. Their task was very large, like a decades-long emotional science project. They believed they would be endlessly robust; they believed the same for their texts.

In a sense, time was their medium. They wanted glamorous seminars to fling open and demolish all expectations regarding the regularization of time. They wanted the spontaneous eruption of intense intellectual newness. Time spontaneously translated to new time. Some of them wanted to experience historicity as radically simultaneous: the medieval wandering poets would be among their most urgent contemporaries, or the epistolary writers of the long eighteenth century, or the gentlemen naturalists of early Romantic England meandering up Adanac Street, or the baroque philosophers tracing their ellipses in the forests of UBC. To help the collapse of time as metrics, and encourage its transformation into a luxuriously distributed lubricant, an enticingly shimmering and moving fabric, a shared yet contested décor, the collective welcomed end-narratives: the end of femininity, the end of nature, the end of work. They believed that each ending was necessarily the site of a transformation. They were good at surviving.

Actions create language in the present at the same time that their historical traces paradoxically remain latent within language across long durations. I think language is a mobile, immaterial archive of a very long history of human gesture. The collective linguistically seized the paradoxical status of the universal commune; now, because in their shabby neighborhoods they moved into then-unknown social futures, because they made poems from these movements, intense collective potentials hover as forms in the present. These forms animate the knowledge that the poem is the opposite of capital.

They said that the task of each minute was to differentiate between the mind's thought and the state's thought. They said the state's thought is an inert placebo for an actual relationship with form. Capital gives everything its emptied double—form can't live there so relationships won't change. Thus, there are two thoughts. One took place in low-budget shadow. This is a theory I wish to open. In the current era of capital, it could be that the mind's thought must live in hiding, in inconspicuous parallel to the official institutionalizations. Their shabby, difficultly accessible rooms were spiritual havens, as in the Epicurian mandate: live in hiding. Because they could recognize, originate, and exchange the mind's thought, time in the collective's spaces and texts was the highly diversified energy of combined innovation and contemplation. Time was not the metrics of the reproduction of capital. They weren't strivers. They scorned tenure. They had arrived at this obscure place by exercising their shared piety for horizontal discursive extremes in others. Lovingly they addressed the future.

From the present point of view, it might seem that what the collective produced, and what remains of both its covert and its gregariously public activities, is a catalogue of linguistic and intellectual artifacts: the poems, essays, journals, chapbooks, and various paper ephemera that will show up in personal and institutional archives, or slip from the pages of casually retrieved volumes of American Language poets, or Frankfurt School theorists, or Montreal feminists, as well as the concepts associated with these movements and texts. All this will remain in circulation for at least the near future. But now I believe that what the collective produced most importantly was a mode of autonomous, plural existence. Deeply, almost like animals, they understood how to live together. They made for a moment a precariously inhabitable social sculpture. Since a way of living is the more evasive and inconspicuous artifact, more evanescent than the texts and material detritus, it is what I wish to describe. This living shall be traced through bodily memories of gestures, of caresses, of mythic spills, the charged air in certain rooms, the movement of thoughts and objects and texts across neighborhoods, transformations in relationships and self-perception and recognition. How do people find each other, recognize afresh the secretive necessity, proliferate and associate with almost painfully new ideas? How do they make situations for one another's most exigent and elegant strangeness? How do these spaces exist in contradictory relation to the dominant histories and economies, evading, for dizzying spans, the oppressive propaganda of institutional assimilation? What is transmission? Must transmission be unbroken or regular in order to be actual? I think not. It will fountain, unannounced, unanticipated, by means of desire.

If there was conflict, it was because of the complex nature of the desire that indeed manifested itself in an irregular continuousness. Part of their work was to learn how to recognize new desire, and carefully to separate it from hegemonic compulsion. That was an ongoing task. It was sometimes tiring. They drank and they puked and they judged and often they were not kind. They enjoyed it. They often didn't like things. There was conflict because there were many desires, erotic imaginations of new forms of intellection, interlocution, composition, and political movement in the city. To bring these multiple desires into temporary resonance was the repeating collective task. Fights could erupt. In this way, an undulant social harmonics was composed, a vibration that provided a buzzing ground for the individual compositions. The collective made a space where the extremities of a multifocal yearning were sheltered by the shared belief in its political necessity. This was a value. Tent-like, its space needed to be repeatedly reinstated, re-erected, since the materials, structure, and dimensions underwent permanent improvisation, as thought veered, as the city transformed, as the economy mushroomed. They dissociated the political from the economic without abandoning the critique of materiality and its relation to power. But their living-together opened the certainty that a part of political practice is immaterial.

I'm insisting on the word *desire* because of the feeling that was in the air in those shabby rooms, both in the collective spaces—the meeting rooms, bookshops, galleries, and bars—and in the apartments the poets moved among. Their rooms were livid with sparks. They rendered defunct the boundaries between the intellectual, the political, the aesthetic, and the erotic. Who kissed whom, who proofed whose texts, who collaborated in what studios, who moved in together, which bands made their ears ring for days after the concerts, who fought at kitchen and bar tables over the vocabulary of political analysis—I can't separate these queries from my imagination of those spaces. They enjoyed the sensation of being impassioned by an idea; they throve in the defensive ambiance. Ambiguity, cathexis, and dispute were expressions of collective love and hate, where love and hate changed places with always unanticipated thoroughness. Any evening, any meeting, any table could achieve the character of an eruption. I heard that somebody punched someone as they smoked on the street between readings. One wrote scotch-tape sonnets. The other invented virtual coalitions. One is still working; the other has disappeared.

As well as disappearance, shared boredom was a content. They passed much time each month hunched over long brown Formica tables, hung over, folding eight and a half by eleven sheets of paper twice, to fit into business envelopes, as the scent of stale beer drifted from corners. Those were the press releases, typed on Selectric, scarred by white-out, their authors decided by consensus at the long, frequent, meandering meetings, as were the rosters of readers, lecturers, workshop leaders, panel conveners, and so forth.

The collective expression was contingent on leisure as a rescued value. Beyond financial and demotic metrics, they made time to spend together, and time to individually think. This time had a particular stretchiness, an opacity, an intensely deregulated quality. It was synthesized among thinking bodies. Late starts, overlong readings, closing down bars, thence to crowded kitchen tables and two a.m. call-in beer delivery, the long sleep-ins, the sleepovers on hard futons and sprung couches, the afternoon reading groups or editorial meetings extending again to the small hours of the following morning, spontaneous road trips to Seattle or Portland to ferry visiting poets, lying at border crossings, deferred degrees, unconventional domestic structures, suspension of reproduction, underemployment, nonprofit work, chosen self-employment and freelancing, low rent, welfare, sharing: they made themselves time-rich through the avoidance or lack of conventionally defined work. And here I should mention that their unstymied reproductive self-determination, via free and open access to birth control and abortion, played an important part in the advancement of poetical agendas. This access was enabled by still other collectives—the Vancouver Women's Health Collective and the Pine Free Clinic occupied cluttered upstairs spaces that didn't feel dissimilar to the ones the poets frequented. If the work of thinking together was gloriously careening onwards, it's because the reproductive labor of capital was ignored, in as many ways as possible. The collective produced leisure, willfully. Leisure had specific textures—worn-out, silk-thin band T-shirts under mended overalls, plaid on damp plaid, Styrofoam cups of Kelowna wine, sentences without subordination. Leisure anticipated new composition. It opened the possibility that language belongs to those who divert its energies toward the multiplication of collective joy.

As resurgent as it surely was, as synchronic in its expression of a recursive communal necessity, there is something particular about the historical time of the collective—it surged into being in 1984 in its province as the government was systematically replacing responsibility toward citizens with the overarching, non-responsive rationality of capital. They did not then know the term neoliberalism. They called it Capital. A rural university in the interior of the province was closed down because it failed to produce profit. I recall how weird and irrational this politically constructed reason then seemed. The students quickly understood the danger, without realizing that such edicts would accumulate into the single banal and smothering fabric now termed global. Protests, letter-writing, and fundraising readings followed. The government wouldn't budge; the arts program in the mountains folded. The disbanded students regrouped independently from the recognizable institutions. They moved to the city, associated themselves with the artists, found a cheap downtown space, installed a telephone, a desk, and a meeting table. They researched new funding structures, found a pro-bono leftwing lawyer, and succeeded in acquiring a nonprofit status. They bought a few dozen black wooden folding chairs. They formed a mailing list and sent out press releases. They taught each other how to write grants. They taught each other how to read and how to argue. And they did argue. They documented everything in bulging spiral-bound ledgers, in poems, and on cassette tape.

Henceforth the collective traced an irregular path, in shifting nodes of six or ten members, and audiences of one to several dozen, depending. The site drifted among several upstairs spaces, most within a three-block radius, in a poor neighborhood which back then didn't have a name. They shared crappy storefronts with galleries or bookshops. Lulls and disquietudes and uncertainties were interspersed with unparalleled intensity and rushes of rigorous excitement and consequent activity, continuing in this way for around thirty years, collective members holding on, disappearing, announcing and renouncing one another until, grants tapering off, no longer able to afford to rent a meeting space, its library in storage, its archive shunted off to the university special collections, it dwindled and fizzled. I recently heard in an email from a longtime member that the collective is now defunct. Defunct was his word.

Here I want to consider that the apparent failure of the collective is actually a condition of potent latency. In the way that the Paris Commune of 1871 expressed afresh an altered form of eighteenth-century revolutionary citizenship, which itself responded to the brief English Revolution of the seventeenth century, future communes will announce themselves in manifestations as-yet unrecognizable. Resurgent collectivity will burst afresh when an intensity stumbles on a snag in the machinations of the political economy, and people decide on a dime to coax open that potent flaw to create a site. Continuity must be irregular in order to effectively cluster the potencies of linguistic subjectivity and political life apart from capital's metrics. Continuity must be vulgar.

The duration of the collective, from 1984 until 2016, is the period that saw the deepening and zenith of the political and administrative expression of neoliberalism globally, and also particularly in the real estate markets of their city, a place historically determined by impolitical and socially violent real estate practices since its colonial "founding" on indigenous territories in 1886. For a long time, the financial colonization was incomplete, but I could say that now the price of everything has made leisure defunct. In the current city, any residual underemployed working class is displaced by the rents. Bookshops close and discourse narrows. It's a way of outlawing non-financialized leisure. It isn't unusual that the collective should have dwindled as the economic rationalization of political life usurped the active practice of the public. It began with such an incipient financialization, in the cauterization of the role of higher education; it ended at what appears to be the new liberal economy's full realization. The fabrication of a description of this thirty-year moment will yield information about the relationship of subjectivity and its formations and movements to neoliberal determinations of political personhood. I use the word *subjectivity* in a resolutely collective, un-private, and non-possessive sense, considering that it is the historical energy that travels between voices. For three decades, the collective exponentially expressed and opened the incompletion and inefficiency of the liberal state, by producing new forms of linguistic subjectivity. No takeover is ever entire.

Now I think that the collective's most important trait was its vehement resistance, coupled with its gregarious linguistic inventiveness. They were resisting the totalizing movement of capital and its usurpation of both individual and collective time, but they were resisting by widely varying means: Marxist class critique, avant-garde experiment, conceptual rigor, feminist rejections of gendered hierarchy, woman-centered editing practices, queer identity explosions, postcolonial and anti-racist actions. Some used images, or alcohol, or archives, or housing, or sex as the resistant material, experiencing these inseparably from language. Myriad groupings of identifications and practices ripped through and animated the collective fabric. Part of what this new subjectivity showed them was the absolute profanity of happiness, and the existence of that happiness outside of duration. Resistance became a form of life, a form of lived co-existence. This form of life included the structure of group conversations, the improvised ways decisions were made and tasks were allotted, the manner in which records were kept and events and meetings were documented, how a generous unspoken agreement to take each person's intellect completely seriously underwrote the most glorious arguments, conflicts and inventions, as well as the ways ideas moved or were blocked between smaller friendship dyads or triads and the larger group. It would include the ways they cared for one another's health and appetites, the ways they helped each other's animals and plants and households, the kitchen haircuts they excelled in, the thrifted garments they exchanged, the various textures of relationship with other collectives and groups. Most of them survived. Many of them later scattered. Some returned. The collective translated communal time to the radically leisured time of the poem.

A question remains open. What is the relation between the poem and a form of life? What are the terms and means of this vital translation? I believe that this is the query that the collective elaborated and refined. That immaterial phalanstery still guides the trajectory of my own activities in poetry.

(2020)

The Woman in the Wilderness

Peter Lamborn Wilson

The subject of this lecture is American utopian communities but with a very special focus, which is reflected in the title "The Woman in the Wilderness." This was, in fact, the name of the community that I will get around to describing in some detail, but I also find it an interesting metaphor for an entire sub-tradition, or perhaps even *underground* tradition, in what is *already* an underground tradition. In other words, the story of American intentional communities and utopias is *already* pretty submerged, but within that story there's an *even more* submerged story, and I would account for this by saying that (this is an oversimplification, but) there are two kinds of utopias: the Platonic utopia and the anti-Platonic utopia. History usually concerns itself with what it calls "success," so that what it calls "failure" disappears from history, and the only utopian ideas that have ever had *any* success at all are in the Platonic or authoritarian or hierarchic school, and in fact that utopian tradition is usually studied to see what our modern society got from it.

And, in fact, our modern society *did* get a lot from the Platonic utopian tradition—like, for example, the way factories are organized, with strict timing and strict production schedules and so on. This social planning for order in society reflects right back to Moore's *Utopia* and to Plato's *Republic*. Garden cities, traffic planning, social welfare programs: lots of things in our modern society have, in fact, utopian origins. They were at one time high ideals held by somebody and now have become entrenched bureaucracies, for the most part.

So, within this vaster utopian tradition of so-called "success," there's a more hidden utopian tradition of so-called "failure." I say "so-called" because the criteria for success or failure in an intentional community are very arbitrary. You could say, as a book I was looking at this morning in the library does, that any community that fails to last twenty-five years is a failure and that any community that lasts more than twenty-five years is a success—a purely arbitrary time division. So, this author had some communes, which no decent human being would want to live in but which lasted a long time, some of the really hyper-pious Christian, extremely authoritarian communities—awful failures from our point of view—these are accounted as "success." But communes that lasted fifteen or twenty years, or like Brook Farm lasted eight years—and the people who were there remembered it all the rest of their lives as the high point of their lives—these are accredited as "failures," and I've always considered this to be somewhat unjust.

Another reason why certain communities disappear from history and are to be found only in obscure little magazines of local history is either because they're distinctly non-authoritarian or anarchistic, and that *by definition* is just unspeakable to official history, or they were run by women, which makes them automatically uninteresting failures to official, consensus history.

What I wanted to do here was trace a certain strand within the utopian continuity having to do with two utopian qualities which are usually not considered relevant. One of those is called, for lack of a better term, the "feminine principle," and the other you might call "the wilderness," as opposed to culture or to the cultivated state.

In America, there's a very strong relationship with wilderness, but generally it's a sort of love-hate relationship. On the one hand, you have the Puritans who looked on nature as a "howling wilderness" populated by savages who are in fact devils. (By the way, I would point out that the Puritans were an intentional community themselves, but extremely authoritarian, hierarchical, patriarchic, etc.) Then, on the other hand, you have the whole American *romance* with the wilderness, the Davy Crockett/Daniel Boone kind of angle on the wilderness, the love of going out into *terra incognita*, the fascination with the frontier, which is very often a very destructive fascination. Even as American white males experienced the frontier, they actually ate it up and excreted it behind them, so that gradually (to extend this rather disgusting metaphor) the whole country became covered in shit, moving in a gradual progressive wave from East to West, until finally there was no more *terra incognita*, there was no more wilderness.

So once upon a time, there was wilderness in America. But American history, official consensus history, is made up of a lot of dichotomies, and I've been talking about one, the culture versus nature dichotomy. You could say that these all fall into the basic rubric of good versus evil. You have male versus female, and the whole American tradition has been to distrust the female principle, or whatever you want to call it, and look on it as allied with darkness, with wilderness, with chaos. Certainly, if you read any Puritan literature, there you find it just laid out flat; this is the founding myth of America: it has to do with the evil of the feminine.

If you want to find a prime example of what I'm talking about, just read a few pages of Cotton Mather, the Puritan divine from the early period of New England, who saw a witch in every woman, and a devil in every Indian, and a force of chaos in everything that did not adhere to the Puritan vision of the City on the Hill. That was their kind of poetical-metaphorical name for what they were doing. Semantically, it's an interesting construction: it's a city rather than any other kind of place, so it's a highly organized structure and controlled vision; and it's elevated, on a hill, which makes you think of hierarchy and authority, and even perhaps of maleness.

Cotton Mather had a very interesting experience in one point of his life with one of the famous women captives of the Indians. One of the earliest forms of American literature are the "captivity narratives." They're about women and children who had been kidnapped by Indian tribes, who were quite used to enlarging their own populations when necessary by taking captives. They indulged in the same kind of relation with the early European settlers, who were not so militarily well-prepared during the seventeenth century as they later became and were quite susceptible to these raids and kidnappings. Large numbers of, almost inevitably, women and children were carried off. Later on they would be "rescued"—usually dragged back to civilization kicking and screaming. This is an interesting point.

Late in the seventeenth century, one of the Puritan divines (it might have been Mather) pointed out with disgust that he knew of innumerable cases of white people becoming Indians but not one case of an Indian becoming white, by which he meant adopting our way of life. What he was really talking about were competing ways of life.[9] It was quite apparent that a great many of the captives, being women and children and having suffered under the Puritan regime, were *only too glad* to discover that life was not all slopping floors and drudgery and learning to read the Psalms and being penitential and

---

9 Cotton Mather (1663–1728) was born in Boston, a third-generation Puritan in America. In 1689, he preached a sermon concerning the "criolian degeneracy" he saw as a threat to the community's identity since, by that time, the majority of colonists were American born.

worrying about whether you had been saved or not. I don't want to romanticize the Indian way of life, but it was clear to these folks, after they got over the initial shock and learned the language and so forth, they usually settled right in with the Indians, and they liked it, and they usually lamented being "rescued" by the men-folk.

Mather got into a really weird relationship with one of these women who had not wanted to come back from the Indians, and he decided she was a witch, because she didn't like white male Puritan society anymore. And so, he put her through the tortures of hell, keeping her up all night questioning her. His really fascinating thesis about America was that it was a country where invisible warfare would be carried out between the forces of God and the Devil, but that it wouldn't be an open warfare, it would be a warfare of magic and struggle for people's souls and intelligence: a very interesting theory of American history. So, the idea of becoming an Indian is just like the myth of "invisible warfare"—one of the origin myths of America culture.

A great deal of the American intentional communitarian or utopian tradition is based on a very clear recognition that there already was something that appeared to be a utopian tradition here, by comparison with the miseries of European civilization, and that was the tribal life of so-called "primitive" horticultural or hunter-gatherer societies. Europeans of the sixteenth and seventeenth centuries had not expected this at all, and many of them, far from experiencing the Indians as devils living in a howling wilderness of evil, quite to the contrary, experienced them as humanity perfected, as the "Noble Savage," to use [Jean-Jacques] Rousseau's term. Rousseau is the culmination of this particular school of thought. So, there was kind of a weird schizophrenic idealism going on about Indian life, that it was either diabolic, on the one hand, or angelic, on the other hand. This dialectic informs a great deal of American experience, thought, and literature.

I should add that the "the witch" is, for the American mythopoesis, a figure of equal importance with the Indian and is almost, in fact, the female version of the Indian. The obsession with the witch in early New England society mirrors exactly the obsession with the Indian. It's not just a transplantation of the European witch craze; it has a specific New World aspect to it, and that aspect is the connection of the feminine culture of the witch with the apparently feminine culture of the Indian (in the sense that it's not European patriarchal, etc.).

The witch is the liminal figure, the threshold figure, that stands with one foot in cultivated space and one foot in the space of wilderness, who mediates between culture and wilderness and brings wilderness experience back into the realm of culture and cultivation. And when a society is no longer able to deal with its witches in any way except by exterminating them, by burning them at the stake, then you have a culture that wants to cease to have any relation with the wilderness, which sees itself as pure civilization, pure culture—nothing left of the wild, the chaotic, the watery, the feminine (the *yin* principle, to use Chinese terminology). So, in America, the stage was reached almost immediately, with the Indian wars (1636–38) and the extermination of so many women as witches (1692–93). Here you have the *active* suppression of the feminine principle, and that's what official American culture begins to base itself on.

Because I have to rush through a lot of history here, I've decided that since the community I'm going to talk about is one of the very earliest intentional communities in America, I'll go backwards in history and get to it at the end of the lecture. So, I'd like to begin that trajectory of tracing the "female wilderness," if I can use that shorthand phrase for this alternative tradition. I'm going to trace backwards through time and try to define what I'm talking about through examples.

Starting in the present, I'd like to say that the intentional community movement is by no means dead and disappeared, as a lot of people would like you to think—there are thriving utopian stories going on. One I would pick as being particularly apt in this discussion would be the Permaculture communities. This is like the culmination of all the alternative sustainable agriculture ideas from the '60s and '70s, now more or less systematized, theoretized, and applicable to any kind of bioregion or ecology, both to individual and to group needs—very interesting, very poetic, and, at the same time, excellent biology. That whole idea of respect for the earth, respect for Gaia that informs a lot of Permaculture thinking, seems to me to resonate with what I'm calling "the female wilderness principle."

I could go on and describe neo-pagan communities, which are also feminist or at least fem*inine* in their orientation—"goddess-oriented" let's say. We could talk about ecofeminism. These categories meld into each other and have informed intentional communities that exist now. There are neo-pagan rural, queer, shamanic communities founded by the group called the Radical Faeries, a very appealing group, one with a lot of good consciousness and also with a great interest in dancing in the forest at night, that kind of thing, so a *very* clear-cut example of what I'm talking about.

Going back from now, take a leap to the sixties, which was the last period that most historians agree to have been a period of communes and intentional community formation, the counter-cultural communes of the 1960s. "Countercultural" already says in a negative sense what I'm trying to describe in a positive sense by referring to a female wilderness principle. If "culture" is civilization, and if civilization is this male-dominated, linear thinking, grid-work concept of society, then anything which is "countercultural" must be *counter* to that and have this kind of snaky sinuosity and feminist gender ambiguity and so on. If you look at the hippie communes this is exactly the kind of style they manifested.

I'm sorry to say that in other respects, political consciousness was not so great back in the sixties: there was a lot of hippie male chauvinism, which a lot of people find annoying—I still find it annoying. So, even though this was my formative period, I am by no means asserting that is was utopia, especially not for women. Nevertheless, there was an attempt at what you might call a Neolithic revival, a revival of the early agricultural, idealized peasant existence, and that was reflected in hippie style. You remember all those peasant shirts, peasant blouses that people wore to make a style statement about what they believed about ecology and the land. And, on the other hand, there was what you might call a Paleolithic revival, an Old Stone Age revival, and a growing fascination with hunter-gatherer tribes. This expressed itself on the psychic level more than on the economic level, because for the most part the communes of the sixties were economic disasters. But on the *psychic* level, there really was a sort of hunter-gathering spirit in the self-conscious tribalism of the hippies, in which attempts were made to actually make contact with Indians, to learn about tribal social structure, to get inspiration, to become Indians once again in that good old American way.

The example I particularly experienced was Millbrook, where Timothy Leary and the League for Spiritual Discovery were constantly engaged in psychic hunting and gathering, as you might say. There was, in fact, a building on the grounds in which at any given moment, night or day, someone was in there on two thousand micrograms of acid. That was said to be the psychic center of Millbrook. If that was not going on, then Millbrook was not alive. And I see that as a constant search for some kind of vast archaic consciousness that was supposed to be rediscovered through these completely disorganized and anarchic and actually, in many ways, counterproductive insanities that went on at Millbrook. So once again, not putting that up as utopia, but just to point out that in a certain strange way it belongs in the history that I'm discussing.

I would like now to take a jump to the next period back in history, which is usually thought of as a golden period for community formation, and that would be the mid-nineteenth century. There was a tremendous movement in America at that time called Reform. It's usually known as the Reform Movement, which makes it sound kind of weak and watery, but it was anything but that. We'd probably be much more correct to think of it as a social revolutionary period in American history. There was a great idealistic ferment of myriad complexes of social issues: abolitionism, women's rights, socialism, anarchism, free love, anti-money, phrenology, made-up alphabets and languages, hydropathy, Graham crackers. (Dr. Graham, the original health-food nut, invented Graham crackers to reduce sexual desire. He was of the anti-free-love contingent.) There was no great agreement about anything, but there was this great surge of excitement about the possibility of reshaping society. So, all kinds of utopian schemes were tried during this period, and I would like to focus on one or two of them that I think are interesting from this particular line that I'm trying to trace.

I would mention Stephen Pearl Andrews and Victoria Woodhull as two very fascinating figures. Woodhull is a great hero of mid-nineteenth-century feminism. She was the first woman to run for president in America (1872), even though it was, of course, illegal for her to do so. She was, for a long time, a member of the First International, until Karl Marx discovered she believed in free love and anarchism and kicked her out, along with Stephen Pearl Andrews.

Andrews was her speechwriter, and he too was a kind of eccentric anarchist who synthesized many schools of thought. He had been an abolitionist and remained one to the end. He introduced Pitman shorthand to America, because he thought it would be a revolutionary way for the poor to become literate. (It became an adjunct of capitalism, secretarial shorthand.) He read Charles Fourier, he read Robert Owen; he hung around with Josiah Warren who was the first person to use the *word* "anarchist" to describe himself in a positive way.

Pearl Andrews and Victoria Woodhull were exponents of free love. Now, it's hard to say exactly what "free love" meant in the nineteenth century—it didn't mean quite the same thing that it meant in the 1960s and '70s. It was more of a critique of marriage and the nuclear family, which was then coming into existence as a direct result of late-capitalist economic pressures on the extended family. So it had to do with the desperate pressures on the American woman, who no longer had the support of an extended family full of aunts and grandmothers and cousins, because the family had been reduced to this hideous triangle of male, female, child, in which the male was on top and the child toward the bottom, as property, and the woman somewhere in between. This was experienced by American women at that time as a kind of rape. And men were exceedingly ignorant about women's sexual pleasure, did not understand the female orgasm at all. You couldn't talk about these things; you couldn't write about them. If you tried to even disseminate really innocent birth-control material at this period, you could be arrested and thrown in jail.

So, it's not easy for us to talk about free love, or to know what was even *meant* by it, because people had to be so restrained in their language. But there are a few examples that would help us to figure it out. One of them was the utopia that Pearl Andrews and Woodhull were involved in, called Modern Times, which was out in what is now Brentwood, Long Island. It lasted from 1851 to 1866, exactly fifteen years. This is one you'll never read about in American textbooks, because it was a "failure." It was a failure *by definition* because it was anarchist. It went along quite happily without leaders, without money, without any kind of preordained structure. It eventually fell apart because some hysterical puritans in New York began a free-love scare, and people began flocking out by the newly built railway to Modern Times, I guess in sort of the way a lot of assholes went to Berkeley in 1968 "looking for where the action was," and thereby destroyed all possibility of real action. Modern Times had to retreat in confusion in the onslaught of scandal, but even after the official disbanding of the community a lot of the people continued to live there, and their descendants are living there today.

At Modern Times, there was not "giving" or "taking" in marriage, as the New Testament puts it; liaisons were completely free between men or women or, one presumes, between women and women or men and men; although if heterosexuality was a taboo discourse in that period, forget homosexuality—there's no way to learn anything about it, but you just have to assume that gay people would have been attracted to a situation like this. It's something I'd like to be able to research, but it's difficult—you just have to go on tragic little clues, there's not much more than that.

Another interesting commune was Oneida (est. 1848). That was in upstate New York, and it still survives today as a community based around a factory where Oneidaware (dishes, pans, flatware) are produced. They're still making Oneidaware after over a hundred years since they broke up their experiment but continued as a joint stock community around a factory. Initially, they had been something far more loony and interesting, and that was a community which practiced complex marriage. It meant that every male in the community was married to every female and vice-versa, at least potentially, and that actual sexual liaisons would be worked out in open discussion—kind of Maoist self-criticism sessions, actually under the direction of the founder John Humphrey Noyes, who was a brilliant man. This was *not* an anarchist community. Noyes was *the leader*, but as far as I can make out, he was not very heavy-handed: he always let the community discuss things before decisions were made; he was very popular and charismatic, and he fathered a *great* number of children at Oneida.

The one point that I really want to make is about the great role that women could have in a situation like this, so different from what they could have in outside society. The key to complex marriage at Oneida was "male continence." This meant that, in theory, while making love, the male would not experience orgasm. And it was discovered by people at Oneida (Noyes himself did the preliminary research) that this could actually be a very satisfying form of sexuality. As far as I can make out, it was similar to Taoist or Tantric ritual intercourse, which goes on for hours and hours. Women could have orgasms this way; they could have multiple orgasms, which was something outside society didn't even believe in. According to some inside gossip I've heard from Oneida, one of the big keys to the success was oral sex, which they could not discuss in their literature. This was a tremendous step forward in women's freedom, because it meant not only multiple orgasms, it also meant birth control. Every time you had an orgasm, you didn't have to pay with a baby. So, this was one of the most radical and pro-female social experiments of the whole period.

I would also mention the Fourierists. Charles Fourier was a French utopian socialist, who actually invented the term "féminisme" (in 1837) and said that his way of judging any society was by the position of women in it, and on that basis he condemned modern Western civilization utterly. So, his followers in the communes where his teachings were propagated were also on the road to feminism, let's say, and on the road to a kind of orgiastic concept of free love. But this was America, this was Protestant, Puritan America, and none of these things ever got off the ground. They were never really given a chance. I mean, the torch-wielding peasants *always* show up at Frankenstein's castle, you know what I mean? And they did at Oneida, and John Humphrey Noyes fled to Canada. The whole thing fell apart, and they decided to change it into a joint-stock factory cooperative and give up the complex marriage in 1881. Oneida lasted through the Civil War; it was Modern Times that died on the eve.

One of the interesting points about this mid-nineteenth-century movement is that it was all destroyed and buried by the Civil War. All of the reform movements were reduced to one, which was anti-slavery. Those who made the argument that wage slavery was just as evil as chattel slavery were no longer listened to; the radical abolitionists like William Lloyd Garrison, who were in fact out-and-out anarchists, were not listened to; John Brown the anarchist was not listened to; Henry Thoreau was not listened to. The communes, the intentional communities, were destroyed or died away one by one. All of the intellectual energy was whipped up into a hysterical frenzy about preserving the Union, and it was not just the South and its seceding states that this control mechanism was aimed at—it was aimed at *any* group that would attempt autonomy, on any level. We no longer understand this, because we've been taught that the Civil War was a Manichean struggle between good and evil, and that good won.

Now, you know bloody well that history is not like that: it's a dialectic situation in which incredible complexities of positive and negative forces can be separated out depending on who you are and who's doing the separating, who's doing the questioning. In the 1850s, there was a powerful radical feminism in this country, represented by people like Victoria Woodhull, but after the Civil War there was nothing of that left except a "votes for women" movement, as if that meant *anything*. You know, it's a purely symbolic little tidbit that's thrown to the women to make up for their disappointment at seeing the entire women's liberation movement destroyed during the Civil War and the woman turned into the image of the mother, the suffering mother, the self-sacrificing nurse, instead of the complete, autonomous human being.

So, all groups, *all* autonomous groups were destroyed by this cataclysmic orgy of *unity*, of political, economic unity. This is what paved the way for the rise of high classical Capitalism as analyzed by Marx and Engels. This is the dark shadow side of the Civil War. Once again, this is something I could talk about obsessively and I'd better just leave it.

Now, out of all early nineteenth-century utopias that we could talk about, which are associated with women as leaders, there were the Shakers, who were founded by Mother Ann Lee, and there was Jemima Wilkinson, the Universal Friend, who had a community in upstate New York. (A lot of these communities were in upstate New York, by the way. It's sometimes called the "burnt over district," because one enthusiasm after another, like prairie fires, would just sweep across upstate New York.)

The most interesting to me, however, is a very short-lived one (it only lasted three years, therefore a "failure") called Nashoba. It was in Tennessee, and it went from 1825 to 1828, so we're back into the early period of nineteenth-century Reform enthusiasm now. Frances Wright was a highly intellectual Scottish-born woman who came over to participate in Robert Owen's big utopian socialist experiment at New Harmony. She founded Nashoba in Tennessee which was, first of all, a very rare move, because the southern states had almost none of these intentional communities. It was one of the very rare ones that happened in the American South. But the purpose of it was to set up a community for emancipated slaves—I guess you would almost call it a "halfway house" concept these days—to help them reintegrate themselves into an economic freedom.[10]

It came to a very speedy demise, because Frances Wright published some incredible magazine articles in which she discussed her feminist free-love and anti-racist ideas, and immediately after these articles appeared, the America public began to imagine *you know what* going on there—"miscegenation," you name it, all the *deep horrors* of the American consciousness. She was literally forced out of America and had to return to Europe, where she continued to have a very interesting and exciting life. A fascinating woman, an interesting writer. Nashoba was rural, it was in the wilderness, it was run by a woman, it believed in free love and anti-racism, and I think

---

10 Wright, like many early anti-slavery advocates, believed that Blacks would never be successfully integrated into white society. She published a plan whereby slaveholders would be compensated for their economic losses and Blacks would be settled in Africa or Haiti. She purchased ten enslaved persons and advertised for free whites and Blacks to join the commune. At Nashoba, the plan went, the slaves would help make the farm profitable by their labor, to recompense Wright, and to help finance their relocation, while learning to be independent workers. Her friends Jefferson and Monroe approved of the experiment, and Andrew Jackson advised her on where to buy land. When the commune failed, Wright chartered a ship to take her enslaved persons to freedom in Haiti.

we can see that it has significance for this radical anarchist feminist wilderness tradition.

Before I leave the nineteenth century, I should just make one little note about Thoreau, whom I mentioned before. It's interesting to think about Thoreau as the founder of the utopia of one, very much a wilderness-oriented utopia. Traditionally, we're taught to believe in it as a "utopia of one," however some recent work (which I haven't gotten my hands on yet) has been leading some people to think of Walden Pond as a utopia for *two*. Thoreau had a very dear friend, who visited him a lot, spent a lot of time out there at Walden, a young man from Concord. And Thoreau was, as we know, always hanging out with the young men of Concord. He never married. He loved to go on canoe trips in Maine with Indian wilderness guides. On his death bed, his last words, which I've always thought were so wonderful, were "forests, Indians." So, it's kind of interesting to think of Thoreau as anti-patriarchist, which of course any conscious homosexual in the nineteenth-century would have been, a kind of secret Whitman (Whitman himself was a secret Whitman), very much oriented toward the idea of becoming an Indian, living alone or with your beloved comrade in the wilderness, and so I think Thoreau also deserves to be included into the line of thought that I'm trying to trace.

Now, going back from the nineteenth to the eighteenth century, we find Christian Priber, a German who, as far as we know, showed up in Georgia sometime in the 1740s and was known as a savant. He quickly taught himself Choctaw and Creek and produced one of the first dictionaries of an Indian language, which unfortunately was lost. He intended to go out, live among the Indians, learn their languages, and convert them all to communism. He believed in the community of women and of children, which was sort of an old-fashioned communist idea that all women and children were held in common, so to speak. It's far from being a feminist ideal, but in fact the way it's supposed to work out was by no means to enslave the women and children but to free them. What Priber didn't understand was that without birth control and sexual freedom, a system like this would only add to women's burdens.

Nevertheless, I think his heart was in the right place. He arrived in Georgia, gave away all his property, dressed as an Indian, and disappeared into the woods. A couple of years later, he reemerged having written a book about his experiences. Any American historian would give their right arm to find that manuscript, but it's gone, along with his dictionary. He was immediately arrested by James Oglethorpe, the colonial leader of Georgia, and thrown into prison where he languished for a few years and then died in 1744—interestingly enough, right around the time that the American revolutionary struggle began. The people who arrested him pointed out that he had come to look exactly like an Indian. This was very shocking to them, that his skin had darkened through exposure to the sun, that he spoke their languages very well, and that he in fact seemed to have taken up the Indian way of life.

Going back a little farther in time, back to the Puritans again, I'll quickly mention Thomas Morton of Merrymount (1579–1647), who was immortalized by Nathaniel Hawthorne in his short story "The May-Pole of Merrymount," which was a fictionalized version of Thomas Morton's experience. He was a jolly English libertine, a kind of Episcopalian neo-pagan if you can imagine such a thing, a tepid Church of Englander whose real interest was in classical pagan culture and wine-bibbing. He arrived in America in 1624, and set up his own little community, and *hated* the Puritans. These were the pilgrims actually, the Pilgrim Fathers under William Bradford. And so, he removed to Mount Wollaston, which is now a suburb of Boston, and started a community called Merrymount where everyone would be merry—that was his idea. He put up a Maypole and he invited all the Indians from round about to come to a big May Day celebration. It was the first May Day celebration in America. I like to say, an inter-racial neo-pagan be-in. The very first in American history. The following May Day, as a good time was being had by all, the famous

Miles Standish showed up and arrested Morton and dragged him off to jail. They made him go back to England and he wrote a book, a wonderful, surprising little book called *New English Canaan*. He identified as a Canaanite pagan in reaction against the Puritans, who identified themselves as the Israelites. If you know your Bible history, you know this was a very shocking thing to say, that one identified as a Canaanite. He called the Indians the red-skinned Canaanites and he said he would prefer a thousand times to live with them rather than get anywhere near Miles Standish and the Bradford fathers.

I'd like to remind you once again, going back in time, about the captivity narratives, about the women in the wilderness, the *literal* women in the wilderness, the women and children who had experienced what they felt as the obvious superiority of Indian culture vis-à-vis the position of women and children in Puritan society, who really were the first literary examples of what became a kind of American child's mythic dream of becoming an Indian, running away into the forest primeval and dressing in animal skins and feathers and having wonderful adventures. This is a myth that's been perpetuated, experienced, and appropriated in myriad different ways, from the Boy Scouts on up.

So, keep that *real* story of the real women in the real wilderness in mind, as I bring you back to 1694 and the foundation of a commune called "The Woman in the Wilderness." Actually, its real name was The Community of the God-Fearing Beloved, or something like that, but it became The Woman in the Wilderness after a passage from The Book of Revelation (12:1-6; 13-17) that was always being quoted by them, about the woman in the wilderness, that symbolized a number of things for them.

The founder's name was Johannes Kelpius (1667–1708). He was like Christian Priber, a German savant, a very learned man. He had studied the sciences because of their occult connections. He had read deeply in all kinds of mystical literature. He came out of the German Pietist tradition, which also produced Johann Sebastian Bach. In fact, when I play some of his music, you'll hear certain dim reflections of Bach-like tradition. Kelpius was the first American composer, the first person as far as I've been able to make out to write music in North America, I mean aside from the Native traditions, of course—the first person to *write* music, let's say. They were all hymns. A friend of mine and I made use of a facsimile edition of his hymnal and we restored some of his hymns; I'll play them for you in a little while.

The Woman in the Wilderness was, I call it, a Rosicrucian communist society. Rosicrucianism was a mystical occult movement that had sprung up in Europe in the earlier part of the century. It was alchemical, it claimed initiatic sources in the East, it had an alchemical mystique and legend about it. It was a secret society, nobody knew who belonged, and anonymous manifestos would appear and cause great excitement. Frances Yates, a wonderful British scholar whose work everyone should know, wrote a book called *The Rosicrucian Enlightenment* (Routledge, 1972), in which she pointed out that the real hidden agenda of Rosicrucianism was in fact political. It was to try to reconcile the split between Catholicism and Protestantism, which had plunged Europe into at least a century of the most horrible wars and, in a way, the first world war. The greatest disaster known to any sincere Christian was this awful split between Catholicism and Protestantism, Luther and Calvin, and the Rosicrucians were devoted secretly to healing that rift. So, they tended to be very latitudinarian, very open-minded, very tolerant of varieties of religious experience and varieties of religious ideology. They were one of the first liberal Christian movements.

Kelpius had studied in Germany with a man named Zimmerman, who was going to be the head of this expedition to the New World but died. Kelpius took over, and they had both been very closely connected to the Baron Knorr von Rosenroth, who was one of the most important German Rosicrucian thinkers. Rosenroth wrote hymns, and Kelpius based his hymns on Rosenroth's hymnal, some of which is still used amongst the German pietistic sects which, by the way, still survive in groups like the Mennonites. The Amish are modern heirs of this tradition.

So, they were radical Pietists. They were occultists and they brought all of their alchemical equipment with them. They brought a telescope (which may have been the first telescope in the new world), they brought an organ and a virginal (a small keyboard instrument, which may have been the first keyboard instrument in the new world), and they brought books. They brought seeds and planted medicinal herbal gardens and began to research Native American herbs. And what was the purpose of all this interesting intellectual activity? Actually, they were waiting for the end of the world. They had originally expected it to happen in 1694, and for mystical reasons they thought that they should be in the wilderness when the world came to an end. So, they had to go to America because that was where *wilderness* was.

So, they came. There were forty of them (forty being the correct mystical number), they were chaste (they did not have sex at all, at least in theory), and they built a house forty feet by forty feet by forty feet, a sort of a Kaaba or cube of logs in the wilderness. On the roof, they mounted their telescope, and every night Kelpius would go up and study signs of the approaching end of the world. I love to think of him up there. And then during the day he would do good deeds (for instance, they started schools).

He wrote a dictionary of an Indian language. It would have been, I guess, the local Algonquian language—Delaware perhaps? It is now lost. He was extremely and outspokenly pro-Indian. He realized right away that Indigenous culture was vastly superior to European culture in a lot of ways and said so in so many words.

In 1694, of course, the world did not come to an end. They expected it to happen on St. John's Eve, which is Midsummer's Night, a great pagan festival which was still celebrated in Germany and northern Europe in general, and is still celebrated to this day with remnants of pagan custom and ritual, like bonfires. And the Woman in the

Wilderness group were very fond of St. John's Eve and celebrated it every year with big bonfires and scared the more pious Protestants in the region into thinking they were witches or neo-pagans of some sort, which in fact they were actually, but they did a very good job of disguising that behind all of their good deeds: setting up of schools, teaching the Bible, and so on.

Along with alchemy and Gnosticism (they also seemed to have discovered a few basic things about Gnosticism) and astrology and so forth, there was also a radically anti-hierarchical mystical aspect to their teaching and experience, which led them to hold all their goods in common, a radical egalitarianism that can only be called communism. Of course, it never had a chance to work itself out in any economic way because they really had no interest in being a self-sustaining, self-perpetuating community—they expected that at any moment the whole show was going to be wrapped up, and they thought that the most important thing to do was to meditate, to try to do alchemy, to transform one's own soul in preparation for the coming of the bridegroom, the apocalyptic final moments. And when you hear Kelpius's hymns, you'll see what a vivid and living idea that was for him.

Kelpius eventually found even the forty square foot building to be too busy a place for himself and retired to a little cave in the wilderness, which I've seen. It's in Fairmount Park, Philadelphia. The American Rosicrucian Society AMORC (Ancient Mystical Order Rosae Crucis) put up a memorial slab in the middle of the woods there, next to the cave. It's still a magical little grove. You can see why he was attracted to it. There he developed his mystical system based on the three-fold wilderness, the three aspects of the wilderness.

The first aspect was the wilderness of sin, in which you find yourself, as Dante says at the beginning of the *Divine Comedy*, wandering alone in a dark forest, in the middle of your life, besmirched by sin, so to speak—which, for the mystic, of course, means the forgetfulness of God-consciousness; rather than any specific sinful act, it means a state of consciousness which is unaware of God. Then after that, comes the wilderness of solitude, in which, you might say, the self-reproaching soul takes up residence away from the hurly-burly and distraction of human, quotidian, daily, banal existence and goes to the wilderness as a special place, to experience this direct communion with the divine principle *in the wilderness*. And the third level of wilderness is the wilderness of the God-intoxicated soul, who has in fact made the breakthrough and has experienced God as a god of *Nature*; instead of a city, the heaven of the Puritans, Kelpius experienced God as god of Nature, of the forest, of the living—the "biosphere" you might say.

Again, I don't have the time to go into these ideas in any great detail, but I would point out that when we get to the hymns, he distinctly wrote these hymns to the male God-principle as well as to the *female* God-principle. *Sophia*, as mentioned in the Old Testament, becomes for Kelpius almost a female God, a Goddess. And so, he places a great emphasis on experiencing the divine principle as somehow feminine. I like to think of it as a wonderful, hidden, and forgotten beginning to this great underground American tradition that I've been talking about, of the female wilderness aspect of utopia. This is it; this expresses it explicitly. The very phrase "woman in the wilderness" is the dialectical opposition to the phrase "city on the hill." So, it's the beginning of a mystical, insurrectionary, pro-feminine, pro-wilderness, pro-Indian tradition. I can't think of any other word to describe the continuity and this lineage (as they like to say at Naropa) that leads from one such person to another, as I've done backwards through time, arriving at Johannes Kelpius.

I would like to turn, in the last time that we have, to playing these hymns for you. Please don't expect great music, OK? There are some very bizarre chord changes if you listen for them, almost unpleasant, and that could be in part, I suppose, because Kelpius was just a bad composer. He was a gentleman amateur. These poems, these hymns, in that doggerel German umpty-dumpty tri-meter, just poured out of him in his cave in the wilderness. In fact, the first hymn that I'll play for you, before I took out my scissors, had fifty-three verses; I've cut that down to five. So, you're not getting the *full* Kelpius experience, and thank your lucky stars for that.

But the hymns and the hymnal are both very interesting, very moving to me, very moving to think of this guy in his cave playing his little virginal, and his weird hymns to Sophia filtering out, and perhaps some American Indian hunters passing by on their way to the camping grounds and hearing this and thinking about this strange white magician who had come to live amongst them and who was by no means disliked by them. I think the Indians probably thought that these people were completely *loony*, but they could undoubtedly see that they were not *nasty* like the Puritans, or William Penn and his little militia, or the white men that they had come across whose only interest was to either convert them forcibly to Christianity or to destroy them. Kelpius was by no means in that category, so I think we could almost take him, in his naiveté and in his period, as an avatar or even a kind of patron saint, of an anti-racist, pro-feminist, magical, wilderness tradition in the story of American utopias. I find Kelpius a very sympathetic and moving figure, despite his obvious nuttiness. I don't think there's any other way to put it, but, you know, "he who persists in his folly becomes wise," and I think that Blakean, utopian concept was very well exemplified by Kelpius.

He died as a young man, probably from overexposure, spending winters in this little cave, and he was not a very healthy guy to begin with. He was delicate. So, the Woman in the Wilderness dissolved around 1708 and was carried on by some of Kelpius' disciples, including one who was a native English speaker and translated his hymns into English in the same umpty-dumpty meter, and that's the text that I used. Just as the sort of last gasp, around 1712–1714, some more German Pietists came over expecting to find Kelpius and to learn about his tradition and were disappointed to learn that he had died a long time before. But they did pick up on some of his teachings from some of his disciples and some of his manuscripts, and they went off and founded a religious community called Amana, which lasted until the late nineteenth century. So, in fact, there was a Pietist tradition stemming from Kelpius that was very "successful" (if you count longevity as success) and only recently vanished from the world. Kelpius was remembered by these German-speaking Pietists, although he was very thoroughly forgotten by most students of American history. I first came across him in a book by Arthur Bestor called *Backwoods Utopias*, which has one or two little paragraphs on Kelpius—that's what got me interested.

Now, I'd like to play one of these hymns for you. The singers are Carol Wilson (no relation) and Peter Becker. The recording is thanks to Paul Ruest and George Wellington of Pacifica Radio in New York. I'd like to thank Steven Taylor for finding the facsimile of the hymnal for us, and Anthony Piccolo, who edited the music, rehearsed the singers, and is playing the electric harpsichord on this tape.

This hymn is intellectually perhaps the most interesting, as it deals with our principle. It's called "Of the Wilderness, of the Secret Private Virgin Cross Love," and it's about the wilderness. These are the words:

> *The true friend came to see Johann in his recesses*
>   *Of quiet solitude in lonesome wildernesses,*
>   *For he was deadly sick and lonesome day by day.*
>   *For joy to see his friend he fainted quite away.*
>
> *The friend embracèd him with trying to relieve him,*
>   *And 'twas a pretty while before John could perceive him.*
>   *"Johannes," says the friend, "I know what troubles thee,*
>   *What makes thee sick. 'Tis love, which now thou canst not see."*

(Here's the pre-Blakean lines:)
Consider the sunflower in dark and cloudy weather.
How faithfully she turns her face to her dear lover
Until she's pregnant grown and bears him like a seed,
Then rests she and does bow in gratitude her head.

Me only thy sunflower, let after thee be turning
    [get that? Let me, as thy sunflower be turning after you,
        divine sun]
And in the pensive night and darkness for thee mourning
Until thy form in me thy Christus hath full power
And then stand thy still in thee, I only thy sunflower.

But thou divinest love who thyself has begun it
This work of love in us so strengthen us to run it,
Perfect it quite, and let us plainly see this is
In this way of the cross the love its wilderness.

(1993)

Reality Is No Obstacle

A Poetics of Participation

Cedar Sigo

> Because the deepest revolution is not social.
> —Will Alexander

Revolutionary Letter #62

Take a good look
at history (the American myth)
check sell out
of revolution by the founding fathers
'Constitution written by a bunch of gangsters
to exploit a continent' is what
              Charles Olson told me.

Check Shay's rebellion, Aaron Burr, Nathan Hale.
Who wrote the history books where *you*
               went to school?
Check Civil War : maybe industrial north
needed cheap labor, South had it, how many
sincere 'movement' people
               writers & radicals played
               into their hands?
Check Haymarket trial : it broke the back
of strong Wobblie movement : how many jailed, fined,
killed to stop that one? What's happening to us
has happened a few times before
               let's change the script

What did it take to stop the Freedom Riders
What have we actually changed?
               month I was born
they were killing onion pickers in Ohio

Month that I write this, nearly 40 years later
they're killing UFW's in the state
I'm trying somehow to live in. LET'S REWRITE
the history books.
History repeats itself
only if we let it.

I have wondered if this piece of writing could more accurately be described as a speech rather than a lecture. The recently insulting and polarized political climate has struck a chord inside of me. Is this a need to articulate my resistance or just a willingness to begin to ask new questions? When does the word itself become action? This is a question I encountered in a lecture by the poet Lorenzo Thomas titled "How to See through Poetry: Myth Perception & History."

It's a question he never really answers and one that I think must be haunting all of our minds. Every day our phones or televisions call up new images and actions of dehumanization—barring whole populations of countries from entering the United States, images of makeshift concentration camps posing as immigrant detention centers (this is happening under a bridge in El Paso), yesterday's threat of defunding the Special Olympics [August 2019], the possibility of being able to deny health-care services on the grounds of some newfangled moral objection from the religious right. These are extra classy, shockingly evil deeds, and I think somehow strategic choices. Let's do the most heartless thing. The headlines no longer pile up, they disappear, and we are feigning shock at this point.

This mindset has caused me to confront the parts of resistance that my poetry has left undone. My work has always placed its highest premium on delaying the meeting of edges in collage, until they fall to form the final image, or is it better to say, the unlocking of collage through the inflection of voice? This is likely due to the way I take in language before attempting to lift it up and set it back out into reality. A variant of this energy is released through the public reading of the work, lending an acoustic sensation of going elsewhere, or that, in fact, the poems are reading themselves. This is a piece from Amiri Baraka's essay "How You Sound??":

> I make a poetry with what I feel is useful & can be saved out of all the garbage of our lives. What I see, am touched by (CAN HEAR)…wives, gardens, jobs, cement yards where cats pee, all my interminable artifacts…ALL are a poetry, & nothing moves (with any grace) pried apart from these things. There cannot be closet poetry. Unless the closet be wide as God's eye.
>
> And all that means that I *must* be completely free to do just what I want, in the poem. "All is permitted."

For the purposes of this lecture I will focus on a new kind of correspondence, another dance that my work is just now beginning to uncover, whose ultimate and desired effect is to build coalitions among people and to keep that spark active and available within poetry. Poetry is never simply a set of words living alone upon the page. It exists as a perennial light in the mind, a tool of recognition that we must press into the hands of others. Teaching poetry as I do now, most often in short stints and out-of-the-way places, I have taken to sharing American revolutionary poets like Audre Lorde, John Trudell, Diane di Prima, Amiri Baraka, Margaret Randall, Jayne Cortez, Tongo Eisen-Martin. I hesitate to immediately stamp their work as political anymore, especially when introducing their poems to students. Such naming at this point feels like imposing an immediate paralysis or unnecessary ceiling when in fact these poets hand us forms that we can carry as amulets, seemingly simple exercises that we may call upon to redefine what revolution means. Taking on reality in luminous particulars, startling us with bound-up images unleashed. That is really the pleasure of the poet anyway: to redefine our engagement with the way language comes to guide our lives.

Revolutionary Letter #100: Reality is No Obstacle

> refuse to obey
> refuse to die
> refuse to sleep
> refuse to turn away
> refuse to close your eyes
> refuse to shut your ears
> refuse silence when you can still sing
> refuse discourse in lieu of embracement
> come to no end that is not
> a Beginning

I was listening to a recording of Diane di Prima reading at Berkeley in 2008. At one point she speaks about the origin of her ongoing series *Revolutionary Letters*:

> What happened was somebody in New York hired a flatbed truck, Sam Abrams—a poet—and a generator that would run an amplifier, and we went out, some folk singers who were considered very radical, gorilla theater people who did Street theatre and poets, and we went all over New York, this was those years of assassinations around '67, '68 or so, not the first wave, but the second wave of assassinations and we would just perform places and I realized the poems I had were too intellectual for that kind of performing so I started to write things that were something you could hear on one hearing, on the street, something more like gorilla theater even though it was poetry and that became the *Revolutionary Letters*.
>
> So, there were a lot of those. They would go out to something called The Liberation News Service which would send them to 200 revolutionary newspapers. People would print what they wanted and that went on every week or so and eventually I put out a book of them in 1971 with City Lights.

I love di Prima's concept of writing work that we can make use of after one hearing. It is an interesting intention to place over the process. Plus the poet is almost expecting that her words will be blindly broken off at some point, so the listener may only get a shard of the poem, and writing with that in mind to begin with. She also describes what sounds like a very deliberate cross-pollenization of the arts. As I begin to imagine this flatbed truck I also begin to question the difference between protest, performance, and actual battle. When di Prima references this second wave of assassinations she is not only speaking of Malcolm X, Martin Luther King Jr. and Robert F. Kennedy, but also of the deaths of seventeen-year-old

Bobby Hutton, the first recruit of the Black Panther Party, as well as Fred Hampton, chairman of the Illinois chapter of the Black Panther Party, who was gunned down in his own home in December of 1969 during a raid ordered by the Chicago police department, who had been working in conjunction with the FBI for their COINTELPRO operation "to investigate 'radical' national political groups for intelligence that would lead to involvement of foreign enemies within these programs." So essentially agents would infiltrate the organization as undercover Panthers, obtain information, begin to divide and conquer, to jail, and to assassinate.

Revolutionary Letter # 36

who is the we, who is
the they in this thing, did
we or they kill the Indians, not me
my people brought here, cheap labor to exploit
a continent for them, did we
or they exploit it? do you
admit complicity, say "*we*
have to get out of Vietnam, *we* really should
stop poisoning the water, etc." look closer, look again,
secede, declare your independence, don't accept
a share of the guilt *they* want to lay on *us*
MAN IS INNOCENT & BEAUTIFUL & born
to perfect bliss they envy, heavy deeds
make heavy hearts and to *them*
life is suffering. stand clear.

The poem is instructive for the way in which di Prima begins to interrogate the reach of pronouns, her own complicity, which leads to throwing out questions about her own origins and then eventually wonders how "we" can even identify any longer with the criminal acts "they" think that they are slipping by as mere legislation. I am also so enamored with the way the pronouns first feel haphazardly talky and strewn about the poem. Though actually they are carefully lighted upon, leaned against, forming the literal crux of the music, *Do you admit complicity?* All explanations are finally ground down to a last dusting of liberation philosophy. "Stand Clear." The reader is placed inside the mind of the poet as strategist, and environmental activist, espousing lists of theories on how we might survive as well as ways of continuing to force change.

When Diane di Prima left the East Coast to move west in 1968 it was primarily to work with a group of San Francisco activists known as the Diggers. One of their founders, Peter Berg, had once teased di Prima on an earlier reading trip to the Bay Area, "Your writing helped bring all of this about, now come and enjoy the fruits." The Diggers would initially proclaim their presence by serving free food in the long and shaded park adjacent to Golden Gate known as the Panhandle. Berg has said that they were actually more interested in getting the attention of the people in cars driving down the street, passing the food line. He hoped that they would wonder why these young people were standing around outside and eating and that eventually they would see no reason not to join them. Placing the word "free" in front of anything was another tactic of theirs; they operated a free store in the Lower Haight, an on-the-spot art experiment which ran for three years. A lot of its goods were donations from large supermarkets, crates of melons, things that would go to waste otherwise. And the Diggers would also spread the donations to a network of communes that had sprung up around San Francisco.

The original mimeograph edition of *Revolutionary Letters* was published in 1968 by the Diggers' own imprint, Communications Company. Subsequent 1968 editions were produced by the Poetry Project at St. Mark's Church in New York City and the Artists' Workshop Press in Ann Arbor. The first international edition was produced in 1969 in London by Long Hair Books. I love that three separate, rabid underground printings of the book began almost immediately, a palpable sign of oncoming insurrection. Di Prima has described her outlook on publishing and distribution of the *Letters* as being tied to her early anarchist beliefs:

> People could hear them and would do whatever they wanted with it. I'm an anarchist, my grandfather on my mother's side was an anarchist who wrote with Carlo Tresca for his newspaper, and I tended to have that way with my politics. I never joined anything but I wrote a lot and put it out to be used however.

What feels most important to say is that *Revolutionary Lett*ers remains an ongoing series. Despite di Prima adding new poems with each subsequent edition (six editions in all now), people tend to confine its concerns to the late sixties or early 1970's, almost to freeze it where it began at those first nine flatbed truck poems. But in fact, the "Revolutionary Letter" is a form di Prima would take with her on the road when she began to work with Poets in the Schools, from 1971-78. This outreach would take her all over the country, including teaching in the Hopi and Navajo reservation schools, and teaching the children of farm workers in Salinas, California. I want to be sure and get a few of the later *Letters* in here. This is dated August 2, 1984:

Revolutionary Letter #72: A Spell for the Children of the Poor

Here
is a camera for Obsidian
of Thunder Mountain, Nevada, tour guide
who cares for her mother & all
her brothers & sisters, whose eyes

turn always toward the highway;   & a
lifetime supply of charcoal & pens
& brushes for Melissa, black girl who lives
next door to me in the Fillmore where the grocer
refuses to give her eggs if she's 2¢ short   & she's always
2¢ short,   her mom
spent the last five dollars on codeine
'cause she hurts.   &

notebooks by the dozen for Erlinda
Shakespeare, Shoshone, age 12 who was
afraid to write more on her great
long poem 'cause the notebook we gave her
(Poetry In The Schools, 1972) was running out &
notebooks
            cost 35¢

          There *is* enough paper
Erlinda, and paint, and a violin
for your brother
        & all the leotards
anybody wants
        on Webster St, in
Hunters Point.
     Here's a drum set,
another,   take the whole damn
music store,
     what are we
holding onto when you guys

are the only art that's News

This is a poem in the form of a giveaway, a potlatch that becomes a series of portraits calling attention to poverty. What are we holding onto? This is a great question to take up in poetry and one that might actually speed up a poem. Di Prima becomes intensely critical of the ways in which we allow class structure to deny various forms of expression to children of color. Di Prima makes class distinction seem in the way of possible greatness. She manages to convey a great sense of boredom about such values. Near the ending of the poem she restores us by saying the possibilities we place in the young go beyond class and that really what we need is access, literal paper and supplies and space and time. She assures us that the instrument can offer a pathway into the arts and that the greatest gift we can offer is a discipline. When I first read *Revolutionary Letters* in my twenties I seemed to miss out on the grief and compassion that so inform the sequence. "A Spell for the Children of the Poor" is a political poem but so personalized and well dispersed as portraiture that it slips in to do its work almost unnoticed, and the heart is reached.

Are the best of di Prima's poems those that compel the reader to act? The recurrent listing throughout the book helps to invite the reader into enacting the aspirations of her words. I think of the activist Assata Shakur's incredible statement, "I see myself struggling /in whatever way/ I can." I feel the same pulse running throughout di Prima's work, that to struggle or to be in the movement is an eternal and aspirational state, wherein poetic forms themselves are offered as strategies for change. I think again of Amiri Baraka, at the end of "A New Reality Is Better Than a New Movie!" where he attempts to refine and question our present-day movements and strategies for liberation:

> If you don't like it, what you gonna do about it. That was the question we asked each other, & still right regularly need to ask. You dont like it? Whatcha gonna do, about it?? The real terror of nature is humanity enraged, the true technicolor

spectacle that hollywood can't record. They cant even show you how you look when you go to work, or when you come back. They cant even show you thinking or demanding the new socialist reality, its the ultimate tidal wave. When all over the planet, men and women, with heat in their hands, demand that society be planned to include the lives and self determination of all the people ever to live. That is the scalding scenario with a cast of just under two billion that they dare not even whisper. Its called, "We Want It All…

The Whole World!"

We understand the way the frame hangs together throughout, that once a point of view is unlocked through a prompt, through a line, it becomes accessible and part of our new armory of voices. The list, the portrait, the chant: these are individual variations to our line that we must test our line against. Gaining and maintaining a stylistic virtuosity is part of revolutionary poetry, part of making it new for yourself. This is a quality of energy that the great poets can scare up over and over. "Revolutionary Letter #110" is an elegy, written after Baraka's death in 2014. He was an early collaborator, ally, and lover of Diane di Prima's, father of her second child, Dominique. I will read just the tail end of the poem:

> what matters:
>
> > every place
> > you read
> >
> > every line
> > you wrote
>
> every dog-eared book
> > or pamphlet
> on somebody's shelf

every skinny hopeful kid
you grinned that grin at

while they said
> *they thought they could write*
> *they thought they could fight*

they knew for sure
> *they could change the world*

every human dream
you heard
> or inspired

after the book-signing
after the reading
> after one more
> unspeakable
> faculty dinner

What matters:
> the memory

of the poem
> taking root in

thousands
> of minds…

• • •

The Cancer Journals came to be written as an attempt to break one silence, one aspect of the kinds of silences that we partake in as women. But I was also thinking as the announcements went on, Sarah mentioned Botha's visit here. Actually, it was not the prime minister, it was his brother, who was the foreign minister. I mean, well, it's about keeping it in the family. But it's pretty much the same. This has been in the wind for weeks, and I wonder how many of you agree, think it's fine, think it's wonderful, that even now, the policy of this country, which at least on paper was not accepting or underwriting apartheid in South Africa, is now in the process of being turned around . . . right? Do you know about it, how do you feel about it, how have you made your feelings known? Even a postcard, right? To Washington, that this is not acceptable, that South Africa is not to lie down with us . . . right? Or at least when it happens that there are people, there are voices in this country who resent it, who do not want this to happen. I mean, once we start thinking of ourselves as active people, once we realize that we have a power and that that power is relative, that we have a responsibility, I have a responsibility to speak out about what I feel, about what I think, that each one of you do, then the climate, then the whole aura begins to change. It becomes not one of simply acceptance, right?

What can we do about it? But a different stance, which is, I have a voice and I have to use it. So it's just something that I'd like you to keep in mind when you hear announcements, when you recognize things are happening that you do not wish to happen, that it's not enough just to say, "Isn't that terrible?" You have a responsibility to yourselves, to our lives!

That is from a 1982 Audre Lorde reading, from in between poems, speaking out on aparthied and the U.S. diplomacy around it. Apartheid would go on (officially) until April 27, 1994.

I have come to realize that my dream is not simply to turn students into revolutionary poets, but to turn them into compassionate teachers and publishers of the art themselves, not only teachers that land jobs at the university level, per se, but those with visions that are tied to the other kinds of community, purposely forming a free workshop. Establishing a time and meeting place for those that need to hear poetry in a group. Giving precedence to the emerging smaller networks just to see what happens. Or letting poets pay what they can. There is a long tradition of poets teaching out of their apartments, or their friends' apartments, having the same students for ten years or more.

Poetry has always been such an underground endeavor in my life, meaning that the tradition I stepped into was always excited to make its own stapled books. This impulse to have a press of my own was partly inspired by Diane di Prima's work as a printer. She would operate the Poets Press from 1964-1970, publishing over thirty titles. Once I read all of her poetry collections I looked into the books she herself had published, books like *Hunke's Journal*, Timothy Leary's *Psychedelic Prayers* and David Henderson's first collection, *Felix of the Silent Forest*. I was also inspired by the more punk aesthetic of *The Floating Bear*, a mimeographed newsletter of new writing that Di Prima would edit with Amiri Baraka (back then he was still LeRoi Jones).

I began to get caught up in the mythologies of these underground presses and their various overlays and offshoots. That is to say they began to occupy my imagination. Poets Press books are now relatively rare. Di Prima printed a lot of first books by poets as a way of offering not simply an object but an actualized pathway to the writer.

Di Prima published Audre Lorde's first book, a collection of poems titled *The First Cities*. The book was published in 1968, the same year di Prima began to write the *Revolutionary Letters*. She provides a short, illuminating, two-part introduction to Lorde's work. The first part is simply a catalogue of what di Prima finds appealing about the poetry:

> Audre Lorde's world is all colors. Its songs move through large areas of light & darkness.
>
> They take us with them through the landscape, which is circular like Chinese painting.

Part two simply says:

I have known Audre Lorde since we were fifteen, when we read our poems to each other in our Home Room at Hunter High school. And only two months ago she delivered my child.
   A woman's world, peopled with men & children and the dead, exotic as scallops.

The birth mentioned is that of Diane's fourth child, Tara Marlowe. She was delivered by Lorde on December 23rd, 1967, at The Albert Hotel, which was a residential hotel on University Place in the West Village. Di Prima would actually hold poetry readings in an old trunk room there during her year-long stay.

Di Prima's intro to *The First Cities* is prophetic of the work Audre Lorde would go on to do throughout the 1970s and into the '90s.

In her introduction to Lorde's collection of essays *Sister Outsider*, the editor of the Crossing Press, Nancy Bereano, writes tellingly of working with Lorde on the manuscript:

When we began editing *Sister Outsider*—long after the book had been conceptualized, a contract signed, and new material written—Audre Lorde informed me, as we were working one afternoon, that she doesn't write theory. "I am a poet," she said.

So then, for all of her transformative work in teaching, organizing, writing speeches, editing and publishing, all of this is regarded as belonging to the work of poetry. In fact, Audre Lorde was famous for how she introduced herself as a Black, lesbian, mother, warrior poet. The following is from an anthology titled *Woman Poet: The East* published in 1981. This is lifted from a section titled "Biographical Notes":

I am a black woman warrior poet doing my work. For poets and other live human beings, those designations used to widen and expand identity are precious, but those categories used to restrict or narrow identity are death.

In the interest of expanding identities, poetic and otherwise, you can say Lorde is woman, black lesbian, urban, mother, cantankerous, warrior, revolutionary, uppity, feminist and fat—all precious and inseparable aspects of my living that infuse energy into my work.

I write as I live, teach, love, garden, etc.—with the absolute conviction that all my activities are only different faces of the same task, surviving and spreading the word (teaching as a survival skill, the task facing all of us). By us I mean those who are moving through the categories meant to divide us, toward an acceptance of the creative need for human difference and the value of change.

I love her use of the phrase "moving through the categories meant to divide us," meaning that all of us must put in check that sense of obstruction when we first meet, that conditioning, whatever it is we can't get over or see past. Poetry is again helpful at showing ourselves. If we choose to meet and to study, together, we can't help but reveal something in common. The workshop becomes an arena so attuned to listening, especially as you get into the second, third, and fourth meetings. It is not just the writing element that sparks a trust between participants, it is also the reading of our work, sounding it out together. I try not to crush them with feedback; it can seem inorganic. I seem to prize a poet's simply reading yesterday's assignment aloud, in order for the mind to click forward.

I find the concision of language within her essay writing to be so disarming. The best description I have come across of first reading Audre Lorde's work belongs to the Afro-Caribbean writer and activist M. Jacqui Alexander who wrote: "But in honoring Audre

Lorde we are also honoring ourselves, our struggles and our victories, for whether or not we know of Lordes work, we have lived it."

When I first began to read her essays, Lorde's perceptions around race, sexuality, and class seemed to put me within reach of emotions I have kept buried for twenty years. Her writing has aided in dissolving some of my own (deranged) interpretations, thinking that I am in fact kept safe by not discussing aspects of race and sexuality, and largely because these elements get paraded around, or instantly processed as a rare and blinding amusement. I sensed this after going away to college and was bored immediately and never wanted to see that narrative again. I was already signaling (through the flames) against tokenism far into the future.

In her essay "Poetry is not a Luxury" Lorde writes:

> For women, then, poetry is not a luxury. It is a vital necessity of our existence. It forms the quality of the light within which we predicate our hopes and dreams toward survival and change, first made into language, then into idea, then into more tangible action. Poetry is the way we help give name to the nameless so it can be thought. The farthest horizons of our hopes and fears are cobbled by our poems, carved from the rock experiences of our daily lives.

Lorde has also helped me to see that terms like "confessional" are often class-ridden designations designed to divide us. Sometimes poets can literally not afford to shroud their language in objectivity. The source of the poem can be pain, and arranged into an object we cannot turn away from, like strains of a popular song stuck in your head. Audre Lorde has terms like "difference" and "survival" and "silence" that reoccur as strands throughout her essays. This sense for constant redefinition builds a coalition across her books. I would like to read what is perhaps her best-known poem. One that I began to cling to after the very first hearing. This is from Lorde's 1978 collection, titled *The Black Unicorn*:

A Litany for Survival

For those of us who live at the shoreline
standing upon the constant edges of decision
crucial and alone
for those of us who cannot indulge
the passing dreams of choice
who love in doorways coming and going
in the hours between dawns
looking inward and outward
at once before and after
seeking a now that can breed
futures
like bread in our children's mouths
so their dreams will not reflect
the death of ours;

For those of us
who were imprinted with fear
like a faint line in the center of our foreheads
learning to be afraid with our mother's milk
for by this weapon
this illusion of some safety to be found
the heavy-footed hoped to silence us
For all of us
this instant and this triumph
We were never meant to survive.

And when the sun rises we are afraid
it might not remain
when the sun sets we are afraid
it might not rise in the morning
when our stomachs are full we are afraid

of indigestion
when our stomachs are empty we are afraid
we may never eat again
when we are loved we are afraid
love will vanish
when we are alone we are afraid
love will never return
and when we speak we are afraid
our words will not be heard
nor welcomed
but when we are silent
we are still afraid

So it is better to speak
remembering
we were never meant to survive.

"We were never meant to survive": a million forms spring up around that statement and then get narrowed depending on who the "we" is. Who is the we? In my case it brings to mind the reality of the Suquamish People, our history as it is transposed to the present day. The fact that our longhouse was torched by Catholic missionaries in 1870, our ceremonies and songs and dances outlawed, our children forcibly removed from their parents and relocated to boarding schools, flagrant attempts (laws) to starve us out at every turn. It reminds me of the famous chief of the Suquamish and Duwamish tribes, Chief Seattle, and his speech during the treaty negotiations of 1854: "These shores will swarm with the invisible dead of my tribe.... In all the earth there is no place dedicated to solitude." This feels similar to Assata Shakur's statement, one I was leaning on earlier, "I see myself struggling in/ whatever way / I can" For those of us who continue to be imprisoned and harassed, silence becomes impossible, and moving toward insurrection becomes the only viable option. Or as Lorde would come to remind us so often in her collection *Sister Outsider*, "Your Silence Will Not Protect You." She provides her readers with so many lines to carry in mind. "The Master's Tools Will Never Dismantle the Master's House" is another classic. They tend to stick in your head after the first hearing.

I teach "A Litany for Survival" not only to allow students to feel acknowledged, but also to encourage them to speak out. This is why I say I cling to it. The transformation it brought to my writing hinged on the realization that I could use poetry to address personal and historical trauma, and that this could be an interesting objective going in. I was able to find a little background on the composition of "A Litany for Survival" in an essay of Lorde's titled "My Words Will Be There," first published in 1983:

> I went through a period when I felt like I was dying. It was during 1975. I wasn't writing any poetry, and I felt that if I couldn't write it, I would split. I was recording these things in my journal, but no poems came. I know now that this period was a transition in my life and I wasn't dealing with it.
>
> Later the next year, I went back to my journal, and there were these incredible poems that I could almost lift out of the journal; many of them are in *The Black Unicorn*. "Harriet" is one of them; "Sequelae" is another. "A Litany for Survival" is another. These poems were right out of the journal. But I didn't see them as poems prior to that...
>
> I write this stuff in my journals, and sometimes I can't even read my journals because there is so much pain, rage, in them. I'll put them away in a drawer and six months, a year or so later, I'll pick up the journal and there will be poems. The journal entries somehow have to be assimilated into my living, and only then can I deal with what I have written down.

It did not surprise me to learn that this classic poem almost went unrecognized. When we write poetry we sometimes have to lock it away at the ending stages, almost with the intention of letting it dry like glue or a piece of pottery. It's a recognition that art might have to catch up with our experience of everyday reality. The poet is so far out in front but doesn't quite realize it until later.

Audre Lorde and Diane di Prima would continue to work and read together until Lorde's death from liver cancer in 1992. Lorde would publish di Prima's work as poetry editor of the feminist magazine *Chrysalis* in 1980. Di Prima would publish an additional collection of Lorde's poetry titled *Between Our Selves* in 1976 on her new imprint, Eidolon Editions. These poems would later be incorporated into *The Black Unicorn*. The cover for *Between Our Selves* is a drawing by Lorde of a symbol she had discovered in Ghana, depicting two crocodiles whose trunks intersected. Di Prima remembers Lorde being very particular as to the color of this image. "Audre said that she wanted an all brown book." Here is the opening stanza of the title poem, "Between Our Selves":

> Once when I walked into a room
> my eyes would seek out the one or two black faces
> for contact or reassurance or a sign
> I was not alone
> now walking into rooms full of black faces
> that would destroy me for any difference
> where shall my eyes look?
> Once it was easy to know
> who were my people.

Lorde herself would start Kitchen Table: Women of Color Press in 1980. This was a press collective founded and operated by lesbians of color, including Barbara Smith, Cherríe Moraga, Hattie Gossett, Leota Lone Dog, and others. Lorde's essays "Apartheid U.S.A."

and "I Am Your Sister," later included in *A Burst of Light*, were first published as Kitchen Table Press pamphlets.

I did want to speak more pointedly about the list, the chant, as repetition is a common formal element in much of the poetry I have read tonight. The fantasy of a truly binding tracery of light. The poet Joy Harjo writes beautifully of both its influence and its effect:

> Incantation and chant call something into being. They make a ceremonial field of meaning. Much of world poetry is incantation and chant. The poem that first made me truly want to become a poet was sung and performed by a healer in Southeast Asia. He appeared in a documentary I found on television. As he sang and performed the poem he became what he was singing/speaking, and even as he sang and spoke, his words healed his client.

Both *Revolutionary Letters* and "A Litany for Survival" are good examples of a poet becoming what she is singing/speaking. We write the world we want to live in, calling it into being, and then make that dispersal available as a book, a recording, a form to step right into. The list can become a deceptively simple entrance.

It is often dependent on a short, recurring, breathless rhythm that feels easy to depart from and even easier to shoot right back into, with time allowed for minor excursions. It can be put to work as an invocation, a repetition pushed to the point of delirium which reads as pure freedom or free union. This is a poem titled "Complicity" by Jayne Cortez:

> Who likes to glitter
> Who likes to smell blood
> Who likes to be real imperialistic
> real corrupt
> Trade all the gold for a mercedes-benz

>   Trade all the oil for a Peugeot
>   Trade all the uranium for a rolls royce
>   Trade all the peanuts for a villa above the Riveria
>   Trade all the cocoa for a ski lodge in Grenoble
>   Trade all the traditional art for a case of champagne
>   Trade all the cobalt for a swiss bank account
>   Who will buy the outmoded mold
>   Who will buy the outdated rust
>   Who will make a billion dollar deal
>   to store radioactive waste
>   Who likes to glitter
>   Who likes to smell blood
>   Who likes to be real imperialistic
>   real corrupt

If you think up a good title, a filter in advance like "Complicity," you can coax your imagination word by word or action by action as in a play. Reading a list poem aloud can help to negotiate the bare bones of narrative. It clings to and flatters those rhythms that tumble out easily. The reader is allowed to climb back down from the apex and the path is always kept clear.

This refining through repetition reminds me of another quote I have been carrying around recently. In an interview, Joy Harjo was asked what she felt was possible at this point in terms of reclamation through Native poetry. Harjo remarked that her intention is "not to reverse history but to draw out the strength." This is the continuous, transformative duty of the poet, to find the poetic *means* by which we can draw out further strength.

Diane di Prima has a great refrain throughout one of the longer, later *Revolutionary Letters*—#105, titled "Fire Sale"—in which she keeps repeating, "we need to look / *Not at what's wrong / But what is possible* // What wd your fantasy   your imagination say / if reality were no obstacle."

Or Audre Lorde again, repeating what is at stake: "Teaching as a survival skill, the task facing all of us."

In a journal entry dated December 16, 1985, Lorde writes:

> Even *Our Dead Behind Us*—now that it has gone to the printer—seems prophetic. Like always, it feels like I plant what I will need to harvest, without consciousness.
>
> That is why the work is so important. Its power doesn't lie in the me that lives in the words so much as in the heart's blood pumping behind the eye that is reading, the muscle behind the desire that is sparked by the word—hope as a living state that propels us, open-eyed and fearful, into all [of] the battles of our lives. And some of those battles we do not win.
>
> But some of them we do.

(2018)

On Property and Monstrosity

Julie Carr

> If you asked me what God I believed in in political philosophy, it would have to be the notion that there is no such thing as individual freedom, that human freedom is finally, always, a project of making a world with others.
>
> —*Wendy Brown*[11]

We bought a 1954 gas station surrounded by fruit trees—apple, pear, peach, plumb, apricot, and cherry—planted a decade ago by Dan, the previous owner, who, in addition to gardening, made soccer goals there (Goal Oriented was the name of his business). Three years ago, Dan's wife died and, after that, he let things go. Compass weed (an opiate) and thistle (good for tea) grew thigh-high all around the

---

[11] Wendy Brown, et al., "Learning to Love Again: An Interview with Wendy Brown," *Contretemps* 6 (January 2006).

trees. Volunteer elm sprung up to compete for light, water, and soil. Berry vines choked tree trunks, spiraling, twining, and scratching our ankles with their thorns. All of this had to be cleared, once in the fall and then again when it all came back in the spring.

There was also a vegetable garden to recreate—beds to clear (again, the weeds)—raised beds to build, soil and compost to transport in our little Ford pickup with its broken doors, broken blinkers, broken window, and broken bed gate, so that we had to stand in the truck bed shoveling the soil and compost out, one heavy shovelful at a time. There was planting to do—some things went in too early, others maybe too late—an irrigation system had to be created and then, when the dog got to it, repaired. The strawberry patch weeded and then, when the birds ate the berries, netted. Rose vines, mostly dead wood, grew up and into and around the chain-link that surrounded the garden, and for many days, weeks really, we cut away the dead wood and tied up the vines to the fence again where, miraculously in June, they all bloomed—tight little red ones, outrageous orange, flimsy white, baby pink, sexy pink, and even creamy yellow. Finally, after all this, with everything coming up, we turned to the area outside the fence.

Two great big apple trees grew from what could have been the sidewalk, but where there was no walk, only weeds and the trees. Russian sage, mint, compass weed, various grasses, and dandelion. The trees hadn't been pruned for so long they were almost unrecognizable as apples, so thick with shoots and so entangled with the mess that surrounded them. It was daunting to begin, but we did begin, spraying vinegar on the weeds first, so we could yank them more easily, then, armed with clippers, saws, shovels, but mostly just our gloved hands, yanking and hacking away.

I say we, but at first it was just me. HR was planting wildflowers around the rose bushes. Jessica, with her eleven-month-old baby on her back and her five-year-old by her feet, was sawing the dead branches we hoped to turn to mulch. Sam was working the irrigation system. Petra was planting more spinach and carrots. I was sitting alone, cross-legged in the shade of the tree, smelling mint and sage, pulling from the roots—then, when I got tired of sitting, standing to pull, then sitting again. There were so many weeds I didn't have to move much to get them, just shift a bit my angle and I'd meet a whole new crew.

But gradually, I was moving in toward the trunk of the tree, into its dark cool center, which at first I could not see. And then, there was an object. I startled. I was, of course, afraid, as if a suitcase out of place were a body out of place, and not just the sign of one. A suitcase—a pretty nice one, zipped up—a shoulder bag, also zipped, and a plastic bag holding a pair of sneakers. These items were neatly arranged, not tossed. They belonged to someone.

No body, though perhaps a body's markings—the weeds near the bags had been flattened. It seemed someone had been sleeping there in that quiet cave of leaves.

In May 2012, Denver City Council approved an urban camping ban, an ordinance sponsored by Councilman Albus Brooks. Other cities have them. In fact, thirty-four percent of American cities ban camping in public; eighteen percent ban sleeping in public.[12] Making it illegal to sleep outdoors means, to state the obvious, that those who are unhoused have to sleep in a shelter (that there are not enough beds does not even need to be said), risk arrest (and the subsequent criminal record as well as fines), or find a place to hide. Some cities don't have such bans and instead designate areas for the homeless to sleep, providing services in these locations, but Denver has gone the other way.

The building was for Counterpath—the nonprofit community art and performance space my husband, Tim Roberts, and I run—in

---

12 Tony Robinson and Alison Sickels, *No Right to Rest: Criminalizing Homelessness in Colorado,* Denver Homeless Outloud, 20.

which we'd recently hosted "Neighborhood History Day," "A Blind Date with Democracy," "The Open Opening" (to which anyone could bring art to display, art of any kind), a feminism and philosophy conference dance party, the launch for eleven-year-old Patrick's online journal of jokes, magic spells, acrostics, and palindromes, and many other such events for poets, performers, activists, and artists. The garden was for anyone who wanted to work in it and eat from it. A portion of all food grown would be donated to soup kitchens in the area. The idea for the apples was that once we'd cleared the area around the trees, we'd prune the trees back to health. I didn't know if it would work, but I hoped that the trees would produce fruit in abundance again. And maybe the kids who lived on the block, Cornelius, Cordelia, Cortrelle, and their cousin Asia, or just anyone walking by, could eat that fruit next September and October, and I could make applesauce and pies.

But when I saw the bags, I didn't know whether what I was currently doing made any sense. Gently, I pushed the bags further in—and what, exactly, did this accomplish? Was there some lesson waiting to be learned from the suitcase under the tree, for example, or from the other thing on my mind—that I was clearing these weeds and making this garden in the immediate wake of a massacre—forty-nine people who went only to dance and to be with one another, mostly young, gay, trans, Latinx, all already by this country at this time punished, made vulnerable for nothing but being? I was clearing these weeds and making this garden while every seventeen minutes somewhere in the country another person was shot. Though humble, and maybe stupidly so, I hoped that the clearing was a peaceful act, an act *for* peace, and not just a private one, one that would extend, more than many things I did, beyond me.

It seemed, even, there could be a parable, or more modestly a metaphor, in such clearing. And then, there was, but it wasn't the metaphor I had imagined.

Days later the bags were still there, untouched, and still I did not remove them, even as I removed sage, brome, shepherd's purse, mint, and cut the dead branches from the tree, cautiously, slowly now, with less certainty, less pride, trying not to cut any healthy branches, any with apples, failing in this regard.

I once had a friend named Itty Neuhaus, an artist who specialized in placing objects where they should not be. Her breakthrough work, "Padded Landing," suspended an entire car frame in a net from the underside of a bridge in Manhattan, traffic flowing over top. This unlikely act, placing the car under instead of on the bridge, set her career in a particular direction. When I met her, she was soaking the oddly named "husbands"—those pillows with the little arms that people used to lean on in bed. Itty placed three husbands in a kind of circle, like a witches' coven, and then, methodically, got them wet—sprinklers set up in the gallery to rain.

Itty was interested in the body, too, particularly the female body, because of how it swells and shrinks, in puberty, in pregnancy, but also just in the less predictable ways of weight gain or loss. The swollen soaked pillow, the suspended car, the distended body, and bread dough—one of her central materials in those years—all of these things, in their ungainliness, their monstrosity, their escape, you could say, from form into new form, or formlessness, were her muse. Mostly, she was interested in instability or dissonance, how a house made of bread dough would rise and then rot, how a pillow soaked would expand and then collapse, and how placing an object where it did not belong made the space itself unstable, even untenable, no longer itself. All this came to mind as I considered the suitcase under the tree, unwilling to move it or look inside.

"The body presents the paradox of contained and container at once. Thus our attention is continually focused upon the boundaries or limits of the body," writes Susan Stewart in her essay "The Imaginary Body." And then later, "We want to know what is the body and what is not."[13]

But what if the body was never this thing—never a form that could be provoked or perverted into a monstrosity—entered and expanded, soaked or cut, and thereby un-made or made other? What if the form of the body or the form of the city is already not and will never be what we thought it was, what we are told it should be: a clarity, a perfection, a completion? What if there really is no shape of a tree to prune for, no garden to reinvent, and therefore no weed or brush to clear, no health or wholeness to return to?

In her seminal essay analyzing the particular cruxes of patriarchy and white supremacy in America, "Mama's Baby, Papa's Maybe: An American Grammar Book," Hortense Spillers considers the difference between body and flesh. "But I would make a distinction in this case between 'body' and 'flesh' and impose that distinction as the central one between captive and liberated subject-positions," she begins, and then goes on to note William Goodell's 1853 study of the American Slave Code, in which he details the precise acts of terror that will turn body to flesh: "The smack of the whip is all day long in the ears of those who are on the plantation, or in the vicinity; and it is used with such dexterity and severity as not only to lacerate the skin, but to tear out small portions of the flesh at almost every stake."[14]

Reading this, or reading so many things available if we should seek them out, is to be reminded, if we need to be, that the fantasy of a whole and un-ruptured *social body* is a fantasy that rests, in the history of our country, against the forced flesh of the slave, just as the fantasy

---

13   Susan Stewart, "The Imaginary Body," in *On Longing: Narratives of the Miniature, the Gigantic, the Souvenir, the Collection* (Durham, NC: Duke University Press, 1992), 104–105.

14   Hortense Spillers, "Mama's Baby, Papa's Maybe: An American Grammar Book," in *Black, White and in Color: Essays on American Literature and Culture* (Chicago: University of Chicago Press, 2003), 207.

of the well-functioning affluent city, the dream city we are trying to make, is built on a foundation of criminality, on land that was only ever stolen.[15]

To discover the suitcase under the tree, to read the massacre's list of names, to remember that it is precisely when the border between inner and outer is broken that the body becomes flesh, is to know once more that the collective that is our dream-nation is *already* broken, already torn by its own brutality, both historic and present. To clear land Tim and I as Counterpath have purchased, is, in some sense, in the context of our city, to add to such brutality, even as growing food for the families of our friends and neighbors, for the students, or for others who we do not know is some attempt to heal what we, even before such purchases were made, have already done or already are.[16]

My copy of William Carlos Williams's great book *Paterson* shows the signs of my needs. The pages are marked, Post-its adorn it, dog-eared corners rip at their seams, fallen out pages have been stuck back

---

15 Who is the "we" that needs reminding? Anne-Lise Francois speaks of the "open secret" as that readily available information that only those with power can choose not to see. What I'm calling Spiller's "reminder" of the material history of flesh-making will only be a reminder to those of us who can, for reasons of wealth or whiteness or both, afford to forget. Anne-Lise Francois, *Open Secrets: The Literature of Uncounted Experience* (Stanford, CA: Stanford University Press, 2007).

16 My own great-grandfather, Omer Madison Kem, was a homesteader, moving from Indiana, where he'd been a destitute farmer, to the "free land" in Nebraska, free for whites because taken from the Otoe Indians. This land he also failed to farm. Instead, he turned to the far-left anti-capitalist political party, Populism, running for and winning a seat in the House of Representatives, which he held from 1891–1897. The success of his political career allowed him to purchase land near Montrose, Colorado, the former home of the Ute Indians. On this land he, like his great-granddaughter, attempted to raise apples.

in upside down or in the wrong place. I have written so much in its margins that it's almost a kind of journal.

What might be in that book that answers such needs, or at least describes them? The book, already a monstrosity, becomes more so each year that I pull it apart to teach it, to learn it, again. A book like that, read so many times, starts to draw apart from its author. It's not that it becomes mine, but that it becomes an appendage of myself, a growth of me from outside of me.

Paterson opens on monsters, a giant (the character "Paterson" himself) lying along the falls. And beyond him, "oozy fields / abandoned to grey beds of dead grass, / black sumac, withered weedstalks, / mud and thickets cluttered with dead leaves—"[17]: a place a lot like the place I'm in, crammed with growth not wanted, or not called for, uncalled-for excess that threatens to burst the word "field" or the word "garden" and destroy it.

A few pages later, we find "a monster in human form," he is twenty-seven years of age, his face, from the upper part of his forehead to the end of his chin, measures *twenty-seven inches,* and around the upper part of his head is twenty-one inches: his eyes and nose are remarkably large and prominent, chin long and pointed. His features are coarse, irregular, and disgusting, his voice rough and sonorous. His body is twenty-seven inches in length, his limbs are small and much deformed, and he has use of one hand only.[18]

This composite man, who lies in a cradle but cracks jokes with clerics, presents a problem of truth. Though this description is lifted directly from Neil Baldwin and Henry Howe's *Historical Collections of the State of New Jersey (1844),* the coincidence of the number twenty-seven makes of the man's "monstrosity" a myth and a metaphor. And,

---

17 William Carlos Williams, *Paterson* (New York: New Directions Publishing, 1946), 7.

18 Ibid., 10.

indeed, Williams provides us with what could be called his "tenor" in the very next prose paragraph, which details the town of Paterson's population just seventy years after Alexander Hamilton saw fit to fund its development into America's first planned industrial city: "There were in 1870, native born 20,711, which would of course include children of foreign parents; foreign 12,868 of whom 237 were French, 1,429 German, 3,343 English—(Mr. Lambert who later built the Castle among them), 5,124 Irish, 879 Scotch, 1,360 Hollanders and 170 Swiss."[19]

That such rapid and diverse growth is seen by Williams as a kind of perversity is underscored by the third prose passage in the group. Here, he borrows a news item from 1817 that describes the catching of an enormous 126 lb. sturgeon under the heading "The Monster Taken."

But what is Williams's attitude toward these "monsters"? How are we to understand his feelings about his rapidly grown mash-up of a city (and book)? Such instability is, we learn, his source, his muse. The monstrous, the obscene—of poverty, but not only poverty, also grieving, age, sexuality, even childhood—provides him with the "things" or "facts" he needs to write from.

> A delirium of solutions, forthwith, forces
> him into back streets, to begin again:
> up hollow stairs among acrid smells
> to obscene rendezvous. And there he finds
> a festering sweetness of red lollipops-
> and yelping dog:
> Come YEAH, Chichi! Or a great belly
> that no longer laughs but mourns
> with its expressionless black navel love's

---

19 Ibid., 10.

deceit...
They are the divisions and imbalances
of his whole concept, made weak by pity,
flouting desire, they are—No ideas but
in the facts...[20]

A man cares for a younger man in the café where I write. The man being cared for doesn't speak, rocks back and forth, makes unexpected and loud noises, stands suddenly and bursts for the door. In another age, he might have been considered dangerous, he might have been kept away, he might not have been cared for at all. Today, the man caring for him catches his elbow, gently restraining. The younger man, groaning, pushes the other's hand off, so that the caring man takes his waist instead. Again, pushed off. Standing in the way of the door, he speaks urgently but quietly: "I'm down with going wherever you want to go, but you just have to tell me, you can't just jump up!" After a longer struggle involving various attempts to bolt, the first man coaxes the other back to the couch where they settle, finally, into reading. The agitated man is lying down now, his head resting in the lap of his caretaker. The reading man's hand lies on the other's forehead exactly as if checking for a fever. He reads out loud, pausing to drink from his water bottle (using only his reading hand, not moving the other from the forehead), until finally the other man is asleep. The first man continues to read, but now silently, with the younger man's head in his lap.

A week later, Counterpath sets up our performance tent at City Park Jazz, the free summer concerts we'd been invited to collaborate with. For ten consecutive weekends, we publish a chapbook that corresponds with a performance or installation in the tent. This time, two dancers, Lauren Beale and Brooke McNamara, dressed in golden

---

20 Ibid., 27.

bathing suits, perform; the tent's been set up to look like a fifties living room. Meanwhile, Hazel Miller sings on stage, and I wander down through the picnicking people so that I can also dance with the collective of kids, couples, and folks on their own, barefoot or in cocktail dresses, in their flamboyant freestyle or dance-class swing. There, I see the young man from the café, dancing with a woman who appears to be his mother. She moves her body in a kind of semicircle of protection, dancing with him, but also around him, so that, I guess, he can't easily bolt. But he doesn't seem to want to, they are having so much fun. Her necklace of beads swings free of her chest; his curls bob. Their private agreement extends into the crowd: everyone gives them a little extra room, as if dancing were a brief and contingent healing, a slipping stroke, and care itself only and ever a momentary and minor gesture.

Williams' interest in dissonant, out-of-place, or monstrous events and entities runs throughout the five books of *Paterson*. One could say it is the work's central theme. A lakebed writhing with eels, a man's body caught between logs and dangling above the falls, a dead horse in the sewer, the "deformed and mutilated verses" of the Greek poet Hipponax, the monstrous acts of the natural world—fires, floods, and earthquakes—and of the human—murders and rapes.

Significantly, one of Williams' later objects of fascination is the irradiated and pregnant body of Marie Curie, her "fetid womb"—a metaphor for the world itself—which occupies the better part of the second section of Book IV, dated 1951. But to say "metaphor" is too simple here. In the fourth book of *Paterson*, "constellation" is probably the better term, as womb/world/bomb/atom/book link together, versions of one another or parts of a whole. One could say that in this section, Williams' interest in monstrosity becomes monstrous in itself, as physics and chemistry in their most heinous application become symbolic of human and creative transformation. Or, as Williams put it, rather horrifically in 1948, "one great thing about 'the bomb' is the awakened sense it gives us that catastrophic… alterations are also possible in the human *mind*, in art, in the arts…

We are too cowed by our fears to realize it fully. But it is *possible*. That is what we mean. This isn't optimism, it is chemistry: Or better, physics."[21] As Marianne Boruch acerbically noted in 1985, "It's hard to think straight—that is kindly—about such remarks."[22] And yet, with Boruch and others, we recognize that Williams was not blithe in his engagement with science, whether medical or atomic. The engagement was deep, and the connections he tried to draw between twentieth-century eruptions in science and those he instigated in poetry were in no way trivial. Further, his relationship to the bomb as "image" shifts significantly over the years. In *Paterson*, we find an early, hesitant, and in many ways uninformed application. But for this reason, in particular, I turn to it, trying to find there an indication of what a poetics of dissonance, of fission, of monstrosity might deliver. Perhaps even more to discover "how the twentieth-century mind becomes alert to its own recklessness" (Boruch)[23] in order to become more alert to my own.

The section opens on a rare scene of paternal attention. Williams remembers taking his teenaged son to a lecture on atomic fission. And yet, this scene begins quickly to break apart into a confused or "fetid" swarm of references—parenthood, poetry, Curie and the 1943 film *Madame Curie*, Billy Sunday's evangelism, and finally a letter from Williams' other (true?) son, Allen Ginsberg. At one point, a "poem" emerges, recognizable as such by way of indentation and Williams' use of his "triadic-line":

---

21 William Carlos Williams, "The Poem as a Field of Action" from *Selected Essays of William Carlos Williams* (New York: New Directions Publishing, 1954).

22 Marianne Boruch, "Williams and the Bomb," in *In the Blue Pharmacy: Essays on Poetry and Other Transformations* (San Antonio, TX: Trinity University Press, 2005), 38.

23 Ibid., 41.

> A dissonance
> in the valence of Uranium
> led to the discovery
> Dissonance
> (if you are interested)
> leads to discovery
> —to dissect away
> the block and leave
> a separate metal:
> hydrogen
> the flame, helium the
> pregnant ash[24]

This description of the transmutation of the unstable element uranium was written, of course, in the wake of Nagasaki and Hiroshima. And yet, the "dissonance" of uranium is evoked here, as throughout, more for its potential to bring forth the new—for the "pregnancy" of its ash—than for the cataclysmic damage that its "little boy" had, only a few years prior, wreaked upon an entire nation.

Images of perverse or violent (re)production occur over this handful of pages with an alarming range. Here is just a partial list: a nurse with abdominal "disturbances"; Curie's own laboring mind, her "ponderous belly, full / of thought"; the city itself, "that complex atom / always breaking down"; the sun parting the "labia" of the "shabby" clouds (echoing the rapes of previous pages); and, finally, the developing debt required to fund the Cold War, which Williams equates with uranium, presumably for how debt is both generative and destructive. None of this resolves. To resolve would be, in fact, to belie the aesthetics of fissure, which only wants to mushroom outward and upward in never-ending expansion, just

---

24 Williams, *Paterson*, 175.

as the "spreading" "splendor" of America's cities grows and grows, fueled by the "radiant gist" that is national or personal debt.[25] Which is to say, in this section of *Paterson* we are given to understand the core of violence that both sustains and damns the fecundity we enjoy.

Property values in Denver have been rising this decade at faster rates than in any other non-coastal city in the country—marginally outpaced only by Seattle, Portland, and San Francisco. In 2015, the average home price in Denver was $500,000, with one-bedroom apartments within a ten mile radius of the city averaging $1,600 a month in rent. Meanwhile, a full-time minimum-wage worker earns just $1,300 a month (the problem was growing increasingly worse).[26] On Colfax Avenue, one block north of the garden, runs a two-mile stretch of one- and two-story motels: Sand and Sage, Airway Motel, The Branding Iron, The Driftwood. These motels with their evocative names are the topic of much conversation at neighborhood meetings. On the one hand, prostitution and drug-related activities; on the same hand, homeless families.[27] There are currently 23,300 documented homeless students in Colorado's public schools, a number that has tripled during the same decade that Denver has "enjoyed" its real-estate boom.

> Here's to the baby,
> may it thrive!
> Here's to the labia
> that rive

---

25 Ibid., 176–85.

26 Statistics from Denver Homeless Outloud and Chad Kautzer, eds., *The Struggle for Space: Homelessness and the Politics of Dys-appearance in American Cities*, Denver Homeless Outloud, 27.

27 These motels are also the topic of the excellent short documentary film, *Colfax Motels*, by Corky Scholl.

to give it place
in a stubborn world.
And here's to the peak
from which the seed was hurled![28]

This brief and aggressive celebration of sexual reproduction from Book IV is nestled between two tributes, the first to the Passaic River: "My serpent, great river! genius of the fields," and the second, an almost verbatim steal from an early twentieth-century text titled *A Little Story of Old Paterson as Told by an Old Man*, which describes the town of Paterson as it might have looked circa 1700. The striking aspects of these otherwise pastoral idylls are the vicious histories they almost casually allude to. For the tribute to the river opens with a reported conversation with a "Jap": "Yellow, for genius, the Jap said. Yellow / is your color."[29] We are reminded, if elusively and with unclear intentions, of the period's anti-Japanese sentiment. We are reminded, too, of the true horrors of the bomb that in previous pages has only been discussed in scientific or metaphoric terms. This is, in fact, Williams' only mention or allusion to Japan, and though it is unclear what work he thought it was doing, the moment presents an undeniable and bitter cry. The passages taken from *A Little Story* nostalgically mention "branching trees and ample gardens," but also make reference to "The wigwam and the tomahawk, the Totowa tribe," as well as to the "colored slaves" of eighteenth-century Paterson.[30] Again, intentionality is vague, but effect is clear. There is no growth, no Paterson at all (as there is no Denver), without the stolen lands and stolen bodies beneath, behind, and within its history.

---

28 Williams, *Paterson*, 192.

29 Ibid.

30 Ibid., 193–94.

What am I to do, then, with this book and its strained and "vulgar" attempts to bring together, between its pages, the brutally murdered, the beaten, the silenced, the disregarded, the forgotten and violent histories of a town, all while it attempts to make of such monstrosities an adequate and productive metaphor for writing?

Paterson dwells in monstrosity in order to find in difference a source of energy, even health. But, despite how uranium's "dissonance" seems so conveniently to fall within the range of dissonances Williams celebrates, the bomb can never *be* an image, can never really *be* a metaphor. And perhaps no act of violence, no matter how local, how precise, how unintentional, can be harnessed for its metaphoric uses without doing further damage to the flesh that suffers.

Counterpath took root in a rented storefront, a building purchased in 2014 by developers who immediately quintupled the rent. We were lucky enough to buy outright the 1954 gas station, drawing on. We bought the building with the savings tax-deductible donations from Tim's business had put away, in case his business (academic book production and university press publishing) fell into hard times, and with some money from my parents, who had just sold the building that had housed my father's business (the architecture firm of Stephen Carr and Kevin Lynch, themselves seminal theorists of participatory urban design) for over thirty years. That is, we bought the building with family wealth and job security, as it's only my tenured job that allowed us to take that risk. The diseased tree hiding the baggage that I will not open, that belongs to someone who does not return for it, grows along the border between public and private land, though in fact, the property, being owned not by us but by the nonprofit that is Counterpath, hovers between these two poles.[31] The tree's seeming

---

31 Because the property belongs to Counterpath, we as individuals can never profit from its sale. Any profit would have to be folded back into the organization. This legal detail does not, however, make any difference at all to the person who had been sleeping under the tree.

illness, its monstrosity, how it is barely recognizable as a tree, is, it now seems, a kind of health for how it has sheltered someone's survival. And yet, even this health hides a greater illness, for it's a city's lack of structural care that makes such fragile temporary shelter a solution.

In my effort to heal the tree, cutting layers of blight away branch by branch, I perform a service and a disservice. In pruning it, I find myself unwittingly enacting the very "pruning" that my city has chosen as law. "To be situated in a position of greater social power produces the social privilege of not seeing how the interests and concerns associated with one's…social location have deeply informed the physical and social world to the disadvantage of those occupying different social locations," I read,[32] and do not know what to do. It had seemed that if I could heal the tree, then I could heal something else as well. It had seemed that the apple tree in its eternal metaphor might, once producing fruit, represent the hope for a healed body, a healed city, a healed country. And in that dream, children emerge from the houses—my children, the children of my students and friends, the children from across the street, and those in the motels on Colfax—they all come to eat. But the tree was never really a metaphor, or its metaphor was, by me, misread. Porous, soaked, rotting, blighted, sending out shoots, trying to live, the knowledge it offered was not waiting to be uncovered like some pure and virginal body, but was there all along within its depths, in its imperfections, in its flesh.

(2016)

---

32 Chad Kautzer, "Homelessness, Dys-Appearance and Resistance," in *The Struggle for Space*, 12.

Collective Action

Jos Charles

In the description for this panel, I was struck most by a word that did not appear but seemed to haunt it—or I thought it appeared, but when I looked back it wasn't there—a word perhaps out-of-fashion or charged. The word I'm thinking is *community* and how it lingers in words like gathering, collectivity, comradeship; the way it has become both disavowed and therefore fixed and overdetermined. I focus on community because in that word—I feel it—is the kind of question which concerns us here, of how to give credence to the gathering, the collective, and so on, without giving way to hegemony. Now, we know, there is no such thing as counter-hegemony—no police except *the* police, no prisons except prisons. Which is to say, I do not mean to suggest communities across power and historical and cultural relations are the same. I mean to try and suggest something about this word here and now, the sense in which it is not spoken at times and yet at others too spoken, aspirational, ahistoric. For we also know that hegemony swallows those in resistance to it, whole communities, it can and it has, and one of the challenges in collectivity is precisely how to anticipate its relation to the powers that be, the unceasing electoral representations and voices hegemony speaks even while continuing its old violences. Utilizing Georges Bataille and Jean-Luc Nancy as a starting point for terminology rather than as an embrace of their stance, I'd like to consider this word *community* we state and don't state, even now, as I speak across such distance, imagined but real distances, to you today.

When I began writing this, I was struck by how difficult it is to begin without defining community and how much more difficult it is to define. This is in part due to a metaphysical tradition—even, or especially, in its so-called end—which has presupposed a detached individual who freely enters and exits communities, engaging in contracts, markets, intracommunal ethics, and relations, only to leave and enter consensually anew, rather than an individual coterminous with community, emerging and differentiating itself from community, even as individuals come to shape it. Therefore, the constitutive capacity of the community has been left largely unthematized, even as some of the resistances within and to this tradition have been. Even in the systematic treatments dealt with here, the meaning of community is generally assumed as given. However, given the proximity of Bataille and Nancy's texts used here to 1945, a sense of the community as the fascist state eagerly wishing to (re)establish itself pervades these texts, pushing the operation or work of community to the fore, community as the work of its continuance. As such, however, there is also a distrust toward the idea of community which may be lost on the word today: considered more often as elective, a chosen set of practices or identities, than fascistic.

Which is to say community is something disavowed, as exemplified in the former, even as it is central, as the latter, to current political concerns. For instance, even as the left comes to rearticulate, and most pressingly, the abolition of prisons, police, borders, and so on, one of the primary disciplinary mechanisms of the left remains a kind of discard or exclusion—a labeling of present members as "not representative of the beliefs and practices of the community," as production studios and academies and governments and businesses love to say, but that they are rather contagious, unethical, have "bad politics," have been fired, sent away, excluded.[33] Restoration and reparation, meanwhile, confront the community with the inaugural capacity of such absences, revealing the crises, striking the community precisely where operation and inoperation, work and mourning, meet. If I may provide a thesis, I mean to question what discarding such "contaminants" does to the community—the inaugural gesture such exclusion performs. It is the fiction of the *pure* community I want to address, one with a purity of ethics and presence, one devoid of contagion, the insistence, performed again and again through mourning and abandonment, on the purity of its presence.

While this thread of engaging, and yet mystifying, community is much older than Georges Bataille, he is the beginning of a particular theoretical engagement, involving the development of a set of terms, figurations, and problematics. Explicitly, Bataille is writing against the left's embrace of "what one might call a certain community, a certain sociality that is to come (that is not yet determined)."[34] While the targeted site of the caution, for Bataille,

---

33 I am less concerned here with the quality of life of the "excluded" from, especially, the most represented, public commons (Louis CK, Harvey Weinstein, etc.). Though, it is worth noting what accepting such expulsions as a disciplinary mechanism means to the "excluded" in other communities—might I say "our" communities; for instance, expulsion is performed likewise in the academy, leftist organizations, identity-based political actions, and so on, at times targeting those most vulnerable, already, to structural alienation (who are often without recourse to accrual—social, capital, familial, and so on—that the above public figures retain). Abandonment is much more simple and pleasurable after all; it solidifies the rest of the community's position as "good" and, above all, inaugurates or confirms something like sovereignty: a right to its gathering.

34 Stella Gaon, "Communities in Question: Sociality and Solidarity in Nancy and Blanchot," *Journal for Cultural Research* vol.0 no.4 (2005) 387-403.

is Soviet communism, a target we might, especially given Bataille's track record, distrust, the engagement targets more accurately communities, especially "modern" ones, oriented more generally toward a coming community, fulfillment, sovereignty. It is, like such secular projects, a Christian one.

One of the key problematics taken up by Bataille concerns communal operation—the work the community gathers itself around, how it preserves and creates both continuity and discontinuity from itself, how it individuates and renders as interchangeable its members. Community, here, concerns itself with those fascistic things mentioned earlier: preservation, continuance, production. For instance, in his seminal *Eroticism*, Bataille characterizes death as a threat to work in terms of (dis)continuity:

> It is my intention to suggest that for us, discontinuous beings that we are, death means continuity of being. Reproduction leads to the discontinuity of beings, but brings into play their continuity; that is to say, it is intimately linked with death. I shall endeavor to show, by discussing reproduction and death, that death is to be identified with continuity, and both of these concepts are equally fascinating.[35]

Rather than writing of death as an anxiety of communal closure, Bataille orients one toward community's necessarily intimate and constitutional relation to death as exemplary of absence. It is by death, after all, the community is confronted with the interchangeability of its members, the positionality of those within the community. In distinction, reproduction and birth (and, to a certain extent, the entrance of any new member to the community) reveal the excess

---

35 Georges Bataille, *Erotism: Death and Sensuality* translated by Mary Dalwood (London: Penguin Classics, 2012).

and individuation of each member. And yet, the death of another, an interruption, an interruption to the work the community concerns itself with, a threat which must be incorporated into that work if it is to be moved past. If left unincorporated, the loss of a community member brings anxieties concerning the (dis)continuous relationship of those left to "deal with" the death: "the community brought into being by work considers itself essentially apart from the violence implied by the death of one of its members."[36] That violence, the disconnect the remainder encounters in the death of another from the community, is intimately tied with taboo for Bataille, as violence "is what the world of work excludes with its taboos, [...] this implies at the same time sexual reproduction and death."[37] Violence, as exemplified in death, aggregates a set of prohibitions, taboos, exclusions around it so as to mitigate its interruption of communal work. In short, taboos interpolate absence as presence. Reproduction and death merely are, for Bataille, exemplary of the threat of interruption to communal order. It is here, for Bataille, various prohibitions emerge in order to maintain continuity while, simultaneously, containing discontinuity, as much as the community can, by incorporating it into communal work.

Sexuality and death are positioned external to the community even as they are internalized through operation, with taboos emerging around both, and, often, accruing together. For instance, homosociality—that is, proper relation between sexes, heterosexual relations prescribed for only "after hours" with likewise the prohibition on homosexuality, injunction of patriarchal submission of women to reproductive labor, and the whole of the kinship structure—emerges as, in Bataille's treatment, the *container* which

---

36 Ibid., 42.

37 Ibid., 46-7.

regulates sexuality's possible interruptions to communal work. Death is similarly contained through certain restrictive, prescribed forms of mourning. Contagion becomes a key term for Bataille, for describing the prohibitions surrounding death, which, in his formulation, is "a supernatural peril which can be *caught* from the dead body." Rather than burial as a response of *where to put* the corpse, or even into a historical or temporal continuity for the community, the corpse is buried "less in order to keep it safe than to keep [other members of the community] safe from its contagion."[38] These taboos, in other words, exist precisely to incorporate and regulate "containable" forms of death and reproduction within the community itself.

While less relevant here, this interplay of death and reproduction, sedimented into prohibited and permitted forms, is what Bataille characterizes as the erotic. It is from this idea of the erotic as a site where lovers negotiate these prohibitions and permissions that Jean-Luc Nancy takes up, again, this terminological formation of community. Published as an essay initially in 1983, and as a full-length work in 1986, *The Inoperative Community* seeks to readdress these (dis)continuities of community, again as exemplified through Soviet Communism, having since passed through 1968, the emergence of the New Left, and the impending fall of the Soviet Union. While, for Bataille, the coming community of Soviet Communism makes the error of conceiving community as a work or operation left outstanding, therefore reaffirming these interruptions (the erotic) as amoral, Nancy considers community in opposite terms of inoperation and worklessness. In a return to this work years later in *The Disavowed Community*, Nancy writes his motivation, in part, was to write against less a European idealizing of Soviet Communism as a reemergence of a fascistic impulse toward "the lost" or originary community.

---

38 Ibid., 45-7.

Fascist communities are exemplary of how all communities function for Nancy. Therefore, community as such presents itself as "a work to be realized" through the constant creation and imagining of a monumental past "as suggested by all the national palaces, forbidden cities, capitals, Kremlins, and all the images of an essence of common being (*res publica*)."[39] Rather than being merely oriented toward a future fulfillment of work, as Bataille has it, Nancy's community imagines the "lost" past it seeks to ally itself as continuous with, and further, too, that it will some day in the future return to—disavowing its very production of the origin in the present. Monumentalizing, in other words, is the form of a certain sovereignty which anticipates, or can, a kind of fascistic disavowal of its own discontinuity.

I would like to think of the name of the community, as well as the "word" here as it exists today—elective, aspirational, nigh synonymous with friendship or its possibility—as this kind of monument. Such names, like all names, are monumental after all, they create the origin they claim is antecedent to it. One lives up to one's name is something I recall hearing. I would, however, rather than conclude merely on the fact that community risks fascism, a sad and old thought, like to orient us to another thinker, one who—rather than Nancy, who frames community in these terms of the constant fascist impulse at the community's heart—orients us to another potential in the gathering, even as the gathering risks the above. I'm thinking of Édouard Glissant, who writes in *Poetic Intention*, "Our necessity today: to affirm, not one community *facing another*, but *in relation to another*."[40] I think here, too, of the liberal idea of listening and speaking, of mutual sharing, of "telling one's story" or "one's truth" that

---

39 Jean-Luc Nancy, *The Disavowed Community*, trans. by Philip Armstrong (New York: Fordham University Press, 2015).

40 Édouard Glissant, *Poetic Intention*, trans. Nathanaël (New York: Nightboat Books, 2010).

so often begins to look like when an edgy comedian, after offending those within their audience or general market, claims to be "starting a difficult discussion," or when an academic institution hell-bent on disciplining a set of students calls it "dialogue." And while telling a story, for instance, about oneself is not bad per se, the injunction, and the subsequent sense that the injunction is good, I believe are. This kind of pretense toward "mutual listening" is often, really, precisely such a monumentalizing demand by those in power to make those who suffer legible within and by and through hegemony, to make their suffering available according to the community's terms, to work it out, pound it out, in language, according to the rules of legibility of the community, its syntax, which is, precisely, one of the things contributing to such suffering in the first place.

An example. Where I live in Long Beach, there is a public square where people once resided. It had lemon trees, benches, an awning. Recently, the city government "renovated" it, tore it down, replacing it with a flat slab of concrete, nominally for "community events," a sign states. The corner is called Equality Plaza and features a portrait of Harvey Milk. And, indeed, I imagine city officials do feel a little bit more equivalent to who they'd like to be equivalent to now—a picture, a name, a vow, which comforts them more than this community they further solidify the conditions of. I know these are not new occurrences, the various US assassinations, coups, and so on, of the past decades being these public acts of monumentalizing as well. In short, rather than face the absence the community makes, or even those "natural" losses it didn't, the community often chooses abandonment. It is the cruel logic of melancholia combined with the power to enact the most violent of its fantasies.

Glissant speaks of something else—not a disavowal of discontinuities or loss—but another kind of relation to them. This is because we are not only a part of those within whatever community in question, nor are we only that part of the community or ourselves we disavow, nor yet again are we only the other, all a kind of oneness, whether intra-communally or extra-communally—but, as Glissant writes, speaking to a hypothetical, in his terms, Occidental subject:

> We are all, and at the same time, the fallow aspect, the unconscious, the unknown and excessively known part of the other. Was not what you would call History incomplete, not only in reach but yet in "understanding"? Is there not in your weary disdain for the historical a sort of affront to those who never had a history for you? The history you ignored—or didn't make—was it not History? [...] Might you not be more and more affected by it, in your fallowness as much as in your harvest? In your thought as much as in your will? Just as I was *affected* by the history I wasn't making, and could not ignore?[41]

I do not mean to suggest, then, that there is no such thing as contagion, that there is no day of fallowness. Nor do I mean to suggest expulsion is not at times needed—depending on the community, depending on the power-relation, depending on the one expelled. Nor do I mean to affirm, on the other extreme, that the current hegemonic sense of what is contagious is correct—all the antiblack, colonial, transmisogynistic, ableist, and other ideology that pervades us. Rather, I hope to suggest one of the great values of such collective abolitionist projects is not merely that those narrated as contagious are not, but that another relation to loss, mourning, another is possible.

For example, it is not only that police unjustly target trans women, particularly Black and brown trans women, as de facto sex workers, nor yet again the criminalization of sex work, though both these are unjust—but the relation which enabled them, too, is unjust, wherein all that interrupts or could interrupt the actions

---

41 Ibid.

of the community is contained, regulated, surveilled, expelled, and denied sovereignty (that others might be sovereign). Even as we gather to abolish these, and we ought to, we must also ask how we relate to not only one another we consider within the community, but who isn't before us, who can't be before us, who we do not want before us. I would that alongside these we ask what is aspired to and disavowed even in the "we," even as it for the first time becomes utterable. And as someone whose state identification bares such old and familiar wounds, monumentalizations too, that a name might bear, I ask too what is required to change a name, one's relation to it, to depart elsewhere, to be, no, not free of the name, but in a mutuality, to be not face-to-face, to be not bearing a word, to communicate nothing legible, to turn one's eyes away. For, as Glissant continues, and I will end with this: "What is necessary here for one and other, communities heavy with history and despoiled communities, is not in effect a language of communication [...] but on the other hand a possible communication between mutually liberated opacities, differences, languages."[42]

(2019)

---

42 Ibid.

From
8 Reflections on the Ugly Beautiful

(a book in progress)

Tonya M. Foster

This talk is incomplete. This talk is out of tune. This talk is me talking *with* you—second person singular/plural as you may be—and with Frederick [Douglass], with Thelonious [Monk], with Hortense [Spillers], with Gwendolyn [Brooks], and with the now that we together make and forage and forecast.

1. Illegible Tunings

> They would compose and sing as they went along, consulting neither time nor tune. The thought that came up, came out—if not in the word, in the sound; and as frequently in the one as in the other…
>
> > "I am going away to the Great House Farm!
> > O, yea! O, yea! O!"
>
> This they would sing, as a chorus, to words which to many would seem *unmeaning jargon*, but which, nevertheless were full of meaning to themselves. I have sometimes thought that the mere hearing of those songs would do more to impress some minds with the horrible character of slavery, than the reading of whole volumes of philosophy on the subject could do.
>
> > —*Frederick Douglass,* Narrative of the Life of Frederick Douglass *(1845)*

[Aside: And what is a self, what is selfhood to the slave, to the noncitizen but orchestrated mystery or noplace? Thing. Th. Thing. Ing. Thing. When asked how s/he is, the slave must conceal, must perform contentment or risk being beaten or sold, must respond only in conscripted formats. The slave does not speak. What is the self, what is selfhood to the enslaved, to the prisoner, to the immigrant but warmth to be secreted, to be masked, to be nourished in the hush-harbor, to be loved despite wounds, despite marks, despite fields, despite walls, despite what is read as brokenness, to love and be love. The enslaved keeps still, sometimes quiet, sometimes makes what is read as noise.]

2. Out of the Frame

One scene in the canceled TV show *Underground* depicts a gathering of well-situated white women in a plantation home parlor. The home is outfitted in period splendor, as are the women. It is summer, and the women fan themselves with delicate but ornate fans and discuss concerns befitting their station—home, children, their views on slavery. Within the camera frame, for a time, are the women and what we are meant to believe is much of the room. One of the characters in the scene seems a bit distracted. She is the only one of the antebellum-referencing quartet who delicately suggests that the abolitionist cause should be considered. The other women mock her childlessness and suggest that if she were a parent, if she were a mother, she might follow southern form and understand slavery's necessity. She appears to half-listen, is slow to respond. Her gaze is directed to something outside of the frame, something offscreen, upper right, not in the direction of the women. As the camera moves in on her, we hear the voices of the other women prodding a response, but the actress and the camera make apparent that her attention is *elsewhere*. The voices of the other women are faint and so sound far away. The camera pulls out to take in more of the room than we had imagined was there, including, this time, the object of the nascent abolitionist's gaze. Upper screen right is a boy of about ten. He is seated on a small platform. One realizes that, in the fiction of this scene, the enslaved child's task has been to fan the women throughout their gathering with a large feather contraption.

What we see is rarely where the vision lies. Attend to what is not seen. What is unseen maps much potent, cosmic terrain. The broad field of the unseen contains multitudes of observed pastures. Pay attention to the spaces between the notes.

3. In the Din

> Din is discourse ... since speech was forbidden, slaves camouflaged the word under the provocative intensity of the scream. No one could translate the meaning of what seemed to be nothing but a shout. It was taken to be nothing but the call of a wild animal. This is how dispossessed man organized his speech by weaving it into the apparently meaningless texture of extreme noise.
> —*Édouard Glissant*, Caribbean Discourse: Selected Essays

> English
> is my mother tongue.
> A mother is not
> not a foreign lan lan lang
> language
> l/anguish
>   anguish
> —a foreign anguish
>   —*M. NourbeSe Philip*, "Discourse on the Logic of Language"

> But there exist other values that fit only my forms.
>   —*Frantz Fanon*, Black Skin, White Masks

As children, my sisters and I could drive each other crazy by mimicking each other, repeating every word and gesture, again and again. We took great pleasure in using repetition and mockery to make language we all knew strange—pleasure in accentuating the strangeness of words, and in holding up that strangeness like a slide to the light. Through mimicry, the familiar and *original* word, or statement, or gesture, as well as the originary voice, are rendered strange. The idealized original is transformed, somewhat and somehow disfigured, made different. This notion of an ideal reconfigured through mimicry seems to be a key strategy in child's play and an important component of colonial discourse. Homi Bhabha writes of mimicry's importance in "Of Mimicry and Man: The Ambivalence of Colonial Discourse" in his book *The Location of Culture* (2004). In assessing the function of mimicry in colonial and postcolonial spaces, Bhabha explains that "in order to be effective, mimicry must continually produce its slippage, its excess, its difference."[43] According to Bhabha, mimicry's effectiveness depends on its capacity to highlight difference between the authoritative and the non-authoritative, the commanding and the weak, the major and the minor or marginal. Two tongues do not and will not tell the same tale.

At age eleven, one of the times I was chastised for "acting too grown," was when I responded to family remarks about how much I ate (a lot) and about how skinny I was (very) with the "my-man-doesn't-complain" comment that I had heard an older cousin use to defend herself. This first-cousin-once-removed was about forty years older than I was. Her whiskey-raped voice and tongue that knew no Sundays were antithetical to the well-behaved, boyfriendless, eleven-year-old that I was. I knew in the moment before I said anything that something out of the ordinary was about to happen, that I was "fixing my mouth" to say something I had never said before. I was letting something unfamiliar slip off the tongue and into the worlds I thought I inhabited. Yet it was the only thing I could *think* to say in order to respond. I had seen the effect of Cousin Butsie's off-the-cuff remarks. However, two tongues do not and will not tell the same tale. Will is simultaneously specific to a person and a more generally constructed concept.

My mother, disturbed and bewildered by what she heard, asked, "Man? What man? What do you know about a man?" In trying out

---

43 Homi Bhabha, "Of Mimicry and Man: The Ambivalence of Colonial Discourse" in *The Location of Culture* (New York: Routledge, 2004), 114.

Cousin Butsie's words, I began to hear the possibility of my own voice as distinct from those around me and as distinct from what I knew. Speech has a force, a weight. Words have a potential for impact within the world. What is the distance between being and the speech-act as a mode of being? Amiri Baraka, Leroi Jones at the time, points out that we daily change the word *yeh* from "simple response to stern challenge by moving the tongue slightly."[44] My tongue (in its prepubescent, eleven-year-old mouth) had changed the cadence, the context, the affect, and thereby, the meaning of Cousin Butsie's words, and her words in my mouth had rendered the me everyone thought they knew unrecognizable. In the slippage, difference and a certain illegibility become evident.

Rather than functioning as an act of repetition or mockery, mimicry, in this instance, highlighted the differences between Cousin Butsie and me: age, life experience, social position, and power. This was a moment of "talking back" which reflected a coming into existence of my imagination through language as my shaping power. It was a kind of linguistic becoming. The paradox was that in order to "talk back," I had to first mimic the language and voices of home, a home that wasn't all my own or all myself.

---

44 The complete quote from Leroi Jones's "Art Not Artifact" in *Americans from Africa* (ed. Peter I. Rose), also in *Blues People*, may be particularly useful in thinking about what haunts Black expressive culture's expressions of what Du Bois calls "double consciousness." The possibility of slippage in this doubleness produces the kind of signification that Henry Louis Gates describes as constitutive of a specifically Black expressive culture. Leroi Jones writes, "In African languages the meaning of a word can be changed simply by altering the *pitch* of the word or changing its stresses—basically the way one can change the word *yeh* from simple response to stern challenge by moving the tongue slightly. Philologists call this 'significant tone,' the 'combination of pitch and timbre' used to produce changes of meaning in words. This was basic to the speech and music of West Africans, and was definitely passed on to the Negroes of the New World" (94).

What happens when, because of historical accident and/or brute force, the language one must echo is both a mother/father language and a foreign language, language imposed by force, however distant? What happens to ideas of the self under the demands of a language, which nurtures, disciplines, and casts one as other? What if the language is, as NourbeSe Philip writes, "[a] foreign languish/anguish"? What happens to ideas of home? What, under these terms, is legible to whom, and in what context? I had uttered a certain noise.

4. Waste and Excess Sittin' in a Tree...

Play the Vaughan tune:

In the 1957 version of "How High the Moon," Sarah Vaughan (also known as "Sassy," as "The Divine One," and as "Sailor," for her salty, scatological speech) references Ella Fitzgerald's scat singing. She also references the apocryphal story of scat-singing's origin, signals scatting as a stand-in for the forgotten. "I don't know the words to this song, but I'm gonna sing 'em anyway. I hope you enjoy it. Hope you enjoy it." The sentence's "it" points to both the song and the singing. Vaughan goes on to make explicit in the song, in the singing, relationships among listening yous and a singing I and within a community of singing I's. "Ella Fitzgerald sings this song..." Through narration and performance, Vaughan places her own rendition within a context of singing that marks the forgotten. What is the voice's relationship to the song emptied of the *words* as we've known them? What is the knowledge lost and gained in this reformation of the song, of the words? Are these sounds the discourse of the tossed off, the remaindered, the emptied out? "I hope you enjoy it," she sings. What pleasure is to be found there, in the space of the forgotten?

There is in scatting, in this performance, a focus on form that reconfigures traditional inheritance and meaning. Refusing the lineage that most easily confers legitimacy or legibility, Vaughan's scatting instead points to the capacity and impulse to make the conventional individual, specific, conversational, and to signal shifting potential relative to form and material. That transfiguration is only possible within the social and cultural contexts in which the convention is operative and understood. Within the world of music—Jazz. Among Jazz musicians—vocalists. Among vocalists—Ella and Sarah (and echoes of Louis Armstrong). Vaughan's narration turns its (and our) attention to the discrepant performance as such. She prefaces and references Ella Fitzgerald's version (and her own imitation) as "real, real, *real* crazy." In this multivalent performance, Vaughan, through scatting and exchange, makes a place and a language, in this song about music and love, for the unexpected and the unreasonable (or the differently reasoned), for the *real crazy* noises. Scatting as process and articulation works, not to maintain tradition nor to establish an easy counter-tradition, but to offer possibility for individual, crazy interpretation within a community of interpretations and interpreters. Local specificity instead of universality. "I" is articulated in the public sociality that produces it, even as parts of the I remain illegible behind the opacities that are aspects of being and of beings. Vaughan emphasizes the one *among* the many.

"Scatting," in my estimations, may be read as an assertion in the defacement (and knowledge) of absence and invisibility. Scatting is potentially the kind of improvised assertion of sonic possibility that breaks open space within narratives of legibility, legitimacy, and the reasonable—space for what has been disappeared and laid waste—space for scat. The "real, real, *real* crazy" emerges within and out of what might be understood as wasteland, waste, detritus. It is "talking shit" as modifier and as cultural practice that talks about and with and around and back to, circumnavigating and disrupting the regulatory and limiting functions of language. Ideas of the "ugly beautiful" are bound up with notions of the liberatory.

This kind of invention and reconfiguration is a feature of Black expressive culture, wherein a site of degradation, which also may be read or (mis)understood as a site of valuelessness, is insisted on and recognized as a site of beauty. Indeed, the degradation, of memory or material, may be a constitutive component of the ugly beautiful.

Anthony Reed notes that "Black experimental writing at the level of form, advances an aesthetic of what Erica Hunt has called 'unrecognizable speech' and that the hiatus of recognizability can spur new thought and new imaginings, especially the (re)imagining of collectivities and intellectual practices."[45]

I think of Frantz Fanon's *Wretched. Les Damnés.* Sylvia Wynter makes the point that there is an ever-expanding global configuration of *les damnés*, which draws together "refugees/economic migrants stranded outside the gates of the rich countries…with this category in the United States coming to comprise the criminalized majority of Black and dark-skinned Latino inner-city males now made to man the rapidly expanding prison-industrial complex, together with their female peers…with both being part of the…global, transracial category of the homeless/the jobless, the semi-jobless, the criminalized drug-offending prison population."[46] Wynter goes on to link the groups of people with "Third- and Fourth-World peoples of the so-called 'underdeveloped' areas of the world."[47]

How are those designations materially, semantically, syntactically, sonically, and visually produced, invoked, and reconfigured? What

---

45 Anthony Reed, *Freedom Time: The Poetics and Politics of Black Experimental Writing* (Baltimore: Johns Hopkins University Press, 2014), 2.

46 Syliva Wynter, "Unsettling the Coloniality of Being/Power/Truth/Freedom: Towards the Human, After Man, Its Overrepresentation—An Argument" in *CR: The New Centennial Review* Vol. 3, No.3 (2003), 262.

47 Ibid.

are the spaces of *les damnés* in relation to scat and scatting? To what does the poem attend?

Which strategies are brought to bear in simultaneously collapsing and delimiting the territories between waste and excess, between genres, between parts of speech, between personal memory and historical narrative, between the individual and the nation-state, between the lyric and the narrative, between sense and nonsense, between fact and speculation?

Attend to what has been/is being dis'appeared or laid waste.

6. The Ugly Beautiful

Play the Thelonious Monk tune "Ugly Beauty" (1968):

How is "talking shit" the kind of invention and reconfiguration of beauty that appear as principal features of Black experimental and avant-garde expressive culture, wherein sites of degradation, which also may be read or understood as sites of valuelessness, trouble the designations "beautiful" and "valuable"?

What's apparent in the work of Black artists and performers is the sense that ideas of the "ugly beautiful," of the rough cut, of the discomforting joy are bound up with notions of the liberatory. Indeed, the degradation, of memory or material, and discomfort may be constitutive features of beautiful (and liberatory) places as configured by Black artists across a range of fields and disciplines.

7. Location, Location, Derivation, Deviation

We often locate notions of "the authentic," particularly when it comes to non-white peoples, in the street. In contrast to Kantian ideals of beauty which insist on harmoniousness, some artists articulate a "street" aesthetic of beauty that is partly constituted by the turned away, by the repelled, by the cast off(s), the scat, and the scat-singing.

At a time when the rate of incarceration for Black and brown peoples is five times that of whites, and reports of death at the hands of increasingly militarized police are regular features of the nightly news, an interrogation of Blackness in its myriad guises and meanings, an interrogation of the discursive structures that legislate, regulate, and narrate racial (and spatial) formations may have, to use the word that recurs throughout Henry Dumas' poem "Mosaic Harlem," "news" of state and individual power relations. Are there discursive strategies that might be understood as challenges and that resist broad social-metanarratives of categorization and hierarchy that continue to operate in various sectors of Black life, even in this post, post-Jim Crow era?

8. Yes, Virginia, Dreams are Colder Than Death

Arthur Jafa's *Dreams Are Colder than Death* opens with shots of Black men, women, and children in various states of engagement—a man standing alone in front of a wall faces the camera, young people play in a pool, a woman and a girl walk up a road, various people walk down a street. The first voice we hear is that of theorist and cultural critic Hortense Spillers. We hear her voice before we see her. Who and where is this knowing "I." She begins, *"I know."*

> I *know* we are going to lose this gift of Black culture unless we are careful. This *gift* that is given to people who don't have a *prayer*...Frederick Douglass...Black people, Black people two hundred years ago didn't have a prayer. Beat our skin off our bodies, skin us. Kill and rape our mamas. In *front* of us. We didn't have a prayer. Now we're the head of international courts, President of the United States, sitting on

the United States Supreme Court, presidents of universities, CEO of American Express, you name it, some Black person is it. Wow...but the price of *that* is to lose this precious insight that connects you to something human and bigger than white folks, and I don't give a f*#k what color the folks is, something bigger than that. We're losing that connection because we are buying this other shit. I know that. I *know* that.

Simultaneously, articulating distances of time and space, we faintly hear the recognizable voice of Martin Luther King Jr. intone:

> I have a dream that one day this nation will rise up and live out the true meaning of its creed: "We hold these truths to be self-evident, that all men are created equal." I have a dream that one day on the red hills of Georgia, the sons of former slaves and the sons of former slave owners will be able to sit down together at the table of brotherhood. I have a dream that one day even the state of Mississippi, a state sweltering with the heat of injustice, sweltering with the heat of oppression, will be transformed into an oasis of freedom and justice. I have a dream that my four little children will one day live in a nation where they will not be judged by the color of their skin but by the content of their character. I have a *dream* today! I have a dream that one day, down in Alabama, with its vicious racists, with its governor having his lips dripping with the words of "interposition" and "nullification"—one day right there in Alabama little black boys and black girls will be able to join hands with little white boys and white girls as sisters and brothers. I have a *dream* today!

This sonic layering and juxtaposition collapse time and social and political space, and puts contemporary Black cultural concerns in immediate conversation with/alongside political and aspirational traditions of rhetoric about freedom and justice that are central to Black intellectual life.

"Black study is the critique of Western civilization," says Spillers elsewhere.

"Black culture is critical culture," says poet, critic, theorist Fred Moten elsewhere.

Jafa makes a space in which these sayings are happening *together* and *in* the same time-space-ethics field.

9. Gwendolyn Brooks: Who Ya' Talkin' With?

> Symbolic struggles are always much more effective (and therefore more realistic) than objectivist economists think, and much less so than pure social marginalists think. The relationship between distributions and representations is both the product and the stake of a permanent struggle between those who, because of the position they occupy within the distributions, have an interest in subverting them by modifying the classifications in which they are expressed and legitimated and those who have an interest in perpetuating misrecognition, an alienated cognition that looks at the world through categories the world imposes.
> —*Pierre Bourdieu*, The Logic of Practice

I was, at some point, waiting with friends to be seated for dinner. An early evening. We waited outside of a restaurant on a West Harlem corner, around the block from where I once lived. The night air was cool, the streets busy with passersby. The friends are poets and artists from Paris, Peoria, and New York. One couple was there with their ten-year-old son who was filled with a ten-year-old's energy. He'd laugh and then do a cartwheel or a handstand as the adults talked but kept an eye on him to make sure that he didn't tumble too far out of reach or into someone. For some reason, he stopped tumbling, stood next to his mother, and recited Gwendolyn Brooks' "We real cool." The adults stopped to listen. His mother was surprised. She didn't know that he had memorized the poem. At ten, S is tall, dark-skinned, with joyful dimples, remarkably playful. There was something in his recitation of the poem, his articulation of and attention to the line-breaks and stresses. It was strange, wonderful, and devastating.

Play Gwendolyn Brooks' reading:

We Real Cool

The Pool Players.
Seven at the Golden Shovel.

We real cool. We
Left school. We

Lurk late. We
Strike straight. We

Sing sin. We
Thin gin. We

Jazz June. We
Die soon.

Hearing Brooks' remarkable music, what she later called *blackblues*, coming out of the mouth of a ten-year-old African American child is both beautiful and jarring. The recitation, coming as it did from an ebullient boy, made apparent the poem's blues aesthetic, proffering a difficult beauty. The poem articulates an epistemology of the Black

American lived experience. Ten years old seems too young for that knowledge, and yet Black American children are rarely afforded the child's innocence which combines an absence of guilt with an absence of knowledge. There is a Black American particularity that emerged in S's performance. Something in his recitation, a combination of content and form of presentation, gave voice to the social and political precarity of Black American lived experience. A poem written in 1959 speaks to the conditions of Black life in America even today, and, in its seeming simplicity, in the language a child can understand, gives voice to knowledge that should be beyond the experience of childhood. And yet, it isn't.

Hortense Spillers observes that the simplicity of the poem is stark to the point of elaborateness. Less than lean, it is virtually coded. Made up of monosyllables and end-stops, the poem is no nonsense at all. Gathered in eight units of three-beat lines, it does not necessarily invite inflection, but its persistent bump on "we" suggests waltz time. If the reader chooses to render the poem that way, she runs out of breath, or trips her tongue, but it seems that such "breathlessness: is exactly required of dudes hastening toward their death. Deliberately subverting the romance of sociological pathos, Brooks presents the pool players—'seven in the golden shovel'—in their own words and time."[48]

Spillers notes that the poem is *their* situation as *they* see it. It is also their situation as the poet reconstructs it, narrates it, imagines it. Those words and the arrangement of them are "determined

---

48 Hortense Spillers, "Gwendolyn the Terrible: Propositions on Eleven Poems." in *A Life Distilled: Gwendolyn Brooks Her Life and Fiction*, ed. Maria K. Mootry and Gary Smith. (Champaign, IL: University of Illinois Press, 1987), 120.

by [Brooks'] feelings about these boys, these young men."⁴⁹ An increasingly particular "we" that includes the players and the lyric voice is apparent by the time we reach "Die soon." Observer and observed are in community in their march toward death, in *our* march toward death.

What's also remarkable about the poem is that it follows multiple aesthetic tracks. As a younger poet, Brooks insisted that poetry is a combination of truth and beauty, yet for the younger Brooks truth was no substitute for beauty which could exist without truth. In its rhythms and language, the poem is beautiful and may render a truth of experience. Like William Blake's *Songs of Experience* and Langston Hughes' *Weary Blues,* the poem maps the difficulty of being embodied.

We know poetry in the context of other poetry. In a statement Brooks made in 1950, she wrote, "But no real artist is going to be content with offering raw materials. The Negro poet's most urgent duty, at present, is to polish his technique, *his way of presenting* his truths and his beauties, that these may be more *insinuating* and, therefore, more overwhelming."⁵⁰ There is a commitment to interrogating the possibilities of language and form, and already an idea of affect. How does the poem impact the reader?

In 1972's *Report from Part One,* Brooks amends her concept of poetry by first reiterating her sense that a poet has a duty to words, and that words can do wonderful things, and it's too bad to just let them lie there without doing anything with and for them.

But something different is happening now. Black poets today—

---

49 Gwendolyn Brooks, *Report from Part One* (Detroit: Broadside Lotus Press, 1972), 156.

50 Ibid., 140.

when I say black poets, I mean something different from that old phrase "Negro poets"—black poets are becoming increasingly aware of themselves and their blackness; they are interested in speaking *to* black people, and especially so they want to reach those people who would never go into a bookstore and buy a $4.95 volume of poetry written by *any*one. And I think this is very important.

Brooks emphasizes the "idealized beloved" to whom the poem is pitched. *To* whom and *with* whom the poem is speaking changes/challenges the form and language that make the poem the poem, and that render legibility and illegibility across time.

10. Community

The poem depends on/in shifting community. The poem is a community of voices and impulses and linguistic structures and maneuvers. The poem, in as much as it is, speaks in a community of other poems, and of poets composing poems. The poem is a community of wills and words, of thoughts and possible thoughts. The poem is the song sung anyway in the forgetting of the words meant to define and dictate; in the presence and opacity of the feelings that can/must remain unspoken (quasi-forgotten) yet remain felt (and sung in peculiar ways), as long as the person is and feels; and, if felt, can/must be somehow survived. The community is in the poem's possible configurations of now and when, of singing anyhow.

(2019)

Identity in the Capitalocene

. . .

While the political discourse of identity politics seems to have been more recently co-opted by neoliberalism, the past year has made us consider more deeply the role of identity in the *capitalocene*. The movement of Black Lives Matter, the fight for transgender rights, and other strategies being implemented to combat discrimination and marginalization have defined our recent experience. We return to the Black feminist lesbian collective who wrote "The Combahee River Collective Statement" in 1977 and coined the first use of identity politics. We consider our roles in acknowledging our own socio-locations, and question whether the current manifestation of identity politics is a productive avenue toward social justice. Identity is something fractured and multivalent. What does it mean to have a female body under capitalism? How can we take a stand against institutional racism and other forms of injustice? What role does poetics have in emboldening our tenacity to do so?

> With "The Capitalocene" we intend to name and sound a terminological rhyme—a repetition but with variation—to The Anthropocene, the name for our era and understanding of global conditions and ecological ramifications, in which everything is tampered with by human agency writ large. By calling the epoch The Capitalocene, we aim to call attention to how life is under the regime of capitalism, rather than humanity as a global-scale phenomenon, that is the disordering force of the life of this world; and further, we mean to gainsay the idea that the end of the world is easier to imagine than the end of capitalism. But what are the means and strategies by which we'll find ourselves capable of this counter-vison, a vision of life in which the world is teeming, diverse, beautiful, strange, and survives—and the destructive capacities of capital are overturned? In this vision of a refreshed ecology of living, the

care and long work of subversive remedy required to unmake the violences of racialized capitalism will be a signal activity. How can writing be a catalyst for bringing these new forms into being? How can these energies be leveraged as subversive remedy? And how can we write with an urgency that is not merely a reflection of the grammar of crisis that constitutes capitalism itself? How can writing be a technology for sounding out both affective being, and the complexities of the political—how to write (collectively) now? We invite writers, and students, and thinkers, and performers to continue the lines of critical voicing, creative work, and spiritual sensibility that have defined the Summer Writing Program since 1974.

—from the 2018 Summer Writing Program catalogue

We reject pedestals, queenhood, and walking ten paces behind. To be recognized as human, levelly human, is enough.

—The Combahee River Collective

· · ·

*Figure 5: Poster made in the Harry Smith printshop during
Aaron Cohick's workshop in the 2019 Summer Writing Program.
Photograph by Anne Waldman.*

Consenting to the Emergency / the Emergent as Consensuality

J'Lyn Chapman

> There was
> The space between [her / his] face and how I felt about it
> where sunlight condensed from what once was sun
> a perspiration of minutes sweating between us
> the door love practiced in me swung open
> to look at you and lodge it in my heart
> an attitude of love, called Ritual Disaster
> —*Eleni Sikelianos*, Body Clock

After nearly five years of trying unsuccessfully to get pregnant, and what seemed like the failure of science to explain why I hadn't gotten pregnant, I suddenly was. Between these two states—not expecting and expecting—I first wanted something I couldn't have, and then attempted the process of accepting the reality that I wouldn't have it. Sometimes it is difficult to categorize the parts of reality that are the most real. Prayer and in vitro fertilization were possibilities and, given the arrogant male doctor who would only address my husband as he discussed my ovulation as well as the enormous fee he charged us for a procedure that was not guaranteed to work, to rely on either possibility felt like what Lauren Berlant calls "cruel optimism" or "the condition of maintaining an attachment to a significantly problematic object."[51] Heteronormative cultural expectations had nearly convinced me that there was a right way and a wrong to start a family. I began to fear that if I got pregnant the wrong way, the pregnancy would be cursed by the means by which I got pregnant, because it would force something into being that wasn't "meant to be." And anyway, I wondered, wasn't it dangerous to bear a child to a world in a perpetual state of emergency?

When I did get pregnant the "right way," the comforts of spontaneous joy *and* conformity to the status quo could not allay the fear that I had provoked an emergency by getting exactly what I wanted. While conception and a healthy full-term pregnancy seemed to make accepting the reality of infertility unnecessary, it drove the need for inquiry deeper into the emergency of my own thinking, and it made so obvious that to encounter the emergency of life, I need to do more than accept reality; I need to consent to it.

Let us begin with two parallel notions of emergency: the first, public and broad, relates to Western culture's increasing awareness and even initiation of the emergency of environmental, political, and humanitarian disaster; while the second, private and specific, derives from the individual body's response to extreme internal and external conditions, such as those during pregnancy and delivery.

---

51 Lauren Berlant, *Curel Optimism* (Durham and London: Duke UP, 2011) 24.

I want to talk about the idea of emergency, not merely as disaster, but also as an occasion for emergence, as is the case in childbirth. Emergence, as defined by the *OED*, is "the process of coming forth, issuing from concealment, obscurity, or confinement." In this case, exposing oneself to danger, putting oneself at risk, what we call endangerment, is a vital part of the emergent process. *Emergence* is also a term shared by science, philosophy, art, and systems theory to generally describe the phenomenon in which "the whole is greater than its parts." Another way to put this is that "emergent properties arise as the consequence of relationships between entities," according to scientists Ursula Goodenough and Terrence Deacon in "The Sacred Emergence of Nature," and that the sum isn't just greater than its parts, it's different from its parts—it's something else entirely.[52]

The private notion of emergency is not relegated to the event so much as it is the psychological recognition of crisis, the feeling of indeterminacy that takes over when a new reality usurps the old—the presence of another being in the body, the seeming inflammation of time as one life overlays another. Even in the event of delivery, the emergency burgeons from the mother's body and its response to otherness—its own, as well as that of the fetus—and the fissure that occurs when the body of the baby separates from the body of the mother. And while pregnancy is an event (advent) of extreme, irrecoverable changes in the bodies of mother and child, the emotional feelings that accompany these changes are at once ordinary and novel. There is a feeling of universality that, in its expansiveness, creates a pressure whose catharsis could only occur through an impossible articulation.

---

52 Ursula Goodenough and Terrence W. Deacon, "The Sacred Emergence of Nature" *The Oxford Handbook of Religion and Science*, ed. Philip Clayton (Oxford: Oxford University Press, 2006), 855.

I am interested in quality over quantity—the feelings that surround an emergency or disaster rather than the emergency itself, even as one is compelled to index catastrophes to both justify the sense that this is a unique moment in history and to stabilize the contingency of it. Such an index attempts to create a shared representation of truth and the preclusion of (more) disaster. But the index as a mode of interpretation is useless in the face of a catastrophe that occurs outside of representation and, therefore, intelligibility. After all, ours is a culture in which reality is obfuscated and disorientation capitalized to manipulate emergent events or the event-as-emergency for economic and political gain—what Naomi Klein calls the "shock doctrine." Which is to say that in the event of disaster, it is the *aftermath* that matters, evidenced by the identification, and exploitation, of feelings, shock, and disorientation by "disaster capitalists."

And while the disastrous event is increasingly marked by its exploitation, it is also marked by a kind of divine omnipresence. It is as if we are born into disaster, so that to speak of a specific disaster is less relevant than speaking of disaster's ongoingness. Because the emergency takes the form of the event and, also, is always already present, the feeling that there is an emergency is perhaps more relevant than the concrete identification of one. If so, this feeling is not intellectual but rather produced by the intelligences of the whole being—body, mind, and soul. There's much to be said about this kind of intelligence, automatic and intuitive; for the purposes of this essay, I understand it as an intelligence that is particular to the mother and measured in the literal beating of the heart.

Two personal instances of emergence that began in my body and then resonated outward in feeling: an episode of prenatal anxiety, in which I perceived I was in a state of emergency, and the delivery of the baby, in which I consented to the contractions of the body. In the former, emergency feels like threat and horror, rejection and rupture. The fear is, ultimately, that I am isolated from others, unable to connect, love, or share their experience, which, in turn, isolates.

In the latter, emergency is the consent of the whole being to the contractions of the body during labor. Paradoxically, rupture is also at work in this consent—but in this case, the self, that is, the mother, experiences an ongoing separation, a dispersion and uplifting of meaning through the new existence, the new self, of the child.

I enter my thoughts about emergency at my own risk; I consent to the disaster of my own thinking. This consent is difficult to parse from those other moments when my anxiety produces the impression that I am in an emergency when I am in fact *not* in an emergency, as was the case with the prenatal anxiety. It's important not to equivocate about reality and non-reality, and there's nothing propitious or interesting about feeling oneself in a constant state of danger. It's debilitating and destructive, a tautology in which the feelings of endangerment anachronistically produce the disaster. Yet, the feeling does not have to remain at the level of panic or fear, nor even of loss or depression. But even more importantly, I want to propose that it is possible to both feel one's own emotions, regardless of their "legitimacy," to have one's own personal experiences of pain and loss, and to sense that these private events—even as they might be entirely located in the body and mind—relate in some way to the larger emergency of being in the world with others.

From this place, in which both public and private emergency results in a feeling of division and separation, even when separation is the process by which the self dissolves in order to come into wholeness, I wonder:

Is it possible to maintain the "complex feeling" of the emergency, to borrow philosopher Jean-François Lyotard's language, to allow the sensation of emergency to keep our response to crisis supple and quick no matter how uncomfortable, so that out of the emergency there could be an emergence—a coming forth, a revelation that proceeds swiftly, urgently? And, if emergence depends on the relationships between entities, then how can we allow emergency, which not only feels but often *is* debilitating, to produce something else entirely, something new and constructive, from the interconnectivity of the individual with other individuals?

Goodenough and Deacon usefully advocate for an "emergentist perspective" on nature, in which "emergence can be thought of as nature's mode of creativity"[53] and the human as not "above" nature but "remarkably 'something else.'"[54] Thinking of the human being as a consequence of nature's creativity occasions spiritual responses of enchantment, transcendence and reverence, and gratitude, as well as moral responses that include moral behavior toward other humans and ecosystems, or ecomorality.[55]

In the sixth month of my pregnancy, I began to feel dread that at once seemed to descend on me and rise from within, which is to say I was immersed in it. In retrospect, I can identify a series of events that stressed me (buying a house, conflicts at work, students encountering their own crises). I assume that at the end of the second trimester, there was also a change in hormones that influenced the thoughts that, until this point, had been remarkably light given my initial concerns around the pregnancy. I have always struggled with anxiety and can identify periods in my life that resembled this one. But regardless, the fear, which I tethered to observable changes in my body, overtook me, not suddenly but with a feeling of suddenness, and while my medical care had been thorough and trustworthy, I encountered an emotional change that was seemingly untraced to a cause.

It is difficult to transform an emotion into a meaningful experience if it cannot be traced to a cause, if it does not have a sign that can contain it. In this way, the emergency of which I speak was a terrifying

---

53   Ibid., 865.

54   Ibid., 867.

55   Ibid., 870.

dispersal of meaning that I attempted to stabilize by compulsive examination of my body, of the spaces I occupied, of authoritative texts about pregnancy. My obsession with knowing and certainty were an attempt to make the emergency I felt in my body but could not locate an object to be handled and expunged, and in that transformation, I reasoned I could care about it less.

There is actually something very therapeutic about the transformation of the feeling into the object. This occurs in meditation when, for instance, a thought is observed or when one can imagine it as a thing, when one allows it to drift by without grasping at it. Sometimes I imagine being immersed in deep water and watching objects float above me. I recognize the objects but do not grasp at them. It's like a flood has taken place, I have drowned but remain sentient, and I watch the banal objects of my life drift by without trying to save them or to use them as life rafts. In the disaster, there is a kind of calm acceptance of reality and letting go. To already have been submerged, to already have met my fate.

This meditative practice hastens the inevitable reification of thought for the purpose of calming the body or the soul, for the purpose of clarity. Thought has a tendency to eventually petrify; the meditation makes it happen more quickly, more deliberately, and within a set of artificial constraints, such as the image that I produce. Yet reified thought has the tendency, as Emerson writes in the essay "Circles," "to solidify and hem in the life," as in, "for instance, an empire, rules of an art, a local usage, a religious rite."[56] In this case, the feeling of the emergency dissipates and so, too, do the emergent possibilities for transformation. Heavy as stone, the emergency settles into silt and sand bars.

---

56 Ralph Waldo Emerson, "Circles" in *Emerson's Essays* (Philadelphia: Spencer Press, 1936), 207.

Two early definitions of *emergence* relate to buoyancy and, more specifically, "to come up out of a liquid in which (the subject) has been immersed." Consequently, one definition of emergency is "the rising of a submerged body above the surface of water." It makes sense and feels good to detachedly watch the emergency float above me, to accept that I am waterlogged debris, to feel nothing for the objects to which I was once attached and to merely watch them. But it is also worthwhile to engage in the emergency, to rise to the surface with the mercurial world that gathers in the grates and the roots of trees. To allow the loss of self and, in this debris, which includes me, to allow something else entirely to emerge.

Perhaps pregnancy could be thought of as an emergence in its resemblance to those "synergistic wholes that are composed of things of 'unlike kinds,'" as Peter A. Corning argues.[57] The single human body is itself an emergent phenomenon, Corning explains, with its "ten trillion or so cells...specialized into some two hundred fifty different cell types that perform a vast array of important functions in relation to the operation of the whole."[58] My daughter and I were two like humans, as the ultrasounds revealed, with our four-chambered hearts, guts, and limbs, and, also, unlike parts of a whole in our different uses of our shared organs, one of which we produced solely for the purpose of this doubling, in our consciousnesses, and in our very different trajectories. And despite these vast differences, I found it possible to differentiate prior to delivery only in the rhetorical gesture of apostrophe, in which I fondly called out the other body's movements, said, "I love these."

---

57 Peter A. Corning, "The Re-emergence of 'Emergence': A Venerable Concept in Search of a Theory" *Complexity* 7.6 (2002), 24.

58 Ibid., 24.

Delivery could not have been more predictable or average. There were no complications, and the day progressed as days always do, until twenty-four hours later, the baby emerged with wide eyes. And yet my body was the site of an emergency, and if I did not stay ahead of it, the pain overwhelmed me, sending me into three-minute intervals of panic. Halfway into the labor, as the pains ascended and the contractions occurred more frequently, I was sure my body was tearing apart from the descending pressure, and my instinct was to recoil—grit my teeth, hoist my body onto my toes, hold the weight of the pelvis in my shoulders, and push sound through the roof of mouth. The labor, then, was a process of giving over my body, allowing gravity to take the baby while also relinquishing the muscle control that had for so long now kept us upright. I stood flat on my feet, bent my knees, let my shoulders drop, droned sound against my diaphragm.

Emergence seemed to occur distinctly differently at the moment that I perceived as the emergency of labor, when our bodies worked in concert to go our separate ways. The obvious analogy is the breaking of waters or the crowning head; less obvious is the enlistment of will to navigate the birth canal, which the baby experienced as physical boundary and I experienced as sheer pain. And while the baby's new life might be a dedication to survival, mine is now dedicated to the ongoingness of that emergent moment.

Consenting to the emergency is also consent to the duration of emergency. This leads us back to the public view of emergency—the world into which one gives birth to life is a world in emergency, and the emotional and psychological feeling-through this world is uncertain. Western capitalism is a salve in its promise to anesthetize and outsource this pain, yet it still bears down and threatens to exceed our boundaries. An emergentist perspective of nature cannot solve the problem of pain and emergency, but it can help us to live through it with one another.

I am still not sure what this means. But over the course of several months of sleepless nights, I have been compelled to light a candle so that the flame within me might have a conversant. And what I've overheard has something to do with emergence. That is, I need you, although sometimes I don't want you, and you make me nervous. On my own, I am precise in my history and memories, but what I am is not my purpose or trajectory. I must be willing to be with you and to become something else entirely.

Motherhood is both the metaphor and practice of what this could mean—in the self-sacrifice that produces pleasure, as well as in the negotiation of contingency that an ongoing emergency, both boring and surprising, necessitates. This being together could almost be religious. The miracle is not the other's coming into being but that I could survive the emergency of it with her. That I could go down deep and rise again.

(2019)

INVESTIGATIVE POETICS

Imagination and Documentation

Ronaldo V. Wilson

I thought I would use this occasion to open up an old or formative piece and to talk through it. So, I'm just going to read this, It's pretty F-R-E-S-H. Fresh. Fresh. Fresh. *Maybe.*

"Poetics of Delusion, or After Bitterness." There are versions of a self here which I'd like to obviate. A self that says, "I'm attached to a history of undeniable oppression." A force so systematic and relentless that I've had to master an ability to speak from inside this force without cause to display much reflex or alarm.

In my search for what and for whom I hate or why I'd like to speak after bitterness, I find terms like tragic-comic or note how one is bolted to the blues and that another never seems afraid of being read as calm and cool and the whirling winds of it all. Because one is best met as a survivor or carefully on edge which is slightly different than being a winner, a chair, or a recipient.

I once took a bus to Paterson, New Jersey for a poetry symposium. It's famous. One poet who edited many anthologies which feature underrepresented folk, many women, many of color, some queer, and all from the same and yet wide and varied diaspora, was on a panel about the production of such anthologies. She said she was tired of the same questions again and again, and I loved her answer, "Who's in? Who's out? Who cares?"

My oppression, one says, I must make beautiful, palpable even. A-void. A-void. This here? This here, nigga... is a version of a self that attempts to translate pathos but is often caught up in the bog of what gets so quickly equipped for market, performed in the line of such predictable narratives like I am a boy who was beaten to a pulp and/or I pray or pray just after this beating or I can't wait to sing this in the tune of many songs that I come from, many that you will recognize. Songs. A song that will punctuate my formation into or as the material of what's left behind.

Piece of shit. Pile. Bile. Vile.

In my dissertation orals, I defended three lists. 20th Century and Contemporary African American Poetry, The Black Body in Contemporary African American Visual Culture, and Myth, Memoir, Manifesto. Some of the details are important here. That I was the first in my doctoral program to use visual images in a defense. These stand out.

Serena Williams, blonde then and young, pounding a backhand so that her muscles ripped perfectly into the shot. Another of the artist Adrien Piper, in her mythic being series, *Thin*. Donning a great afro, full mustache, and aviator shades, flipping by tryptic an equally thin white man to the ground. Second, I described how a number of critical arguments about race and abstraction, loss and defilement, in both poetry and prose, informed these photographs, were at least my beginnings of an argument about them.

How I was starting to imagine writing a poetics of the Black body as a field of reiterative violation. Serena, Piper, as interventions. I received highest honors for my defense. On cloud nine, after such a *win*, I cruised down the elevator to the end-of-the-semester party where two of my friends in the program volunteered to DJ the event. I don't recall the details of why this happened. Maybe it was about us keeping the music hip hop or house, and I gained some wishes, or I was feeling super aggressive or too happy or dancing too hard, when one of the students in my program thought I was a part of the DJ crew. Of which he though none of us were graduate students. Too rich. Too urbane. Maybe the help. And I was the jig and hype man, not taking his request for whatever the fuck—seriously.

Maybe I told him to wait, that he can't have *everything*. Maybe I said, my body is code, my refusal reveling in winning distinction. You piece of shit. I don't recall how close I was to his face. Or if I would really hit him. Or if I told him I was a student there. But I did say that language between us now has failed. That violence is the only answer to what he called me. It's inevitable but I asked him quite plainly, shaking, puffed like a baboon. Should I hit you in your jaw? Primate, back down. [Shifts to singing] *Back in black mountain, a child will smack your face. Back in black mountain, a child will smack your face, baby's crying for liquor, and all the birds sing bass.*

Though I think that if I perform this enduring ballad of my sadness that you will buy it and celebrate it. Especially if I recount other instances of my needs in living like this along the way, those that make me nice, those that make me like you. Or smile mostly real some quick facts that you must already realize is, I listen to all types of music or I have a father to whom I am estranged and/ or in my lack of silence I project my regret and subservience in a worn form that is recognizable from start to finish. I'm continuous, stanzaic. I couplet, I title each. I'm full of it. I will not kill you. Love leads me. I will not murder when you least expect it. You will not be face-raped. Nor will you feel ashamed for looking so closely at my file, my absent hair, my chest, look into my eyes. I work hard. I'm an open book. I want to work for your institution even though you say to me over breakfast in the shiny hotel that's not where I'm staying, it's all luck.

And when you call, I miss the call because I'm teaching and you say, "call back," and you leave your office and your cell and you do call me back and it's not too long a wait just enough time for me to imagine carrying your 3'3" load on your back. But when you catch me where I wait like a baby bird starved and in a packed nest, you don't say "Ronaldo, we can offer you the position." Or, "Ronaldo we've offered it to someone else," like you said you would say. Because I had another opportunity in the wings.

You say, "We've decided to run the search again next year." Funding, schmunding. Liar, liar, pants on fire. I wiki-see you did select, and yet another of the same, someone who looks like another version of you. Or maybe a little tougher version of the same, the voice still save the credentials the calls don't matter clever beaver chomping at the bit in the fast food joint. How typical.

When they say, "the right fit," it matters. When they say, "you can't go into the pool until we are finished," the slime burns into your eyes even though you've never seen one, for real, up close, in the actual life. You learn to make alternative moves. Elide history. Improvise. Interrogate. Start over. Run wind sprints. No matter what, get the run in. Return to language. [Starts singing] *Don't worry about a thing, 'cause every little thing it gonna be alright. Don't worry about a thing, 'cause every little thing it gonna be alright.*

All sociological/ideological analyses agree on the deceptive nature of literature, which deprives them of a certain pertinence. The work is finally always written by a socially disappointed or powerless group. Beyond the battle because of its historical economic political situation, literature is the expression of this disappointment. So says Roland Barthes and Bernstein in a poetics that strives two distinct camps of poets, those that refine tradition, and those who are dissatisfied. Neat plates for sure. But it keeps my eyes on the prize no matter the shards on my fractured face. I don't say but you know how you made me feel. I am proud to be a finalist again, forget serendipity. I want you to feel safe. And when you hear me sing, you should lie back and feel in every case smoothed. Imagine hard, me reading so many books and internalizing so many ideas and trudging so long a road just to slip in by the skin off on my back to your front door. And even though in most cases it's shut, or one will lie in your face, one self blogs about his success, "I did not get the fellowship I wanted but I got a job!"

And then prattles along, describing the campus. This is it. Cheerily feeling like it was like being on a cycle of dates. Falling in love again and again with each of the hiring committee. Finally, it says, "Mission Accomplished." *Certainly*. I do enjoy lots of things that mark me as refined. Such as shifting to sauvignon blanc at the first hint of spring. While in winter you should know that I used to drink only red, but now have decided to go only as low as an oaky chardonnay white white white in even the deepest of freezes.

My gums are clean and pink and even though the dental technician asked me if they bleed when I floss, to which I answered "no," she charts out the smallest indentations on my teeth, threatening a protective coating on the one or two abrasions, I fail to schedule an appointment on the way out because the actual dentist congratulates me, no cavities, there is no need to return.

I choose to write in form once and a while to test my skills. To keep me on my toes. And as a formalist, I try pantoums, villanelles, or sonnets, to test my accuracy, to challenge my ear. I'm good enough to capture the extent of the problem, its circularity, its condensed force. Despite the potential of my language and its expansive girth growing in my rotting stomach. I hold my art in my arm like a proud mom or dad and spread word of its dissemination. I'm so proud. This means I will never be a problem for you. I will say, "I got this. I want that. I'm tenured," and the sound will reverberate in my body or resound innocuously as the gliding car down the road, or the child screaming on the deck of the suburb from which I emerge, leave, transpire, and drift.

I choose poetry to test my limits of a fractured self. Or I write to see how the fracture looks within the assumptions of a poetic stability though I do often rattle some deep belly blues song once and a while as it belies my complexity to balance in saying. A self that imagines at this point that it can say this and looks out the window and into the memory of saying close to exactly that. And the Skype scream mine background is design behind me. So, in front of you, you will see a stack of neat books, a vast and unseen shelf out of the frame, papers wagging out like dead, tired tongues. Who are you? as you close in on the frame to hear this is why I want to go there. This is why I want to be there. To say that I'm this for you and any form you imagine, you know, I'll say anything.

(2011)

ANCESTORS

Eliot Weinberger

I want to begin with the title of a book—not the book itself, just its title, and more exactly, just one word in its title. It's a book of poetry by Nathaniel Mackey, published recently, called *Blue Fasa*. Mackey, as you know, is an African American poet and novelist who has brought a great deal of African and African diaspora culture into his work, and who also has an encyclopedic knowledge of jazz and world music. In the introduction to the book, he tells us that the title is partially an homage to an old jazz album, Kenny Durham's *Blue Bossa*—"Bossa" as in Bossa Nova—but it's the second word, "Fasa," that interests me. It's a word that many American poets once would have recognized, but it's doubtful they still do.

It comes from a narrative poem, "Gassire's Lute," that Leo Frobenius collected in Togo in 1909, sung by a master griot in Soninke, the language of the court of the vast empire of Ghana, which lasted a thousand years until the fourteenth century, when it was conquered by the Malinke, the people of Mali. The elite speakers of Soninke went into exile, and for centuries their griots—their traditional poets—sang laments for the lost land of Wagadu, as they called it, and its lost capital city, also called Wagadu, in a language that no one in their audiences understood.

Frobenius, who was born in Germany in 1873 and died in 1938, was the first European scientific exponent of African civilization. He spent thirty years roaming the continent, amassing notes on hundreds of thousands of file cards. He published twelve volumes of African folktales and, among many other books, an enormous cultural atlas that compared the artworks and everyday objects of scores of cultures. He believed, long before Leakey, that humanity had originated in Africa and, moreover, that there was, in deep history, what he called a "Eurafric" civilization, whose remnants were the quite similar rock drawings found in caves from South Africa to Lascaux, and that its memory trace was the myth of Atlantis, which, he thought, had actually existed in present-day Nigeria. Apollinaire took Picasso and Matisse to see Frobenius' collection of African masks. His writings were inspirational for Léopold Sédar Senghor, Aimé Césaire, and the other founders of the Négritude movement in the 1930s. Senghor wrote, "No one did more than Frobenius to reveal Africa to the world and the Africans to themselves." Senghor tells us how thrilling it was, as a young student in Paris, to read Frobenius' words, "The idea of the 'barbarous Negro' is a European invention." Even if his account of Atlantis is no longer—or was never—believed, his insertion of African civilization into pre-colonial European history was radical and shocking to the North's narrative of itself.

Here, briefly, is the story: Gassire is a brave warrior, the son of an extremely aged king. He is eager to ascend to the throne, but a wise man tells him that he will never rule. Instead, he will learn the language of the partridges and become a singer of the *Dausi* epic. Kings and warriors die, the city of Wagadu will be destroyed, but the *Dausi* lives forever. Gassire has a lute made for himself, but the lute is silent. He is told that the lute is just a piece of wood, that it cannot sing if there is no feeling in it. Gassire must take the lute into battle with him. It must hear the clash of swords, absorb the blood that flows and the breath of the warriors. Gassire's pain must become its pain, his glory its glory. It must become his own flesh and blood.

Gassire slings the lute on his shoulder and takes his eldest son into battle. The son is slain; Gassire carries him home and the son's blood trickles into the lute. The scene is repeated until seven of his eight sons are dead. The people of Wagadu are sick of war and send Gassire into exile in the Sahara Desert. There, he finally hears his lute sing. Meanwhile, Wagadu, unprotected by Gassire, is destroyed. In order to become a griot and sing the *Dausi* epic, Gassire has sacrificed his sons. His city—his whole world—has perished. He is nowhere with nothing but his song.

Wagadu will be obliterated and then rebuilt four times, each under a different name, and the poem has a refrain: "Hoo [meaning 'hail!'] Dierra, Agada, Ganna, Silla! Hoo Fasa!"—"Fasa" being the name of Gassire's royal family.

Ezra Pound had a long correspondence with Frobenius and with his American colleague and translator, Douglas Fox, beginning in the 1920s—the letters have yet to be published—and Gassire's lute appears in the cantos that Pound wrote while incarcerated for treason in the cage in Pisa at the end of the Second World War. Gassire turns up in the 1960s in Charles Olson's *Maximus Poems* and in an unpublished collage piece, "Origo," mentioned in his letters; in Paul Blackburn's *Journals*; in Robert Duncan's *The H.D. Book* and in the "Of the War" section of his *Passages*.

Nathaniel Mackey is one of the last in the American mythopoetic lineage of—to mention only the dead—Pound and H.D. and Muriel Rukeyser and Kenneth Rexroth and Olson and Duncan. He has often written about Gassire, beginning thirty years ago, in an early section of his serial poem, "The Song of the Andoumboulou"—the word comes out of Dogon mythology—and he has a long essay on Gassire and

Duncan's Vietnam War poems in his book *Paracritical Hinge*. (And, as Mackey once told me, there is an unexpected conjunction with another component of his worldview: Frobenius was friends with a tribal chief in the Congo. At the time, it was still the practice that when the chief died, the eldest son succeeded him, and the younger sons were put to death to avoid possible contention. Frobenius' friend asked him to rescue his youngest son, Joseph Tchicai, by taking him to Germany. As an adult, Joseph lived in Denmark and married a Danish woman. They had a son, John Tchicai, who would become a prominent saxophonist who played with John Coltrane on "Ascension" and Albert Ayler and Archie Shepp, collaborated with Amiri Baraka, and founded the New York Art Quartet. Frobenius, then, was instrumental, so to say, in the "free jazz" he could never have imagined.)

When I went back to look at these things, I discovered that I had remembered most of the Gassire story but had completely misremembered the various poets' response to it. In my mind, there were two aspects: first, like Gassire in the desert, the exiled poet in a time of war or in the ruins of war: Pound in the cage in Pisa, Duncan and the others in the alienation of, or self-exile in, America during the Vietnam War. This was similar to the traditional role of the griot in West African cultures, who, along with blacksmiths and leather tanners, was both feared and forced to live as an outcast, apart from the rest of the village, for all three are sources of power: the blacksmith makes the weapons of war, the tanner makes the shields, and the griot makes the poems. (Griots were traditionally buried upright in a hollow tree, so as not to pollute the earth or a body of water; they returned to the wood of the instrument that they played.) Second was Gassire's lute itself: the almost unbearable thought that the poet needs this blood of war, the blood of his children, to make the poem sing.

Frobenius and Gassire appear at various times in Pound's *Pisan Cantos*. Here is a passage from "Canto 74":

A man on whom the sun has gone down
nor shall diamond die in the avalanche
          be it torn from its setting
first must destroy himself ere others destroy him.
4 times was the city rebuilded, Hooo Fasa
          Gassir, Hooo Fasa dell'Italia tradita
now in the mind indestructible, Gassir, Hoooo Fasa,
With the four giants at the four corners
and four gates mid-wall Hooo Fasa
and a terrace the colour of stars
pale as the dawn cloud, la luna
          thin as Demeter's hair
Hooo Fasa, and in a dance the renewal
          with two larks in contrappunto
          at sunset

To run through it again:

A man on whom the sun has gone down

(A line that's repeated elsewhere—presumably Pound himself in the cage.)

nor shall diamond die in the avalanche

be it torn from its setting
(What endures despite disaster: for Pound, this means ideas, the true meanings of words, which is the Confucian "rectification of names," and great works of art.)

first must destroy himself ere others destroy him.

(A heartbreaking reference, given the context of the writing, to Mencius: "A man must first despise himself, and then others will despise him. A family must first destroy itself, and then others will destroy it. A kingdom must first smite itself, then others will smite it." This is James Legge's translation, the one Pound used.)

> *4 times was the city rebuilded, Hooo Fasa*
> *Gassir, Hooo Fasa dell'Italia tradita*

("of Italy betrayed": this is "Canto 74," the magnificent elegy that begins with the death of Mussolini: "The enormous tragedy of the dream in the peasant's bent shoulders." Which reminds us again that—as is so often the case in modernism—horrendous politics made great poetry.)

> *now in the mind indestructible, Gassir, Hoooo Fasa,*
> *With the four giants at the four corners*
> *and four gates mid-wall Hooo Fasa*

(Wagadu had four gates, as did the prison at Pisa. The giants, who also appear elsewhere, are apparently Pound's invention.)

> *and a terrace the colour of stars*

(This is Ecbatana, the city in western Iran built by Dioce in the eighth century BCE, described by Herodotus, and a recurrent theme throughout *The Cantos*, as the image of the ideal city. Meticulously planned as a map of the universe, it had seven terraces, corresponding to the seven planets.)

> *pale as the dawn cloud, la luna*
> *thin as Demeter's hair*
> *Hooo Fasa, and in a dance the renewal*
> *with two larks in contrappunto*

("in counterpoint")

> *at sunset*

Although the exile of Gassire and the blood that feeds the lute song may be implicit, what is explicit is the city of Wagadu itself. In the "Gassire's Lute" section of the *Dausi* epic—most of the rest is now lost, though some say it never existed—Wagadu is destroyed by vanity, another key word in Pound—the vanity of Gassire, who has sacrificed his sons and the city itself in order to sing his poem. It is built and leveled three times more, each time under a different name, each time facing another direction. After vanity, it is destroyed by the loss of faith, then by greed, then by strife. But, the poem says, "Wagadu was not actually built of stone nor of wood nor earth. Wagadu was the strength that dwelt in the hearts of men. At times it could be recognized... sometimes it could not be seen because it had fallen asleep, exhausted and bewildered by the lack of human restraint... But if Wagadu were to be rediscovered for a fourth time, it would live on in man's mind with such vigor that vanity, lack of faith, greed, or strife would never again be able to harm it." What Pound sees in the story of Gassire is Wagadu, like Ecbatana, as the image of the city as paradise.

Duncan picks up on this in *The H.D. Book*: "The lost city that is also the strength of those who live in the thought of her." And more: "The Wagadu of *The Cantos* is the lost city not of a tribe but of a kindred among all men, an 'aristocracy of emotion' Pound called it." "The people of that city, the people of a dream of a kind of human life once known that perished as the dominant way and is yet carried forward in the minds and hearts of certain devotees, this people remains... intensely aware of themselves in their allegiance to an invisible city more real than the city in which they are."

This echoes in "Passage 24: Orders," one of the "Of the War" passages, written during the Vietnam War, which sets the US invasion of the Dominican Republic in 1965 against a vision of what Duncan calls the "great household": "There is no / good a man has in his own things except / it be in the community of everything." (It should be remembered that the US occupied the D.R. in the fear that it was turning Communist, like nearby Cuba, and that Communism, for Duncan, is less its Marxist-Leninist-Maoist realities and more an image of *communitas*, of communalism.)

From house to house the armd men go,

      in Santo Domingo hired and conscripted killers
       against the power of an idea, against
      Gassire's lute,   the song
        of Wagadu, household of the folk,
      commune of communes

hidden seed in the hearts of men

        and in each woman's womb   hidden

They do not know where It is…

(The lines "hidden seed in the hearts of men / and in each woman's womb hidden" are quoted from the Gassire poem itself.)

    Gassire's appearance in Olson is too long to read here—it's in the third volume of *Maximus*, "130," a late Olson vortex of energy and free association. Gassire's fate is "FA"—the Latin root of prophecy, utterance, and fate: "to s-i-n-g [Olson spells it out] the / root of / the Well of the / Liquid of the / *Eagle's mouth*." This is Norse mythology: Odin sacrifices one of his eyes in order to drink the water from the well at the foot of Ygdrasill, the World Tree, and gain wisdom and the knowledge of his own fate. Odin changed himself into an eagle to steal the magic mead of the power of poetry; a few drops fell from his mouth, which was how humans were first given the ability to compose poems. This leads, among many other things in the poem—including magic mushrooms—to the eagle that Chaucer sees in a vision in the *House of Fame* who teaches him to write. The partridges in the Gassire story remind Olson of the partridges he heard in Gloucester, unable to speak their language, and that birds are our Muses. There is the Olsonian obsession with fathers and sons: Gassire's father declaring that the son will never be king, Gassire drinking metaphorically from the well of his own sons' blood. And there is the Olsonian obsession—some would call it a delusion—that true power resides with the poets, not the politicians, that Gassire has become more powerful than his father: "Prince in another / vocabulary / ... / agent of / all other persons for a superior / purpose."

Wagadu and the Fasa clan only appear a few times in Mackey's *Blue Fasa*, in the context of exile, wandering, and the nostalgia for the lost city. But Mackey discusses Gassire in the preface to the book and makes an interesting connection of Gassire's sacrifice of his sons with the blues singer Robert Johnson at the crossroads selling his soul to the devil, and the African American tradition of paying your dues to sing the blues. This, in turn, reminds me of the work of Sylviane Diouf, who has taken the origins of the blues back beyond the "shouts and hollers" of slaves in the cotton fields to the Muslim calls to prayer in West Africa—thirty percent of the slaves were Muslims—and the translation of kora music to guitar music. There is an archeology of everything: layers and layers to uncover. It is not the so-called "ambiguities" that New Criticism taught to unravel—it is the culture that is the latest result of many cultures that is embedded—reenacted—in any given poem.

I'm following one small word in a few poems, and it's taking me down various tracks. There are the historical and mythological particulars, and then there are the larger meditations: a Utopian city and the longing for a lost paradise, a communal poetry, the exile of the poet in the time of war or ruin, the sacrifice—however extreme in the case of Gassire—necessary to write poetry, the powerful, magical roots and nature of poetry itself.

This is the kind of thing that poetry does, or can do. It has always been not only something one reads to a lover under a tree, or alone late at night as a confirmation of, or a solace for, one's sadness—though of course it can be that. But poetry was also traditionally the archive of everything a culture knows about itself: the histories, mythologies, the customs, the daily life. Poems were an integral part of what Leo Frobenius called the *paideuma*. If Hegel's *zeitgeist* was an abstract and passive spirit of the age, Frobenius' *paideuma* was more concrete, what Pound called the "gristly roots of ideas in action"—with an emphasis on "in action." (It's reminiscent of Olson's injunction that we have to get down to the roots with the dirt still clinging to them.) The *paideuma* of a culture is in the ideas expressed, not necessarily consciously, by its artifacts, and to understand the age, you have to look at those artifacts, from high art to utilitarian objects, all of which are connected to one another. Not William Carlos Williams' "no ideas except in things," but ideas through things. This may seem obvious now, but Frobenius was the first to say it, and it raises a question: at any historical moment, in any culture, there are poems that epitomize the age. So, what are those poems, right here and right now?

The received idea among ethnologists in Frobenius' time was that cultures independently follow a kind of Darwinian evolution, from hunting and gathering to the pastoral, to the agricultural, to the mercantile with its towns. Frobenius, though he perhaps took his diffusionism to an extreme, maintained that no culture—no matter how seemingly "primitive"—has evolved or exists in isolation. In that, he was the mirror or product of modernism, which arose in a globalized world and expanded the mandate of the arts from the individual culture, from which its artifacts were created, to humanity itself. In what Duncan called the "community of everything," the subject became everything.

The task, then, for the modernist was not only to make something new, but to recover something old or neglected from one's own tradition or from other cultures: a place where Frobenius' African masks could become inspirational for Picasso. And American poetry, beside opening out into history and natural history, mythology and anthropology, politics (whether good or bad) and philosophy, rediscovered whole worlds of poetry: classical Chinese, the Provençal troubadours, the English Metaphysicals, Japanese haiku, the oral poems of tribal cultures, the Mesopotamian epics, the unrestored fragments of ancient Greek. All of these pointed to new ways to write. All of these were new ideas discovered in the old. All of these were based on the idea that one must learn from the ancestors.

With a few important exceptions—the rereading of Emily Dickinson as a radical poet, initiated by Susan Howe, is an obvious example—this has largely dropped out of American poetry. The reigning dogmas are imprisoned in an eternal present: at one end, autobiographical anecdote or rumination, written under the mantra of "writing what you know" (not what you imagine, or want to find out about); at the other end, the selfless and ironic luxuriation in the disposable language of this very moment—a poetry with a built-in obsolescence. (Another camp, the self-named formalists, while claiming adherence to tradition, seem to be merely reducing the aesthetic and political radicalism of English Romanticism to its metrics.)

Moreover, the reliance on personal experience—writing what you know—inevitably makes the poem culturally bound, fixed not only in the present but in the immediate world of its author. This, in turn, has spun into two odd and unhelpful concepts. The first is "authenticity," the belief that, since literature is the expression of the personal or a narrowly defined group "identity," certain subjects are the property of certain people and are stolen—"appropriated"—when used by others. The second is that a poetry that reflects social or political realities is somehow more valid when written by a "witness"—someone who was actually there—and it tends to regard those who weren't as inauthentic interlopers.

Of course, some writing is a detailed self-investigation, and, of course, great works have been written out of wars and the Gulag and the concentration camps, but it's hardly a rule to be followed: Dante never went to Hell; Homer never witnessed the Trojan War, not to mention the Cyclops; the "plague year" so amazingly documented in Defoe's "journal" occurred before he was born. (And all autobiographical writing, anyway, by its nature, is a form of fiction where the characters have their real names.) So, it's time to say that, in the arts, everything can belong to anyone who spends the time to learn and think about it. There are no border walls. And even more, the infinitude of possible border crossings—among groups and within individuals—is what enriches a culture and enriches a person. Among groups, nearly every Golden Age of a national literature has not coincidentally been an age of intense translation: Elizabethan England, German Romanticism, the Tang Dynasty, American modernism, to name a few. The astonishing variety of English-language literature today is largely due to the English being written by writers in or from South Asia, Africa, and the Caribbean—however the fruits of a sometimes monstrous colonial past—and the immigrants in the US and the UK who are writing in, for them, a second language. In the current nationalistic manias, it's worth saying that, along with all its other benefits, immigration is one the best things that could happen to a national literature. A culture stagnates when it never hears what other people have to say.

On the individual level, crossing the border from one's own culture or one's own experience is a way—these days perhaps the only way—to understand one's own world: the endless reverberations of contexts, contrasts, and similarities. As in Duncan's poem, you go back to traditional Africa and Gassire's lute and you go to present-day Santo Domingo to understand what is happening in America right now.

To be a writer, you have to go in search of your own ancestors, as, in Native American initiations, one had to go into the wilderness to find one's totemic animal. These ancestors are not the so-called canon, which is someone else's pantheon of ancestors. This is a personal tradition—or lineage, in the Buddhist sense—of kindred spirits, from which you learn and of which you feel you are a continuation. Although certain technologies change, the arts are all ancient arts, as old as humanity. They do not exist in some hermetically sealed chamber of the present. The artist or the writer is merely the latest in a long line, and one needs to know what that line is. And, moreover, be daunted by it.

And, to say it again—it should be obvious, but unfortunately it has no longer become obvious: one's own private tradition is not bounded by one's own collective or genetic identity. Quite the opposite: it should be entirely unbounded and not determined by the circumstances of one's birth or one's life, nor should those circumstances be relevant to a consideration of the actual work. In art, unlike economics, there is no appropriation, there is only inclusion—and the rallying banner since the birth of modernism has been the inclusion of everyone, particularly those who were excluded.

The art of one's own time exists simultaneously in two times: the present moment and a deep past, the wellspring from which art draws its power. It is both an artifact of its time, an expression of the *paideuma* of its time and culture, and something beyond. Pound's line "in the mind indestructible" is both a memory of the ruined city and a vision of the future Utopian city. To imagine the future, to imagine anything, to understand our time and to understand all times, one needs memories that are more than personal memories. Literature has traditionally been a way to hear the dead speak, to learn of what they've seen, to hear their stories. It lives in a haunted house. The ancestors you choose will determine the writer you become.

(2015)

What's the Frequency?

Trends in Contemporary Poetry

Alan Gilbert

On the evening of October 4, 1986, as *CBS Evening News* anchorman Dan Rather was taking a walk along Park Avenue, he was attacked by two men. As the primary assailant punched and kicked Rather, he repeatedly asked, "Kenneth, what is the frequency?" The two men disappeared and were never apprehended, until a person named William Tager shot and killed an NBC employee while trying to gain access to the *Today* show television studios in August 1994. At that point, Rather identified him as the man who had assaulted him eight years earlier. The second man, who Rather says didn't physically accost him, and may not actually exist, has never been identified or arrested. Tager targeted Rather, and later the *Today* show, because he claimed that the media was watching him and broadcasting messages directly into his head. Although the consequences of his actions were deadly serious, it's difficult not to note that he seems like a character straight from a Philip K. Dick or William S. Burroughs novel, two authors very much attuned to the relationship between messages and control. Poetry, perhaps more than any other artistic form, has the ability to scramble the relationship between messages and control, to create static within it, and it partly does so by putting the body—the body of the poem, an extension of the body of the poet—between them. Maybe that's one reason why Burroughs liked to hang out with poets. For a brief time early in his writing life, Philip K. Dick was a roommate of San Francisco Renaissance poets Robert Duncan and Jack Spicer.

All art is, in certain ways, about the body, because dominant ideologies seek to both fix and mark the body, and the more "othered" the body—by ethnicity, class, gender, sexual orientation, war, geography, age, etc.—the more deeply inscribed, which isn't the same as legible, the marks. Whiteness aims to be the invisibility of marks. If language—or, more precisely, discourse—is the tool of this inscription, then poetry is the writing of scars. "My vocabulary did this to me," Spicer famously said on his alcoholic, ruined-body deathbed. Spicer also famously compared the poet to a radio receiving messages from the Martians, an idea partly inspired by a scene from Jean Cocteau's film *Orpheus*, in which a poet transcribes coded messages from a car radio. This is Spicer's notion of poetry as dictation. In a Spicer poem entitled "Sporting Life" found within his larger serial poem "Thing Language," a title that evokes the poem as physical object and body, he writes, "The trouble with comparing a poet with a radio is that radios / don't develop scar tissue."

Hip-hop star Young Jeezy evokes this as well in his recent single "Lose My Mind," when he raps, "I'm hearing voices in my head think I'm schizophrenic / I swear they're saying let's get it from another planet." Of course, there's a rich tradition of interplanetary communications in recent African American culture, from Sun Ra and Parliament Funkadelic to Afrika Bambaataa and the Jonzun

Crew. In *How to Wreck a Nice Beach: The Vocoder from World War II to Hip-Hop, The Machine Speaks,* Dave Tompkins quotes Michael Jonzun of the Jonzun Crew describing the song "Ground Control" from the album *Lost in Space*: "'I thought it was time to leave Earth,' he says. '"Ground Control" was the sad intergalactic feeling of slow-moving time. Earth has a lot of problems.'" There's an ethics—and maybe an ecopoetics—here of learning to be a stranger in your own land or in the land in which you were born (which aren't always the same) while dreaming of a better place. Indigenous cultures frequently perceive themselves as custodians of the earth, not possessors of it. When Native American societies signed treaties with European colonizers, they had very little concept that the land they physically occupied could be owned.

In a short poem that opens "Thing Language," Spicer describes poetry as "White and aimless / signals"—the "white" perhaps signifying white noise, although it might be read ethnographically as well. Spicer then writes, "No / One listens to poetry," which doesn't so much signify cultural irrelevance as the idea that poetry speaks without a listener and sometimes without a poet (earlier in the same poem Spicer says that no one listens to the ocean, either). In other words, a poem is as much about the saying as the said. This idea goes back at least to Romanticism but takes on a whole new meaning in the media age, with its televisions and radios, its satellites and internet, its smartphones and unmanned drones.

At some level, William Tager was right: we are constantly surveilled and datamined, perpetually bombarded by messages from the media that in most instances are designed to feed consumer capitalism but which, post-9/11, also contain the most sinister note—the threat of stripping any individual of her or his rights, of making her or him disappear, of torturing and even killing her or him after this individual has been transformed from a political subject into a body subjected to the conditions of bare life, as the Italian philosopher Giorgio Agamben has carefully detailed in books such as *Homo Sacer:*

Sovereign Power and Bare Life (1998) and *State of Exception* (2005). It's only a slight exaggeration to say that José Padilla could be any of us, though some of us more than others.

Dan Rather, like any prominent TV personality, began to be inseparable from the media that produced him—and that eventually destroyed him in the wake of a misguided 2004 *60 Minutes* report on George W. Bush's record with the Texas National Guard during the Vietnam War. Rather was brought down by a right-wing media empire that from the start hasn't hesitated to blur the lines between news and entertainment, and, more deviously, between fact and rhetoric, between ideology and performance. Rather once appeared onstage with the band R.E.M. during a November 1995 sound check at Madison Square Garden and sang part of the song inspired by the attack on him. Or at least the title was: "What's the frequency, Kenneth?" A clip from Rather's performance was broadcast on *The David Letterman* show. At this moment in history, which is another name for story, news and entertainment become indistinct yet again.

Michael Stipe, lead singer of the band R.E.M., described the song "What's the frequency, Kenneth?" (which obviously doesn't quote the original quote exactly), as about "a guy who's desperately trying to understand what motivates the younger generation, who has gone to great lengths to try and figure them out, and at the end of the song it's completely fucking bogus. He got nowhere." I'm here today to talk about trends in contemporary poetry. And I'm going to take as a thread this idea of what frequencies we tune into, and tune into us, as poets and as global citizens. These frequencies used to be called history; in the Marxist tradition, historical materialism; and for anyone interested in psychoanalysis in the twentieth century, trauma.

History has now been replaced by a media, culture, and economic apparatus so massive that it compresses everything into a perpetual present, which Marxist theorists such as David Harvey and Fredric Jameson have been saying for decades. Poets are wrestling with this phenomenon in different ways: embracing it, resisting it, both.

The poetry movement known as Flarf submerges poetry within the post-spectacle online world. Manipulating Google searches and appropriating posts and comments from fan sites and chat rooms, Flarf aims to expose both the shiniest surfaces and darkest unconscious impulses of what was recently known as postmodern society. As a result, Flarf is meant to be both seductive and offensive. In taking seriously the idea that language—or, more specifically, discourse as ideology and material effect—determines, locates, and speaks through the human subject (which is another version of frequencies), Flarf may be the most direct heir to Language poetry, even if it originates in parody, and is very different in both intent and result.

Digital poetics sometimes applies the idea of frequencies directly. Young-hae Chang Heavy Industries' *BUST DOWN THE DOOR!*, originally made in 2000, signals back to the Kwangju rebellion (and massacre) that figures prominently in Cathy Park Hong's hybrid poetry book *Dance Dance Revolution*, while also anticipating the Bush Administration's condoning of extraordinary rendition, torture, and murder as part of the soon-to-be-implemented war on terror. Young-hae Chang Heavy Industries, formed by US poet Marc Voge and Korean visual artist Young-hae Chang, exists on the border between visual art, net art, and digital poetry. In both visual form and narrative content, the work manifests the tension between command and escape. The detainee in *BUST DOWN THE DOOR!* dreams of a better place while the barrel of a gun is jabbed into her or his back and the captors' spit drips down her or his face.

In the essay "'*Omnes et Singulatim*': Toward a Critique of Political Reason," Michel Foucault succinctly describes this relationship between power and resistance: "There is no power without potential refusal or revolt." Kamau Brathwaite outlines this relationship between power and resistance, colonizer and colonized, master language and creole in the poem "Negus" from the book *Islands* (1969), which is part of his *The Arrivants: A New World Trilogy*, originally published in 1973. The poem "Negus" mentions both TV and radio, and Brathwaite's poetry in general is filled with references to various media devices, most recently computers. In fact, he invented a font called Sycorax, which references an invisible character in Shakespeare's *The Tempest*. In the *Barabajan Poems* (1994), Sycorax the character directly transmits an alternative history of the Caribbean via Brathwaite and his computer. Along with serving as a visualized version of a transmission device, the Sycorax font emphasizes a material page in which body and place are brought into a more immediate, yet fluid, relation—"tidalectics," Brathwaite calls it, in obvious response to Hegel's dialectics. Repeating the phrase "I / must be given words" in the poem "Negus," Brathwaite explicitly addresses the idea of the poet as transmitter and as a radio responding to the depredations of both nation-state colonialism and transnational capitalism.

Over the years, my own poetry and thinking about poetry have moved from a documentary-based work engaged with history and politics, to an interest in the everyday, to one that absorbs the contradictions and confusions of life in an information-saturated and media-addled culture. Sure, it's given me some ADD, but I've got some OCD to hit back with. "The poet is a radio. The poet is a liar. The poet is a / counterpunching radio," writes Spicer in "Sporting Life." Like most of the writers I'm talking about today, I'm interested in how bodies insert themselves into this culture and get inserted by it, and I'm fascinated by the ways in which bodies physically retain history and memory. Because in a culture in which, increasingly, culture is what's for sale (as opposed to the traditional objects of traditional manufacturing—Taylorism, in other words), questions of desire become central. The danger isn't that the mass medias brainwash or indoctrinate, it's that they attempt to hijack our desires, and desire in a consumer-dependent society is directly related to what gets purchased, whether literally or symbolically.

But desire is complicated. There aren't always answers to desire, and I find myself moving away from poetry that provides answers. I want a poetry that provides complications, that reflects our fundamentally compromised lives. For myself, one of the most useful ideas about poetry is a fairly old one and a relatively simple one: John Keats' notion of "negative capability," which he briefly defined in a letter to his brother in December 1817: "Negative Capability, that is when man is capable of being in uncertainties, Mysteries, doubts without any irritable reaching after fact & reason." For Keats, the prime example is Shakespeare, whose work puts conflicting characters and forces into motion without necessarily choosing sides, and who was able to give full life to a character as wicked as Lady Macbeth and as sweet as Cordelia.

I'll close with a video that, for me, is an excellent example of "negative capability" in the present moment: Young Jeezy's "My President is Black," directed by Gabriel Hart. In it, Jeezy expresses some of these contradictions in the chorus, "My president is Black, my Lambo's blue" (meaning his Lamborghini). There are also references in the song to selling drugs amid chants of praise to Obama. I think a crucial component of any progressive politics is the ability to admit that one can be wrong, that one is fallible. The rhyming and prosody of hip hop sometimes seem to exclude it from serious discussions of "advanced techniques" in contemporary poetry, but in actuality these are tools for reinserting the material effects of the body of the poem—and by extension the body of the poet—by a community whose bodies have been the recipient of deadly material effects for centuries.

Hip hop is definitely one of the most important trends in contemporary and recent poetry. Young Jeezy's video also happens to be one of my single favorite political artworks in any medium during the past couple years. It's not a political work of condemnation, or mourning, or elegy, or judgment—in other words, it's got "negative capability"—but one of celebration. We need more ecstatic politics.

As the Situationists proclaimed in 1968, "Under the paving stones, the beach." We need more people in the streets. I also like the way Jeezy says at the beginning of "My President is Black" that this is "the realest shit I never wrote," probably meaning that he wrote it in his head and not on paper, a compositional method in hip hop that reminds me of Spicer's theory of poetry as dictation.

In my mind, "negative capability" is a form of dictation, which implies a writer tuned into various, perhaps competing and contradictory, frequencies. Some of the poets I've talked about today might be understood in terms of "negative capability," and some of them might not. But that's okay. Being able to encompass both is itself a form of "negative capability," functioning like some weird amoral and rhizomatically wobbly, occasionally punch drunk and irredeemably broken dialectic.

(2017)

Lyric Embodiment

Hoa Nguyen

Lyric, Music, Poetry

Music initiated me into poetry. Sung lyrics. Human experience and stories told and sung as song. Poetry as music and language, transformed. Those songs I sometimes call talk songs. Songs that split off from human words into a new language inside of song. A calling to orders of self beyond self. Let's call it a nerve ghost that sings.

In Vietnam, traditional folk poems are memorized and sung. A tonal language, it's one that I learned and lost, the ghostly imprint through which I heard a relationship of music and language as something I shared with origin and kinship despite loss. An articulation and tonality waiting to be writ and sung, an orientation to linkage, patterns, and ruptures.

In 1994, I was figuring out how to become a poet. That year, Naropa's Jack Kerouac School of Disembodied Poetics celebrated twenty years of brilliance and I attended the Summer Writing Program as a visiting graduate student. I was barely prepared for the richness of the programming, studded with a long list of literary giants. It was during that summer that Nathaniel Mackey's gave his lecture on Lorca's *duende*, a presentation he named "Cante Moro."

In his talk, Mackey addresses Lorca's consideration of the so-called "dark" or "black sounds," the sounds of *cante jondo* or deep song, and "the quality and condition known as *duende*..." The title, "Black Song," refers to "dark" or "black" song as "Moorish singing." This naming, originally used by Roma artists, acknowledges Spain's "deep song" tradition, one that is linked with the impact of the Moors in Spain. By doing so, this gesture, says Mackey, "acknowledges the hybrid, heterogeneous roots not only of *cante jondo* but of Spanish culture generally, of, in fact, culture, collective poesis, generally." His talk went on to discuss the influence of African diasporic "presence and persistence" as that "of the otherwise excluded, the otherwise expelled," and how this influence participates in these soundings. As music, they are sounds beyond language, an essential source; duende is linked to trouble, deep trouble, "a struggle, not a thought" that concerns loss. The surfacing of this loss comes with meaning and resonance. It is *itself* a meaningful and resonant cause.

As a Vietnamese American diasporic poet, I was drawn to the formulation of cultural bearings—the past and the relationship to language and its musical charges and capacities. In poetry, I've long been interested in the connection between the living and the dead inside of this struggle, with place and history, with speaking beyond the immediately known to the perceived elsewhere, of reading the patterns inside of cyclical systems, and in poetry's enduring relationship to the mediation of past, present, and future. Adjacent to this, as a maker my attentions remain on language's performative possibilities of utterance and syntactic turns and timbre and how sound coheres as we move inside architectures of meaning.

Of Spain's singers of flamenco, Mackey says: "The voice becomes troubled. Its eloquence becomes eloquence of another order, a broken, problematic, self-problematizing eloquence." Mackey is speaking here of the presence of duende in flamenco singing, a necessary friction that has the effect of increasing its difficulty rather than promoting any clarity. He writes: "One of the things that marks the arrival of duende in flamenco singing is a sound of trouble in the voice, the voice becomes troubled. Its eloquence becomes eloquence of another order, a broken, problematic, self-problematizing eloquence."

Hiccup and Hauntings

My first attempts at writing creatively explored loss, home-lessness, and disfluency. My young self wrote short stories and created characters who struggled into articulation and belonging. Looking through the lens of "Cante Moro" to these young stories, I see my protagonists, including one named "Hiccup the Frog," a frog who has a speech impediment of hiccupping when nervous. Funny now, reflecting back, I can see how this character aligns with an understanding or inquiry toward a "limping eloquence" alluded to in the essay "Cante Moro." While mine was a talking frog, the disfluency is similar: a self seeking to go beyond language, a self struggling into articulation, "resounding inside of interruption/repetition." The nerve ghost lives inside two worlds, crossing realms with necessary articulations.

Language ghosts can arrive as intertextuality. For a public park installation in Philadelphia, pavers have been inscribed with lines of poetry. My paver includes the lines from a poem from which half of the language belongs to Shakespeare's "Sonnet 86" (echoing the lines "by spirits taught to write"), stating:

> Spirits taught me to write   countless spirits
>   writing this

As part of a current creative research, I'm studying the indigenous religions of Vietnam and their occult aspects (spirit mediums, spirit possession, divination, talismanic blessings, etc.). Ceremonially, observances may involve elaborate costuming, genderqueer shaman, and pageantry and music, while others are conducted without instrumental accompaniments or devotional decorations aside from flowers and incense. Spirit communications are important in all Viet indigenous religions.

Many are what are generally categorized as "folk" systems, ancient beliefs held in the commons, practiced in public and private. These systems of practice can be described as one of engaged relationality rooted in nature—often with an appreciation of ancestors both human and non-human. In the West, these practices are called "animism" and "ancestor worship." My earliest memory is an attempt to venerate my Vietnamese great-grandfather. I was five and created a ritual with water where I evoked his presence. This is a different kind of record keeping, articulated through the body, with language and something beyond language.

It seems to me that speaking beyond the immediately known to the perceived elsewhere is a constant preoccupation when it comes to a formulation of a poetics with the lyric. Sometimes this elsewhere speaks from "extra-human" sources. As poet Alice Notley writes in an interview:

> I sometimes think that good poets open themselves to all the voices in the air, and they are there, of the live and dead, of animal and plant and inert matter, of whatever inhabits the rest of the universe. And to a vast unconscious or sleeping assemblage of souls. My job has become to interpret the nature of the cosmos as it is presented to me by these voices, but I suspect that "the dead" speak through the voices of any poets that are open to them, the way you can open up when you write a poem and tap words from just anywhere.

In music, this other voice can be sources in an instrument; as Mackey writes of the slide guitar, that slide technique is applied in order to produce "a more human (but not quite human) sound out of the guitar, out of the instrumental line—human-but-not-quite-human speech as well as human-but-not quite-human cry." The slide guitar's use in American Blues is linked to the diddley bow, a West African instrument that allows the player to bend strings. Like the diddley bow, the đàn bầu is an ancient monochord zither. It consists of a single bent string over a resonator; the string is manipulated by a stick. Use is typically for songs of lamentation, traditionally sung by blind players. The folk origin story tells of the monochord as an invention of a woman, a widow who made it while her husband was at war to fight the invading Chinese as a way to support herself and her children. It is estimated to be at least one thousand five hundred years old. The flexible rod causes the tension of the string to vary, the pitch may be made to rise or fall, the note may be lengthened or shortened, and trills may be played, producing a "human (but not quite human) sound out of the guitar, out of the instrumental line—human-but-not-quite-human speech as well as human-but-not quite-human cry."

Earth Dragon Aquarian

In preparing for this talk, I thought about this tale and I thought about women, and how often their contributions are not counted or remain anonymous. I'd like to bring forward a woman singer, gospel great Dorothy McGriff (who later went by Dorothy Love Coates) with a voice that exemplifies "eloquence of another order, a broken, problematic, self-problematizing eloquence."

Born in Birmingham, Alabama on January 30, 1928, like me she was an Aquarius of the first decan. She was also born a lucky Earth Dragon in the lunar system. Here you'll want to cue the song "99 & A Half Won't Do" and listen with me.

I think of her voice as something torn yet rising up. Striving for that last step which maybe feels out of reach. But the rising voice, reaching voice, is what goes beyond the given. Nathaniel Mackey speaks of this, also: the falsetto, the rasp—how the voice stretches into a song in search of the lost ground, lost twin-ness, lost union—a "wish to be we," converting the loss of a larger collectivity into song that sings toward the "longingly imagined, mourned or remembered place, time, state or condition." She could outsing the male singers of her era. Her spirited singing would lead her off stage, so drawn by this lost striving; her Harmonettes would lead her back on. (James Brown copied this as a performative act; in Coates, it was genuine). A skilled songwriter, she also became active in the Civil Rights Movement, working with Martin Luther King Jr., and addressing political issues, speaking out against the war in Vietnam, racism, and other evils.

READING PATTERNS INSIDE OF CYCLICAL SYSTEMS AS A WAY TO RELEASE CONTENT & FORM

> Divination is working with things to release the content and form of a future or fate, sometimes bringing up what we choose upon a conscious impulse, sometimes drawing the sorts by chance to bring a foreign element into action.
> —*Robert Duncan*

The card Judgment in the tarot deck is the number twenty; two turns of the wheel (or spiral), the Fool, who is fully awake to consciousness. Awakening is the name given this card by tarot adept Rachel Pollack. Others name this card as Discernment. The meaning is the same: a rising up of an insistent previousness that will animate the future—life that functions to animate the yet-to-be. We learn from the past, from living traditions, and create our own actions based on a psychological outlook of our culture in order to bring us back to life.

Awakening is not the small death of lovers' union nor the acceptance of death as change, but the ability to move from a fragmented state to a state of wholeness. But as with Osiris, can we, as writers (God Thoth of the myth), animate the dead, move from fragmentation to incomplete wholeness?

Isis, "Queen of Heaven," performed the rite to reanimate Osiris (opening of the mouth ceremony) with Thoth. As bird, as soaring wailing kite, Isis not only lamented and purified Osiris, but ferried Osiris to the underworld.

A lyric as song that recalls echoes in lyric poetry's seriality. A "telling in articulacy."

Why does the lyric, the cry, resemble a call that is pre-utterance or re-utterance? How to ring in order to awaken? Ring: "to crow, caw, croak, shout." I maintain that the lyric, to call into an uprising, must be a braid of vocality: complex, scrapingly dissonant, a polyphonic "affectivity of the ghost" as Fred Moten writes of moaning in Black song.

THE LYRIC OF UNKNOWING

I was born in the Mekong Delta. Delta means change, and I'm interested in lyric poems that are designed to invite complex relationships between stable, less stable, and unstable meaning-environments as a parallel experience of a diaspora marked by kinship, rupture, and loss.

> Wandering Souls' Day is the second largest festival of the year. (Tet is the first.) Though it falls on the fifteenth day of the seventh month, it may be celebrated at any convenient time during the latter half of the month. It is not just a Buddhist holiday but also celebrated by all Vietnamese who believe in

the existence of God, good and evil. They believe that sinful souls can be absolved of their punishment and delivered from hell through prayers said by the living on the first and fifteenth of every month. Wandering Souls' Day, however, is believed to be the best time for priests and relatives to secure general amnesty for all souls. On this day, the gates of hell are said to open at sunset and the souls fly out unclothed and hungry. Thus, plenty of food is left at family altars.[59]

Wandering Souls was also the name of a psychological warfare operation designed to exploit this belief system to encourage defectors. It was not successful and when the ghost tapes were played from US helicopters (the voices and funeral music simulating lost, wandering souls of killed unburied soldiers), the response was very heavy ammunition fire.

I tend to articulate the trauma of the Viet diasporic experience inside of what is hidden—what the trauma of loss and rupture confer—including essential ties to kinship, the severing of kinship ties. I hate that the last paragraph ended in ammunition fire. Sometimes I say seeds and crumbs. Robert Duncan's "speaking of more than one knew what."

A displacement and loss of language, land, life ways, a loss that is sensed as "phantom limb," a term used by Mackey in reference to an African American diasporic experience…that can include a wooing of the other unknown voice, "an alternate voice, that's so important to *duende* has as one of its aspects or analogues in poetry that state of entering the language in such a way that one is into an area of

---

[59] "Trung Nguyen, Wandering Souls Day", Offroad Vietnam, https://offroadvietnam.com/vietnam-info/festivals-holidays-and-recreation/wandering-souls-day

implication, resonance, and connotation that is manifold, many-meaninged, polysemous."

In the preface to his poems in *Splay Anthem*, Nathaniel Mackey quotes Edward Dahlberg: "Memory is our day of water tutored by want."

This is interpreted by Robert Creeley as, "We remember what we have because we do not have it."

(2018)

from FROM THERE TO HERE TO WHERE

Robin Blaser

So, I was born in 1925, in Denver, Colorado. I was illegitimate for five months before my father decided to be respectable. If you will, go back to 1925 and think what an utter disgrace that was. And for my mother, who had been in a convent, a Sacred Heart Convent, in Provo, Utah—The Sacred Heart Sisters are Jesuit Sisters. I am deeply indebted to that tradition, for the history of that thing I'm always hanging on, and that is why we must know how old we are. And that was a way to begin. It also meant that I was made to learn the mass in French and in Latin as we didn't have an English mass then. And, so there were things to do, things to be, things that I do not let go of and say thank you for, for all of my distance from that.

I was born in The Great Depression, and there is absolutely no help in that great depression. In fact, we need to get to Franklin Delano Roosevelt in 1933 before any help would have come and any great vision of social justice began. All of it is now being torn down here, and up there, as a matter of fact. And, what's fascinating was my grandmother, they had been, they'd come from at least a very comfortable level economically, when everything broke down. And, she must have had, though I have not the story from her, she must have had the contacts to get a position, a job. She became a telegrapher. And, I wanted to bring the telegraph key, and especially for those of you young enough not to know, that there was once upon a time, no net; and once upon a time, a lot of other things, and so that you handled the trains by way of a telegraph key, with Morse code. I have her telegraph key, and it has a wonderful sound [knocks a moment of Morse code on the table]. And, so, I was taught that, and that was perhaps an early, an early learning of language which was not itself.

She wound up first, and I think this is where my mother got fucked, she wound up in a place that was given the name Blaser, which is my last name, and, as I've said before, if you look in the Rand McNally Commercial *Atlas*, it's the only atlas in the world that would name Blaser, Idaho; and, as I've said elsewhere, it will tell you there is no population. And let me tell you, there is no population. There is also the river, the Portneuf River, which runs right along the place called Blaser, and there is a highway called Blaser Highway; so you might wish to drive it someday. It's charming: on one side sage brush hills, on the other, the river, and then some mountain. And then you wind up in Bancroft, a town named for the great historian. Someone ought to help that little town. That's where my great-great-grandmother, my grandmother, and uncle Mitch, who wrote westerns, that's where they are buried.

Now, those westerns, there was an entire trunk of them. One of those trunks, what do you call that when they weave the heavy branches? Wicker branch. And my father, now he's married my mother, you see. And when it came time to move my grandmother from Orchard, where she had managed on this salary. Of course, women, there were other women, but getting jobs, women would be stuck out in these little places with populations of nine, or nineteen or something. And what they did there was to send the telegraph messages back and forth, and so on. And then they had big bamboo hoops, so when the train came rushing by, because this is being sent to an agent some place on the telegraph lines. So it wouldn't be going to the train directly. So they would go out, I can't believe this thing they told me: they go out with this hoop and there's this little wonderful grandmother, Sophia Nichols, she would hold the hoop up while the train roars by, and the engineer would put his arm through the hoop and get the message, which was on a very special yellow paper. And then throw the hoop out into the sagebrush. That was my job: to find the hoop. I thought that was absolutely marvelous. Splendid. And I have an absolute love of sage brush.

I'm trying to, you see, I'm after the "there." And so, I've gone all the way back, and especially to her. Now, they're broke, and they didn't get much to take with them from the better life that they had once led. The telegraph key is missing because I was afraid they would think it was a bomb, in the security system. And even if I tried to explain it, they would see there was some wires on these things, and arrest me immediately. So, the telegraph key is waiting for me to send you a message when I get back. The other thing was, a few pieces of furniture were there. At one point you'd find me under the library table, you know a library table's the one that has a shelf at the bottom to put the magazines on and so on, and the rest was a writing top and all this kind of thing. Well, they had that, and a rocking chair. And the rocking chair, this is the back of that rocking chair [holds up a square of canvas with a dark portrait painted on it]. So that in my childhood, this was my companion. If you look at it, you can't escape him. He never lets you go.

Now, the housing. Let me tell you about the housing. What the Union Pacific did was to take old railway cars and stick them right by the railway tracks and turn them into housing. And sometimes, if you were lucky, you'd get the dining car, so you'd have a few more windows. You know, it was quite good, but they were narrow. And the library table and this chair, and you never see me alone, I'd go all the length of this railway car, painted yellow, Union Pacific yellow, and I'd try to get away so I'd get under the library table. That gave me a few moments respite. So, now, so much for that part of it. And I wanted you to recall whether you call him Wandering Jew or Wandering Nomad. The stories of him all of you will know. The Nomad. I am the nomad, now, and will be the rest of my life. Many of you will be too. We are wanderers, and that is where we stay. Now, I told you that there is a Blaser, Idaho, and Orchard, Idaho. There were other places: Kimama and so on. All of this is Idaho landscape. Now, grandmother Sophia Nichols. Oh yes, there were a few books that she'd managed to keep from a better life. And those few books, there was a set of Poe, that little set you'll still see in used bookstores in ten volumes in red. Absolutely invaluable. Poe. There was some Hawthorne. That made me imagine that I'd be able to go to Bowdoin College someday, but I never got there. But I got to some other good places, and then went to Bowdoin to see what I'd missed. And I had missed. There was some Emerson there. And most of all, this back of the chair. Of course, I put that in literature. And then we had something that utterly fascinated me. And this was my first sense of poetry. Apart from my grandmother liking to quote a little bit of things to me and these other books. And it was (she pulls out something, the sound of large pages turning is heard. It's Dante, illustrated by Doré. And the book is large, like a full-sized art book). Now this is the size of the book. And this book was more than half my size! I started reading at about four. But before that, I was after this book. This is *The Inferno* in this instance, and it's a marvelous edition. This is a translation by Henry Francis Cary, early in the nineteenth century, this particular edition. And then the illustrations are later in the century, by Gustave Doré. And you can find them around, and so on. All three were done but *The Inferno* is what fascinated me, with the scariest pictures you can imagine. And put angels permanently in my life, and I wasn't quite understanding then that people were really being magnificently punished. It was in later years that I discovered more of the volumes of *The Comedy*, *The Purgatorio*, and *The Paradiso*. And here, I want again to draw attention to the marvelous study of Philippe Sollers of Dante, that our poetic condition is that of purgatory. You try to think of a paradise. You try to write a paradise. I suggest you try a purgatory first because I think we talk the inferno all the time. The purgatory is a life you live that is a matter of a debt and a necessary transformation. We would be hard put to it to write that paradiso, though I like to read and reread Dante's and remember its possibilities. *Paradiso* 27, lines 4-5, Dante says "what I saw seemed to me a smile of the universe." I'm so touched by that.

(2003)

News Bulletin

kari edwards

I had a couple people ask me, "Why do we need to worry about words when people are starving?" I went home early last night because I was exhausted and depleted and starting to get cold, and I had a news bulletin, I mean, it came over the wires, I didn't make this up, this is real: in Cortez County yesterday, they found a teenager bludgeoned to death who was thought to be a homosexual because this individual had plucked their eyebrows, had makeup on, and had a purse. And this is no joke. They really just found this person totally brutalized out in the woods. And the other thing about words is why, when we hear about other people being murdered, do we have to hear about their clothes or their makeup? Why does that happen to anybody who's queer? Oh, they were wearing this, or they wore this. So, I was really taken back by how easy it is to sort of make someone look like a target, and it also, it's also a way to tell all queers, "if you dress like this, this is gonna happen to you." So, I have a little thing I want to read. But I just wanted to … since we stayed here and we didn't get to hear the news, I wanted to pass that on.

I was thinking: Narrative. Isn't that the sort of thing that forms identity? Maybe I was thinking of another narrative. Whatever the case, I see narrative as something that needs to be troubled, discarded, and sent through the shredder. I personally attempt to find the edge of narrative, where it starts to disintegrate into a Dadaist manifesto and end up negating itself. Well, that's not quite right. I attempt to find the edge where narrative turns into an endless cycle of rejecting, appropriating, and expelling. Digressing from the thread of the possible to the impossible, to the utopian, that at any moment can turn to the depths of the torturous shadow. Did I mention that Brandon Teena was beaten, raped, then murdered? I'm not sure I said that. Anyways, at the same time, I want to try to maintain a thin connective tissue to a narrative, to the object at hand, so I don't lose myself in a lack of gravity, fear, or some trumped up charges listed in the *Diagnostic and Statistical Manual for Mental Disorders*. But the question is, how loose can the connective tissue be and still maintain a sense of cohesion? Does it need to even be a narrative? Could it be lists, phone numbers, or instructions on the impossible? I don't know how many panels I've been on, speaking on gender, linguistics, and performativity, and how everyone cross-dresses no matter what, and so on and so forth. And after every other queer on the panel has told their coming out story, complete with details about their urinary tract and what brand of makeup they use, someone turns to me, "So, what's your story?" I always wonder if they want me to lie, or for me to sit here for the next forty-five years and tell my story. I think this kind of "what's your line?" narrative is either a Foucauldian confession centering on a narcissistic rendezvous with one's kinship, or reiteration of some mythic telemarketing scheme trying to perpetrate the social contract. Then maybe the other type of narrative, the big grand master narrative. I'm not sure. They both seem so similar to me and reinforce each other's schema. If I say homosexual, does that not reinforce heterosexual? Did I tell you gender is surgically enforced on infants? I'm not sure I told you that.

In reading way too many biographical coming-out stories, I'm finally a woman, a man, gay, lesbian, top, bottom, leather, king, drag king, I've always wanted to be stories, of those that have been labeled, or labeled themselves, transsexuals, transgender. I was a secret transvestite for the SS. What I found for the most part is a struggle to speak themselves into existence without their voice emanating from the great medical model, or to say it differently, their internalized, colonialized body. I'm speaking about individuals such as Jan Morrison and Christine Jorgensen, trying to escape the symbolic, only to have their legs caught in a bear trap of the binary. If you're not this, then you're that. Did you know Joan of Arc was burned at the stake for wearing men's clothes? Did you know that in the 1960s and '70s, gender clinics enforced stereotypical gender behavior? I'm not sure I told you that. The first crack in the gender narrative was *Gender Outlaw* by Kate Bornstein. That's not really the first, but I think *Gender Outlaw* did irrefutable damage to the narrative. A truly postmodern text that weaves indeterminacy, drama, theory, and a short section on S&M, into a multi-textual experience. The text's construction reflects the experience of Kate. A little bit from here, a little bit from there. A sort of cut-up, paste thing. I always thought the cut-up and paste thing was sort of ironic. Get it? Cut-and-paste? *Gender Outlaw* can be seen as a mirror of no gender. Dysphonic, slightly out of phase oscillation with a light reliance on narrative, chopped up and reassembled, but nonetheless narrative. I wanted to see if I could bring the experience into the structure of text. A sort of text of and on gender and language with the inhibition button released, where it becomes a joy ride through the absurd. Did I tell you that that's what it's like? I mean, here I am riding along in my car, and the gender police pull me over and demand that I circle either "F" or "M." And I don't. And I am informed I won't receive my pension, subscription, monthly medication, food stamps, taxes, student loan repayment plan if I don't. And you know I have to laugh since I know and you know, this gender thing's all made up. I know I was never a boy, and I know I was never a girl. So, hey, where does that leave me? Lying on my gender exam. Or, so, if I'm lying, what else? I want to know who else lies on their gender exam. Go, ahead: raise your hands. Oh, got a couple. Great. It's fine. The destabilization process has already started. Did you ever see the movie *The Invasion of the Body Snatchers*? The other question, then: if gender is made up and strictly reinforced, you have to wonder what else is made up. How deep is the conspiracy? Is the world really flat? And what if the words that bind us are released? What would the world be like? Better yet, what are the possibilities of sex if we don't have language differences, male, female, man, woman, gay, straight. Oh, I was talking about narrative and identity. Well, if narrative is here to reinforce identity, and identity fluctuates depending on one's mode of expression at the time, and the gaze one receives from others, then there's no such thing as gender or sexual categories. And identity becomes indeterminate as narrative. Well, that doesn't quite sum it up. What we really need to do is send the super ego on a permanent holiday.

(presented at the panel: Identity, Narrative, Anti-Narrative, 2001)

Narrative and Fragment

Robert Glück

For no reason in particular, I'm going to begin with something, just because I like it. It's a little snippet from one of the gnostic gospels, The Gospel According to Thomas:

> Jesus saw some little ones nursing. He said to his disciples, "what these little ones who are nursing resemble is those who enter the kingdom." They said to him, "so, shall we enter the kingdom by being little ones?" Jesus said to them, "when you make the two one and make the inside like the outside, and the outside like the inside, and the above like the below, and that you might make the male and the female be one and the same, so that the male might not be male, nor the female female. When you make eyes in the place of an eye, and a hand in place of a hand, and a foot in place of a foot, an image in the place of an image, then you will enter the kingdom."

Thank you, Jesus. Kristeva, Julia Kristeva, that would certainly be her idea of paradise. She's writing quite a bit about the breakdown of ego boundaries, and in particular about the breakdown of boundaries between a mother and child.

I teach fiction writing in an MFA program, and very often during the course of a class discussion, I find myself engaged in such questions as "Would Norma really say that to Ted, when Ted said he was going to fix up his cousin Al with Norma's best friend, Nancy?" It's fun, and it's a little like doing crossword puzzles, and I think of it as cultivated entertainment. It's mostly what fiction is. It's cultivated entertainment. It's a couple degrees better than television, usually. And it's terrific, you know. You read it and while away the time. But there's no doubt that it supports the status quo, what a self is, and what governs our lives. The way a story is told is the way a self knows itself. How it perceives experience. By the same token, I don't think fragmentation and disjunct forms, which, after all, are taught also in schools, along with other approaches to writing, automatically exempts a work of literature from the category of cultivated entertainment. So, what does Louis Althusser winningly put in his essay called "Ideological State Apparatuses?" He said, "Ideology is the imaginary resolution of real contradictions." "Ideology is the imaginary resolution of real contradictions." That's a statement that was very important to me in the late '70s and '80s when New Narrative writing was getting going. And it seemed to give a permission for the interpenetration of the fiction of self, to see the self as a fiction, and for that to interpenetrate other kinds of fictions. Ok, so, for ideology, substitute writing: writing is the imaginary resolution of real contradictions. Then substitute the self: the self is the imaginary resolution of real contradictions. If the self is a fiction, an imaginary resolution, is it the same as the fiction one may be writing? Writing that knows itself allows these contradictions to be resolved. What contradictions? The self versus the community, the self versus the state, the unified self against the self as an ensemble of social forces and interactions—that phrase, "ensemble of social forces and interactions," is actually from an essay by young Marx, a very repulsive essay, actually, called "The Jewish Question." Nature versus society, the life of the senses versus the distance of history, sense and nonsense, class conflict versus the rhetoric of classless society, the violence of our country versus the rhetoric of peace, or versus the suburbs, the desire to live versus the desire to die, local culture versus turbo capitalism, the word and the thing it identifies, the writer and the reader, timelessness and time, duty versus self-interest, which you could see, for example in [Jean-Baptiste] Racine. And in general, writing as a made-up thing and writing as a depth. There's a phrase I like by Robert Duncan. He's talking about the poem, but I also think it could just as well describe the self: "a made-up thing and a depth in which my being is." I would like to gather all these contradictions under the heading of autobiography, which is the problem of the self. But you can see it differently. By autobiography I mean dreams and daydreams, the relationship to the reader, the clash of flesh and culture, the self as an ongoing collaboration, the self as fragmentation, and the enjambments of power, family, and history. At any rate, I look for writing that makes such contradictions visible. So, disjunct writing describes a fragmented self. By disjunction, I mean a break in narrative expectations, like switching point of view mid-sentence, as Juan Goytisolo does in *Makbara*, mixing of genre, working with the sentence as a palette, working below the sentence, working with collage and appropriation, seeing character as an environment, as one of my students today said. The fragment is used to combat. So, we have fragment...there's a lot done with the fragment. It just doesn't sit there. It's used to combat patriarchal linearity, convey spiritual states, describe the porousness of women's experience, make writing know itself, examine the way narration makes meaning by obstructing that process, portrays a desolate breakdown of character and society, celebrates a polyvocal approach to writing and the world, and the collapsing of categories. The mobility of, like, my would-be saint, Marjorie, who ran around the holy land in Europe in the fifteenth century, is part of the process of mobility that allows the surrealist image to travel anywhere, or the signifier and the signified to come unstuck. I can find my being in the movement of a story, or in the silence between fragments. Do I live in a coherent narrative? Sometimes. Sometimes it is important for a group to tell itself its own story, especially for a group fighting for self-recognition. A community may be conservative in that it conserves a certain kind of self. Narrative can bring new matter into language, a new way of being, an ethnicity or a sexuality, gossip.

Something I'm very interested in is the way a community tells itself what is inside and what is outside, and so an interesting place to write from. The other night, Robin [Blaser], David [Farwell], and I were walking across the street and a truck bore down on us, and we ran across the street, Robin taking the lead. At that moment, I think, his self was very united, and in general I think danger may unite the self in self-preservation, and when are we not in danger? So, there's narrative. A work of literature can be as complex as a person. I want both narrative and fragment. In writing, you can have your cake and eat it too. I see a lot of work, now, that seems to take for granted a high level of disjunction with rich narrative elements—work by writers here this week—and that is very interesting, as it describes and summons into being what could be called a community of doubt. I'd also like to mention Pamela Lu's book *Pamela*, Dodie Bellamy's *The Letters of Mina Harker*, and Camille Roy's *Rosy Medallions*, Gail Scott's *My Paris*, and Lawrence Braithwaite's *Wigger*. One time I was interviewed by an editor from *Cups Magazine*. Do you know what that is? It's like a coffee house magazine and he, in the middle of the interview, said "you're for unsafe sex, right?" And I was dumfounded. And then I realized that he wanted me to give him a recipe for transgression, that he wanted me to give him some kind of junior woodchucks manual on how to be transgressive. So, what is transgressive writing? Well, in my view, it's writing that describes the present. That is the shock of transgressive writing. That is the shock of Baudelaire, of Kathy Acker. The present is not yet described. The present is shocking. It has never been described. The language has yet to be invented. We have to make one up. There are no forms that describe the present. That is always the case. You know, why would there be any shock, for example, when the Impressionists showed work, and it was just a bunch of fuzzy haystacks. Why would anybody get upset? Well, it was telling people they were perceiving the world in a way that they haven't yet realized. And that was very upsetting because it was telling them they didn't know who they were. They were looking for recognition, and they couldn't find it. By describing and so creating the present, I include such interventions as translating a Palestinian poet, or reconsidering a moment in history, testing the borders of the acceptable, the exploration of shame and breaking down, as Eileen [Myles] spoke about this week, breaking down that is. We're all united in that. I am looking for an anti-narrative that brings into language the contradictions and imaginary resolutions of the present. A writing, as Robin said, that is not as we have been, but relates to the condition we are in.

(2001)

GRASSES GRASSES GRASSES

Fred Moten

1.

Because I know of no typography that corresponds to the topography of Layli Long Soldier's *Whereas* and the existence with which it is concerned, the invention of an alternative system of marks, or another repertoire of marking, is required. And this is to say that the malady of not marking must be voided, with the settler's mouth full of grasses brushing through the skin, unsettled mouthfeel whatsaid violently in Long Soldier's saying. When she writes of a writing without words—of the rites of such writing, of the wrongs it bears, of its rupture of and by the brutality of the philosophy of right—it makes you wonder what comes first: the necessity or the exhaustion of transcription and translation. Because I cannot even write the title of the first poem of *Whereas*, not only not even knowing if it's accurate, let alone true, to speak of it as a first poem, its putative singularity given in numbered sections so that it seems always to be arriving before itself; because insofar that it appears, or they appear, as a named section of a larger field or plain that defies its name in sounding the depths of its doubleness, which is as numberless as grass, as the grassesgrassesgrasses; because I am enjoined and seem unable to make room for it in my mouth as it flares down to the tips of my fingers; because I cannot type what I also cannot pronounce, so that I can neither rewrite nor recite *Whereas*, I cannot read *Whereas*.

I am compelled to write about *Whereas* because I cannot read it; that I cannot read it is given in that I cannot write it down or ride it across. After having begun many times, there's a title that appears to be made of two words; but I don't know if they're two or if they're words. This estrangement with which I begin is a barrier to communication that tells of radical communicability. There's an undeniable circulation of feel which also stops in its tracks anything like a tendency to assume or enshrine some fundamental distance between me and what I can't read, or write, and where it comes from, and/or from whom it comes. This is a matter of approach, something in the distance, a topographical existence, a sudden rise. It's not that there it was, word for word, the poem that took the place of a mountain; rather, it's that poem and mountain and the theft of the mountain and the erasure of the people's approach to it which is given in its approach to them are held and unheld in a double displacement. *Whereas* is such displacement's plainsong and what I am trying to say is that its name—and the name of the poem with which the poem begins again; and the name of the mountains with whose misnaming the poem begins again and again; in the name of the indigeneity, the irruptive presence, and the Blackness of the mountains; in the name of the mountain and the poem and their mutual approach and shared indigence, "sleek in the rise of both," a twoness both imposed and already given in what can only pass as one passing through the passion of the numberless—is a name that can neither be read nor written from my position, or from any position that can be held. Hence the terror, and terrible beautiful necessity, of "this unholding":

> Hĕ is a mountain as hé is a horn that comes from a shift in the river, throat to mouth. Followed by sápa, a kind of black sleek in the rise of both. Remember. Hĕ Sápa is not a black hill, not Pahá Sápa, by any name you call it. When it lives in past tense, one would say it was not Red Horn either; was not a rider on horse on mount and did not lead a cavalry down the river and bend, not decoy to ambush and knee buckle
>   to ten or twenty, perhaps every horse face in water.
> Its rank is a mountain and must live as a mountain, as a black horn does from base to black horn tip. See it as you come, you approach. To remember it, this is like gravel.

A huge part of what's at stake is the nature of this approach. Does approach, in this regard, imply distance? Can there be an approach that doesn't imply or bear, dragging awkwardly behind it, a position? What is it to be in the presence of another cosmology? The appearance of the mountain is all bound up with seeing it as you come, with the nature of your approach. What is the nature of seeing as you come, of approach, if one accepts the indivisibility of things, given obliquely when "he is a mountain as he is a horn that comes from a shift in the river. Followed by sápa, a kind of black sleek in the rise of both," where "both" is indeterminate in number or marks a meta/physical undecidability? The rise of both, of its appearance, of their showing up, is incalculable, uncountable, and this problematic of the incalculable, this preservation of the uncountable, is motive and motif in *Whereas*.

2.

There's an intensity regarding this problematic of how things, in their indivisibility, show up, to which Rei Terada, by way of Cedric Robinson, pays beautiful attention, allowing us to see the compatibility of indivisibility and incoherence, as well as to see (through) our regulated and regulatory surprise at that compatibility, that going together, that "black sleek in the rise of both." What we're speaking of is regulatory violence done to the irreducible irregularity of metaphysical violence, whose ruptural totality is given in never having "allowed for property in either the physical, philosophical, temporal, legal, social, or psychic senses." Here, in the possessive economy of subjects and their positions, Robinson and Long Soldier will have been unavailable to one another; but a mutual approach, a wounded profanity of share, sleek in the (sudden) rise of both, is given in the general absence of even the "slightest conjunctions." Begin there, in that deprivation, with the mark of what is missing: "*But /* is the small way to begin."

But:

> …*drag* changes when spoken of in the past i.e. he was *dragged*
> or they *drug* him down the long road, the pale rock and
> brown. Down dust, a knocking path. And to *drag* has a begin
> point (though two are considered): begins when man is
> bound; begins also with one first tug.
> So we take the word to our own uses and say:
> it begins with his head on the ground with his hair loose
> under shoulders and shirt with snaps, they're mother of pearl.
> Then begins a yank
> and slide, begins his skin and scalp—
> begins a break a tear, red to pink
> to precious white; then begins what is
> his skull, glisten of star
> to bone.

This execution, this laying down of the law comes back to us emphatically in another poem, within this infinity room of a poem, called "38." It begins, "Here, the sentence will be respected," and ends with a recitation of another poem that constitutes and redoubles the sentence, executing it in the redoubled but anticipatory execution of a man, a bound man, the man.

> One trader named Andrew Myrick who is famous for his refusal to provide credit to Dakota people by saying, "If they are hungry let them eat grass."
>
> There are variations of Myrick's words, but they are all something to that effect.
>
> When settlers and traders were killed during the Sioux uprising, one of the first to be executed by the Dakota was Andrew Myrick.
>
> When Myrick's body was found,
>
>   his mouth was stuffed with grass.
>
> I am inclined to call this act by the Dakota warriors a poem.
>
> There's irony in their poem.
>
> There was no text.
>
> "Real" poems do not "really" require words.
>
> I have italicized the previous sentence to indicate inner dialogue, a revealing moment.

NEW WEATHERS • 331

But on second thought the words "Let them eat grass" click the gears of the poem into place.

So, we could also say, language and word choice are crucial to the poem's work.

Things are circling back again.

Sometimes, when in a circle, if I wish to exit, I must leap.

And let the body swing.

From the platform.

    Out

                to the grasses.

The sentence that is respected, here, is a death sentence. And what is it for one to speak of a thing with regard to when that thing "lives in past tense"? And what is it to speak of that as, or in the shadow of, what one has become? And what is it to drag around bound man, which is drag's begin point, where two are considered, the one dragging, the one dragged, in the past, in the (old) beginning of a "switchback trail to follow," this turn on returning looked back on from can't turn back? But this is inseparable from the "small way to begin," "but," the ghost connection, the mark of conjunction's absence, which remarks a turn, an overturning, a catastrophe's double edge, the terror of again beginning given in this imperative of drag, this dragging of the man behind, our baggage, our burden, the execution of his sentence, his uncrowning, which redoubles her coronation, which is beginning as a failure to begin because of all it carries. This isn't preface to a discourse of forgiveness, that duress; but it bears, in dragging him behind, this failure:

> But I failed to begin there, with this
> expanse. Much as I failed to start
> with the great point in question.
> There in muscle in high inner flight always
> in the plunge we fear for the falling, we buckle to wonder:
> *What man is expendable?*

See, it's the burden of anticolonial morality, which Long Soldier sounds so deeply, that we must also try to misunderstand. To bear his body, and a feeling about bearing his body that constitutes no challenge whatever to the execution of the sentence, while also having to account, now, for the question of a man's expendability or non-expendability, which exists not simply as the residue of his having brutally shown up but as a function of the brutality of a certain modality of things showing up, severally, in severalty's ongoing imposition, in the very divisibility of things that constitutes Andrew Myrick as man, as trader, as settler. And see how terribly beautiful it is that his execution is redoubled in domestic care, loving violence bearing a trace of violent beginning in an ongoing effect of violent foreclosure:

> I kneel in the hairline light of kitchen and home
> where I remember the curt shuttle of eyes down, eyes up—
> where I asked, *are you looking at how I've become two?*
> This one combs and places a clip just above her temple,
> sweeping back the curtain of *why*
> and *how come.* I kiss her head I say, *maybe you already know.*
> Born in us, two of everything.
> As in, each born to our own crown—the highest part of the
> natural head.
> And each born to our own crown—a single power, our
> distinction.
> But I'm ragging myself, the other me, every strand up to the

surface. I remember
very little. So I plunge my ear into the hollow of a black horn,
                                                listen to it speak.
Not one word sounds as before.
Circuitous   this
I know.

One asks this catastrophic question concerning knowledge of having become two having left unasked the question of having become one, catastrophe's anticipatory double, which is recounted in and through this dragging of your murderous double, having forcibly let him eat grass as your beginning, given, again, in a conjunction you cannot have. If there is a catastrophe that manifests itself as the absence of a conjunction with which we might begin, there is also a catastrophe given in the impossibility of partition, which is manifest in and as (the desire for) what we s~~hare~~. Long Soldier thanks Zitkála-Šá for guidance through the catastrophe of words, sentences, their execution and for the dual annihilation of connection and separation that is both given before and imposed by colonization, and which renders decolonization all but impossible and anti-colonialism irreducible uneasy in their catastrophically counter-catastrophic tendency "to other   wise   put—."

Holding is defined variously as an area of land, as property, as possession, as detainment. It implies a certain logical consistency that will have come to legitimize, in its legal definitions, a court's determination of a matter of law or whatever legal principle that might be drawn from a judgment. But can a principle, either legal or paralegal, be drawn from the law Long Soldier lays down? Here she is in the more anti- and ante-lawyerly mode her work takes up toward its conclusion:

WHEREAS the word whereas means it being the case that, or considering that, or while on the contrary; is a qualifying or introductory statement, a conjunction, a connector. Whereas sets the table. The cloth. The saltshakers and plates. Whereas calls me to the table. Whereas precedes and invites. I have come now. I'm seated across from a Whereas smile. Under pressure of formalities, I fidget I shake my legs. I'm not one for these smiles, Whereas I have spent my life in unholding. *What do you mean by unholding?* Whereas asks and since Whereas rarely asks, I am moved to respond Whereas, I have learned to exist and exist without your formality, saltshakers, plates, cloth. Without the slightest conjunctions to connect me. Without an exchange of questions, without the courtesy of answers. It is mine, this unholding, so that with or without the setup, I can see the dish being served. Whereas let us bow our heads in prayer now, just enough to eat;

By way of Mahmoud Darwish, Nouri Gana requires us to ask whether one (people) can love life without access to it? But what if the life we have to love *is* this lack of access, "this unholding," which is the refusal and the effect of settlement. The exhausted life of "this unholding," the poverty of and in this violent fecundity of grasses, is laid bare, here, now, as where we are required to examine our decolonial and anti-colonial desire then, there, unburdened by the coloniality that infuses them, which is given in the way, in the divisible appearance, of things.

3.

Long Soldier brings another phrase of Robinson's to mind: "the eternal internal alien," a figure who will have obliterated, by virtue of its presence in and against order, a crucial distinction in Carl Schmitt's work between *hostis* and *inimicus*, the public and the private enemy. If colonialism can be characterized as an ongoing regime of exclusionary inclusion, of possessive dispossession, then that distinction was never operative. This is another aspect of the imperative to think what it is to take the outside in, what it means to sing the inside out, a dual activity by which poetry can be characterized. The poetics of Schmitt's distinction are difficult; they seem both to follow and deviate from Cicero, who distinguishes between the legitimate enemy (the one who can become a partner, or a friend, by treaty, given a fundamental equality that is most precisely expressed in conflict, where legitimacy is manifest in a proper, common, but divisible publicness that constitutes the same) and the pirate, who will have been, in their inappropriateness, more properly known as (the cons)piracy, which is the enemy, insofar as it is the essence, of all, (not-)being beyond all boundaries, outside all law, but whose delineation in theory moves by way of the language of the internal, as one's interior deviance or paramour, an impropriety that will have already invaded the proper from inside as domestic fugitive, as eternal internal alien, as when G.W.F. Hegel writes, in the *Aesthetics*, and Judith Butler echoes in *Antigone's Claim*, of those who "are gripped and shattered by something intrinsic to their own being" or when Prospero is forced to acknowledge the thing of darkness as his own or when the blackamoor inside the cave that constitutes Denis Diderot's interiority turns out to have given not only the final but the first of Wallace Stevens' paramouric soliloquys. In this regard, the shared undecidability of *hostis* and *inimicus* constitute the indigenous, indigent breakdown of inside/outside. Consider what it is to be gripped by what is inside, to be held by what one holds, as if what one holds, because it holds you, is an already given exteriority; and to have one's capacity for holding together destroyed by the thing that one holds, by which one is also held. What one holds tears one apart, in a potentiality, an eventuality, an already given event that is far more than mere exposure but is, rather, the necessary condition and enactment of force, of φύσις, of (meta)physics in its irreducible and irregular experimentality. The *inimicus* is held within, as the impossibility of being held together, in an inevitability of being-shattered that is, in the end, a shattering of being inside and outside, a catastrophic rending of ontological interiority and non-ontological exteriority. It's hard to conceive of this condition as stasis because what is held within is differentiation, given away in and as an exile whose depth is so hyperanoriginary as to exhaust itself. We might speak, along with Nathaniel Mackey, of this profane, invaluably expensive, and intrinsic exteriority as fugue statelessness, which Long Soldier offers in an ani*mate*rial, plenipotentiary poetics (under)grounded in impersonal, topographical sociality. Hannah Arendt, after Alexis de Tocqueville, can only foretell of this by way of anti-Blackness, giving us a chronicle of this death foretold, this internal dispersion, this anexilic spray that leaves settlement's vicious (dis)placement of indigeneity unremarked and unremembered. This prophecy is, for example, what *On Violence* is, revealing it as the extension of a colonial operation. Her work is continually undone by what it buries, which is violence itself, namely, unnameably, the condition in which *stasis* is already given over to *polemos* (whose warlike regulation, Terada teaches us that Robinson teaches us, is the political itself). The doubleness of irregular violence and the brutal, regulatory violence it produces, which will have been understood as its inimical other, is what Long Soldier radically, critically, and beautifully misunderstands with "this unholding" in her impersonal, revolutionarily suicidal leap "out [from the outside] to the [numberless] grasses."

To lay the law down in long grassesgrassesgrasses, in small, statelessly exceptional inadherences to the laws of the sentence, in the passing of sentences and in their recitation: this is the physics, the ante/meta/physical violence, of Long Soldier's poetry. This horizontalization of law bears a jurisgenerative grammar and gravity, a violence of stories unheld in narrative occupation. To do so, as she describes early in "38" by way of its inveterate curving of the sentence in the interest of clarity, or of, at least, the navigation of the sentence's murky waters, is to appear to have agreed to a kind of self-regulation, a kind of legalism, a clipping of the imagination's wings. Again, this liminality that is given in switching back, this severe meandering, as if along the path of a river, is something Long Soldier remarks and echoes, memorializes in action, with Zitkála-Šá's guidance, by way of her (extraordinary rendition, and rendering, and rending of the) example. But their back and forth in twoness, as two, as in the twoness of the poem "38," its straightforward wandering, its duplicitious unanimity, it's all but divine criminality can't be accounted for. Consider that the imposition of a twoness that was already there and which, now, is mobilized against whatever singularity, is as innumerable, as unanalyzable, as violence, whose other name is poetry, whose other name is Blackness, whose other name is indigeneity, whose other name is grassesgrassesgrasses, whose other names, in radial and radical exhaustion of naming, bear all that all these names can bear. "38" is not a poem; it is writing that describes one poem as unwriteable and indescribable. Its words are murky, its syntax wanders, but all that backtracking and circling in and by words is to get us to that anamemorial enactment of the poetry that requires no words. The mouth is for eating and drinking and not just talking. There's an intensity here. It is also for starving and for dying. Mouth and throat are present for holding, and for this unholding. An argument for the extra-legal is made—anamemorially, retroprospectively, topoietically—by paralegal means.

Will the circle be (un)broken? This leap by and from the brutally juridical puts one in its place, which is a noose, a circle, that is given for the exiting of circles. Fly from the platform. Out to the grasses. Long Soldier isn't happy with the poem, which is a thing made out of words. So, *Whereas* cuts itself, too. Both "that being the case" and "while on the contrary," it sets the table as and for this unholding. The law holds, all but never in holding for the plaintiff, but even in holding against them. But they are unheld by the law. And what's the relationship between unholding and non-standing?

Is there a dispossessive/non-possessive modality of resistance that disrupts the standing of one's ground, that refuses standing and the possession of ground by way of another metaphysical sociality, one that is, in its irreducible difference from itself, like something going through a double slit, both before and after the fact of colonization, so that what comes out is nothing at all, nothingness as all? This unholding sounds this liminal criminality, this paralegality, this non-being against the law, this abandonment in and to a non-juridical non-being, to a radical unprotectedness remaining, somehow, that from which the law can provide no protection, thereby inciting the sovereign violence of the state, where violence become genocidal regulation responds to an existence without formality, without the slightest conjunctions to connect me, that it imposes brutally, but impotently, against our enactive claim of it as the ongoingly annihilative ante-colonial preface to our anti-colonial beginnings and ends.

(2019)

Writer's Block

William S. Burroughs

I want to start with sort of a brief recapitulation of my teaching here at Naropa. I started out giving a course in creative writing, and I've come to doubt whether writing can be taught in a classroom. It's like saying, "Can you teach someone to dream?" Well, Don Juan[60], of course, would say "yes," but it was a long process between the student and the shaman, and certainly not suitable for a classroom.

So, I tried to arrive at the concept as to whether there was any technology for writing. I mean, anything that could be taught, say, comparable to teaching someone to fly a plane, or teaching someone to be an engineer, and I don't think that there is any such technology. There are just little bits and pieces here and there. Contraindications.

Sinclair Lewis always said … someone asked, "What should I do if I want to be a writer?" and he said, "Learn to type."

---

60 The fictional protagonist of Carlos Castaneda's *The Teachings of Don Juan*.

But he also said that, if you've written something that you think is just absolutely great, and you just can't wait to show it to somebody, throw it away. It's terrible. I found that that is often, though by no means always, true.

There are of course these books on writing and all these writing courses. One thing they don't take up is writer's block, which I think is very important because it happens to most writers at one time or another. Suddenly they just can't write. And I found that the way to get around this is not to try to force yourself, but to do something else, like reading, or whatever you can get into, photography, something. And then let it just take care of itself.

Well, I did arrive here at Naropa at a number of very important concepts, I mean, important to my way of thinking. One is that I arrived at a concept as to what the function of art and of all original thinking (that would include scientific thinking, I would say all creative thinking) is to make people aware of what they know, and don't know that they know.

The people on the seacoast in the Middle Ages, they *knew* the earth was round. They *believed* the earth was flat, because the Church said so. And Galileo was nearly burned at the stake for saying the Earth was round.

Well, after a certain length of time, of course, a new concept—once the breakthrough is made—becomes a part of the general awareness. There still is a Flat Earth group, but they're not very influential.

In the same way, when Cézanne's paintings were first shown, people were so incensed that they attacked the canvases with umbrellas. They couldn't see that this was a lemon or a fish seen from a certain angle in a certain light. But now any child can see Cézanne.

So, once you make people aware of what they know and don't know that they know, there's a period of resistance and protest until the new concept becomes part of an expanding awareness.

And Joyce, of course, made people aware of their own stream of consciousness on the verbal level. That's only one level of consciousness, and he was accused of being unintelligible—but now, I don't think any anybody would find *Ulysses* a difficult book. *Finnegan's Wake* is another matter.

So that's a trap that writers can get in, spending twenty years on the great book that nobody can read. One of many traps.

In the same way that when Brion Gysin and I came out with the cut-up method, we were accused of promulgating a cult of unintelligibility. But the cut-ups have been more and more accepted. They were used in *Performance*. No, not *Performance*! Yes, *Performance*. Mick Jagger and Nicolas Roeg, yes. He used the cut-up method in that film. I mean, Antony Balch showed him how to do it.

So, another concept that was evolved here is the concept of seeing living creatures as artifacts created for a definite purpose. And then by comparing where an artifact is, you can see where we are, in fact. You're comparing technologies.

For example, you have an artifact like a flintlock rifle. You take one look at it, and you see that it's got a long way to go before it's practical. Water can get into it, they become quite inoperable with a driving rain behind, and misfires, and so on and so forth.

Now you look at an artifact like the bow. Well, what's wrong with it? Well, very little. It's gone about as far as it can go. Because there's a basic limitation there, that the more energy you want to put into the projectile, the more energy you have to put out to pull the bow. Whereas it takes the same amount of energy to pull a trigger. Anyone can pull a trigger, but not everyone can pull a bow.

So, it's gone as far as it can. And we may possibly be getting close to the limitation in small arms with, say, modern automatic rifles.

Now, if you look at the human organism, and you ask yourself what's wrong with it, well, just about everything. Consider a creature that can live on the seacoast watching ships come in day after day, year after year, and still believe the earth is flat, because the Church said so. They *knew* the earth was round, they *believed* it was flat.

Or an artifact that can use cannonballs for five hundred years before the idea of a cannonball that explodes on contact blossoms in this barren soil. I could go on and on.

So why has the human artifact stayed back with a flintlock? Well, I'm advancing a theory that we were not biologically designed to remain in our present stage any more than a tadpole is designed to remain a tadpole. The human species is in a state of arrested development. Now, that describes an organism fixated at what would ordinarily be a larval or transitional phase. Ordinarily a salamander starts its lifecycle in the water with gills, and later the gills atrophy and drop off, and the animal develops lungs and comes up to land. Well, then they go back and they spend the rest of their lives in the water, but they have to come up to breathe. There are certain salamanders who never lose their gills, and they never leave the water, and they are, of course, in a state of arrested development.

The axolotl salamander, found in Mexico, is an example. Scientists, moved by the plight of this beautiful creature, gave him an injection of hormones, whereupon he shed his gills and left the water after ages of arrested development. Whether for good or for bad, who knows.

But this is very important, that evolution is a one-way street. Once you lose your gills you can never get them back. So, we know that the whale was once a land animal, because they have lungs.

I think it's a little too much to hope that we could be jolted out of this by a single injection, but by whatever means the change takes place, if it does take place, the change will be irreversible. The axolotl, once he sheds his gills, can never reclaim them. This law of evolution, it seems to be a real law. Of course, there may be exceptions.

Now, when we consider these evolutionary steps, one has the feeling that the creature is tricked, in a way, into making them. Here is a fish that has survived droughts because he has developed feet or rudimentary lungs. As far as the fish is concerned, the feet are simply a means of getting him from one water source to another. But once he leaves his gills behind, he has made an involuntary step. I wouldn't say forward, but a step. Looking for water, he has found air.

And perhaps a forward step for the human race will be made in the same way. You see, the astronaut is not really looking for Space, he's looking for more Time to do exactly the same thing. They want to start building factories up there. You see, he's equating space with time.

The Space Program is simply an attempt to transport all of our insoluble problems, our impasses, and take them somewhere else, where exactly the same thing is bound to occur. However, like the walking fish, looking for more time, we may find Space instead. And then find out there is no way back. Such an evolutionary step would involve changes literally inconceivable from our present point of view. I quote here from a work-in-progress called *The Place of Dead Roads*.[61]

> As a prisoner serving a life sentence can think only of escape, this is my hero. So Kim took it for granted. so Kim took it for granted that the only purpose of his life was space travel. He thought of this as not so much a change of locality, but as a change of dimension. The basic change of it being, with all its surroundings, like the switch from water to land.
>
> But that's where you start. There has to be the air-breathing potential first. So, the first step toward space exploration would be to examine the human artifact with biologic alterations in mind that would render our human artifact more suitable for space conditions and space travel.
>
> Now, we are like water creatures looking up from here at the earth, and the air, and wondering how you could survive in an alien medium. Well, fish didn't have the capacity to do that. We do.

---

61 Novel published in 1983, the second book of the trilogy that begins with *Cities of the Red Night* and concludes with *The Western Lands*.

The water we live in is time. That alien medium we glimpse beyond time, is space, and that is where we are going. Kim read all the science fiction books and stories, and he was stunned to find the assumption, the basic assumption, that there is no real change involved in space travel. Same Jerry people playing out the same tired old roles. They're gonna take that dead act into space. Now here they are, light-years from Planet Earth, watching cricket and baseball on a vision screen.

You imagine taking their stupid pastimes light-years into space.

Well, you see, they're not in space. It's like the fish is saying, "Well, you put an aquarium out here on land," and he's got everything he needs in the aquarium. But, he hasn't left the water. So, while I think that it is a tremendous achievement to get man off the planet at all, and worth all the twenty-three billion dollars it cost (it's one of the few government expenses I don't begrudge), still, they were traveling in an aqualung. They hadn't really moved into Space.

There are lots of things, of course, to consider. One of the most important considerations, of course, is weight. Your human organism not only weighs about a hundred and seventy pounds, but it also has to encapsulate its entire environment, and transport that environment with it. So, it mounts up to, of course, more and more weight.

We have a model of a much lighter body. In fact, a body which is virtually weightless, and I'm referring to the astral dream body, which some scientists (or most scientists) don't believe in. But this model gives us a clue to the changes we must undergo. When I say must, I am speaking not in moral, but in biologic terms.

And I think dreams also give us an insight into space conditions. Recent research has established that dreaming is a biologic necessity. They can tell when an animal or person is dreaming by the REM brainwaves. If they wake the animal up every time it starts to dream, no matter how much dreamless sleep it is allowed, irritability, restlessness, hallucinations, and eventual coma and death would result. They've done the same experiments with people.

So, Kim saw dreams as a vital link to his biologic and spiritual destiny in Space, and deprived of this airline, we would die.

The way, of course, to kill a man or an animal is to cut off their dreams. That's the way the Whites took care of the Indians. They cut off their dreams, their magic, and, of course, they tended to die out.

So I am making here a basic assumption which, of course, many of you perhaps cannot accept: that our destiny (again, I'm talking here about our biologic destiny) is in Space. And that our failure to achieve this is the basic flaw in the human artifact. So that's why we are back down there with the flintlock, and we obviously have a long way to go.

(1981)

Notes of a Dirty Old Man

(Who Masturbates in Public)

Samuel R. Delany

Opening remark: "Since I was quite young, I've suspected that the wisdom of the elderly came largely from the fact that, after a certainly age, when we've become quite forgetful, we tend to speak in generalities and thus, somehow, appear wiser than we are. Here, at seventy-three, I admit I haven't had much evidence to change that opinion."

1.

The referent for this title, of course, is not me—but rather Diogenes of Sinope, a one-time slave who lived rough, slept among dogs in a discarded bathtub, and taught in a market in Athens—not Plato's

Agora, though if what comes to us from those who wrote down some of what he said can be trusted, the two philosophers overlapped in time and knew one another. For many years, when the rather unsettling side of his sexual habits was more or less restricted to those who could read Greek and Latin, Diogenes was represented as an old man, walking around ancient Athens, with a lamp in his hand, in bright sunlight, looking for an honest man—a classical image of the Quixotic futility and irony of all philosophy, if not of life itself. But there *are* other correspondences between us, however, documentable enough. Plato, Heraclitus, and even Aristotle were noblemen. My own grandfather was a slave in this country, before he went on to become the vice principal of a southern Episcopal college for Black students and the first Black suffrage bishop of the Arch Diocese of North and South Carolina. As well, much of the writing I have done, especially in that published over the last forty years, has been insistently about the mechanics of sex—much of it gay, so that more than one critic has accused me of *practically* masturbating in public, if not, like Diogenes, actually doing it. What makes this array of similarities of interest is the almost endless number of differences that can be inscribed between them, as it were, differences which give each of us, the philosophical clown Diogenes, and the science fiction writer Delany, his own meanings and provide contexts that distinguish us so greatly—a relationship between similarity and difference that I consciously borrowed, on a day back in April 1993 from the philosopher and critic Gayatri Chakravorty Spivak, when both of us, among several others, were giving presentations at a Yale conference on "postcolonialism." At the same conference, Spivak said that the proper description of "postcolonialism" was the failure of recolonization to reestablish itself in a formerly colonized country. Both strike me as equally insightful articulations.

2.

In the eigteenth century, author of the novels *The Sorrows of Young Werther, Elective Affinities*, and *Wilhelm Meister*, as well as the epic dramatic poem *Faust, Part I* and *Part II*, and the first artist to become an international cultural hero, Johann Wolfgang von Goethe wrote, "A man of fifty knows no more than a man of twenty. They simply know different things." I quote it, because, yes, I think it is right. Somehow, though, I do not think that is a very daring belief.

3.

The other utterance that remains most clearly with me from that April '93 conference, however, was said to me by the Egyptian novelist and psychiatrist Nawal el Saadawi. After our session, a bunch of us had gone out for pizza, and pausing before a bite, she turned to me on her stool and said, "You know, Chip, if you had presented that paper in my country, at the University of Cairo, say, at three o'clock in the afternoon, likely by four you would have been in jail." Now that refers to a situation that obtained twenty-two years ago; nevertheless, it is small contextual moments that make me feel that—just perhaps—that initial literary reference for some will have some resonances. All I can do is feel humbly grateful that I don't live there and have been allowed to write as freely as I have.

But I am also aware that that is far more luck than any sort of bravery or courage.

4.

What everyone seems to overlook is that "homophobia," certainly today, and the "unnaturalness" of homosexuality are not about someone of the unexpected sex hitting on you or even about procreation. It's about production (and, specifically, reproduction) for profit. On any farm or in any wilderness, animals are always "hitting" on other animals and other sexes than the ones with which they will produce offspring—all the animals, no matter how many legs they use to walk or run. (If you are looking for a reference, see Bruce Bagemihl's very fat book, *Biological Exuberance: Animal Homosexuality and Natural Diversity*. My copy was given me as a birthday present toward the end of the last century by a midwestern Baptist divinity student then studying Greek and Hebrew, among the many other subjects required of it, in New Orleans divinity school—the same languages that my ex-slave grandfather had to learn, along with Latin, and Aramaic, to become a bishop.) As soon as the farm becomes caught up in an economic process that privileges the production of young (to sell, to eat), heteronormativity (and soon species normativity) quickly becomes privileged. (The same thing happens when a country becomes war-like—that is to say, needs to produce cannon fodder—unless, like Sparta, they work homosexuality in as a fundamental part of the military.) First, all non-reproductive sex becomes "non-serious" or "playful" or "marginal" and, as the pressure increases to produce, eventually "forbidden" and/or "unnatural" and/or "unspeakable." However, as the Roman poet Horace put it, who died nine years before the birth of Christ: "*Naturam expellas furca, tamen usque recurret, et mala perrumpet furtim fastidia victrix.* / Drive nature out with a pitchfork, and she will hurry back and burst through your futile contempt, the victrix." In short, anyone who has observed the actual world without the socioeconomic pressure to make it yield up its young will realize there's nothing unnatural going on when a dog humps your leg. Usually, homophobia is about the guiding patterns we form to justify our production goals (we call them ethics or morals)—and often work them into our religions to stabilize our economic system. (That's what we have always called "natural." Nothing less and nothing more.) This, indeed, is how it relates to the pathologizing of onanism from biblical times up through the nineteenth century. Briefly, what's important to remember is not so much that varieties of sexual interest and orientation are natural, but that homophobia is specifically cultural, whether it is manifested in *Leviticus* or Uganda or 1950s Boise, Idaho—or even the current Republican party's attempts to roll back same-sex marriage—or, indeed, whether the particular instance of homophobia noted foregrounds the same pattern or different ones. Right now, however, that is provisionally the more useful piece of adversarial data.

5.

Is this the only reason for homophobia? No. But if only because it is a result of the silent workings of power, it is often a decisive one in terms of the place discourse works to stabilize infrastructural patterns long after we have forgotten or even never noticed the relation.

6.

Dozens of unquestioned assumptions lie behind an argument such as mine. It will not hurt to look at a few here.

First, we are not talking about prediction; we are talking about an explanation for what has already happened, again and again.

Second, the cultures entailed must know that sometimes sex produces offspring. This is not something that anyone is born knowing, any more than anyone is born knowing they will die. Both can be found out in many ways, from experience embedded in language or from language alone. In many western cultures, the latter is passed on in the very bedrock of the language which names human beings as "mortals"—those who will die. It is a fact we carry around with us as soon as we learn what our category is. The former, which is more complex (that sex can sometimes produce offspring) requires more complex language structures and acts to convey. But rhetorical hints of the transition between not knowing and knowing both come up in texts as old as the J-Writer's tale of the Garden of Eden that begins in the third chapter of Genesis—initially a text from approximately eight centuries before the start of the Christian Era, to an early Greek novel from a thousand years later, *Daphnis kai Chloe*. We get hints of the second having been forgotten and relearned, and taught to others, in both.

7.

Even the first chapter from P-Writer, from three hundred years after the J-Writer (the time between Shakespeare's death and us, today), whose account Bishop Hieronymus Eusebius—with his pet lion at his feet (St. Jerome to you and me)—decided to leave at the head of Genesis, starts off with the suggestion that language is the creator of the world.

> *en arche en ho logos kai ho logos en pros ton theon…*
> In the beginning was the word and the word was with God…

In short, the privileged language, the language that counts, the language that (if you want to take the step into theology) is holy, is the language/logos that explains how the world works—as opposed to "chatter," the words of ordinary folk, gossip, and bragging, and—dare I say—the stuff of novels and poems since Archilochus or, indeed, Longus of *Daphnis and Chloe*: or, if I may, the tension between literary language and the language really used by men. It's very hard to keep them apart. What we recognize as literature seems to begin with their constant crossing.

But this is how, more or less contemporary with the P-Writer and writing only a few hundred miles away, Heraclitus uses the word "logos," among the fragments of his that we still have, including this one that Aristotle was generous enough to quote, and tell us it was the opening of Heraclitus', today, long-lost treatise, named for the poem by Parmenides, "About the Material World," ... the "*Peri physeos.*"

> The logos is eternal
>> but men have not heard it
>> and men have heard it and not understood.
>
> Through the logos all things are understood
>> yet men do not understand
>> as you will see when you put acts and words to the test
>> I am going to propose:
>
> One must talk about everything according to its nature,
>> how it comes to be and how it grows.
>> Men have talked about the world without paying attention
>> to the world or to their own minds,
>> as if they were asleep or absent minded.

Basically, this is a description of language that-explains-the-world and what happens to that language in the world. But as a philosopher who, though he occasionally laughed, along with others, at the silliness of the gods, Heraclitus was not pushing for one of them (or even, as in his later years, Xenophanes was, to have one instead of many); Heraclitus was more interested in the usefulness of this particular category of language than in its holiness. Indeed, more and more, that would become characteristic of Greek philosophy, even before Plato.

8.

How far *is* Ephesus, Heraclitus' home, from Jerusalem…? Six hundred miles as the crow flies, slightly over a thousand by foot. The boat trip, which would have hugged the shore in those days, was in between.

We have no evidence that Heraclitus ever visited Iraq or that the P-Writers or any other priests of the Temple ever visited Ephesus. But probably both knew Greek. It was the trade language—and basically educated people did know it.

9.

"If only I could free myself from hunger as easily as from desire… everything is of one substance. It is custom, not reason, that sets the temple apart from the house, mutton from human flesh for the table, bread from vegetables, vegetables from meat… Give up philosophy because I am an old man? It's at the end of the race that you break into a burst of speed!"

—*Diogenes of Sinope*

10.

One of the things I feel very lucky about is that, at various times in my life I have had good friends who were ten, twenty, thirty years older than I was, who were not my parents but whose company I valued and who were willing to put up with me. Said Diogenes of Sinope, who walked back and forth each year between Athens and Carthage: "There is no stick hard enough to drive me away from a man from whom I can learn something."

Well, sadly I never had Diogenes' tenacity. But from my late teens on, I was lucky enough to have a series of friends, women and men, anywhere from five, to ten, to thirty years older than I. (Marie Ponsot—her first book of poems, *True Minds*, followed Allen Ginsberg's *Howl* in Ferlinghetti's Pocket Poets series—the editor Bobs Pinkerton, and the philanthropist and actress Barbara Wise among the women. And my long-term mentor, Bernard K. Kay, most notable among the men.) One such, I acquired in my late twenties, who was then in his late fifties: the composer John Herbert McDowell. We lunched together regularly over the years, 'til shortly before his death; we spent lots of time talking to each other and I think of him as a man who taught me so much of what I learned during the last years before I went to London to begin a family.

I can remember at one lunch with John Herbert (his name to all friends), when I was in the midst of some young-man's despair about what, today, I remember no details or even the topic, though I was totally distraught, and, lunch done, I asked, "John. Please, tell me. Please, John. Does it *ever* get any better than this?"

On the other side of the restaurant table (Luchow's lunch special for workers in the neighborhood, where you got a three course meal for three dollars—and, at the time, it still had the reputation as one of the best restaurants in the city), John paused a while and considered, as he stared into his martini (extra, but it was practically a triple!) and finally said: "Does it get better? No, Chip. It doesn't—But you *care* less."

Forty years later, I can say John was right. Probably that's the closest to a life-saving piece of wisdom I ever received; as well it helps explain why I maintain such fondness for the fellow who would whip it out and do it anywhere, Diogenes.

(2015)

Homunculus

Margaret Randall

Painters in the Middle Ages depicted children not as infants but as diminutive versions of adults, the boychild—and it was almost always a boychild—with wrinkled brow who might have been pondering some philosophical or financial concern, the head-to-body relationship that of a fully-grown person. This adult-like child has come to be known as a homunculus, a strange term more fitting perhaps for a malignant growth than for a young person. Some define a homunculus as "an ugly child," attesting to the fact that placing an adult face on a newborn erases the sweet innocence generally associated with infancy.

This has nothing to do with those children about whom one thinks: "You can see exactly what she will look like when she grows up." No. Those little ones display a facial feature or set of features that bring a whiff of future into the present. An oddly shaped nose or style of eyebrows, a jut of chin or unusually broad brow. The proportions are still those of a child. With the homunculus in Medieval painting, the adult head is too small to belong to a newborn. The body is also often muscular: a fully developed physique rather than the folds of baby fat associated with an infant.

It is believed that this pictorial tradition came from the Christian need to portray the infant Jesus as fully developed, not as some baby who might share the physical qualities of any other recently born. The explanation makes sense. It wouldn't be the first or last time Christianity has led us astray. In Europe during the Middle Ages, most portraits were commissioned by the Church, and it stands to reason that such orthodoxy would color all cultural manifestations. As more secular influences took hold, artists were free to experiment more. As the Renaissance dawned, it wasn't only the Church but also the Court that commissioned works of art. And many artists gave free reign to their desire to paint from life what inspired them, including babies with their natural features and proportions.

But the idea of the fully developed miniature human didn't disappear altogether. It remained in certain examples of folk art and/or religious iconography in different parts of the world. One of its attributes, in particular, continues to spark my imagination: the image of a small but fully developed person placed inside the image of another's head, no doubt symbolizing the belief that only another brain is able to think our thoughts. It is easy to understand why this belief persisted for centuries, until science rendered it obsolete.

When I see an image within an image, I am reminded of the Dutch Cleanser ad of my childhood, in which a little Dutch girl held a can of cleanser which, in turn, held a little Dutch girl with her can of cleanser... and so forth and so on, until the repetitive sequence faded to a mere intimation of continuity. Some images remain in one's consciousness. That advertisement was purely decorative, though, and didn't signify that one little Dutch girl was thinking the thoughts of her larger homologue.

In Mexico in the 1960s, an elderly man from a remote region of the Puebla Mountain Range lived with us for a few months. He was suffering from tuberculosis of the bone, and we hosted him in order that he see a doctor friend who, finally, was only able to make him more comfortable in his final days. Prior to staying with us, Don Rodolfo had never been in an automobile, experienced electricity or seen any other of the conveniences we take for granted. One night, we took him to the movies. He had no explanation for those people walking and talking on the screen other than believing that living people had somehow entered the screen. In his long life, he had not come in contact with the information that would have permitted him to entertain another interpretation.

In some way, out of sync with our more elaborate contemporary structure of thought, those actors were homunculus, in this case larger rather than smaller than the adults they portrayed.

Art has always created its own variant of reality. This is one of the qualities that makes it art. Cave paintings of bison and other animals rendered forty thousand years ago emphasized movement, what would have been most powerfully present in the scenes those ancient artists conveyed. African masks and other sculptural art exaggerate those qualities—human or divine—most important to their place in the scheme of things. Hindu gods and goddesses are portrayed with multiple arms, symbol of their supernatural powers. Picasso and the cubists dislodged and rearranged the planes of the human face so as to indicate its many angles. Abstractionists are more interested in action than in a static representation of their subjects, while hyperrealists try to paint as much like a photograph as possible. So-called primitive artists privilege certain features because they are most meaningful in terms of the way they see the world. Critics often assume an artist paints in a stylized way because she or he is unschooled or otherwise incapable of rendering a more objective image. I assume they have more interesting reasons for doing so.

Meanwhile, the homunculus lives on in history and in my imagination: an explanation that has given way beneath the march of time and scientific revelation, but that remains an evocative image whose job may yet not be done.

(2021)

AGAINST ATROCITY

Figure 6: Cover of 2019 Summer Writing Program catalogue

• • •

Atrocity: an extremely cruel, violent, or shocking act.

In weaving this section together, we kept returning to that famous provocative statement by Theodor W. Adorno: *nach Auschwitz ein Gedicht zu schreiben, ist barbarisch* ('to write a poem after Auschwitz is barbaric'). We reapproached it as a question: How is it possible to write in the face of atrocity? What kind of rhetoric do we use in writing through such devastating sociopolitical realities? How do we grasp for words when what we are reaching for seems ungraspable? What we found in Naropa's audio archive revealed the responsibility writers feel to address atrocity. It is one of the tendencies at Naropa to search and investigate—whether through documentary poetics, performance, or various other engagements—and, in this search, we can continue to look for our own rhetoric through which to approach the atrocities of our times in ways that are responsible and politically committed.

"With the title 'Against Atrocity,' we mean to signal both a committed antagonism, and a fact of relation: we live, and think, and write in an era of unrelenting ecological and political atrocity; it is the situation, the context, the defining field we're up against…

As a first image for what this counter-urgency might be, we've taken inspiration from Ana Mendieta's 1974 *Untitled (Blood Sign #2/Body Tracks)* performance (and its photographic documentation); which is also to say we've taken inspiration from the archive, that site & source of beginning(s) (again). Inspired by how Mendieta's performance quickens with the refusal of the stance of the spectator, we'll try to take a lead from how manifestly her own body is implicated in the struggle against atrocity—if we can take the field of blood as holding space for the unspeakable, for that which can never be justly represented, a kind of anti-sublime. Crucial to note, also, how Mendieta's own work took inspiration from the long archive of artistic practices, making a unique vocabulary out of Neolithic gestures, performance art (and the temporal layering of documentary media), and an ethos we might now see as beginning a decolonial, feminist criticality."

—from 2019 Summer Writing Program catalogue

• • •

BLACK FREIGHTER

Tongo Eisen-Martin

I guess asylum seekers will have to hang in there under the jail.

I make inaudible rebel art; our revolutionary potentials ground into powder, then mist, then conversation. Conversations emptied into fourth floor sewers (insert fourth floor of any institution here). Conversation topics including the political party within the political party within a society's death date.

When social contradictions heighten, all talents leave the world. All institutions are abandoned (they just don't know it yet). I write poems and see people hooks in people cheeks; see a bureaucracy's bicentennial; one big bible for imperialists. The ruling class disposing of shadows, or artists who need to be shot down. I am running guns in place for a packed theater. I write and participate: the paranoid versus the paranoid proper versus the white picnic. Southern trees bare a strange response to pandemic.

"Capitalism is a death cult," most wisdoms agree. School teachers' faces carved into the handles of our shovels heralding a new change in the division of labor: we will all work only one more time. As imperialism heads toward the final curtain, poets might as well play with fire because, for all of our bibliographies, it will be the bullet. I am hiding from Baldwin Hills friends; hiding from talented Harlem because I no longer have confidence in genius during unorganized revolutionary tides. How do you challenge power only on the page? How do you truly drown a reactionary mind?

In recent decades, oppressed people both lost the class war and opportunity to learn from loss. Ahistorical civilian-saviors flood the streets with their art and intellectual conversations. Very white and white-adjacent. The new city-universe brimming with anti-rank-and-file matter. Around semi-corporate, reused species-beings, I try to write something original; or at least an original reiteration of locales of reality. Half-reading my bus transfer, half-reading the tents; the objective becoming to create art while taking advantage of the fact that we all live in one city now.

My head knows that there has been a dream; but my heart sees no evidence of true political resistance nor the spiritual cultivation of art. I see state power versus tens of millions of door hinges and people who still believe they are not dialectically part of a social side. Citations over Ferguson doorways; apparently our taste of power was only a conversation starter. Well-timed gun fantasies refilling the political void in imperialism's collapsing anatomy. Fishing in gas stations for movie plots, my spirit is not yet lifted. Foundations getting friendly with our comrades; no one fears, nor necessarily has to fear for … the modern poet.

While I do enjoy a multi-vocal free-for-all, I am not a psychedelic writer. I am sure of what world my narrators are living in as well as what carceral proverbs my narrators want to liken society to. It is my business to know the socio-military locations of metaphors; to have a good hand for psyche-art; for facilitating a dual haunting (to be both the revolutionary and the sum of all inanimate objects) in the face of fears of individual and collective annihilation. A poet becomes a house for lightening.

Your craft is your universe. A universe that you interfere with. Acknowledge that. There is no pure third person. If you are not a pure third person, be true to that. Define phenomena through the lens of participation.

Gentrification means that I write poems next to San Francisco. Politicians legislate next to reality. As survivors, we share first-date spirituals. Hopefully, by the time a fascist secures all of their cool points, my love will have found a way to hide me. Or blues people will forgive me for all the wrong turns I took off of the fifth fret of a guitar, like my longitude completely re-colonized. Sweeping my left hand over the frets until there is no city left.

A politician promises to end apartheid soon; shakes the clock parts out of their wig to prove their change of heart.

I am a shell of my former knowledge of hip hop. Forgive me for the living rooms I co-wrote with a day's surrender to the ruling class. Traumatized by a life of open-air intake; losing my grasp of poetry; hordes of voices slipping to the back of my mind like nails falling into construction site dirt.

A poet is a nobody. A vagrant (who enjoyed school) walking in a reader's head; walking up from the back of a reader's mind; or a curious, young mirror image who runs to and from social conditioning; playing your shadow or your subtitle. A fun way to interpret an extinction-level government.

All I see are sharecropper shacks and neoliberal free association. Subject matter come to life only to cut their own lives short. Big names in our genocide. I am a blues person with a slave ship sailing through my motel room. I want to write about someone waving.

What do you read to the blood on the floor?

Will I live to see the best of my generation?

I went to sleep with twenty-first century revolutionary friends and woke up with the sun missing. In several states in the US, Latinx people, on the frontlines of surplus value slavery, are twice the percentage of Covid-19 cases than they are the percentage of the state population. In Louisiana, Black people are thirty-three percent of the population, but seventy percent of Covid-19 deaths.

Throughout the US, similar ratios are the apple pie of the American medical reality. When I write poems, I peel back material reality and get the feeling that a genocidal superstructure is satisfied with disaster, but only for now.

One day I started thinking on paper in a McCoy Tyner kind of way; like Martin Luther King Jr.'s right-hand apparition; or like a gallows koan. In a society of boot-dwellers, my great-grandmother would not want me to call it any other way. Red Summer in my latest chords. Live from late-stage imperialism; the poem goes well for a day or two.

(2020)

Anything is Light When it Bears it Heavy

Etching a Name onto a Malleable Surface

Asiya Wadud

> A *fault plane* is the plane that represents the fracture surface of a fault. A *fault trace* or *fault line* is a place where the fault can be seen or mapped on the surface. A fault trace is also the line commonly.
>
> —*Wikipedia entry for "fault"*

For our entire lives, we advance and retreat, advance and recede across the long plane of our own prismatic geographies. These geographies, multivalent and shifting, bear all of our paths, bear witness to all of our paths, and bear the load of the paths. Some of the routes we take become well-worn because we ferry ourselves across them again and again. Some paths we take only once and perhaps we presume their imprint falls then rests in a gathered heap somewhere in the recesses of our periphery. But I think each of the paths finds a way to engrave itself upon us, embed itself in us, become part of our subcutaneous logic. Sometimes the logic is a fixed engraving onto a firm, certain surface. Sometimes it is onto a mutable object. But always, in our own silos, our own logic becomes calcified, firm, ardent. Every single time we advance, there is a new imprint made, until there is a catalogue of imprints, countless intersection and grids, layered paths that form across the planes of logic, supposition, and summary we inhabit. Even if we take the same course one thousand times, it's never exactly the same, there's always a tiny bit of vagrancy—we stray—somewhere. When we veer from the well-worn path even a little, a new imprint is made to take into account that meander, that striving.

> My inclination is to worry about the (fault) we don't know about yet, more so than about another very large earthquake in this area.
>
> —Jeremy Boak, head of the Oklahoma Geological Survey

On September 3, 2016, an earthquake registering 5.8 on the Richter scale jolted the Wichita, Kansas area and made apparent a previously unknown fault line. The oil drilling and subsequent pulsing effect that happens when wastewater is disposed triggered this earthquake. The fault line responsible for this earthquake is now known to be in Pawnee, Oklahoma. Before the earthquake, it didn't register as a concern, it was a mute factor in our geographies.

Fault lines are tactile objects. As with any rupture, you can touch it. It rises into a gradation; theirs is a haptic, stabilizing knowledge, though revealed only when there is an earthquake.

The fault line is representational—it stands in for the entire field. Boak's "inclination is to worry about the fault that we don't know about yet." What urgency is exposed in the aftermath of the discovery of the new fault? What trepidations insert themselves in otherwise firm footing? Can we assume that the entire field that surrounds the fault line is full of fault as well? How does this question inform our own advance and retreat?

The fault line merely exposes the entire bedrock of bad logic. It is the visible, tactile place we touch, then name. After an earthquake a fault line does not mend, there are no sutures to close up the wound. So, it remains a monument to the skew, the schism, the rift, the break in knowledge. Monuments are places that remind us something happened. Monuments also remind us to not let the thing happen again, they are a vow and a commitment of sorts. Or, if not, then later on, a recompense.

• • •

How do we align our action with our logic, remembering it is possible to scaffold bad logic atop a field rife with faults? For our entire lives, we advance and retreat, because the only option we have is to advance and retreat.

On August 27, 2015, 3 a.m., a driver met seventy-one Iraqi, Afghan, and Syrian refugees along the Serbian-Hungarian border and loaded them into the back of a small meat truck. The space allotted each person was two feet by two feet. The meat truck barreled down the A4 near Vienna; the driver, Mitko, ignoring the urgent need for oxygen for the seventy-one people in the back of the truck.

The fact that all seventy-one people died within the hour, including Lida Rahm, one and a half years old, is an unmitigated horror. To feign shock, disbelief, and incredulity, though, is to ignore an entire, resonate fault plane of accumulated bad logic that resulted in the measures the refugees were forced to take to reach central Europe in the first place.

In Parndorf, in Calais, in the southern Mediterranean, there are fault planes that stretch well past the confinement of these exact sites of migration, containment, and dislocation. The territory extends across an entire landscape of knowledge and topography and reckless, failed empire. The fault plane is rooted in colonial misconceptions that, when accrued, pock the past, mar our presence, and then propel us into the future—but doing so with a fractured knowledge.

· · ·

Today, one of my fourth grade students asked me for good 'O' words for a poem: Optical. Octagon. Octopus. Over. Oblong. Omniscient. Obvious. Omnipotent. Object. Ocular. Ocular, I told her, meant willing to see something, to give it your attention, which is not entirely true. It just means of or related to the eye. But, if we are talking about the eye, I want to know what it sees. If you will yourself to see something, then it's probably not long until you see the fault lines. If you see the fault lines, you acknowledge there is a fault field. If you avow the presence of the fault field, then you are open to the brokenness within you and everyone, and your own faultiness of logic, our misguided rectitude.

1. We Talk About Fault and Blame in One Breath

What is a suitable syntax to talk about seventy-one people dying in the back of a meat truck?[62] No one in the back of the meat truck died with their hands folded, passively, they each died clawing for their last breaths. What is a suitable syntax to talk about seventy-one people dying in the back of a meat truck? What words in our lingua franca do it justice? I pity the words tasked with this. I pity them because the task of these words is to unravel, slowly, carefully, with love and belated eulogy, the anonymous tangle that people fleeing the same horror, mitigating against the same moments, migrating to a new place, become in our ever-waning imaginations.

• • •

Power has to do with a series of accumulated gestures, major and minor, across an entire plane, gestures that vest and reinforce power for some, brokenness for most of us. To vest, maintain, and animate power requires an aseptic refusal to examine the fault plane. This strong-armed vesting of power is not without blame.

---

62 "Police recount journey of 71 migrants who died in Austria as investigation ends," *Reuters*, October 12, 2016.

2. "Anyone Could Begin the Day with His Eyes and End it Blind or Deceased..."
—Terrance Hayes, "How to Draw a Perfect Circle"

Often, we pass through the day with our own accretion of knowledge in the fault field. Nothing happens. We eat, we drink, we sleep, we work, maybe we walk home from the subway, and nothing happens. For one more day, our broken knowledge remains untested, so we don't have to do the work of examining it, we don't even know there's work to do.

What is the lineage of a bad idea? I mean "bad" as in it didn't form well. "Bad" as in it never formed well and, on top of that, it metastasized. How is bad logic allowed to carry on? Are borders evidence of faulty logic, across an entire fault plane? Is this how the logic accumulates? What is the opposite of a border? Is "ocular" the opposite of border?

The fault line is merely the place that represents the fault plane. Logic can build and accrue faultily for a long time, and it's only in the revelation of the fault line that it is revealed. Sometimes faulty logic is a quiet, subdued accretion (accumulation) and the lineage of thought is only revealed at the final moment, in the fault line, in the quake.

. . .

A fault is a rupture, helps us see the other sides—the before and after the fault—plainly, starkly. We are approaching the fault line. Take note. Look to see where it is going to begin. There is an impending crevasse. Where is the resonate, firm end just before and just after the gape?

The fault line is a measure of the past, it doesn't have to demand its presence—its existence as a rupture already commands it.

3. I Know the Center Because I Remember the Periphery

You know worth is also relational, to a fault. Your own worth, everyone's own worth, rests on an attenuated continuum, a fault, along with everyone else. Your position on the continuum is, more often than not, determined by someone who is not you. No one knows your own interiority when they place you on the continuum. With Parndorf, with each kilometer as the truck drove on, the lives inside were of diminishing value. Worth is relative to the value of all other proximal lives.

Is indifference a fault? How about willful, vile indifference? What about irreversible indifference sanctioned from such a distance that to wend our way back through the fault field to attribute blame is always and forever lost in our own sturdy miasma? How about if everyone is doing it? Does collective indifference get recast, renamed as just our country's creed, our own manifested beliefs? What is the opposite of border?

What happens when you worry a fault line, does it become its own accrued border? What does it mean for something to be faulty? Like an entire patterned language you've constructed that is full of holes. Like the patera was ill-equipped to transport people, it was a faulty vessel? Or can something be faulty if we already know it is full of bad logic? Is that just a fault? Or a false start? We thought the engine was good, but it turns out it was faulty. *Faulty* develops in the space where we thought it was one thing, but it turned out to be something else. A fault line is the place of blame. It's the place that we can pin our doubt, mistrust, our own extroverted misery.

4. This Entire Country Is An Assemblage Of Peripheries

Naming a border is a way to rectify and absolve us, it's a way to give credence to our own inaction and to do so without shame. A border can do the job of asserting the limits of our ethical obligation—where we are bound and then miraculously, arbitrarily, not.

What's the name for the space right at the precipice of a fault line? Penultimate fault. Is there a name that acknowledges the winnowing distance between the edge of darkness and copious, prolonged, disciplined light? Caravaggio painted in the bright enclosure of this space, the chiaroscuro, Italian for "light-dark."

Every single time we retreat, we etch something somewhere. Barring prolonged incalculable stagnation, the only option is to advance and retreat, always, for as long as we live. Each time we advance and each time we retreat, something of the moment is etched upon us. What's the opposite of a border? Is "ocular" the opposite of border? Is acceptance of our own brokenness the opposite of border? Knowing we are labile, fungible, futile, but always reaching, the opposite of border?

(2020)

On the Edge of Forgetfulness

Eleni Sikelianos

The question is how to interrogate the remains.

What are the remains? What are the archives that record them?

The remains are things outside systems of institutional knowledge-creation, outside systems of power. We might speak of large-scale history (genocides, wars, mass migrations), and we might speak of small-scale history (events in an individual life). Both the macro and the micro scales matter, and I'm interested in the play between the two. Sometimes a poem more thoroughly resides in one than the other.

Archives on the micro scale may include the individual body as document, and we can think about how to liberate phrenology (whereby you palpate the skull to find out things about the individual) from its racist, sexist past. The body carries its histories. From forensic anthropologists, we know the way soft tissue wears grooves into bone, so that you can tell from a skeleton what kind of works a slave was forced to do and can thus imagine the excruciation of that labor. So, the body itself as an archive of lived experience, and even of cosmic histories, in that it carries remnants and markers of stellar activities. How does the individual bodily archive still see its ancient chemical past?

The micro archival includes the psychic body, and individual memory, and just like the collective or written, it is constantly on the edge of forgetfulness. In our family histories, our ancestors are archives, some with walking stories, some with rubbed-out pasts. Each of these persons is connected to a web of others, and to other stories, the fabric of the world they lived in—that is an archive.

Derrida, in *Archive Fever*, says, "Archive takes place at the structural breakdown of memory." Archive itself invites forgetfulness and thus always works against its own aim, erasing memory as it creates it. What does that mean in our age of surplus information? We're already discovering the ways that solicit both memory and forgetfulness.

And I want to say that the micro and the macro archives can never be extricated, one from the other.

When we speak of the macro scale history, we might speak of archives and the social body, the historical or collective body, the collective body of consciousness, the geological archive, and the archive of fauna and flora. When I think of the war on memory, that is something that absolutely comes to mind, our biological diversity memory. I don't know if some of you read *The New York Times* article about two weeks ago—about a quarter of our mammals are going to disappear in the next two to three generations. And so that kind of archive being lost; and zoos, actually, become a kind of archive, yet they're forced to choose what animals they will keep and what animals they'll phase out. Because there's just not enough room, not enough resources. Who gets to decide, how do we decide what living animal archives to keep in existence?

What, as writers, do we retrieve? What attend to and why?

I just returned a couple of days ago from two countries where archives carry crucial things, for poets and writers, for everybody.

Cambodia's civil war, instigated by the secret bombings ordered by Kissinger, led to one of the most brutal regimes in history. Half the population was killed, about three and a half million people, and in particular, intellectuals, artists, and teachers. Those were some of the first to go, so that systems of handing on knowledge, including knowledge of literary life, have been seriously damaged. And so, literacy is something that is on the edge of forgetfulness in this sort of loss of living archives. Every single person I met had been touched in some way by Pol Pot's terror. Our interpreter's father and siblings had been killed. Our guide's uncle, a poet's whole family, everyone had lost somebody. So, certainly, what they're working on right now is reconstructing and examining and confronting the archives of the genocide.

And then in Vietnam, intellectual and literary life have remained vital, in many ways more so than they are here in this country—poets are published in newspapers all the time—but they are working through a system of censorship and repression of archive and memory. So, different situations. In both countries, I talked about Charles Reznikoff and Lorine Niedecker, among others. And it was interesting to think about this documentary poetics or investigative poetics as a Western phenomenon. Certainly, there are Vietnamese writers and poets who are writing about, say, the American war, but not in the same way that we're consulting archives. Why is that? I mean, why are we drawn to the archives as artists and poets in this nation?

I want to make sure everybody here knows Charles Reznikoff, a poet trained as a lawyer, who was not particularly good at practicing law (he didn't feel he could be responsible for anyone going to prison), but was very good at practicing poetry, who said, "I didn't invent the world, but I felt it." *I didn't invent the world, but I felt it.* What a profound, what an accurate thing to say. He exhaustively consulted the legal archives of 1885 to 1915 to track events, he was particularly interested in what happened in American society in the change from an agrarian society to an industrialized nation. And so, by looking at individual cases in the courts of law, he thought he could tell us something about what happened to our national consciousness as we shifted to industry. He traces the racism, violence, and cruelty in American history that our national narratives do not. He was one of the first white American poets to write starkly about Black suffering. (Charles Bernstein says, "If we can't read *Testimony* then we can't read our own history.") His poems can be excruciatingly accurate, shining a light into corners of the archives our national narratives willfully forgot. *Volume I* begins this way (a jack is a male donkey):

> Jim went to his house
>   and got a pair of plow lines
>   and then into the stable
>   and put one on the jack
>   and led the jack out
>   and tied him to a fence;
>   and put the noose in the other line around the head of the jack
>   and began to pull.
>   The jack began to make a right smart noise.
>
> Its dead body was found next morning,
>   fifteen or twenty feet from the stable door;
>   the neck, just back of the head,
>   badly bruised.

That's it. He doesn't tell us the outcome of the case, or anything about Jim, just the precise action, to devastating effect. Later, he worked with the Nuremberg trials documents to create a series of poems called *Holocaust*. There's a pretty straightforward title for you. He was particularly acute at focusing on the micro to render the macro more real. (I remember Allen Ginsberg loved a poem of Reznikoff's in which he describes a woman chewing on a piece of bacon hanging out of her mouth like a second tongue.)

Paul Ricoeur: "The most valuable traces are the ones that are not intended for our information."

Now, what is the relationship between archive and vision? In Reznikoff, the line breaks carry the brunt of the emotional work. There is so much to say about how he does that, but one thing we could quickly point out is all the "ands" beginning the lines in that opening to *Testimony*, the kind of forward moving tension that puts us in. The fact that they're lowercase, what that does. In general, he follows lines of stark music and surprise. For me, when I'm working on family histories or other documentary-inflected work, the imagination organizes the evidence in various ways. Putting material against material, form against form, creating texture and palpability. See Anne Waldman's *Iovis* as it documents male energy, and how she uses form as an act of the visionary. The imagination inserts itself and expands the real.

Investigation also provides relief from the limiting, all-consuming space of the self and inscribes the self into, relates it to, a larger world and world history.

What interests me particularly is the infection, the mutual infestation between the lyric and the document, the imagination and the artifact. A poem is a fact, wherever it lies. A quote from Renee Green, a complex thinker, multimedia artist and writer, speaking of her work in the historical records: "It is exactly at these locations of limit and even fatigue where it may be necessary to search." And that search, I think for the artist, happens in the glut, in the aporia, in the surplus, and in the lapses in the archive.

We are walking archives of all the nutrients and chemicals we've ever consumed, stories we've been told or lived. The river bottom is an archive. Lorine Niedecker, who worked in the geological archive so often, in natural sedimentation, says this:

> Along the river
>   wild sunflowers

>   over my head
>   the dead
>   who gave me life
>   give me this
>   our relative the air
>   floods
>   our rich friend
>   silt.

    First of all, "our relative the air" should knock us out of our chairs with its beauty. We might make a case for our relatives the whales, the shrews, the salamanders, the plants; we usually forget about the air as our relation, but Niedecker did not. And thus, she reminds me that working in the archive is also a way to rekindle relation, to put back into context anew—not the official context, but to see and feel for oneself what that context might be.

    The Russian artist Ilya Kabakov, who worked with trash and the archives of trash, says, "Should everything without exception before his eyes in the form of an enormous paper sea be considered to be valuable or to be garbage? And then, should it all be saved or thrown away?" It isn't just a receptacle for the dead or forgotten, not a trash heap, but a living network of fact, and fact both in decay and fact in rehabilitation, that feeds us. Kabakov again, "To deprive ourselves of these paper symbols and testimonies is to deprive ourselves of our memories… All points of our recollections are tied to one another. They form chains and connections in our memory, which ultimately comprise the story of our life." The poet sticks her fingers into the holes to find out not what is reported, but what is felt there. She exports and imports language between systems of organization. She reinterprets event, giving it music and heft. She reconfigures and confounds organizing systems to achieve a new method of understanding, so that the forms of history are not dominated by one way of apprehending.

I am a remnant of my ancestors living among the residues of biological and geological and epistemological and political history. A remnant that bears witness to the remnants, as Agamben would have it. Renee Green again, telling us that we must attend to "that small remaining quantity, after so much has been used or sold." The tatters making up a whole.

[Friedrich] Hölderlin, quoted by Giorgio Agamben, quoted by Green: "What remains is what the poets found."

(Presented at the panel: Archival Poetics & The War on Memory, 2012)

Raccoon Magic

Ariana Reines

I remember when referring to the Crimean War was something that you could do to refer to something so obscure, and seemingly without relevance, that it could be a little bit funny. I used to say to my friend, while I was working on the play *Telephone*, "I wish someone could just tell me when the Crimean War was!" The Crimea crisis has induced in me a Justin Timberlake obsession; I don't know if you remember the song, "Cry Me a River." I've been thinking about that because of the way that songs revolve in the mind. Also, because, I think the Crimean War was one of the things that happened before WWI. And it's peculiar to be alive in a time of such transparency or such nudity when it feels as though everything is turning itself inside out—the air itself, all substances, and history, is somehow exposing its guts for all to see. And here again, we have a Crimean crisis; a kind of geopolitical situation, that is so fragmentary/difficult to understand that it makes me recall how little I ever understood about WWI or the conditions that made it happen.

I want to talk a little bit about homelessness, and the phrase "at home in the culture," which is something that used to revolve in my head when I was homeless, and while my mother was homeless…

because one of the things I think about poetry is that it's something utterly portable, or it has to be, in the end. There have been, and are, these archives, these libraries. And libraries are always places longed for, dreamed of, made pilgrimage to...but they're also, places in the mind where the poems, or what little we're able remember of them, revolve. At least this is what the voice in my head says, when I'm going from one place to the next.

On January 12, 2010 there was an earthquake in Haiti and the way I came to hear myself, remembering a song about that earthquake... was that earthquake convulsed the world into a relation with Haiti. That perhaps it hadn't had, or was willing to have, before. Another phrase that revolves in my head is "the shot heard round the world." I'm from Salem, Massachusetts, and they ingrained in us a sense of the beginning of the American Revolution as having begun with "the shot heard from round the world." I thought a lot about was how long it takes to hear a shot, in particular, a revolutionary shot. Haiti's revolution ended in 1804, but I sometimes wonder if the shot didn't begin to be heard round the world until 2010. That was a time that I happened to be in Los Angeles, semi-homeless, and I found myself convulsed into a relation with an idea of revolution, an idea of the world, a place in the world, and also a geological situation. I found it happening to me, for the first time. I mean, even though it had been happening to me and to all of us every day; it happened to me in such a way that I knew it and felt it.

The other date that I was thinking about is December 21, 2012. I don't know if you remember how there had been talk of the world ending on that day. And, in any case, it is the date that the Mayan calendar ends and after which it would reset. And I remember feeling—I guess I'm opening a kind of corridor between January 12, 2010 and December 21, 2012—and this corridor, it's inside me; it's in my body and it's in my mind, and I'm not trying to assert it's in capital "H" History, but I wanted to share with you the way that I feel...this time and these times going through me...maybe as poetry.

I feel like, I came to legal maturity at a time when apocalyptic thinking and feeling in America was just on the up and up and up. It was literally the air; 9/11 happened on the first day of my last year of college. And then the Bush years were both a cruel baptism into an experience of language, that…was so weighed down by mendacity that it was very very difficult to figure out how to be in, and how to use it. I say that, knowing that we're in Gemini time and knowing that language itself is supposed to be tricky; it's supposed to be tricky and dangerous, and not necessarily submissive—to borrow Anne's way of understanding the word "submissive"—language does not submit, but there's a degree that it can be pushed. Like the other elements with which we live in in this world, into a realm…where it can really be warped and changed beyond all recognition. And I feel like that was the world in which I was coming out of adolescence and into some kind of at least legal adulthood, if not spiritual or psychological adulthood.

It was between, it was in that corridor between January 12, 2010 and December 21, 2012, that I started to think a lot about origin stories. Literally just in the simple way, that everyone was talking about the end of the world, I really wanted to think about the beginning of the world; and specifically, to think about…immerse myself in ways that, poetic speech, and also written poetries, have told beginnings. And I found that, just on a purely medical level, I found it to have incredibly salubrious effects on my health. I also started to meditate a lot around how the uttered word, poetic speech when it's spoken aloud whether or not it's in the oral tradition, whether it's something that was written and is then incarnated by the voice or whatever comes out in some kind of torrential pure vision, has a way of gathering culture around it. And there must be a reason why we need these; we need to be told these stories of beginning, and we must have always needed these stories of beginning. It seems to me it's how nations have constituted themselves, it's how languages and cultures and worlds have constituted themselves. I knew that I was desperate to constitute, not only myself, but myself in the world or the world. It seemed both the thing to study and also the thing to apply to myself, like some kind of salve. And it began in the way maybe all documentary poetics begin, which for me—and, I'm doing this with my hands—it's a kind of raccoon magic. I like rooting through the garbage because no one's looking over my shoulder there. And that's the beauty in doing documentary work as a poet is—rather than, say, a journalist, or scientist, or another kind of researcher. I like looking in places, where there's nobody—where I feel nobody is looking at me, and we all know that nowadays it's very difficult to do that or to feel that way. I like to, like raccoons do, I like to clean what I find before I put it in my mouth.

One of the things that is another word or set of words of almost a line but not in poetry exactly, that goes around and round in my head … is the emulsification of worlds. I often feel that that's what the internet is an engine for. Like, literally—like if you wanted to make vinaigrette: you have oil and vinegar, but you need an emulsifier to put them together—and the internet is emulsifying the things of culture and the things of our world in ways that can enter us in altered form. And I discovered that there are online, just like there's everything else, there are also ancient texts and sacred texts that you can read for nothing. That you would have had to be an initiate on a very very high level and in a very restrictive world to even see not too long ago. And to be able to walk into these spaces, these libraries, or archives of majesty in the mind, for hundreds of thousands of years most people could only dream of, or fantasize about, spin poetry out of imagining. We can now just walk into those spaces and encounter at least the skeletons of what they mean, which is the words. And I find that to be intoxicating. And so, with all of the sorrow and strangeness of these times, I also discovered an access to origins, if you want. That I don't think poets have ever had in quite the same way. Certainly, I'm not as learned maybe as a poet might have had to be in those days, once upon a time. And yet, in the times in which we live, our consciousness is so loaded with so much—other kinds of information—especially about what's happening in the present on any day, that I don't know if it's possible to measure the kinds of learnedness or degree of learnedness that poets might have; but anyway, but there's a long tradition of poets being ragtag fakers, and you know wandering liars, and yarn-spinning charmers who maybe aren't even charming and things like that—I think there's a way that the poet is also a kind of gadfly, or like the fool card in the Tarot—can you see it on my hand…what, there's no fool card on your hand—okay, like three people are laughing. More than three, don't feel too awkward.

We carry what little can be carried from one place to the next, I think. I guess I want to gather that in just to close, by invoking the Gemini time that we're in. So, language, it itself is a tricky poet, I think. And it's constantly changing the reality in which we live, and I believe that it's on the level of something coming into being as writing or coming out of the mouth of speech that we're already altering the world. And I know it's not as fast or as drastic as production, what we do with the products of our imagination but, then again, I'm not so sure. And I can't tell if I've completely confused the airwaves with this strange little back-and-forth jaunt through my corridor between January 12 and December 21, between thinking about origin stories and thinking about the present in which there's both an extreme—all of the devastations, I guess, that Anne enumerated and all of us know both in our bodies and in our daily experience, the ways that we experience these things. With all of that, there's also a strange sense that once an origin is sited and spoken and constituted as itself… once we can gather a sense of ourselves around it…there's a kind of identity, or a kind of personhood that can come into being around that. And it seems to me, that it has to be done one person at a time, as things are breaking up. And I find that it's helpful—when I work with people astrologically, to think about—not only think about, but to work with physically—the fact of having been born; it's the most obvious thing of all, but I found it's actually very difficult to conceive of—in many ways, more difficult than to conceive of death which is also what everyone is talking about, and also avoiding. It's difficult for people that are miserable to think of the fact that being born as any kind of a gift, but it is a gift.

And one of the ways that steeping myself in creation stories has helped me is perceiving gifts as gifts, even when they're not ones that one wants. And I like what [Antonin] Artaud used to say, something like: "I am he who has to whip his innateness." I kind of like that—I'd like to whip my innateness. And I think that perhaps the whip of one's innateness is language itself. Because all these other things, they're parasitic in a kind of automatic way they're just feeding off of us, advertising the state...almost like Jack Spicer's ocean, but in the dark, nearer reflected version of that...these things are taking from us but just kind of automatically. Like whereas, in order to touch your root, your innateness, your having-been-born, and trying to reach through that, to some kind of common origin both around which to constitute a future and sense of tradition, I think the whip is language, and it's great to be the one holding the whip of your own innateness...I recommend it...that was a joke, I also meant it.

(2014)

Poetry, Politics, and the Real World

Amiri Baraka

I want to do two things actually, or maybe not two things, but whatever it is. And you're free actually to ask any time, anything, you know. But remember, I can't hear well. I've had to listen to too much BS all my life, so the ear is reacting. But first, I know I was supposed to talk about poetry, politics, and reality, you know, to make certain that you know that they're three vectors of the same kind of thing, but I wanted to talk about first this part, that politics, culture, and art, which is the same thing, and then some notes on that second thing that I said. They're similar, and that's why I said if you got any questions, please ask them.

So, I begin with this little thing, politics, culture, and art: it is material life, actual long-term livingness, that determines everything else. So that the Ten Commandments, actually ancient Egypt's negative confessions, necessary for the dead to recite before entering heaven or the land of the dead, are drawn from what humans were and had been doing for a long time. The confessions were done to codify, make clear the most negative and self-destructive tendencies in the real world, and hear these offenses as destructive to the whole society. So, here, the spiritual is a formula for removing the most egregious self-destructive practices from the society. They also were delivered by the art of writing. The spiritual, even religion itself, in its most rational expression, is a tool used for community uplift. To make God a religion as shapers of the community, to demand stability and positive social organization. The less directly the spiritual relates to the material, the less relevant it becomes. Culture simply helps people live over time, it's character consolidating, it is confirmed and reconfirmed over the years. Politics shapes the culture, in its turn, shaped by it. Ron Karenga said, "Politics is the gaining, maintaining, and use of power," unquote. That's how the forces that govern a particular society became those forces.

US culture, historically, is composed of sharply contradictory forces and tendencies. What aspects of it are most prominent is determined by the political forces that dominate it at any time. US-, Western-, or European-dominated culture begins as an object impacted by a breakaway religious group from the old Church of England, derisively called Puritans. They felt the church had gotten to be too dominated by Rome, as well as by the British monarch. This is what the cry of religious freedom meant. But this breakaway meant more than just seeking another form of religious practice; this movement in itself meant that another kind of culture was developing, one that carried with it the act, and ideas, and spirit of rebellion and pioneering. But also, at the same time, the practice, ideas, and culture of European or white supremacy. That culture would have economic features like its early mercantilism, which would be used to make many of the poor members of the society and prisoners indentured servants, as the white and the Black indentured servant. It also carried with it the idea and act of committing genocide on Native Americans, fastening slave chains on captive Africans, so that a certain kind of daring, even courage, was always mixed with an exploitive and oppressive feature of the developing culture, even as they cried that they were the inventors of free society and democracy.

Mao Zedong, in his lectures at Yan'an, says art is the ideological reflection of real life. The ideological reflection of real life, that is what you are actually doing, transforms your own ideological development. That's what art is. It's not anything from nowhere, it's from you, and society, you know. And, of course, poetry, as I said before, cannot just come from your head. You know, it becomes quickly boring. You have to be able to reflect on the real world, real life, you know.

American art, since its earliest times, was bifurcated by its ideas of liberation and freedom on one hand, and its stiff reactionary formalism on the other. And as you have two forces throughout history in the United States: free, slave. Always, you know. You have great artists like Herman Melville (*Moby Dick*), Mark Twain (*Pudd'nhead Wilson*), have you ever read *Pudd'nhead Wilson*, in here, anybody? Okay. You should read that. That would explain the United States to itself. You should read it. As well as the slave narratives, the narratives written for the slaves, and then the great Frederick Douglass, *The Narrative of the Life of Frederick Douglass*, written by himself. So that's another incremental leap, revealing both aspects of the US city and culture. The fact that Douglass could write this meant another profound development inside US culture, and the society itself. This is great art, but it's deeply political (so is Melville, so is Twain,) you know, deeply political, and even boldly progressive. Emily Dickinson, as well, shows us a new aspect of US culture, presenting the self-life of a young American woman. Or, if you read *Diary of a Slave Girl* by Linda Brent. They tell us something about the minds of the American woman, nineteenth century, both of them: slave woman and free woman. This is the United States, again, developing this dichotomous, this contradictory culture. A painter like Winslow Homer is so extraordinary because American painters of the time refused to paint the most fearsome happening in the American nineteenth century, which is what? The Civil War. Henry Ossawa Tanner, the most famous Black painter of the nineteenth century, carried a middle name which is shortened version of Osawatomie, which is the name that John Brown was given when he opened up Kansas. You see, it's interesting that he would call himself Ossawa, so you would know the identity with the revolutionary forces in… (Do you want to read about John Brown? Read W.E.B. Du Bois, *A Biography of John Brown*.) Melville and Twain, and later Whitman and Stephen Crane, were also anti the exploitation and oppression of their fellow citizens. Douglass and the slave narratives, Frances Watkins Harper near the end of the century. The common themes: slavery versus freedom. Wish there were as many good films about those themes. Most that have been made take up the slave owner's side, whether it's *Birth of a Nation* or *Gone with the Wind*. The actual other side of that struggle has not been documented, so that among this thousands of ugly films that are made, so few are made about real American history and real life of struggle. How you got to be you. How we got to be we. You know, why we are all related, whether we know it, or admit it, or not. You know.

Twentieth century Euro-American Modernism: Pound, Eliot, reactionary US authors. They went to Europe and stayed there. And I'm not saying that to just dismiss them. God knows, all of us were addicted to them, when we were little, you know. They were modern English poetry. That's the time, the era of seven types of ambiguity, Latin quotes. Neo-English poetry followed their example. The academic poets of the US wanted a neo-Anglo poetry of formalism. Southern agrarians openly supported Southern pre-industrial values. They said industrialism was the enemy, meaning the conquest of the old Southern agrarian slave society by the North, and the end of slavery. But struggle is always constant. It always incrementally leaps to the next period. William Carlos Williams and Langston Hughes are the great models for trying to develop an American poetry instead of imitating English verse. They went to Europe but came back home. See, Pound and Eliot went to Europe and stayed. Williams and Langston went over there, and dug whatever they dug, and came back. And their line was, American speech, American speech, you know.

And then, of course, some other things I'll mention: The Harlem Renaissance, what that was, you know. Was it forty years after slavery is over, there's a Renaissance? People moving out of the South moved to Harlem. People from the West Indies, Africa, moved to Harlem. And so, you have a dynamic movement in Harlem in the Black side, at the same time that you had the development of your American modernism, that is, American art becoming modern, you know. If you read early O'Neill, you'll see that. I mean, all of that coming out of the whole European tumultuousness that led to the Russian revolution. Some other things I just want to mention, there, on the way out to another point: Du Bois, from Frederick Douglas. Du Bois. Liberation by true self-consciousness. Read *The Souls of Black Folk*. Read *The Souls of Black Folk*. How does it feel to be a problem? First question. How does it feel to be a problem? You know. The question of the double-consciousness: to see yourself through the eyes of people that hate you. To constantly see yourself through the eyes of people that hate you, to look at yourself with a mixture of amusement and contempt. Whether you're Black, or whether you're an American. We still believe that culture has an English accent. We still believe that England somehow is the creator of cultural values, you know, you see they remove my man King from his ten o'clock show, and now you've got an Englishman there, you've got a Black English woman. I guess they're trying to sell tickets for the Olympics.

The other thing: Langston Hughes, of course the great Afro-American poet, the great poet, the great writer. Zora Neale Hurston, Zora Neale Hurston. Not only great novelists, but a folklore studier, folklore anthropologist. And what's important about that is that the Harlem Renaissance had an international break, because everything we do in this country has an explosive relationship to the rest of the world. So, the Harlem Renaissance, what did it do? They say the Harlem Renaissance. But it also engendered what was called Negritude, you know, in France, Africa, the West Indies. It also engendered something called Indigénisme in Haiti, that they should study their indigenous culture rather than just believe that they're French, you know, it's important. So that when we talk about that what is the focus on ourselves? That we should study our indigenous culture rather than think we have just getting stuff from Europe. You know, we are not Uncle Sam, you know, the hick with the beard in the top hat, you know. We should see what this country's true consciousness is. And even in the Spanish-speaking world, in the Caribbean, you had Negrismo, that is, to look at not just Spain, but the African route. Nicolás Guillén, the great poet. (How many people here have read Nicolás Guillén? You know Nicolás Guillén? Okay. Great poet.) Some of the greatest poets in the Western Hemisphere speak Spanish, you know. Ernesto Cardenal, you know, for instance. And the brother from El Salvador, Roque Dalton, who's related to the Daltons. (You know that—what was the movie where they ride out of there? What was it… I can't think of that. The two guys, they end up jumping off the cliff. Butch Cassidy and the Sundance Kid? Right. The Daltons ride out of there, and then one of them ends up in El Salvador, you know. And he has a son who is a great poet: Roque Dalton.) That's interesting, that's the United States/Latin American thing, you know.

Also, the '30s. The influence of the Russian Revolution, for which we had to pay, still pay. My English professor, Sterling Brown, he was a great poet. I didn't know it when I came there, he was just my English professor, you know. But he's the one who pulled my coat perhaps the greatest understanding of this country when he said, he took us to his house, because me and a guy named Robert Spellman thought we were so hip. We'd heard of Charlie Parker, so we were hip. He says, "Come to my house," he shows us a wall full of records, organized by time, genre, person, he says, "That's your history. That is the music." Says, "That's your history. You want to hear how these people were living? Study the music. That is, in the music is your history. In the music is the history of the United States. If you listen to the music, you will find the history of the United States. Even the slave histories, you know. 'I may be wrong, but I won't be wrong always,' the slave says. 'I may be wrong, but I won't be wrong always. The sun gonna shine in my back door, one day.' And they's slaves saying that," you know, always.

So, the history of this country is always a struggle for liberation against the kind of addiction to slavery. The addiction to formalism. For instance, you know, McCarthyism tried to silence everybody. Why? Have you ever wondered why the United States was allied with China and Russia during the Second World War, or the fight against fascism? But after that, the Japanese and the Germans, who were our enemies, become our allies, and the Chinese and the Russians become our enemies. You ever think about that? What that means? That means that the alliances have switched. You understand what I'm saying? So that no longer are we fighting against fascism, we're fighting to be in control of it. See, that's the point, and that's what you have to realize, that your own life is at stake, your own consciousness is at stake, unless you know what side you're on, as my wife always said, what side are you on? It don't matter about your ethnicity, your nationality, the way you look, it matters what side you are. Who are you supporting? And so, in this imperialist country, which, as it began to have that imperialism dominate, tried to silence the three greatest Black artists, Du Bois, Langston, and [Paul] Robeson, you know. All three, you know.

So, when we come down late '50s, I had just gotten kicked out of college, and then I went to the service, I got kicked out of the service. That's two for two, actually. And went to New York, where I met this lady, and some other folks. The question then was, for are we the sons and daughters of the recent immigrants, remember that. The bill, the

GI Bill, which said we could go to college, you know, that kind of new liberation, it meant that what we reacted to first was this attempt to impose Europe on us. This attempt to impose English formalism on us. And so that was the basis of what I would call the United Front Against Academic Poetry. And who was in that? Well, when I was in Puerto Rico, just before I got kicked out of the Air Force, I heard about a guy named Allen Ginsberg, who had written this poem *Howl*, which was banned, and they wanted to lock him up. I said, "You could be locked up for a poem? That's heavy, you know, you could be locked up for a poem?" I later found out, yes, you can be. But that legacy with Allen and *Howl* and what that was is just the first shot. When *Howl* came out, that was the first shot of that revolution, and I always said, when I read *America*, said, "America, go fuck yourself with your atom bomb," I said, "That's great poetry, right there. I can see, I can feel that." See, I can feel that. That's not about "da-di, da-di, da-di, da-di, duh-da, duh-da, duh-da, duh-da." "America, go fuck yourself with your atom bomb." That's poetry, you see. And that, to me, was always where you had to go. You had to go to the most direct, and out of your own speech, as Olson tried to teach us about the breath phrase, you know. The American speech, the breath phrase, stay close to your own conversational tone. That is the strongest, that's the most important point you could make. You know. Not "O, thou art full of shit," but, "You are full of shit." That means, your own linguistic force.

So, nominally, Ginsberg and *Howl*, the so-called Beats, and the beat thing was just media, except for Al Aronowitz, who took it seriously, and became a beatnik. Reporter from the *New York Post*, he came to interview us, the next thing I know he's a beatnik. And the Black Mountain School, you know, which was very important. And these things should serve as notes to you, to go and look, to find out, to study, you know. Black Mountain. What was Black Mountain? Who came out of there, like Charles Olson? Who was Charles Olson? Who's Robert Creeley? Who's Robert Duncan? You know, find out. What it was, why that made them important. And here I was, a young

Black dude from Newark, New Jersey, who became interested in, first, Ginsberg talking about your own speech. And that struck me as important. Your own speech, what do you mean by that? Don't imitate, "Ooba dooba, dooba dooble dooble..." Start with your own speech. That's where your poetic impulse comes from, your own speech. "Oh, what is that?" Your own speech, not some artificial English-type speech. And then, as I said, Charles Olson's *Maximus*, Olson up in Gloucester. When I was young and published the magazine *Yugen*, because I wanted to be published, I wasn't waiting for somebody else to say, "Oh! You're discovered," said, "I discovered myself," and I published some of Charles Olson's most important essays. The one, *Projective Verse*, which still needs to be read. I published that. *Proprioception*, I published that, you know. We went up to Gloucester to see him, to see, "Who is this guy living up here? What is the point of this?" You know. And that, of course, was very... I wrote an essay recently on the relationship between Charles Olson and Sun Ra. They both talked about space. What space are you talking about? You know, outer space, the space of America, you know.

And who else? The people from San Francisco, for instance, and also Creeley, from the Black Mountain School. They wanted a post-fuel modern integrated as a fundamental of urban life, restatement of a more positive American value system, and because we were fighting for this opposition to commercial anti-spiritual military whore of Moloch, because we were fighting that, there was a sense of unity and struggle. Always the most important element: unity and struggle. What side are you on? When you speak, who are you representing? Who do you think your readers are? Who are your readers? Who are you trying to reach? You know. And Robert Duncan, Michael McClure, Diane di Prima, some of our contemporaries, you know. What split the so-called Black Arts from the Beats and white radicalism was the assassination of Malcolm X. That was the most dominant thing in our lives. I remember I was down at the 8th Street Bookstore at a book party, and a guy named Leroy McLucas runs in and says, "They just killed Malcolm!" And so, we standing there trying to figure out, first of all, what—how come they did that? How come we couldn't help him? How come we couldn't protect him? Why are we down here in Greenwich Village? You know, I left, I went to Harlem the next month. We opened up a theater on 130th Street and Lenox Avenue called the Black Arts Repertory Theater School. Why? Because we wanted to create an art that was, first, Black, culturally and consciously. Because we wanted to fight, you see, because remember: they had already killed John Kennedy. 1963. And then they killed Malcolm X. Said, "Wait a minute, this is some kind of war. We're in the middle of a war." So, you either gotta, you gotta pick. Again, what side are you on? You know, don't take the aesthetic cop-out of not being for anything but thyself. That's why the poetry became so boring, because too many people were talking about themselves, what's in their mind, the confusion, you know, the failure to understand reality, and the fact that reality finally is what matters. That what you think is against or with reality.

So that was the question, now what do we do? We wanted to create an art that was Black; we wanted to create an art that was mass-oriented, that would affect people generally; and we wanted to create an art that would help in the liberation of the Afro-American people. That's what we wanted to do. A lot of people in the village put us down for that, a lot of people, even some of the Black writers, said that we were trying to dictate how they wrote. No, we're saying, "This is what we think is important." I remember there was a story one of my close friends Frank O'Hara, who was, I thought, the leader of the New York School, not John Ashbery, but Frank O'Hara, some guy was telling Frank, "You know, Leroi Jones is saying he's going to kill all the white people." Frank O'Hara says, "Well, I don't think he'll start with us." I mean, that's so Frank O'Hara-ish, man, that's him to the point, you know. But, that question, Black by culture and consciousness, a mass art, a revolutionary art to help with the liberation of Afro-American people, another, again, what side are you on? So, what do we do? We set up this theater. Classes, poetry readings, plays. We sent four trucks out into the community every day. Vacant lots, playgrounds, whatever. Play streets. We sent out four trucks. One truck had poets, and we got all the poets that would come. One poet pulled a gun on me and said he wasn't coming to Harlem. I didn't make it that dictatorial, but anyway. And we sent paintings on another truck. They would stop, take the easels off the truck, and set them up in the middle of the street, where people who had never been exposed to that kind of easel art would see that. The other one had music. We had some of the greatest musicians who we had hooked up with downtown. We brought them up too. Like I said, Sun Ra was supposed to be weird. When we brought him to Harlem, the people thought it was dance music, you know, it's just what's on your mind depends. And music, poetry, theater, drama, graphic arts.

But what broke that up was we discovered that Black is not an ideology, the normal division among Black people is the normal division among any people. You got nationalists, you got Muslims, you got communists, you got Christians, you got vegetarians, you got people who got to say two or three different ideologies at the same time. Get ten people in a room, you probably got fifteen different ideologies, you know, because they not united with themselves. So that's what split that in half, you know. But the turbulence of the sixties, when Mao said, "Revolution is the main trend in the world today," what happened, again, is what we call a Sisyphus Syndrome. From that revolutionary period, rolling the rock up the mountain, then the rock is rolled back down on your head, like the end of slavery: Emancipation Proclamation. You know, the whole ending of slavery. What happens after the end of slavery? What happened to reconstruction? They destroy it. Slavery, you climbing out of that, you get up to this point, reconstruction, bam. Goes down. By 1915, Black people could not vote anywhere in the South. That is, it had gone from the whole question of revolutionary liberation, because that wasn't negotiation, that was actually fighting. People were killing each other. More casualties in the United States than any other war because they were both Americans killing each other, you see. But in that period the art was great because we could see that struggle was important. Whatever you were struggling against. So, our struggle now is to recreate a revolutionary art from revolutionary politics. We see the same contradiction in US culture and US society, you know. [Barack] Obama on one hand, still dominated by the right-wing Republican clan, Tea Party, rich pay too little taxes, poor too much, nine-one-one, the conqueror, the world. And we have to understand that, that the reason that people jumped on me about the nine-one-one stuff is because I was saying, "I don't believe this, but you telling me this." You know, poets have to be very dangerous, because if your vision—if you can see something, you can't really pull punches. I mean, you know what I'm saying? You got to say it. You got to say it. You got to put yourself on the line.

Like 1967, I went to jail for possession of two pistols and a poem. But the judge said to me, "This poem is a prescription for a criminal anarchy." Because the people burnt the town down, Newark, 1967. But because I could see that coming, then he wanted to blame me for doing it. You understand? If you can say, "I see this getting ready to happen," if it happens, they say, "You did it." I said, "Judge, do you think that the people came in my house and read that poem before they went out and set fire? You really believe that?" Three years, no parole, but of course we beat that. You know. One of the things that's interesting about that is the judge had me sentenced for contempt, because he said—to one of his judgments, I said, "Oh, your father." But then I pointed out to him, "No, no, Afro-Americans, we would say, 'Your mother,' we wouldn't say, 'Your father,' you never seen your father. We say, 'Your mama.'" And they threw that out. That's interesting how culture impinges on the law. And then, of course, in 2002, the poem "Somebody Blew Up America." Again, because you can see something happening, and you have to state it. Otherwise, the society has no way of arming itself. If you see it, you must say it, you know, no matter what, you know.

So, for us all, I think that time, the '50s, was so important, you know, and all that stuff, the Rosa Parks, Montgomery, you know, the Birmingham bombing, you know. Did you know Condoleezza Rice's family belonged to that same church that they blew up, was full of little girls, you know, that her father was anti-Martin Luther King at the time? You see, stuff is weird. But all those things, and Malcolm X, Robert Williams, Cuba. I went to Cuba, 1960. I went to Cuba, 1960. I met Fidel Castro and Che Guevara when they were young people, and what I marveled at was the fact that, here's some young guys, young women, who had actually—weren't just talking about revolution, who had actually taken over their country. That was impressive to me. As a matter of fact, I rode a train from Havana to Sierra Maestra, the mountains in the East, right across from Haiti, that's where Fidel gets his political impact, from the Black part of Cuba. And the kids there, oh you know, hundreds of Latino poets from all over the place. They were ridiculing me because I said I wasn't political. See this is… "What do you mean you're not political? You come from the United States, those terrible people." I had to hear that for fourteen hours when we're on the train. And that was important, you know.

So, the question is, of the politics of all this, for the Afro-Americans we're still struggling for self-determination and equal rights, you know. And Obama, for all the things that he does represent that are positive, still cooled out, was a cool out for us, if you understand. I wrote an essay in a Poetry Project publication a couple of years ago called "Why Poetry Is So Boring Again," and that's the substance of it. It's so boring again because it's not focusing on the world, but focusing on the inner machinations of its own fevered minds. When in the turbulent '60s poetry was turbulent, was a reflection of those times, it was a reflection of those times. It was a time when we said, "Revolution is the main trend in the world today," and it was, you know. And so, if you investigate those things: the '40s in China and India, the '50s, the Puerto Ricans when they tried to light up the

Congress and shoot the congressmen, you know, you meet that Lolita Lebrón, the Brown versus the Board of Education, Africa, Nkrumah becomes the Prime Minister and President of Ghana, and we US children of the immigrants, and all the other things that were going on. Montgomery Bus Boycott, you know, the appearance of *Howl*, you know, the fact that it was called a Beat Generation. It's important. And these things, I think I mentioned most of these things before, we wanted to stop the domination of the English departments. The English departments have made a comeback. You see these young poets, and it's disgusting to see this English poetry, you know, again. But I think I'm gonna stop. I got some more to say but I think I'll stop, and if you have questions, you should go.

And one important thing is that there was no draft. They were smart enough to understand that if they didn't try to draft you all, college-types, they wouldn't have to put up with you falling out in the streets, stopping traffic, saying "No draft." That they could proceed with their war by getting, who? The working class, the poor whites, the country folks, that they could offer them, what? Free education if you go get killed. The normalization of revolutionary forces. They just give money, money, money, money. And that's the danger of what we face today. That's the danger, that we will have a corporate dictatorship, a corporate-dominated society. The whole thing that Obama said about "post-racial," that's like farce. That's a farce. I mean, Trayvon Martin proves that's a farce, you know. So, we have to face reality. The US is an imperialist country aiming to dominate the world. They want to dominate the world. That nine-one-one was simply the door to the Middle East, where the oil is. They're gonna sit there. They overthrew Libya, changed, they got Iraq, Afghanistan, and you don't even know who did that. You say, "Somebody blew up America," they say, "It was some crazy militant in Afghanistan." It wasn't all these people, these nuts. But how do we know that? Do we know that? You know. So, that's the question, I think. What side are you on?

(2012)

Transmission Fluid

Thurston Moore

Is the work now different? I don't feel the same. But we are the same. We still like to be looked at. Maybe less now with the realization of complete infiltration. But you'd never know it. Every photo, every move, every twinkle stared and shared. Maybe it's a young person's game. I told my teenage daughter my desire was to be a poet hidden away in a Parisian pied-à-terre off map. Her smile was entirely sublime and was me as female and, like so much of her, the defining light in my DNA. The separation of romance and cash was seemingly easy to negotiate in Paris before reactive displeasure psychosis instigated extreme violent retaliation and murder in the whispering rooms of sophistication and pleasure. No different from the past but the past is beautiful, as is every child. The police are insane and having giggle fits of rotten entrails spewing passerby. Paris will wait while the poet, musician, artist breaks down the capital lexicon into shards of godhead resistance. Most of them are cool, if not innocent. My teenage daughter is not teenage anymore, she's activist and makes thoughtful art and poetry books and sells them for money sent to a fund for migrant women incarcerated in squalid detention centers. Her now makes me both sweet and sour, angry and proud, confused and ready to fight. She's older than I was at her age, but not so old to fully reflect on a history that resounds in stereo spasms. The astounded alphabets and arcs, exasperated lessons of complacent socialist bliss. Who are these people? What records do they like? What art do they love? No words. Only sputtering. Sick cream turned hellish grey ticking across screens, news-cycle a godless snort snort snort. Maybe it's funny, maybe the thought of assassination in the favor of Buddha warrior principle is for real, but it is not. It is all not. So, write a letter to the local DJ. From one vibeologist to another. Eva [Prinz] wants to start a new new record label. To begin with: only women. First up, the all-girl British African punk rock trio Big Joanie from London, for real, who blew our minds in The Angel the other night when they played with old school anarcho-punk band The Ex from the Netherlands. The drummer from The Ex is a woman named Kat and we've asked her to record an LP of healing arts sound therapy. I am always happy because these bands, these drummers, these DJs, these daughters, these poets, these books, these design-delighted visionaries, these deep 'n' shallow delighted scenes shared in an ill-physical wilderness—they will rise above, rise up and reclaim darkness as hot. Loneliness is cool but sleeping with you is all he thinks about. You, the proprietor of the wholly awesome record label. And tapes. The cassette, the mix tape. Fuck the cashish. The squares can have it. I'm voting for the her, beyond sex, skin, real estate, or faith. She's already won, the delivery is essential. So, the work remains the same. I love the punk rock past, I love the holy future, I love your lip bruised from the drunk skinhead fat man annoyed by you and Brix Smith pogo-ing to Public Image Limited at the 100 Club in the year 2018, a giddy surreality if it wasn't so obviously made for us to attend. Is this our present? Who are we people? We are madly in love with protecting our children. Crawling into bed the great reward. Prayers are powerful. And so is the collective chant, chant down the illicit power freak.

There are those who experience horror for no reason besides hate and hate does not exist in true nature linguistics. So, I vote for Alice [Coltrane], her sound and wisdom in John's heart and soul. And Moki, the light and poetry in colors stitched to sheets of vibrational foreverness surrounding the notes of exploration flowing from Don [Cherry]'s pocket trumpet, and Jayne, fire and beauty and love and the kiss heard from the plastic saxophone of Ornette [Coleman]. And she, she, she is the tree outside the academy. Male hierarchy capital obliterating the view to the egoless garden. Today is a perfect day to take the class outside. Inside out the work is immeasurable. Dignity in labor. No one is perfect, hearts failing, cancers attacking, but in unity we are nature's intention, we are happening, and we experience the epiphany that perfection is gleaned from the veriness that is nature, and which is all. My machine is the electric guitar, an axe smashing through speaker cones, screens, clouds. It is a noise of walls dismantling, noise as protest to walls ignorant to the sentient desire for holistic progress, and for divinity. It's not a love thing, hate thing, he thing, she thing, it's a you me thing and long may they wave oh radio wave lover, shut 'em down, lock 'em up, read to them the wild gift of X, stories of dharma grace. Everyone is looking, stroking. Transmission fluid. It is our blood that will save the day.

(Presented at the panel: Urgency & Agency, 2018)

BEYOND SOVEREIGNTY

Aimé Césaire, Opacity, and a Poetics of Invagination

Roger Reeves

RENÉ DEPESTRE: But they have never been published.

AIMÉ CÉSAIRE: They haven't been published because I wasn't very happy with them. The friends to whom I showed them found them interesting, but they didn't satisfy me.

RD: Why?

AC: Because I don't think I had found a form that was my own. I was still under the influence of the French poets. In short, if *Return to My Native Land* took the form of a prose poem, it was truly by chance. Even though I wanted to break with French literary traditions, I did not actually free myself from them until the moment I decided to turn my back on poetry. In fact, you could say that I became a poet by renouncing poetry. Do you see what I mean? Poetry was for me the only way to break the stranglehold the accepted French form held on me.

....

RD: Has surrealism been instrumental in your effort to discover this new French language?

AC: I was ready to accept surrealism because I already had advanced on my own, using as my starting point the same authors that had influenced the surrealist poets. Their thinking and mine had common reference points. Surrealism provided me with what I had confusedly been searching for. I have accepted it joyfully because in it I have found more of a confirmation than a revelation. It was a weapon that exploded the French language. It shook up absolutely everything. This was very important because the traditional forms—burdensome, overused forms—were crushing me.

> —Aimé Césaire, interviewed by René Depestre
> at the Cultural Congress of Havana (1967)

Maybe the greatest atrocity is sovereignty—our belief in its naturalness, its sublimity, its necessity. The sovereign nation, the sovereign subject, the sovereign citizen—we have taken these terms to be our birthright, as coin that has forgotten that it is merely metal. Bound up in our notion of sovereignty, in the ability to decide, is the legal, political, and philosophical fiction of autonomy. In the inhabitation of that fiction begins the atrocity—genocide in its multitudinous forms—because it removes the consanguinity of relations. Quite simply, it removes the con-division, the kinship of friendship, of interconnectedness, which Giorgio Agamben argues, in his essay, "The Friend," is the most political relationship one can have. Sovereignty removes the "polis," the people, from the political.

Thus, the political, the sovereign becomes a manifestation of organizational power, an exclusion of the human—what Agamben calls bare life. In this slippage, we get the State, the un-feeling orgiastic organism of a people-less political will.

So, maybe the State, the nation is the problem—our desire (sometimes mistaken as a need) to reify it. Even in our postcolonial struggles for liberation, in our desire to put the people back in politics, the goal of the postcolony, it seems, is to reify a nation, a State in the image of the people fighting the metropole, the colonizer, the oppressor. But why reify the State if the State, the nation, is the issue? In Haiti, Cuba, India, Nigeria (and the list could go on and on), even after the new nation and its cockchafers of order resemble the people who struggled to liberate themselves from their colonizers, the nation, the State still acts and invokes its own form of bare life, of a peopleless politics, a blur of organizational power. Quite simply, the State enacts atrocity. Again, maybe the State is the problem. Maybe, we need a non-sovereign future, a future of anarchic invagination, a future that doesn't reconvene anything like the nation. But what might that non-sovereign future, non-nation nation look like? In fact, how do we imagine a non-nation nation, a non-sovereign future? Imagining is exactly the issue here, which is why I believe we must turn to art, turn to an artist like Aimé Césaire, someone who might be able to speculate about a future that has not arrived, someone who might be able to make the invisible visible.

Aimé Césaire, a Martiniquan "surrealist" poet, politician, and, with Leopold Senghor and Léon Damas, architect of the Negritude Movement, confronts and grapples with colonialism, a State-sanctioned atrocity, and the attendant discourse of sovereignty. In "Preliminary Question," a poem from the unexpurgated *Solar Throat Slash*, Césaire imagines and enacts an anarchic upheaval of colonial (read: French) notions of the body, politics, religion, order, family, and belonging through marronage, a stealing away, a fleeing, a flight, a renouncing that is also an enactment of what it renounces. As

Yarimar Bonilla notes in *Non-Sovereign Futures: French Caribbean Politics in the Wake of Disenchantment*, "marronage refers to a broad range of practices through which enslaved populations contested the system of slavery across the Americas. This includes permanent acts of flight and the formation of large-scale maroon communities" or "provisional acts of fugitivity," termed *petit marronage*, acts wherein enslaved folks stole away for brief periods of time, in order to recover from illness, to visit relatives, or "avoid being punished or sold."[63] In this discussion, I am particularly interested in this opacity, itinerary, and possible contradiction of a community built in and of flight, the defiant ontology of communal fugitivity in the poetry and poetics of Césaire. As Bonilla notes, maroon communities were entangled with the "colonial order," often creating treaties with the colonial state, a politics of entanglement. Thus, maroon communities participated in a type of sovereignty; however, this sovereignty was not an instantiation or mimicking of French colonial order per se, but an interaction with it, a contamination of it, an establishment of autonomy that was akin to European notions of sovereignty but something wholly different, something more in line with Césaire's notion that in order to write poetry he had to renounce it. Quite simply, the maroon's presence as an absence subverted the colonial order, colonial sovereignty. It, the ontological flight of the maroon, disrupted the purity of French notions of order and governance, which does more than "carve out spaces of autonomy within the colonial system," but overwhelms the colonial order through an invagination and, simultaneously, enacts a beyond, a future. Here is where I extend Bonilla's perspicacious analysis of Césaire and marronage and turn toward Fred Moten playing with, and in the darkness of, Jacques Derrida's notion of invagination. If allowed such an ensemble, such a gathering of matter,

---

63 Yarimar Bonilla, *Non-Sovereign Futures: French Caribbean Politics in the Wake of Disenchantment* (Chicago: University of Chicago Press, 2015), 41-2.

voices, and thinking, then Césaire's poems articulate a poetics of "things which are not"—the not-yet, the not-so thus articulating a future. His poems enact poetics of invagination, a poetics that renounces even as it enacts what it renounces, a sovereignty that is contingent, fleeting, momentary, something that is more akin to an undercommons (to borrow, again, from Moten and Stefano Harney), entangled, contaminated, yet wholly separate.

But what do I mean by invagination? Or, better yet, what do Derrida and Moten mean by invagination? In *The Law of Genre,* Jacques Derrida describes invagination as:

> A principle of contamination, a law of impurity, a parasitical economy. In the code of set theories, if I may use it at least figuratively, I would speak of a sort of participation without belonging—a taking part in without being part of, without having membership in a set. With the inevitable dividing of the trait that marks membership, the boundary of the set comes to form by invagination an internal pocket larger than the whole; and the outcome of this division and of this abounding remains as singular as it is limitless.

Like Derrida reading set theory figuratively as a way of discussing genre and belonging, I am applying a similar sort of reading of Césaire through invagination. As evinced in the interview with René Depestre that appears as an epigraph to this essay, Césaire embraced and championed a principle of contamination, a law of impurity, a parasitical relationship to France and its literary traditions. Césaire states: "I was ready to accept surrealism because I already had advanced on my own, using as my starting point the same authors that had influenced the surrealist poets. Their thinking and mine had common reference points." Césaire "accepts" surrealism because it corroborates an aesthetic and political sensibility that he himself "had already advanced," had already been working toward.

However, he also refuses membership to the group, "to the set" as evinced in the toggling between pronouns—"my," "mine," and "their." In this dialectic, surrealism still lies outside of the pocket his poetics occupies. This "participation without belonging" echoes Césaire's earlier sentiment expressed in their interview: "I became a poet by renouncing poetry," a simultaneous arrival and departure—marronage. In fact, Césaire's explanation of his arrival-departure at something like surrealism is an invagination of the sovereignty of French claims to birthing surrealism. Césaire encircles the movement, invaginates the surrealistic aesthetic by producing a competing narrative, one that does not rely upon his French contemporaries as progenitors. Instead, his narrative centers colonial discontent and upheaval while decentering the colony's civilizing claims of modernity. Césaire's answer to his relationship to surrealism and the French poetic tradition subverts notions of belonging and poetic lineage.

In fact, he revels in that abjection, the abjection of being apart from, being untethered, separate. Abjection, in fact, acts as a primary mode of enacting this invaginative resistance to the colony and its sense of order. In *Notebook of a Return to the Native Land*, Césaire often incorporates and deploys the language of disease as a means of subverting traditional notions of home and belonging. Home is not comfortable or easeful. His island, the towns in it are "inert," "pitted with smallpox," "dynamited by alcohol." The French colonial citizen suffers from and contends with "scrofulous buboes," encounters "putrescible species," "erysipelas," and "malaria." Césaire writes: "[b]ecause we hate you and your reason, we claim kinship with dementia praecox with the flaming madness of persistent cannibalism." This claiming kinship with disease and mental disorderliness expresses and performs the rejection or renunciation of tradition via the metaphor of disease. The "you" here is not identified or stabilized. It could be beauty and reason which had been addressed earlier in the stanza. Or the apostrophic persona referenced could be the European colonizer—France, more specifically. I think Césaire would be interested in this slippery indeterminacy, in this fracture or schism, wanting us to understand his address as speaking to multiple audiences simultaneously, his address mired in and complicit in opacity, in disorderliness, which is a corroboration of his desire to be in "kinship with dementia praecox." It should also be noted that Césaire is interested in a cannibalistic relationship to beauty, reason, and/or France. In other words, Césaire understands the performance of poetry, the making of this type of imaginative non-sovereign sovereignty as an act of cannibalism, an act of repurposing, subverting, marooning, laying waste, disorganizing an original material or substance. But let us also remember that cannibalism also means to absorb, to completely envelop, which can also be understood as an invagination. Here, I put in conversation Césaire's calling for the cannibalistic with his Brazilian contemporary Oswald de Andrade's *Cannibal Manifesto*. In *Cannibal Manifesto*, Andrade writes:

> Only Cannibalism unites us. Socially. Economically. Philosophically.
>
> Against all catechisms...
>
> Against all importers of canned conscience...
>
> We want the Caríba Revolution. Bigger than the French Revolution. For the unification of all efficient revolutions for the sake of human beings. Without us, Europe would not even have had its paltry declarations of the rights of men....
>
> We were never baptized. We live with the right to be asleep. We had Christ born in Bahia. Or in Belém de Para.
>
> But for ourselves, we never admitted the birth of logic....

In Andrade, we see a polemic articulation of Césaire's poetic work—a disavowal of Europeanized logic, an inversion of wakefulness as a type of sleep, a subversion of order, a renouncing that is also an enactment. The aesthetic of the cannibal is against catechisms or doctrine, against prescription, against "canned conscience." The cannibal aesthetic practices a "parasitical economy" much like invagination. As Andrade offers later in the manifesto: "We had the right codification of vengeance. The codified science of Magic. Cannibalism. For the permanent transformation of taboo into totem." That moment of transforming taboo into totem, the right to practice this transformation is prescient for Césaire, one might even say essential in his disruptive, convulsive, anarchic poetics and politics. For example, in "Preliminary Question," of which I will do a much more thorough close-reading later in this essay, Césaire's speaker transforms his excrescence into a camel bearing a pope, which also leads to the speaker vanishing in a row of fig trees that convulses to strangle the pope "in a beautiful tropical balancing act."[64] The sacred is rendered profane and profaned. Taboo totemed. Liberation is embedded in disorderliness, in disorder.

In Césaire's poetry and poetics, the logics of Western, rational order are inverted or displaced. And there is a way in which that displacement might still seem like a belonging, like being part of the set through the touching, through the act of displacement. However, Césaire's participation is without belonging. It is quite literally a surrounding, an encircling. Like Derrida's notion of invagination, in *Notebook*, Césaire embraces the schizophrenia of his negritude, his island that is "not connected with anything expressed," a "throng that does not know how to throng, this throng, so perfectly alone under

---

64 Aimé Césaire, *Solar Throat Slashed: The Unexpurgated 1948 Edition*, trans. and ed. James Arnold and Clayton Eshleman (Middletown, CT: Wesleyan University Press, 2011), 125.

the sun."⁶⁵ Here, in the "throng that does not know how to throng," we glimpse Derrida's notion of "a taking part in without being part of, without having membership in a set." It is strange and contradictory belonging and itinerary—one that is not static, one that is constantly dividing. Division, separation, negation becomes its membership and that begins to "form by invagination an internal pocket larger than the whole."⁶⁶ This moment is best expressed in *Notebook* when Césaire writes:

> What is mine, these few thousand deathbearers who mill in the calabash of an island and mine too, the archipelago arched with an anguished desire to negate itself, as if from maternal anxiety to protect this impossibly delicate tenuity separating one America from another; and these loins which secrete for Europe the hearty liquor of a Gulf Stream, and one of the two slopes of incandescence between which the Equator tightrope walks toward Africa. And my non-fence island, its brave audacity standing at the stern of this polynesia, before it, Guadeloupe, split in two down its dorsal line and equal in poverty to us, Haiti where negritude rose for the first time and stated that it believed in its humanity and the funny little tail of Florida where the strangulation of a nigger is being completed, and Africa gigantically caterpillaring up to the Hispanic foot of Europe, its nakedness where death scythes widely.

Though Césaire draws "a set" of sort, connecting his subjectivity to that of other subjectivities in the Black Diaspora—Guadeloupe,

---

65 Aimé Césaire, *Notebook of a Return to the Native Land*, trans. Mireille Rosello with Annie Pritchard (Hexham, UK: Bloodaxe Books, 1995), 3.

66 Fred Moten, *In the Break: The Aesthetics of The Black Radical Tradition*, (Minneapolis: University of Minnesota Press, 2003), 258.

Haiti, America—he does so through a division, an "anguished desire" of negation. He understands that the division is tenuous, fleeting; however, it exists—as both an absence and presence. It is a maternal anxiety, one that signals filial belonging but simultaneously also signals rupture. This rupture is not only a division between the islands and diasporic subjectivity. It is also a rupture with Europe and European epistemological, philosophical, political, and aesthetic traditions. Again, we can hear the echo of Césaire responding to Depestre's question concerning why he didn't publish some of his earlier poems—the renouncing of poetry in order to become a poet. Or the aesthetic and poetic encomium that also appears in *Notebook* concerning where to begin—by enacting the end of the world, by a division, a participation that is a nonparticipation or fraught or contested participation in European political and aesthetic traditions. Much like Andrade in *The Cannibal Manifesto*, he divides Haiti's negritude and humanity, the humanity of that of his island and others "who mill in the calabash of other islands in the archipelago" from Europe. In fact, he divides all of these Diasporic subjectivities from Europe because they bear the death of "European scythes." Membership into this set is created through negation, through "deathbearing," through division, through a birthing that is also a death, one's citizenship granted through this "sleep," to beckon back to Andrade. Here, in this moment, is also a rejection of sovereignty. This division creates a pocket, a physical place that is the Caribbean, the Black Diaspora more largely or ontologically, but this physical pocket can also be read as an invagination—"an internal pocket larger than the whole." The pocket creates a membership of belonging built upon non-belonging or an estranged belonging. The pocket articulates a subversive iteration of nation, sovereignty, and autonomy. In Césaire geographically sectioning off the Black Diaspora in this fashion, he creates a division that is singular and simultaneously limitless. This invagination is significant because of this limitlessness; he creates and performs an articulation that disrupts form and tradition, thereby creating a new form, a new sense of inhabitation, a future. Maybe something more than future: a beyond. Something beyond sovereignty.

This beyond sovereignty or non-sovereign sovereignty, this invagination, this act of renouncing that is also an enactment of what is renounced can best be glimpsed in "Preliminary Question." Here is the poem in its entirety:

Preliminary Question

As for me should they grab my leg
I vomit up a forest of lianas
Should they hang me by my fingernails
                         I piss a camel bearing a pope and vanish in a row of fig trees that quite neatly encircle the intruder and strangle him in a beautiful tropical balancing act
The weakness of many men is that they do not know how to become either a stone or a tree
As for me I sometimes fit sulfurous wicks between my boa fingers for the sole pleasure of bursting into a flame of new poinsettia leaves all evening long reds and greens trembling in the wind
like our dawn in my throat
                —*Aimé Césaire, from* Solar Throat Slashed

What one notices immediately (if one is reading the poem) are the short lines that resemble something like a poem, a lyric. In fact, syllabically both in French and in the English translation by A. James Arnold and Clayton Eshleman, the first three lines of the poem share the same syllabic count. In French, the line is seven syllables that feels like a trimeter line, one with three accented syllables, and in the English translation the line feels iambic though loosely so. Though I am doing an accentual syllabic scanning or reading of the line, I do that to corroborate that the lines and the poem thus far traffics in what one might call a more traditional lyric tradition of free verse. However, the departure from and subversion of this traditional lyric mode is announced, even if subtly so, in the lack of punctuation. Right away, Césaire signals that he will depart from tradition. However, his departure, the lack of punctuation is not a complete departure from the French lyric tradition, particularly the avant-garde tradition of Apollinaire, one of the progenitors of this sort of radical act of non-punctuation and surrealism. In the first three lines, in both the deployment of line and in the radical choice of non-punctuation, one can glimpse his renouncing of poetry in order to write the poem. When we consider the first two lines imagistically, one also notices what might seems like a surrealistic moment—the vomiting up of a forest of lianas when grabbed by the leg. However, I would like to remind the reader that to give this image and image-making whole-cloth over to surrealism and the French avant-garde tradition would be to dismiss what Césaire himself has said about his relationship to surrealism in the interview with René Depestre:

RD: Has surrealism been instrumental in your effort to discover this new French language?

AC: I was ready to accept surrealism because I already had advanced on my own, using as my starting point the same authors that had influenced the surrealist poets. Their thinking and mine had common reference points. Surrealism provided me with what I had confusedly been searching for. I have accepted it joyfully because in it I have found more of a confirmation than a revelation. It was a weapon that exploded the French language. It shook up absolutely everything. This was very important because the traditional forms—burdensome, overused forms—were crushing me…

AC [on the surrealist approach to consciousness]: This, for me, was a call to Africa. I said to myself: it's true that superficially we are French, we bear the marks of French customs; we have been branded by Cartesian philosophy, by French rhetoric; but if we break with all that, if we plumb the depths, then what we will find is fundamentally black.

In other words, Césaire was already in the zone of surrealistic principles though not in name. He walks alongside surrealists such as Breton; however, he is separate from them as well, "a participation without belonging," to harken back to Derrida. As aforementioned, surrealism as a confirmation or corroboration points to the fact that he's dividing his aesthetic and political practice into something else, something wholly apart, something forming a larger pocket in relationship to "the set," the set in this case being "French customs, Cartesian philosophy, French rhetoric."

This invagination can also be read in the imagery of the poem. The speaker of the poem, as the title of the poem points out, is involved in some sort of inquisition. And I do not use the term inquisition lightly. Someone or some entity has grabbed the speaker by the leg, and in response, the speaker finds it necessary to vomit up a forest of trees. Though the speaker does not tell us who "they" is—another moment of purposeful and deliberate opacity—one can imagine the "they" being some sort of authority figure. "They" can be read as similar to the "them" of African American vernacular culture—the folks, The Man, The Police, the State—or, to go back to opening stanza of Césaire's *Notebook of a Return to the Native Land*, "they" is the "cop," the "lousy pig," "the flunkies of order," "the cockchafers of hope," an "evil grigri," a "bedbug of a petty monk." I bring in *Notebook* here and this catalogue that begins the long poem because, for Césaire, "they" is shifting, and that shifting Césaire understands to be weaponized, an ideological and repressive apparatus of colonial order. In calling them "they," he fixes them in their abstraction, locating them in their shifting, willful political sublimity, calling out their desire to remain obscure, to function namelessly. His subversion of their weaponized invisibility does not stop there. In the action of vomiting up a forest of trees, he himself subverts the "they's" inquiry and their grasp through a surrounding, through an act of invagination. In fact, he doubles down on this radical invagination in the next two lines, which also signals a formal break from the short lines that begin the stanza. Césaire writes:

> Should they hang me by my fingernails
>   I piss a camel bearing a pope and vanish in a row of fig trees that quite neatly encircle the intruder and strangle him in a beautiful balancing act

To continue the line of thinking concerning invagination, Césaire's speaker imagines an escape strategy that will help defy the torturing methods of "they." In the subjunctive imagining—"should they hang me by the fingernails"—Césaire preempts the violence of authority, preempts their conscription, and subsequently imagines an afterlife, a future, a beyond that can subsume the violent imagination of the state, of the colony. Like Aunt Hester's shriek in Frederick Douglass' *Narrative of the Life of Frederick Douglass,* Césaire's speaker disrupts the economy of violence, disrupts and subverts the fungibility, the exchangeability of the body, the Black body in the obfuscatory practice of making an obedient colonial subject. In excrement, in the speaker's piss, in this moment of abjection, the speaker solidifies a "they," a pope, even if aqueously so. However, the speaker invaginates a pope, a metonymic substitution for colonial order, in a row of fig trees and strangles him "in a beautiful balancing act." This act of strangling the pope rebels against the sovereign, neutralizing one of the sovereign's most-used technologies of control—religion. Textually, this rupture, this break is signaled in the change in lineation, moving from a short line to a longer line, a long line that shades over into prose. The line beginning with "I piss a camel" is not left aligned either as the first three lines of the poem had been. Rather, it is tabbed over such that the "I" falls beneath fingernail. This lineation choice, I argue, is a type of marooning; in other words, Césaire maroons the pope figure. However, it is also more than that; the action of encircling the pope in a row of fig trees that the speaker has vanished behind is a bit more violent. It is also a revolt. The poet revolts formally through not only the centering of the line, but also in the sporadic lineation that occurs from then on. In other words, the poem shifts from a lineated poem to something like a prose poem that still retains the haunting, the echo of the earlier short-line lineation pattern. He maroons form, yet simultaneously creates a form that could not be imagined, one that is larger than its origin (free verse), larger and separate from the original set, one that is not entangled but strategically apart.

This apartness is corroborated by the disappearance of the speaker into what I would like to term convulsive nature, the hemorrhaging wilderness. Here, I am borrowing from and putting Césaire's speaker's union with nature in conversation with Michel Foucault's notion of convulsive, disobedient, possessed flesh from his lectures on the abnormal. In these lectures, Foucault argues that possession, particularly that by witches, was a moment of subversion of the Catholic Church's call for order in the governing of souls. The convulsive flesh resisted confession, resisted being hemmed in by dogma, as manifested in possession, thus the shaking disavowed the church's desire for the flesh to become body, ordered, exhaustively known, fungible, circumscribed. Césaire's speaker performs a similar sort of disordering through his disappearance into nature, into "lianas" and "fig trees."

Concomitantly, the trees perform abjectly through convulsion, convulsion in the form of vomiting, pissing, and strangulation. This abjection makes way for more opacity, for a subversive disappearance through a total assimilation of the speaker's body with nature. The speaker's body breaks into a blossom of sorts. Césaire writes: "As for me I sometimes fit sulfurous wicks between my boa fingers for the sole pleasure of bursting into a flame of new poinsettia leaves all evening long / reds and greens trembling in the wind / like our dawn in our throat." In that moment, the speaker is no longer alien from the convulsive wilderness. In fact, he becomes the opposite of what he derides in the line before—"men who cannot become either a stone or a tree." This moment also further corroborates and calls back to Césaire's decision not to use punctuation. The process of becoming the other, in this case, wilderness, is without physical interruption, order, border, or civilizing technique. It is a purposefully indeterminate process, an ending that is also a beginning, an absence and a presence.

This slide into the vegetal, into the wilderness, also evinces the slide from the rational into the crazy. As Frantz Fanon noted, an anticolonial position is one that will be perceived as crazy. However, Fanon understood, as noted by Jack Halberstam, "not to accept this organic division between the rational and the crazy and he knew it would be crazy for him not take the stance [of the crazy] in a world that had assigned him the roll of the unreal, the primitive and wild." In Césaire's speaker, we have a similar sort of embracing of that abjection. The ending of colonial order requires this sort of inhabitation, one that does not reconvene the logics of colonialism, the logics of sovereignty. Writing about Moten thinking through Fanon's embracing of the crazy, Halberstam continues: "In order to bring colonialism to an end then, one does not speak truth to power, one has to inhabit the crazy, nonsensical, ranting language of the other, the other who has been rendered a nonentity by colonialism." Césaire's speaker embraces this sort of nonsensical subjectivity, and Césaire, as poet, mucks about in this sort of poetic and political endeavor and study. Of Fanon's willingness to live in the space abandoned by colonialism, Moten, himself, writes: "Eventually, I believe he [Fanon] comes to believe in the world, which is to say the other world, where we inhabit and maybe even cultivate this absence, this place which shows up here and now, in the sovereign's space and time, as absence, darkness, death, things which are not (as John Donne would say)." Similarly, Césaire, in "Preliminary Question" imagines this non-space, this darkness, this absence.

However, even as Césaire creates and imagines this space, it's important to note that he does not call to order anything like nation or a politics or a rule of law. Though there is a "we" at the end of the poem, a "we" trembling in the wind with dawn in the throat, he does not reconvene an order, a logic that supplants the colonial logic. Instead, the reader and the "we" are left in the break, in the moment of rupture. There has been no resettlement or alternative society made, imagined, or arrived at. Rather, the reader is left in the middle of flight. I think this move is important in that it does not imagine what the "we" might want because the poet is not there yet. As Stephano Harney and Fred Moten note in *The Undercommons: Fugitive Planning & Black Study*, what one wants before the break, before the cut from colonial order might be quite different from what one wants while in the break; and that desire for the future might be quite different when one has made it through the break and is on the other side. Césaire's leaving us at dawn, trembling in flight, having not yet arrived might be a heuristic of how we might think of sovereignty and the future of the nation; that we stay in a state of upheaval, that we occupy this form of debt, the larger pocket, the other world, but we do not do so through the mode of critique and then the reinstitution of an order, that we fully move out of the logic of order.

(2019)

A Condition of Impossibility

Lyn Hejinian

Ilya [Kutik]'s mention, or discussion, of translating into rhyme brings up an issue that is something that has interested and concerned me for a long time, which is thinking about the paradigm of what a poem is, and it's been my longstanding interest to imagine expanding the paradigm of what poetry is and what kinds of projects poetry can undertake appropriately. We have a mutual friend, Arkadii Dragomoshchenko, a poet who does write—well, he doesn't rhyme, let's put it that way, not often—and he was giving a reading in St. Petersburg (then Leningrad)—Ilya also—and at the end of his reading, somebody from the back of the audience yelled, "That's not poetry!" And Arkadii said, "You are right but excuse me please you are also wrong." That is, that it didn't sound like a Russian poem—and for someone who had an expectation of what a poem would sound like, it didn't fit—but it also was a poem if you could expand what the definition of the poem would be, and then it would be a poem because there had been a big paradigm shift. Okay, I say this by way of sort of a preamble to something that I've been thinking about in the last few years, teaching a lot of theory and philosophy in the context of a poetics program at New College. A great deal of French contemporary philosophy, that is Derrida, etc., begins and is somehow anchored in a famous dictum of Theodor Adorno's which appears in *Negative Dialectics*, if anybody wants to check on it, but it says that "to write poetry after Auschwitz is an act of barbarism." That's a line, also, that the very famous Jewish Egyptian French poet Edmund Jabès quoted at the beginning of his enormous multi-volume project, and it's a line that I have thought about a lot because my own coming into adult consciousness as a poet—but, as I hope, a socially responsible one—was in the context of two big atrocities. If you take the Holocaust to stand for itself but also as a kind of metonym for other atrocities, my own coming into consciousness occurred in the light of, or I was shocked into awareness by the two important atrocities in this country, which were the social inequities in the segregation in the South (my earliest political activity was walking around Woolworths), and then the Vietnam War, where the anti-war movement learned a lot from the Civil Rights movement, which was just preceding it. So those two things sort of interlocked in my mind.

So, that's a little bit of background. And then, in more recent times, as I said for the last couple of years teaching all this theory and examining the way it operates and the kind of departure points and arrival points. For any of you who have read Lyotard, Derrida, Kristeva, etc., there's a sequence of arrivals and departures and they often seem to be the same. Endless, like a bird rising from a branch and falling again, but it's not quite the same spot on the branch and the bird's ruffled its feathers slightly differently. All of which I find ravishingly intriguing, and all of these people are terrifically prolific. And I began to think about a double interpretation of this dictum of Adorno's: one would be precisely in the negative sense of what it says, that after atrocity meaning is forever altered and it is altered into a condition of impossibility. That is that we cannot make meaning of an atrocity—to do so is in some way to allow it to exist, it's to accept its terms somehow. But the second way that I thought about it was to think about what barbarism means, and it comes from the Greek word *barbarous* which is an onomatopoetic imitation of babbling. It was the Greek word for people who don't speak Greek, they babble, that is people who don't speak the language. And I've come to think of a possible position for the poet which is precisely to be a barbarian—precisely to refuse to speak the language of atrocity and to endlessly be searching out the other paradigms of language, other ways of speaking that will defy the language of atrocity. And since atrocities replicate themselves constantly, that means that poets are always having to rethink the question of language and position themselves constantly in a kind of barbarian territory which, in this sort of big metaphor that I'm working on, which I'll just mentioned briefly here is a kind of border, a border zone where the barbarian we want is always a barbarian at a border where different languages are encountering each other, mores are confusing, different, etc. And I think that is an important territory for poetry not only to occupy, but actually to constantly recreate.

(1995)

THE QUESTION IS THE BEGINNING OF THE HEALING

Cecilia Vicuña and Anne Waldman on Ritual and Performance

ANNE WALDMAN: First, I was going to highlight some of the parts in your book *Spit Temple* where you speak of your life and performances. There's the occasion of visiting the shaman, Carmela Romero Antivil, who performed healing ritual songs in ceremony, and told you that you should begin to sing, this is in Chile. And then in *Cloud-Net* in '98, you say, "The true performance is that of our species on Earth: the way we cause suffering to others, the way we warm the atmosphere or cause other species to disappear. I cover myself with clouds to feel like the Earth feels."

Later, in *Empire*, this is in a performance with Charlie Morrow in 2002 on the observation deck of the Empire State Building, where he is playing trumpet and bells and you have a poem in your pocket saying that the empire is fear. You speak of embracing our fear. And you say a deep mourning emerged as you performed, and that turns into the skyscraper blues. Out of that, a notion of exactly how can performance, this thing that we've been doing since the Ice Age, how can that provide some kind of healing for this time we're in as we're going through these multiple, really epic catastrophes of pandemic, of uprising, of climate change, of undoing all kinds of treaties around nuclear disarmament? Also, we have earthquakes, as in Mexico just recently?

I've been feeling more and more this urge to somehow connect with all the *kami* [elemental Shinto spirits], all the spirit forces of the earth, and to look into civilization's past, what they've struggled with and endured. I've been doing research on some of the different pandemics and different circumstances there, and how to actualize right now some of that wisdom and awareness, which *you* certainly hold and which you've been activating your whole life. So, I wanted to get us into the present in terms of ritual performance, your thoughts, what you've been working with right now.

CECILIA VICUÑA: Well, everything that you have said brings forth the presence of silence, the need for silence. I think we have been put in a position where everything that we've known and we've counted on is gone, or going. I don't know what is worse, the fact that it's gone or that it's going. And we're pushing it even further by our consumption, by our way of being. It's like every little act that we do, turning on the AC, whatever we do, we are placing the bill on Kora, your granddaughter. We're *placing*—you say in English?—the bill in the future. And so how could we possibly stop that? A year ago, I published a little book—it's a conversation with a dear friend of mine from Chile [Camila Marambio]. And I called the book *Slow Down Fast, a Toda Raja* [Les presses du réel, 2019].

And it turns out that I had actually composed those lines, maybe a few years ago, 2015 I think.

And if you think of what this forced lockdown is doing to us, of course it's separating us, isolating us, but that's not all. It is also reducing us, reducing the scope of what is possible in our relations, in our feeling and sensing the world. And is this an accident or is this a sought-out program? And I think we all feel the answer and do not wish to say it very clearly, because it's too hurtful to acknowledge that we're all complicit in whatever is happening. And hurt is probably the only way to feel what this is really about. So, in order to get to a possibility of healing, we have to go back to that ancient principle of *parar*, to stop.

I will bring the first page that I composed for that little book to the video. It says… This is the little book [holds it up to camera]. And my friend's name is Camila Marambio. It's just conversations. It was published in Berlin and is available online. And it says, "We propose to slow down fast *a toda raja*, before it is too late. Before the nauseating speeding up of our destructiveness kills us all. We can perform it daily and the awareness that others are doing it too will come." It seems like [it was just] written now doesn't it? *A toda raja*… This is very much like what, Anne, you have been doing all your life. La raja is the slit, but it is the rip, the tear, the opening, the slit between our legs.

As I was preparing for our conversation, I opened up one of your books, just by chance, and I encountered this line by you that says, "I feel myself always an open system—parentheses—woman."

So, what does that really mean? That is not just a line of poetry; it's really a program, a program for existence, as I see it. And it is the notion you were speaking of, going back to ancient cultures, which is what I have done since I was a little girl, very much like you have done, Anne.

It's to feel my being as not my being Cecilia, the little person, but my being is all this vibratory immensity of which we are a part.

I could think completely when I was a little girl, and I lived in a space of silence and darkness, because I lived in the countryside away from any town or city. And it was a time when darkness existed. For example, right now, if you ask me what I'm doing now, I am writing the text for a book that is a collective book that I have put together, that is created by the meeting point of indigenous knowledge, and astrophysics and science and astronomy, and poetry. With these three currents, I composed a collective system, I would say, that began in August last year and went on until January 2020, with many people participating, hundreds of people really participating, and that is just because the darkness has been eliminated from the planet.

When you eliminate darkness, it's like you eliminate the Mother, you eliminate poetry, you eliminate half our being. And it's affecting the neurological connections in our own brain, you know, because we have been created by the cycle of day and night. Every creature on this planet has been created by that cyclical transformation of day into night, day into night. So how can we really open up when we have been reduced to a version of being human that is completely inhuman? Just the very question is the beginning of the healing.

AW: We're not experiencing the full picture, and out of touch with our cycle, our life, the day-to-night cycles. And it's said that the so-called *Kali Yuga*, which from some point of view we are already in, is very speeded up. That's one of the qualities of the difficult times, the trouble times, Dark Ages, is that everything is very, very accelerated. And even the predictions for when this would come are sooner than we might expect. According to some of the Buddhist and Hindu teachers, it's happening quickly. It's happening more quickly in our planet. You feel this all the time and the way things are coming on, you know, on top of each other now.

CV: Yes. Perhaps something so simple that looks really idiotic and silly, like *stopping*, is really a practice that we can do at any time.

I remember when I first arrived in New York. I came to give a performance in 1980, and I ended up being caught by New York and am still here, forty years later. And it still feels like an accident to me.

But I remember that one of the things that I did as a practice is to be walking down the street on Fifth Avenue, whatever place, full of skyscrapers. (I mean, complete madness in every possible sense.) And I would stop next to one of those, usually my favorite spot is where the garbage is, those garbage baskets, the metal baskets that they have in New York. And it seemed like an appropriate place for me because I was sort of protected from people walking on top of me, being small, you know. So, it's like I am a little animal right there standing next to the garbage can, and I could suddenly, completely stop my being in order to be. And I could go into a complete trance state, feeling the immense beauty of all that madness, all that passing, you know.

And I think artists and poets are among perhaps the few people on this planet that have not been reduced yet. Because our art and poetry would not be possible if we didn't have the ability to enter into that trance state, into that state of grace which is really what the writing is. It doesn't mean that is—how do you call that?—a sort of nirvana state. Not at all. It can be the hardest, most painful thing as well as the most joyous. But it's not about that. It is not, like the Buddhists say, *this* or *that*. It is something else. Something more beautiful than *this* or *that*. Because it is whole. It is undifferentiated sensing of differences.

I am writing down what I said not to forget it, because I said it and after I said it, I realized that I was speaking to you something that I didn't know was the central poetics of the land where I was born. And I didn't know it rationally or intellectually because it was suppressed, submerged like all indigenous knowledge around the world has been consistently suppressed and submerged by the colonialisms.

But when I came across the naming of this knowledge system, I immediately recognized it. And if you have seen the film *Kon Kon* [2010], which we showed at Naropa, in that film was the first time that I put together that ancient spiritual technology with whatever I was. It's as if I was finding my way to that knowledge through the stupidity and ignorance of my own being, my own not knowing. So, it's a risky thing to say this, but truly for me the most authentic thing is to have gotten to a sliver of understanding through *not knowing shit*. That's me.

AW: You use the term "melodic matrix." Would you see a connection to that through this kind of ancient sort of sounding, and also feeling it's partially the interconnectedness of where you are? I mean, I see you like this little animal. I love that you invoke the *vicuña*, next to the trash on Fifth Avenue. [Laughter.] It's more real than Fifth Avenue. When I last saw it, I was circling the Trump Tower shouting mantras about banishing the con. Con begone con. Not your *Kon Kon*, but the con.

CV: The C-O-N. [Laughter.] The real con of the world.

AW: This matrix, and you mention the slit, coming through the cracks, the interstices, the things that have been so repressed needing to come forth, and poetry which is in some traditions a kind of secret knowledge. And you see it in the crook of a tree or a cloud formation, and it's that act of unlocking through sound, it's up to you to unlock. You unlock it in a way, and it's activated *tibot*, I know we've both referred to that notion of tibot, from Thai poetics and opening sound, the way it hits the whole body.

CV: Tibot!

AW: Yes, tibot. And also, in various traditions you have text, and you have the knowledge, the gnosis, the background, and so on, critical, but you have to *sound* it. You have to sound it to actually make it affective, make it efficacious in the world. Without that you're missing the transmission. Where is that coming from? It never feels external. So it is wired into your systemic conglomeration of tendencies, your sense perceptions, and so on. Interesting where that comes from, and I love your idea when you talk about the quasar, using the word "quasar" as something that's in process, that hasn't become yet. And that's in a more concrete, relative way the poem that isn't locked-in, finished; it's becoming; it hasn't happened. So again, that notion that if it's happened, it hasn't happened, yet where is it coming from?

But one question I want to ask concerns the role of the poet. We invoke shaman, seer, etc. There's a wonderful passage I like to embellish from Robert Pogue Harrison's *Forests: The Shadow of Civilization* which says that it's going to be up to the poets to take the secret teachings, take the treasures, take the libraries, the mental structures, out of the falling city and go to the forest and maintain this kind of gnosis that one might have, and away from what I keep calling the *syndicates of samsara*, these endless syndicates that trap you, and I feel like we're in one right now, because our information is coming mainly from ignorance, aggression, media, and fear, and this is why it seems so important to go to other times and places and seek out a different kind of knowledge. We're so caught in these images that are very transitory, poof! They're like demonic *imposti*, these impostors that are coming at us all the time. So how do we—as people working with language, mind, ritual, remaking, redoing, turning—keep it going? How do we stay able and strong enough to keep it all alive, and not be tricked by ego and "con"? And I think about this with some of the practices and ethos of what we've tried to do in our various communities, but moving forward it looks pretty dark. So, there's one prediction that maybe a third of the planet would survive. How do we carry the knowledge forward? Or maybe it becomes something else, it turns into something else.

CV: Yes. The knowledge carries us if we let it, because the wonderful thing is that as long as we are alive, and as long as we are being human, we have been endowed with two million years of evolution of sensitivity, evolution of the ability to feel. Our thoughts are truly muddled, clouded by all this culture that has been posed through a brutalizing education system, brutalizing communication system, government systems, police system. It's not just the police that are brutal. Everything is brutal in the current world that we live in. But there is something that isn't brutal, which is how we feel. Our bodies are still incredibly fragile, incredibly sensitive, and it is through connecting to that sensibility that is hidden from us *in* us, that there is still a chance.

When it was still possible to be together and do rituals, the last big collective ritual that I performed was in Mexico City [in February 2020]. It was the most beautiful experience to say goodbye to our ritual collective *quipu*.[67] And I don't know if any of you know that Museo Nacional de Mexico, it's in a lava field, a field where ancient volcanos exploded. And therefore, it is a place that has a particular energy, and because the city is so polluted it's always cloudy, but on the day of the performance I called it a *Lava Quipu*.

I invited a lot of people, like a little over one hundred people came to this lava space that was open sculpture called Espacio Escultórico. And when we were arriving, we immediately could see that the two volcanos that were always covered up were present. They showed themselves. These great female volcanos showed themselves. So, we began to weave collectively with our bodies a direct menstrual line of red lava, red menstruation between our bodies and the volcano. And I have to tell you, Anne, that when this crowd completely slowed down, everybody, and even those who were not inside the *quipu*, that were outside, can feel it. The birds, the animals, the snakes, everything and everybody can feel it. And so, we all go together into this space that is beyond cognition, that is beyond names, and the only thing that is part of us there is our state of mind, our sense

---

67 "*Quipu*" or "*khipu*" means "knot" in Cusco Quecha language. A quipu is a record device or type of text made of knotted strings employed among people of the Andes. Similar devices are found in China, Tibet, and Japan.

of touch, and the vibratory dimension of our being, which is the voice. But not the voice for relating words, but the voice for relating something else. And so, we got together and I think everybody who was part of that will never forget it. Like the volcano will never forget it, and the lava itself.

These are the ways in which we create a connectivity with the future, by being present in the site of great antiquity, a place that has been sacred forever. But come to think of it, what place on earth has not been sacred forever? Every place, Manhattan too, is still a sacred place. So, the idea that there is something that is called a sacred space is true, but it's true as a state as much as a space, because a state and space are really one. They're not two things. This notion you find not only in astrophysics now or in quantum physics, but you also find it in indigenous cultures around the world. So, the possibility is there as long as we can breathe.

AW: As long as we can breathe. Yes.

CV: Shall we open it to the people?

AW: Yes. Let's do that.

CAROLINE SWANSON: What's your relationship with the quipu as you're creating it, the materials, the pattern, style, and how those might relate to a kind of semantics for you?

CV: OK. It's something funny that you asked what is my relationship to quipu. What is my relation to quipu? I think it would be more realistic to ask what is the quipu's relationship with me? Because, first of all, when I encountered the quipu, in the '60s, when I was a teenager, the quipu was a completely dead, gone system of knowledge. And how is it that I encountered it at a time when there were no pre-Columbian art museums, no books of pre-Columbian art in Chile, but very few people had a few books. My aunt happened to have one and that's how I encountered it because she was a sculptor. And so, for me, it seems to me as though I'm an old woman recalling how come I devoted my life to something so improbable. And what is it that happened between the quipu and me? How is it that the young girl who encountered an image felt attracted to it?

And it must have been an initial encounter with what I consider to be the living field of any knowledge. Whether ancient or contemporary, all forms of knowledge are *fields*, fields of energy. What was it in this field of energy that sensed the way in which the little girl related to it, with intrigue, with delight, with curiosity, with tenderness? How is it? What was the quality in that little person that the quipu embraced? Because from that moment forward, a long stretch of time moved on inside my own being, because there was no information, there was nothing about the quipu, but I never forgot it.

It was many years after that that I actually constructed my first physical quipu. So, my first quipu was a visual one, an image, and I gave it the name which is *El quipu que no recuerda nada*. The quipu that remembers nothing. That was the matrix of all my quipus, the fact that I was aware that I had stolen that knowledge, stolen that understanding. And if you're interested, Sarah Riggs and Omar Berrada and I recently had a conversation exactly about that subject, about how we have been *extracted* from, all of us, not just ancient people like me, but all of us. It's like this extracting machine; it's not just about extracting meaning, the forest, extracting everything, extracting life from us and so extracting feelings, extracting sensations, memories, dreams, and so whatever happened I constructed my first tactile quipu. It's gone, it doesn't exist, but I do have a picture. I exhibited it in London in 1974. Something happened with my hands and with this creature, but still many years went by until I had to find myself in New York.

I had to find myself completely removed, out of the Andes of the South American universe, in order to feel the need to begin *weaving* people. I began weaving people, weaving my audience, years before I encountered that such kinds of ritual, not exactly like I did, but in a similar spirit did take place in the Andes. So, what kind of memory existing as our body can remember something that our mind doesn't know? Does that help you?

SARAH RIGGS: May I ask a question, Cecilia? I was remembering that you had said in our previous conversation that you discovered that you were indigenous through your mother when you were in your sixties. And I wonder if you could talk a little bit about what lies within each of us in terms or our ancestry and older traditions and how to realize them, because it seems like in some ways you were enacting certain rituals since you were a young girl, since you were five years old? That connection for each of us who may not know what we were composed of?

CV: Yes. I think that's very important, Sarah, thank you very much for asking. Because I realized that there was no chance of people ever respecting or understanding the existence of indigenous cultures, unless they understood that *we* are *all* indigenous. So that became the *leña*[68] we say in Spanish, this log that was the principal expression of my sight. My partner and I, James O'Hern the poet, created our first website work, that was in 2009, and it kept collapsing, kept sort of being hacked or disappeared digitally. It's still up, but the phrase was "we're all indigenous to humanity." And the notion that the word human means *of the earth*, it's not a metaphor, it is not an image, it is not just a phrase, it is actually, literally true. Remember in the beginning I was speaking of the inheritance. Each one of us carries two million years of humanness. That is a gift beyond description.

---

68 "Firewood;" also "beating," as with a stick; rough play; flak; in vernacular: prodding, goading along.

And all that is in *us*. So how can people connect with that? It's only through nakedness. It's only through letting go of the descriptions or definitions of each one of us, like Cecilia Vicuña.

I remember I had a little nephew; he adored me and I adored him, you know, because I don't have children. I really love this little boy. And one day I said to him, "do you know," his name is Mateo, "that you're not really Mateo, like I am not really Cecilia? I am something else." And he looked at me. He was probably three or four years old at the time, and instead of replying with a question or whatever, he looked at me and I could see that he was looking into my eyes, like *piercing* inside of me to see what was in there. And I remembered, when he did that, an exercise that I used to do in high school.

In high school we had something called *recreos*[69] … So I would very often go into the bathroom where there was this tremendous, huge mirror. And I could be in front of the mirror. But what I did in front of the mirror, I did not see Cecilia, the little girl in school. I could go inside inside inside inside, until I would reach the Big Bang inside my skin, inside my bones, inside every molecule and particle of my being. And years later, maybe thirty years later, I encountered that that was actually an exercise. So that's how we discover our humanness, by *seeking* it, [by] opening up to whatever it is that is not us in us.

In this little text that I was reading of yours just before, I found this line of yours, which to me is truly a definition of indigenousness. And it says, this is Anne Waldman, "I am the context of those before me."

AW: Well, it's an aspiration. It's interesting that you brought up the mirror because that is, as you say, a tantric exercise. There is the notion of the *amrit kundali*, which is a ritual of emptiness you do when you first see yourself in the mirror. You try to do this with a child and

---

69 "Recess."

when somebody's very young. You do a ritual sort of blessing with a juniper bow dipped in sanctified water and you sprinkle it to *cut* the fixation of your own image in the mirror or you start not to see it as solid, but to see it as many things, as you were saying. You just go inside the mirror and touch all these other things, but also from the point of view of how to keep living in this continuum, that you don't become fixated on that as a kind of solid identity—it just flips everything around. So that's beautiful.

But this notion of how to work with that, how to work with these systems, even trying to understand them more fluidly, how to be able to enter in the way you do the mirror, and the idea of breaking everything down into the constituent forms, and then what is the love underneath, the compassion, whatever it is, the tantric thread? "*Tantra*" actually means "thread." So, I think of the quipu as well, the thread of things, and then the oral thread that you referred to, almost as if it's part of the threads that you work with or part of the larynx, and then what are the modes we have as poets and artists and feeling inside a continuum of some kind but also with a sense of duty. And I've been going back to some of the early poems of the Buddhist nuns, from the Pali canon. The notion that you reach a certain age and you're allowed, because you fulfilled so many duties, you can go to the forest and just live in silence and kind of leave the world, so to speak. And also, that you've been blessed to see the eyes of your own children, or seeing the eyes into the future, the eyes of the children to come. And so you leave with that sort of mission and it seems not even a mission, there's nothing demanded in a way, what is that? Are you letting go? I've always been curious about these architectures…Indra's net, again, the quipu, the threads that you work with, the interconnectedness of this fabric. How you are inside it, helping make it, weaving it…lots of questions.

EMMA GOMIS: Eleni Sikelianos is asking if Cecilia and Anne could speak about joy?

AW: Joy! Yes. It's so joyous to see you, even in your activated Zoom shrine boxes! I'm feeling so much joy, I was panicked about the earthquake in Mexico. All the earthquakes. And also thinking of all the people I've been with recently. Thinking of the students we worked with in the little village Tlahuitoltepec outside of Oaxaca this last fall, the CECAM school for young musicians. It's so powerful. And the joy of that. The immediate joy, whatever we're facing, but how to face these things with joy. Cecilia, will you tell us?

CV: I think that this sense of joy I can speak…I will go back to the first page of this book because it speaks…It says getting down through the slit, and this is very important that in terms of joy, both men and women are endowed with the ability to experience total joy. But women have a sort of joy organ, which is the clitoris. And so, we have a few poets and artists, women that throughout the millennia have devoted themselves to pursuing that knowledge of the world provided by the clit.

    I recently did, at Serpentine Gallery in London, a performance called *Clit Nest*, where I converted the entire crowd into a collective clit. It was really absolutely delightful. But here, getting back to the joy, what is absolutely magnificent about joy is that whether it is physical or non-physical—and a neuroscientist, I'm sure, would be able to have a beautiful answer for that—it touches a certain dimension of our being like an explosion that breaks open all boundaries. So, if we are removed from this ability to experience joy, how on earth are we going to be human again? How are we going to be able to release whatever it is that we haven't yet released? Because that's what we have to do in order to get to the other side where we collectively decide why this destruction? Why are we burning all the forests? Why can't we stop?

    First of all, we have to believe that this is possible. And second of all, I will go down to this text. It says to slow down as a symbolic active gesture restores paradise on earth. Paradise is a stop and a lifting of the soul, a break with the reign of the lone self. It was in 1966 that I wrote a poem about the word *paraíso*. "What can be constructed by stopping and elevating our being?" And it seems to me that paradise exists already in our being if we can listen to it, hear it again, in our breath. I personally do an exercise that I do several times per day, which is my favorite position in the world. It is *savasana*, the position of the corpse. And it is by becoming a corpse that I cease to be a corpse. And that's how I recover my joy.

(2021)
edited by Steven Taylor

Afterword

It's getting late in the day—
we'll have caviar and champagne—at the edge
of the crater on the Sea of Dreams,
and look down to earth as if it was all one
and the same, and leave our footprints
for those who follow

—Lewis Warsh, "Dark Side of Time"

Feminafesto

Torques of Tongue and Archive and Anthropocene

Anne Waldman

Of late I've been tracking what I'd call the torques of the Mother Tongue. And this project moves itself through various interstices here & now & upon material cusps, here & now & elsewhere (into various poetry cultures here & abroad, and other senses of economy and activism—gift exchange, *sousvellience* and the like) with a driven sense of personal and public duty, & includes the creating & preserving of Archive & other endangered identities of the poetry & poetics work that so many of us have been involved with over the last half century & more. It includes being a kind of ambassador of a "wild mind" lineage and a view of the primacy of imagination. *And the view that there is no human dimension in any period of history without poetry.* And it creates investigative projects that are long poems. It's a radical dimension in that it is a way of life. There's no time off.

It's a "calling," if you will, with a privilege of mobility that I have struggled for in what I am also calling the "activity demon vow." This vow has many heads and thousands of arms, and an imagination or an image of that imagination that strives to operate in eleven tentacular directions at once, like string theory.

Jacques Derrida in his text *Archive Fever* postulates that we should consider the "death drive" as a force, without which there would not be in effect any desire or possibility of Archive or Anthology. The entropy of the death drive is interesting since it provides us with tremendous energy. I exist because of the dissipative structure of Archive. Forget eternalism or nihilism. An archive meditates on memory, religion, time, war, technology. It is a technology of inscription, an inscription of our psychic processes, our utopias, our seed syllables, our cosmic batteries, and hopes of future. Archive is a practice. And through Archive we show humanity—or whatever it is—the consciousness of the future—the post human future—the intelligent slime mold poets of the future—*we were not just slaughtering one another.*

Have you noticed how all the new scientific research is showing us how *smart* animals really are? The Buddhist view, & the increasing scientific view, is that all life forms are interrelated through their evolutionary history, & that human and animal minds are both participants in reality. We share the planet with billions—trillions—of non-human temporalities. Minds exist at the quantum level below the level of atoms of sub-atomic particles. Minds never come from nothing or go to nothing. In terms of the advances of biotechnology—& the extraordinary fantasy feats considering resurrection the DNA of the Tasmanian tiger or the work with hair samples of wooly mammoths to the point where bio-geneticists are able to modify the DNA of a sixty-thousand-year-old creature & place it inside an elephant's egg so it will be brought to term in an elephant mother's body is radical and strange. Impossible? The Industrial age is drawing to a close. Welcome to the scary Anthropocene! This term has been critiqued for its excessive human-focus. We are not the center of the universe by any means, only perhaps its enemy. Nothing without the hand and control of the human. It will be both terrifying and fascinating to see how consciousness is measured in these new engineered life forms that could well outlive their "masters." And heartbreaking to watch so many species go down, as they do, now, daily...manatee, whale, sea turtles and myriad sea birds washing up on the Gulf Coast—just one sign of the enormous ecocide taking place.

We must fight offshore drilling and re-commit ourselves to other life-forms—palpitating non-human temporalities—that suffer & die so hard in the oil and detritus of our "advanced" civilization! And hold BP and other robber barons (Halliburton (Xi) et al.) accountable and bring them to trial.

I see our bodies as ethical matter. *The last threshold of resistance I have is my body* is Foucault's line. The body is radically non-Cartesian. It talks to itself in a continual feed. The brain is not the central planner. There's an inner sense of how the body is located in landscape and space—including gestures of vision & touch and imagination & poetry. This is *proprioception,* an obsession of poet Charles Olson, who saw it as the way "in." *Proprius*—"one's own, and perception." Perception of the body itself in this efficacious time and place which stays alert.

I have always been grateful for the freedom to make my work, & to be part of poetry cultures that have had real presence & force in the world. That continue to provide nourishment &, commitment and the time-tithe on a continuous life adjacent to these feeds. To benefit others. These sites & utopias and resistances and *fellaheen* worlds are practices. They are not pre-cooked. Yet they seem to strive outside the establishment, whatever that is, & outside official culture, whatever that is, outside politics & media (we know what they are!) and stride beyond short-sighted economic blasts in that they are vision-generated, the thrust of our projects is ageless, ritualistic, often endangered. The edge of the precipice.

We need to keep fighting on gender issues, human and civil rights. To keep exchanges going with women in Iran, Iraq, Afghanistan, Tibet, Vietnam, Africa, China. To the Women warriors of Rojava. To the fraught stateless Rohinga women. With our Native American sisters on this continent—and women in Mexico, Canada... to fight for immigration reform. One might also conjure a sense of exile here. As a state of mind, although we all know poets in true & dire political exile, who suffer greatly the lost homeland... we are in a kind of "temporary autonomous zone" exile. You can't territorialize a mind of artistic exile. And the de-territorializing that such a frame of mind engenders which is why one is drawn to poetry, which like music, de-territorializes and gives strength to the practice. And takes one to places of risk and anarchy. Poetry is not empire building. It de-territorializes empire.

(2010)

Morphology of Dust

Emma Gomis

> Sifting daylight dissolves the memory, turns it into dust motes floating in light.
>
> —*Toni Morrison*, Beloved

Dust is a mutable, elusive substance. It resists a fixed shape and is not easily containable. Fugitive dust, or aeolian dust, made of soil and clay, is prevalent in arid-land ecosystems largely due to anthropogenic impact. It swirls in a cyclical nature; we kick it up with our boots. Dust becomes a productive metaphor for thinking about archival practice. Records and boxes too long left unattended acquire a fine layer of dust—abandon, disuse, time passing. Fly ash, coal combustion particulates, contain a material history of our ecological destruction—residue remains like a memory trace which spark moments of archive poesis. What will happen to the archives after we're gone, and who will steward their dust?

During the summer of the first COVID lockdown in 2020, I would wake up in the morning, get in my truck, a 1991 Red Izuzu Trooper, and drive down the canyon into town. In Anne's backyard the rabbit visited us every day, Ed floated in and out bearing treats, the Buddha sat among the greenery.

The forty-sixth year of the Summer Writing Program had moved online. From a tent in a field, we were now scanning the grids on our screens, looking into each others' rooms, contemplating the aesthetics of our backdrops. The voices of the poets who participated in the program still reached us in our isolation. We wished to collapse the distance between us, so we danced with our friends on the screens. Behind the scenes we ate sandwiches and fell asleep on the couch. Our presence dematerialized in the world, the lectures and readings served as punctums for us to escape into. As the summer waned, the fires in California blew their ash into the sky and spread out like a blanket, the sun filtered a red light through the windows. Ashes to ashes, dust to dust.

That summer we often talked about the archive, pressing record on every Zoom session and sending it off to the librarian. Thinking through a post-digital paradigm, I think many poets harbor the fear that every digital artifact might somehow vanish, not be saved, transferred, or recorded. And so, we can think of what is contained within this anthology as an analogue preservation of artifacts that represent a small portion of the history of poetics at Naropa.

To give a complete overview of the Naropa Archive is an impossible feat. To assemble a book that would encompass the whole of the collection is as daunting as summarizing the contents of any archive. Any single excerpt proves an inadequate metonym as each file differs so wildly from the next, each piece adding a new perspective. The act of engaging with the archive became extensive, at times exhaustive, in its sheer dense and lengthy composition. Overwhelmed at making one's way through the endless files, the only thing to be done is to take a deep breath and dive in, knowing that the labor of digging will result in a rewarding find, a nugget that proves to crystallize a deeper understanding.

When Lisa Robertson came to Naropa in 2018 she offered a prompt for thinking of the imagination as a productive organ within the anatomy of the soul. The idea charmed me. She quoted Agamben: "During earthly life, the pneuma is the instrument of the imagination and as such, it is the subject of dreams, of astral influences, and of the divine illuminations." The imagination produces images. It can warp the sensuous, distort the memory, or fabricate things into existence. If the archive forms part of a material representation of the soul of Naropa's Jack Kerouac School of Disembodied Poetics, we brushed off the dust that had settled like film covering some of these pieces and allowed their pneuma to swirl around us again. Each piece conjuring different images of the past. From memory to audio to written record.

Thinking about archive futures, I do not wish to focus on the fact that they are at risk or mourn their loss, but rather to make a case for building resiliency, and equally to stay curious to the manner and cause of their destruction. Are archives, libraries, and storerooms memory palaces? I liken these archive stories to a fairy tale, once you are under their spell, you must finish them, till your heart breaks— you carry on and finish the work you have begun, of inscribing, reading and remembering.

(2021)

Figure 7: Anne Waldman and Emma Gomis visit the Naropa Archives
(Boulder, CO 2020)

Acknowledgments

We are so grateful to all those who helped bring this book to completion.

We want to give particular thanks to Steven Taylor and Laura Wright for their erudition, enthusiasm, encouraging feedback, and editorial support. They have been invaluable in the shaping of this book.

To Jeffrey Pethybridge for helping us organize our production efforts, and for remembering old manuscripts and lectures and for contributing to the Summer Writing catalogue texts. To Amanda Rybin Koob and Jaime Groetsema for helping us navigate the Naropa University Audio Archive and locate files.

Thank you to those who helped transcribe the material: Andrew Hawes, Drew Dean, Peter Belly, Madeline Rose Hernandez, Mayra Rodriguez Castro, Aubrey King, and Alystyre Julian.

PUBLICATION ACKNOWLEDGMENTS:

- "A Poetics of Participation" by Cedar Sigo was published *Guard the Mysteries* (Wave Books, June 2021).
- "On Property and Monstrosity" by Julie Carr was previously published in *The American Poetry Review* (March/April 2017), and in *Someone Shot My Book* (University of Michigan Press, 2018).
- "Dreams, Again" by Alice Notley was previously published in *Talisman: A Journal of Contemporary Poetry and Poetics* (Issue 42, 2014).
- "Homonculus" by Margaret Randall was previously published in *Thinking About Thinking* (Casa Urraca Press, 2021, Abiquiu, New Mexico).
- "Feminafesto" by Anne Waldman was published in a chapbook titled *Feminafesto* (Chax Press, Tuscon, 2011).
- "Syntax and the Event of Reading" by Renee Gladman was published in *Thuggery and Grace* #5 (Denver, 2015).
- "Consenting to the Emergency / the Emergent as Consensuality" by J'Lyn Chapman was published in *Dial 2* and in *To Limn / Lying In* (PANK Books, 2020).

PERMISSION ACKNOWLEDGMENTS:

- From "Footnote to Howl" from *Collected Poems 1947-1997* by Allen Ginsberg. Copyright © 2006 by the Allen Ginsberg Trust. Used by permission of HarperCollins Publishers.
- "We as Witness" by Paula Gunn Allen used with the permission of The Permissions Company, LLC on behalf of the Estate of Paula Gunn Allen.
- "Writer's Block and Neoteny" by William S. Burroughs. Copyright © 1981 by William S. Burroughs, used by permission of The Wylie Agency LLC.

Thanks to the generosity of the authors and estates of authors published in *NEW WEATHERS*.

Gratitude to the year-round faculty of the recent years: Jeffrey Pethybridge, J'Lyn Chapman, Michelle Naka Pierce, Andrew Schelling, Reed Bye, Sara Veglahn, Julia Seko, Brad O'Sullivan, Junior Burke, Bhanu Kapil, and to Ambrose Bye for developing the Summer Writing Program Recording Studio. And to Ed Bowes for his continuous support. Gratitude to Bob Rosenthal and Peter Hale of The Allen Ginsberg Trust and the Committee on Poetry for their ongoing support of the Jack Kerouac School.

The editors would like to extend gratitude to Stephen Motika and to the staff of Nightboat, including Lina Bergamini, Lindsey Boldt, Gia Gonzales, and Caelan Nardone. Thanks also to the book's designers, HR Hegnauer and Rissa Hochberger. We deeply appreciate Nightboat's commitment to demanding and educational anthologies of this kind, that move the century and critical thinking forward on literature, poetics and politics, and on the essential importance of literary and cultural archives.

Deep thanks to Chuck Lief, President of Naropa University, for his enthusiastic support of The Jack Kerouac School of Disembodied Poetics, its resident and low residency MFA Programs, and the Summer Writing Program within the great Naropa experiment.

Anselm Hollo, Bobbie Louise Hawkins, Jack Collom, Lewis Warsh and Diane di Prima in memory.

To listen to more lectures on poetics given at Naropa University, please visit www.naropa.edu/audioarchive.

Biographies

PAULA GUNN ALLEN (1939–2008): Native American poet, novelist, activist, literary critic, feminist, and scholar. *The Sacred Hoop: Recovering the Feminine in American Indian Traditions* (1986) explores the importance of women in traditional Native culture. *Studies in American Indian Literature: Critical Essays and Course Designs* (1983) is considered a landmark text in Native American literary criticism.

AMIRI BARAKA, FORMERLY LEROI JONES, (1934–2014): Poet, novelist, playwright and political activist. Jones joined and was part of the Beat movement, then with the assassination of Malcolm X, he took the name Amiri Baraka and founded the Black Arts Movement. He published many books of poetry and prose including *Black Art* (1969) and *Somebody Blew Up America and Other Poems* (2003), as well as plays, essays, and music criticism.

SHERWIN BITSUI (1975–): Author of the poetry collections *Dissolve* (2019), *Shapeshift* (2003), and *Flood Song* (2009)—which won the American Book Award and the PEN Open Book Award. He is Diné of the Todích'ii'nii (Bitter Water Clan), born for the Tlízílaaní (Many Goats Clan). He grew up on the Navajo Reservation in White Cone, Arizona.

ROBIN BLASER (1925–2009): Robin Blaser helped spark the Berkeley Poetry Renaissance in the 1940's. Author of numerous collections of poetry including *The Moth Poem* (1964), *Cups* (1968), *Syntax* (1983), and *Nomad* (1995). Blaser's poetry and prose has been collected into three volumes: *Even on Sunday: Essays, Readings, and Archival Materials on the Poetry and Poetics of Robin Blaser* (2002); *The Fire: Collected Essays of Robin Blaser* (2006), edited by Miriam Nichols; and *The Holy Forest: Collected Poems of Robin Blaser* (2007).

WILLIAM S. BURROUGHS (1914–1997): One of the primary figures of the Beat movement who popularized the aleatory literary technique called cut-up. Burroughs wrote eighteen novels and novellas including *Junkie* (1953) and *Naked Lunch* (1959), six collections of short stories, and four collections of essays.

JULIE CARR (1966–): Author of *Real Life: An Installation* (2018), as well as six books of poetry and three critical prose and experimental essays. With Tim

Roberts, she is the cofounder of Counterpath Press, Counterpath Gallery, and Counterpath Community Garden in Denver, and is a Professor at the University of Colorado in Boulder in the English department.

J'Lyn Chapman (1977–): Author of *To Limn / Lying In* (2020) from PANK books, *Beastlife* (2015) from Calamari, and the digital chapbooks *The Form Our Curiosity Takes: A Pedagogy of Conversation* (2015) and *A Thing of Shreds and Patches* (2016) from Essay Press. She taught for many years at the Jack Kerouac School of Disembodied Poetics and is currently an Assistant Professor at Regis University.

Jos Charles (1988–): Author of *Safe Space* (2016), *feeld*, a Pulitzer-finalist and winner of the 2017 National Poetry Series selected by Fady Joudah (2018), and *a Year & other poems* (2022). From 2013-18 she served as the founding-editor for *THEM lit*, a trans literary journal. She holds an MFA from the University of Arizona and is currently a PhD student at UC Irvine.

Jack Collom (1931–2017): Poet, essayist, teacher. Author of twenty-five books and chapbooks of poetry, three books on/of children's writings. Most recent collections: *Entering the City* (1997), *Dog Sonnets* (1998), *Red Car Goes By* (2001), and *Situations, Sings* with Lyn Hejinian (2008). He taught ecopoetics at Naropa Institute for several decades, forming an important part of the community.

Samuel R. Delany (1942–): Author of over twenty novels including *Dark Dahlgren* (1974), *Reflections* (2007), and *Through the Valley of the Nest of Spiders* (2011). His shorter fictions are collected in *Aye* (1967), *Atlantis: Three Tales* (1995), and *Gomorrah & Other Stories* (2003). Delany writes widely on the topics of mythology, memory, language, sexuality, and perception.

kari edwards (1954–2006): Artist, gender activist, and author of *post/(pink)* (2000), *a diary of lies* (2002), *a day in the life of p* (2002), *iduna* (2003), *obedience* (2005), and the posthumous *Bharat jiva* (2009). She received a New Langton Arts Bay Area Award in literature in 2002 and the Small Press Traffic's book of the year award in 2004.

Tongo Eisen-Martin (1980–): Author of *someone's dead already* (Bootstrap Press, 2015), nominated for a California Book Award; and *Heaven Is All Goodbyes* (City Lights, 2017), which received a 2018 American Book Award, a 2018 California Book Award, was named a 2018 National California Booksellers Association Poetry Book of the Year, and was shortlisted for the 2018 Griffin

International Poetry Prize. He is the current poet laureate of San Francisco. He is also an educator and organizer whose work centers on issues of mass incarceration, extrajudicial killings of Black people, and human rights.

TONYA M. FOSTER (1966–): Author of *A Swarm of Bees in High Court* (2015), and coeditor of *Third Mind: Creative Writing through Visual Art* (2002). A poet and scholar, her writing and research focus on ideas of place and emplacement, and on intersections between the visual and the written.

FORREST GANDER (1956–): Poet, translator, essayist, novelist. Recent books of poetry include: *Science & Steepleflower* (1998) and *Redstart: An Ecological Poetics* (2012). Novels: *As a Friend* (2008) and *The Trace* (2014). He has won numerous awards, including the Best Translated Book Award for *Spectacle & Pigsty: Selected Poems of Kiwao Nomura* (2011) and the Pulitzer Prize for *Be With* (2018). He holds degrees in both geology and English literature.

ALAN GILBERT (1969–): Author of the poetry collections *Late in the Antenna Fields* (2011), *The Treatment of Monuments* (2012), and *The Everyday Life of Design* (2020), and the essay collection *Another Future: Poetry and Art in a Postmodern Twilight* (2006). Gilbert is also an art writer who has contributed catalogue essays for biennials and various group and solo shows.

ALLEN GINSBERG (1926–1997): One of the most respected Beat writers and a cofounder of the Jack Kerouac School of Disembodied Poetics at Naropa University. He gained significant public attention after publishing *Howl and Other Poems* in 1956. He was a poet, activist, performer and a major counter-cultural icon.

RENEE GLADMAN (1971–): She is the author of fourteen published works, including a cycle of novels about the city-state Ravicka and its inhabitants, the Ravickians—*Event Factory* (2010), *The Ravickians* (2011), *Ana Patova Crosses a Bridge* (2013) and *Houses of Ravicka* (2017)—as well as three collections of drawings: *Prose Architectures* (2017), *One Long Black Sentence*, a series of white ink drawings on black paper, indexed by Fred Moten (2020), and *Plans for Sentences* (2022).

ROBERT GLÜCK (1947–): Poet, fiction writer, critic, and editor. With Bruce Boone, Glück founded the New Narrative movement in San Francisco. His poetry collections include, with Boone, *La Fontaine* (1981) and *Reader* (1989). His fiction includes the novel *Jack the Modernist* (1985) and the story collection *Denny Smith* (2003). Glück served as the director of San Francisco

State's Poetry Center, codirector of the Small Press Traffic Literary Center, and associate editor at Lapis Press.

EMMA GOMIS (1989–): Catalan American poet, essayist, editor and researcher. She has published the chapbooks: *Canxona* (Blush Lit), *X* (SpamZine Press) and *Goslings to Prophecy* (The Lune). She holds an M.F.A. from Naropa's Jack Kerouac School of Disembodied Poetics and is currently pursuing a Ph.D. in criticism and culture at the University of Cambridge.

LYN HEJINIAN (1941 -): Poet, essayist, translator, publisher, and a founding figure of the Language poetry movement of the 1970s. Her lyric prose and descriptive engagement with the everyday have made her an influential force in experimental poetics. She is the author of many poetry collections, including her landmark work *My Life* (Burning Deck, 1980), *The Fatalist* (Omnidawn, 2003), *The Book of a Thousand Eyes* (Omnidawn, 2012), and *My Life and My Life in the Nineties* (Wesleyan University Press, 2013). A native Californian, she teaches in the English Department at the University of California, Berkeley.

LISA JARNOT (1967–): Author of *Black Dog Songs* (2003) and *Joie De Vivre: Selected Poems 1992-2012* (2013). In 2013, her biography *Robert Duncan: The Ambassador from Venus* was published by University of California Press. She lives in Jackson Heights, Queens, and works as a gardener.

KEVIN KILLIAN (1952–2019): Poet, editor, and playwright. His poetry collections include *Argento Series* (2001), *Action Kylie* (2008), *Tweaky Village* (2014), and *Tony Greene Era* (2016). Killian contributed significantly to scholarship on the life and work of Jack Spicer. With Dodie Bellamy, he also edited the literary and art journal *Mirage #4/Period(ical)* and the anthology *Writers Who Love Too Much: New Narrative Writing, 1977–1997* (2017).

THURSTON MOORE (1958–): A musician, composer, performer and founder of NYC experimentalists Sonic Youth (1980-2011). His most recent solo release is *Spirit Counsel*, a three-CD set. He has taught for many years at the Jack Kerouac School of Disembodied Poetics.

FRED MOTEN (1962–): Poet and scholar. His work explores critical theory, performance and Black studies. His critical texts include *In the Break: Aesthetics of the Black Radical Tradition* (2003) and *The Undercommons: Fugitive Planning & Black Study* (2013), co-authored with Stefano Harney, among others. He has published numerous poetry collections including *Hughson's Tavern* (2008), *B Jenkins* (2009), *The Little Edges* (2014), and *The Feel Trio* (2014).

EILEEN MYLES (1949–): A poet, novelist, and performer whose books include *Chelsea Girls* (1994) *The Importance of Being Iceland: Travel Essays in Art* (2009), and *Inferno* (2016). She is often identified with the Second Generation New York School poets.

HOA NGUYEN (1967–): Author of a dozen chapbooks and five books of poetry including: *Red Juice: Poems 1998-2008* (2014), *As Long As Trees Last* (2012), *Tells of the Crackling* (2015), and *Violet Energy Ingots* (2016), and *A Thousand Times You Lose Your Treasure* (2021) which was a finalist for the National Book Award. With her husband, Dale Smith, she founded the small press and journal *Skanky Possum*.

ALICE NOTLEY (1945–): Author of over forty books of poetry, including most recently: *Alma, or the Dead Women* (2006), *In the Pines* (2007), *Culture of One* (2011), *Benediction* (2015), *Certain Magical Acts* (2016), and *For the Ride* (2020). Her experimentation with poetic form blurs genres; often writing in narrative and epic modes which explore the nature of the self and the social and cultural importance of disobedience.

AKILAH OLIVER (1961–2011): Writer, performer, and feminist activist. Author of two books of poetry: *the she said dialogues: flesh memory* (1999) and *A Toast in the House of Friends* (2009), and five chapbooks. She collaborated with a wide range of artists. Oliver founded the feminist performance collective Sacred Naked Nature Girls in the 1990s.

M. NOURBESE PHILIP (1947–): Poet, novelist, playwright, and lawyer. She practiced law for seven years before turning full-time to poetry. Her poetry books include *She Tries Her Tongue, Her Silence Softly Breaks* (1988), *Zong!* (2008), the novel *Harriet's Daughter* (1988), and many essays.

DAN BEACHY-QUICK (1973–): Poet and essayist, author, most recently, of a collection of poetic records of light titled *Variations on Dawn and Dusk* (2019) and a collection of essays, fragments, and poems, *Of Silence and Song* (2017). Some of his other books include: *North True South Bright* (2003), *Spell* (2004), *This Nest, Swift Passerine* (2009), *Circle's Apprentice* (2011), and *Wonderful Investigations* (2012). He teaches in the MFA Program at Colorado State University.

MARGARET RANDALL (1936–): Poet, feminist, historian, and activist. She cofounded El Corno Emplumado in Mexico in the 1960s. She has participated as guest faculty at Naropa's Summer Writing Program for many years.

Roger Reeves (1980–): His first book of poems, *King Me*, came out with Copper Canyon in 2013. His next book, *On Paradise*, is forthcoming from W.W. Norton.

Ariana Reines (1982–): Poet, playwright, performance artist, and translator. Her books of poetry include: *The Cow* (2006), *Coeur de Lion* (2008), *Mercury* (2011), and most recently *A Sand Book* (2019).

Lisa Robertson (1961–): Poet, essayist and researcher. Her books of poetry include *XEclogue* (1993), *Debbie: An Epic* (1997), *The Weather* (2001), and *3 Summers* (2016). Her works of prose include *Occasional Works and Seven Walks from the Office for Soft Architecture* (2010), *Nilling* (2012) and *The Baudelaire Fractal* (2020).

Ed Sanders (1939–): Poet, singer, social activist, environmentalist, author, publisher, and longtime member of the band The Fugs. He is the author of more than a dozen collections of poetry including *Poem from Jail* (1963) and *Poems for New Orleans* (2008), among others, as well as the manifesto *Investigative Poetry* (1976).

Andrew Schelling (1953–): Poet and translator. His recent collection is *The Facts at Dog Tank Spring* (2020). His numerous translations of poetry from Sanskrit and other languages of India include work by Mirabai, Lal Ded, Bhartrihari; among his edited volumes is *Love and the Turning Seasons: India's Poetry of Spiritual & Erotic Longing* (2014). He has been core faculty teaching poetry and Sanskrit at Naropa University for many years.

Cedar Sigo (1978–): Poet, essayist. Raised on the Suquamish Reservation in the Pacific Northwest, Sigo is the author of eight books and pamphlets of poetry, including: *Expensive Magic (2008)*, *Stranger in Town* (2010), *Language Arts* (2014), and *Royals* (2017), and two editions of *Selected Writings* (2003 and 2005).

Eleni Sikelianos (1965–): Author of nine books of poetry, most recently *Make Yourself Happy* (2017) and *What I Knew* (2019), and two hybrid memoirs, *The Book of Jon* (2004) and *You Animal Machine: (The Golden Greek)* (2014). Her work has been translated into a dozen languages, and she frequently collaborates with musicians, filmmakers, and visual artists. Sikelianos has taught poetry in public schools, homeless shelters, and prisons, and currently teaches at Brown.

HARRY SMITH (1923–1991): Collector, artist, filmmaker, musicologist, and polymath. He was an important figure of the Beat Generation. In 1952 Folkways issued his *Anthology of American Folk Music*. He spent his last years (1988-91) as "shaman in residence" at Naropa Institute where he offered lectures, worked on sound projects, and continued collecting and researching.

STEVEN TAYLOR (1955–): Writer, editor, and musician based in Brooklyn. His latest publications are *Don't Hide the Madness* (2018) and *William Blake's Songs of Innocence and of Experience* (2019). He is a member of the seminal poetry rock group, the Fugs. He was on the faculty at Naropa from 1995-2008, and presently teaches at the City University of New York.

EDWIN TORRES (1958–): Author of eight books of poetry, including: *The PoPedology Of An Ambient Language* (2007), *Yes Thing No Thing* (2010), *Ameriscopia* (2014), and *XoeteoX* (2018). He has performed worldwide and taught his process-oriented workshop, "Brainlingo: Writing the Voice Of The Body," across the United States.

CECILIA VICUÑA (1948–): Chilean poet, performance artist, and activist. Recent books include: *Slow Down Fast/A Toda Raja* (2019) and *Spit Temple* (2012). Her work has been exhibited in the Tate Modern, Whitney Museum of American Art, and MoMA, among others.

ASIYA WADUD: Author of *Crosslight for Youngbird, day pulls down the sky/a filament in gold leaf* (written with Okwui Okpokwasili), *Syncope*, and *No Knowledge Is Complete Until It Passes Through My Body*. Her recent writing appears in *e-flux journal, BOMB Magazine, Poem-a-Day, Chicago Review, Social Text, FENCE*, and elsewhere. Asiya's work has been supported by the Foundation Jan Michalski, Lower Manhattan Cultural Council (River to River: Four Voices 2020; Governors Island Arts Center residency 2019-2020; Process Space 2017), Danspace Project, Brooklyn Poets, Dickinson House, Mount Tremper Arts, and the New York Public Library, among others. She lives in Brooklyn, New York where she teaches poetry at Saint Ann's School, Columbia University, and Pacific Northwest College of Art.

ANNE WALDMAN (1945–): Poet, performer, professor, editor, cultural activist, and co-founder with Allen Ginsberg of the Jack Kerouac School of Disembodied Poetics at Naropa University. She is a former director of The Poetry Project, which she helped found in 1966. Author of over fifty books of poetry including *Manatee/Humanity* (2009), *The Iovis Trilogy: Colors in the Mechanism of Concealment* (2011), *Gossamurmer* (2013), and *Trickster*

Feminism (2018). She is a frequent collaborator with poets, dancers, musicians, and visual artists.

PETER WARSHALL (1940–2013): Ecologist, activist, and essayist whose work centers on conservation. His research interests include natural history, natural resource management, conservation biology, biodiversity assessments, and environmental impact analysis, among others. He worked as a consultant for the United Nations High Commission for Refugees in Ethiopia and was elected to the board of the Bolinas Community Public Utility District.

ELIOT WEINBERGER (1949–): Essayist, political commentator, editor, and translator. His work has been published in more than thirty languages. His books of avant-gardist literary essays include *Oranges & Peanuts for Sale* (2009). His political articles are collected in *What I Heard About Iraq* (2005), among others. He is also the author of a study of Chinese poetry translation, *19 Ways of Looking at Wang Wei* (1987).

PETER LAMBORN WILSON (1945–2022): Author, political critic, essayist, and poet. In addition to his writings on ontological anarchy and Temporary Autonomous Zones, Wilson has written essays on other topics such as Tong traditions as well as the utopian Charles Fourier, the poet Gabriele D'Annunzio, alleged connections between Sufism and ancient Celtic culture, technology and Luddism, *Amanita muscaria* use in ancient Ireland. His most recent book is *The American Revolution as a Gigantic Real Estate Scam & Other Essays in Lost/Found History* (2019).

RONALDO V. WILSON (1970–): A mixed media artist, scholar, and the author of *Narrative of the Life of the Brown Boy and the White Man* (2008), *Poems of the Black Object* (2009), *Farther Traveler: Poetry, Prose, Other* (2015), and *Lucy 72* (2018). Co-founder of the Black Took Collective, Wilson is an Associate Professor of Creative Writing and Literature at the University of California, Santa Cruz.

Nightboat Books

Nightboat Books, a nonprofit organization, seeks to develop audiences for writers whose work resists convention and transcends boundaries. We publish books rich with poignancy, intelligence, and risk. Please visit nightboat.org to learn about our titles and how you can support our future publications.

The following individuals have supported the publication of this book. We thank them for their generosity and commitment to the mission of Nightboat Books:

    Kazim Ali
    Anonymous (4)
    Abraham Avnisan
    Jean C. Ballantyne
    The Robert C. Brooks Revocable Trust
    Committee on Poetry
    Amanda Greenberger
    Rachel Lithgow
    Anne Marie Macari
    Elizabeth Madans
    Elizabeth Motika
    Thomas Shardlow
    Benjamin Taylor
    Jerrie Whitfield & Richard Motika

This book is made possible, in part, by grants from the New York City Department of Cultural Affairs in partnership with the City Council and the New York State Council on the Arts Literature Program.